90 0939823 4

KW-438-589

WITHDRAWN FROM
UNIVERSITY OF PLYMOUTH
LIBRARY SERVICES

University of Plymouth
Charles Seale Hayne Library
Subject to status this item may be renewed
via your Primo account

http:/primo.plymouth.ac.uk
Tel: (01752) 588588

POLICY ANALYSIS IN JAPAN

International Library of Policy Analysis

*Series editors: Iris Geva-May and Michael Howlett,
Simon Fraser University, Canada*

This major new series brings together for the first time a detailed
examination of the theory and practice of policy analysis systems
at different levels of government and by non-governmental actors
in a specific country. It therefore provides a key addition to
research and teaching in comparative policy analysis and policy
studies more generally.

Each volume includes a history of the country's policy analysis which
offers a broad comparative overview with other countries as well as
the country in question. In doing so, the books in the series provide
the data and empirical case studies essential for instruction and for
further research in the area. They also include expert analysis of
different approaches to policy analysis and an assessment of their
evolution and operation.

Early volumes in the series will cover the following countries:

Brazil • Germany • Netherlands • Japan • Taiwan • Israel •
Australia • Czech Republic • Belgium • France

and will build into an essential library of key reference works.

The series will be of interest to academics and students in public
policy, public administration and management, comparative politics and
government, public organisations and individual policy areas.
It will also interest people working in the countries in question
and internationally.

In association with the ICPA-Forum and *Journal of Comparative Policy Analysis*.

See more at http://goo.gl/raJUX

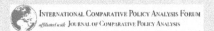 INTERNATIONAL COMPARATIVE POLICY ANALYSIS FORUM
affiliated with JOURNAL OF COMPARATIVE POLICY ANALYSIS

 **POLICY PRESS**
at the University of Bristol

POLICY ANALYSIS IN JAPAN

Edited by Yukio Adachi, Sukehiro Hosono
and Jun Iio

H0030833

International Library of Policy Analysis, Vol 4

PLYMOUTH UNIVERSITY

9U09398234

First published in Great Britain in 2015 by

Policy Press
University of Bristol
1-9 Old Park Hill
Bristol BS2 8BB
UK
t: +44 (0)117 954 5940
pp-info@bristol.ac.uk
www.policypress.co.uk

North America office:
Policy Press
c/o The University of Chicago Press
1427 East 60th Street
Chicago, IL 60637, USA
t: +1 773 702 7700
f: +1 773-702-9756
sales@press.uchicago.edu
www.press.uchicago.edu

© Policy Press 2015

British Library Cataloguing in Publication Data
A catalogue record for this book is available from the British Library.

Library of Congress Cataloging-in-Publication Data
A catalog record for this book has been requested.

ISBN 978 1 84742 984 1 hardcover

The right of Yukio Adachi, Sukehiro Hosono and Jun Iio to be identified as editors of this work
has been asserted by them in accordance with the 1988 Copyright, Designs and Patents Act.

All rights reserved: no part of this publication may be reproduced, stored in a retrieval system,
or transmitted in any form or by any means, electronic, mechanical, photocopying, recording, or
otherwise without the prior permission of Policy Press.

The statements and opinions contained within this publication are solely those of the editors
and contributors and not of The University of Bristol or Policy Press. The University of Bristol
and Policy Press disclaim responsibility for any injury to persons or property resulting from any
material published in this publication.

Policy Press works to counter discrimination on grounds of gender, race, disability, age and
sexuality.

Cover design by Qube Design Associates, Bristol
Front cover: image kindly supplied by www.istock.com
Printed and bound in Great Britain by by CPI Group (UK) Ltd,
Croydon, CR0 4YY
Policy Press uses environmentally responsible print partners

Contents

List of figures and tables

Figures

Tables

Notes on editors

Dr Yukio Adachi is Professor Emeritus of Kyoto University, Japan, and Professor of Public Policy at Kyoto Sangyo University. His academic background is in political philosophy.

Sukehiro Hosono is Dean at Chuou University, Japan, and the President of the Japan Association of Planning and Public Management. He serves on the Advisory Committees of the Ministry of Finance.

Dr Jun Iio is Professor of Political Science at National Graduate Institute for Policy Studies, Japan. He has served on various advisory committees of the Japanese government.

Notes on contributors

Prof Dr rer publ Koichiro Agata is Professor of Public Administration at the Faculty of Political Science and Economics of Waseda University, Japan, and Past President of the Japanese Society for Public Administration.

Takao Akiyoshi is Professor of Policy Studies at Chuo University, Japan. His published book is *Koukyo Seisaku no Henyou to Seisakukagaku* (*Policy Sciences of Policy Change*) (Yuuhikaku, 2007).

Toshiyuki Kanai is Professor of Municipal Government and Administration at the Graduate School of Public Policy, University of Tokyo, Japan.

Hirotsugu Koike is Professor of Kwansei Gakuin University, Japan. Before joining the university, he had covered the policymaking process both in Japan and in the United States as a journalist.

Jun Makita is Researcher at the Faculty of Humanities and Social Sciences, University of Tsukuba, Japan. Formerly he worked as a Secretary to the Minister for Internal Affairs and Communications.

Wataru Sano is Associate Professor of Politics and Public Policy at the Graduate School of Human and Environmental Studies, Kyoto University, Japan.

Mika Shimizu (PhD in International Public Policy) is Assistant Professor at Kyoto University, Japan, and has been a visiting researcher in East-West Center in the US.

Takahiro Suzuki is a visiting professor at Josai International University, Japan. His research interests include political systems, social governance and policy intellectuals.

Hideaki Tanaka is Professor of Public Finance at Graduate School of Governance Studies, Meiji University, Japan. His research interests include public policy, finance and management.

Takafumi Tanaka is an assistant professor of Economics at Tokyo Gakugei University, Japan. His major interest is in Public Economics, especially non-profit organisations and non-governmental organisations, and the economics of the family.

Kimie Tsuchiyama is Associate Professor of Public Policy at Ryukoku University, Japan. Her publications include the changes to politics and autonomy since the high-growth era in Japan.

Makoto Usami is Professor of Philosophy and Public Policy at Kyoto University, Japan, and Adjunct Professor of Law and Philosophy at the Tokyo Institute of Technology.

Satoshi P. Watanabe is Professor of Economics of Education at Hiroshima University, Japan. His research interests include both theoretical and empirical aspects of higher education industries.

Dr Kiyoshi Yamaya is Professor of Policy Evaluation at Doshisha University, Japan. He serves on advisory committees of the Cabinet Office, Ministry of Economu, Trade and Industry, and the Ministry of Defence.

Editors' introduction to the series

Professor Iris Geva-May and Professor Michael Howlett,
ILPA series editors

Policy analysis is a relatively new area of social scientific inquiry, owing its origins to developments in the US in the early 1960s. Its main rationale is systematic, evidence-based, transparent, efficient, and implementable policymaking. This component of policymaking is deemed key in democratic structures allowing for accountable public policies. From the US, policy analysis has spread to other countries, notably in Europe in the 1980s and 1990s and in Asia in the 1990s and 2000s. It has taken, respectively one to two more decades for programmes of public policy to be established in these regions preparing cadres for policy analysis as a profession. However, this movement has been accompanied by variations in the kinds of analysis undertaken as US-inspired analytical and evaluative techniques have been adapted to local traditions and circumstances, and new techniques shaped in these settings.

In the late 1990s this led to the development of the field of comparative policy analysis, pioneered by Iris Geva-May, who initiated and founded the *Journal of Comparative Policy Analysis*, and whose mission has been advanced with the support of editorial board members such as Laurence E. Lynn Jr., first co-editor, Peter deLeon, Duncan McRae, David Weimer, Beryl Radin, Frans van Nispen, Yukio Adachi, Claudia Scott, Allan Maslove and others in the US and elsewhere. While current studies have underlined differences and similarities in national approaches to policy analysis, the different national regimes which have developed over the past two to three decades have not been thoroughly explored and systematically evaluated in their entirety, examining both sub-national and non-executive governmental organisations as well as the non-governmental sector; nor have these prior studies allowed for either a longitudinal or a latitudinal comparison of similar policy analysis perceptions, applications, and themes across countries and time periods.

The International Library for Policy Analysis (ILPA) series fills this gap in the literature and empirics of the subject. It features edited volumes created by experts in each country, which inventory and analyse their respective policy analysis systems. To a certain extent the series replicates the template of *Policy Analysis in Canada* edited by Dobuzinskis, Howlett and Laycock (Toronto: University of Toronto Press, 2007). Each ILPA volume surveys the state of the art of policy analysis in governmental and non-governmental organisations in each country using the common template derived from the Canadian collection in order to provide for each volume in the series comparability in terms of coverage and approach.

Each volume addresses questions such as: What do policy analysts do? What techniques and approaches do they use? What is their influence on policy-making in that country? Is there a policy analysis deficit? What norms and values guide the work done by policy analysts working in different institutional settings? Contributors focus on the sociology of policy analysis, demonstrating how analysts working in different organisations tend to have different interests and to utilise different techniques. The central theme of each volume includes historical works on the origins of policy analysis in the jurisdiction concerned, and then proceeds to investigate the nature and types, and quality, of policy analysis conducted by governments (including different levels and orders of government). It then moves on to examine the nature and kinds of policy analytical work and practices found in non-governmental actors such as think tanks, interest groups, business, labour, media, political parties, non-profits and others.

Each volume in the series aims to compare and analyse the significance of the different styles and approaches found in each country and organisation studied, and to understand the impact these differences have on the policy process.

Together, the volumes included in the ILPA series serve to provide the basic data and empirical case studies required for an international dialogue in the area of policy analysis, and an eye-opener on the nuances of policy analysis applications and implications in national and international jurisdictions. Each volume in the series is leading edge and has the promise to dominate its field and the textbook market for policy analysis in the country concerned, as well as being of broad comparative interest to markets in other countries.

The ILPA is published in association with the International Comparative Policy Analysis Forum, and the *Journal of Comparative Policy Analysis*, whose mission is to advance international comparative policy analytic studies. The editors of each volume are leading members of this network and are the best-known scholars in each respective country, as are the authors contributing to each volume in their particular domain. The book series as a whole provides learning insights for instruction and for further research in the area and constitutes a major addition to research and pedagogy in the field of comparative policy analysis and policy studies in general.

We welcome to the ILPA series Volume 4, *Policy Analysis in Japan*, edited by Yukio Adachi, Sukehiro Hosono and Jun Iio, and thank the editors and the authors for their outstanding contribution to this important encyclopedic database.

Iris Geva-May
Professor of Policy Studies, Baruch College at the City University of
New York, Professor Emerita Simon Fraser University; Founding
President and Editor-in-chief, International Comparative Policy
Forum and *Journal of Comparative Policy Analysis*

Michael Howlett
Burnaby Mountain Professor, Department of Political Science,
Simon Fraser University, and Yong Pung How Chair Professor,
Lee Kuan Yew School of Public Policy, National University of Singapore

INTRODUCTION

Policy analysis in Japan: the state of the art

Yukio Adachi

Synopsis and contents of the book

What are the necessary and sufficient conditions that need to be satisfied in order for a series of intellectual and practical activities to qualify as policy analysis? What mode of thinking is required of policy analysts? What are the core knowledge, skills and ethics to be conveyed through public policy programmes? What constitutes 'good' policy analysis? In answering these related questions, it is important to recognise that there are two main approaches or frameworks in relation to the practice of policy analysis: positivism and post-positivism. Proponents of these approaches are often at odds with one another, especially when addressing the big questions in their field, such as the level of rationality and objectivity that should be applied by policy analysts, how to conceptualise the relationship between facts and values, what weight to accord to quantitative analysis vis-à-vis qualitative analysis, and what criteria to adopt in ranking policy alternatives. The conflict between positivism and post-positivism over these mainly philosophical/methodological issues is important and should not be ignored, but we should also be wary of drawing a definitive line between the two and be prepared to look at their shared characteristics. In fact, a conception of policy analysis that comprises the following three propositions is now widely shared among policy theorists and policy practitioners in almost all democracies, including Japan (Stokey and Zeckhauser, 1978; MacRae and Wilde, 1985; Weimer and Vining, 1989; Patton and Sawicki, 1993; Radin, 2000; Heineman et al, 2001; Fischer, 2003; Geva-May, 2005; Lejano, 2006; Dobzinskis et al, 2007; Adachi, 2009; Dunn, 2011; Bardach, 2012):

- Policy analysis is the 'process by which we arrive at a course of public action that will effect beneficial change in the situation at hand' (Lejano, 2006: 7).
- The primary mission of policy analysis is not to be a substitute for democracy, but to complement it by providing major policy actors with evidence-based policy options.
- Policy analysis is composed of three main processes or phases: analysis of the problems to be tackled; examination and selection of policy objectives; and conceptualisation and selection of specific prescriptions.

It should be noted, however, that among the democracies where the previously mentioned conception of policy analysis is widely acknowledged, there are some significant differences with regard to the nature and quality of policy analysis, its influence on the policy process (if and to what extent policy analysts' voices are genuinely listened to and used in the policy process), and the method of instruction. Hence, there is a vital need for close examination of the intellectual and practical activities carried out in the name of policy analysis in each target country, with a comparative policy analysis perspective in mind. Application of the comparative perspective is expected to make a considerable contribution to improving the quality of policy analysis and its instruction.

To put it bluntly, meta-study of policy analysis is still at a primitive stage of development in Japan, lagging far behind the US and many other countries where policy analysis has been successfully established as a profession. Studies in those countries have moved some distance towards an assessment of what constitutes good policy analysis, and the results of this have been integrated into the design of educational and training programmes for professional policy analysts. In Japan, policy analysis has rarely been taken up as an object of systematic analysis. Herein lies the raison dêtre for this book, the aims of which are as follows: first, to identify and examine the kinds of policy analysis that have been practised in Japan and by whom; and, second, to deliberate on and propose a host of institutional and substantial reform measures that should promptly be taken up as means to improve the quality of policy analysis, thereby enhancing its influence at each stage of the overall policy process, especially when formulating policy options.

The book is divided into four parts. Part One deals with the styles and methods of policy analysis in Japan. In Chapter One, Jun Iio provides readers with a historical overview of the types of policy analysis that have been practised in Japan since the end of the Second World War. Based on his experiences as a political and policy adviser to Diet members and central government bureaucrats, he stresses the urgent need to restructure the policy process to ensure that policy analysts' voices are listened to much more attentively by key policy actors. In Chapter Two, Sukehiro Hosono, one of the leading policy analysts in Japan, reflects upon the striking shortage of quality policy analysts in Japan. He identifies this as one of the key explanatory factors behind the limited role played by policy analysts in the Japanese policy process. This situation is in a sharp contrast with the US and some European countries, where the overdependence on formal analysis is often criticised. One of the unique features found in policy-analytic activities in Japan is the existence of a robust 'policy research movement', which was initiated in the 1960s by local government employees and has been tenaciously carried on, propelled by the decentralisation that has taken place since the beginning of the 1990s. In Chapter Three, Kimie Tsuchiyama analyses how and why this movement was born and what historical changes it has undergone. She concludes by setting out a number of directions that this movement could explore in the future. In Chapter Four, Wataru Sano, a policy theorist who continues to stress the vital need for formal policy analysis to be complemented using the post-positivist approach, discusses the 'pragmatic' nature that underpins the Japanese policy culture, taking welfare benefits policy as an example. Here, this pragmatism is presented as a problem, represented by the tendency to tinker with such problems rather than finding robust solutions. In Chapter Five, Makoto Usami, a legal philosopher, looks at the contrast between the 'principled' legal and the 'opportunistic' approaches employed by policymakers. He argues that legal theorists and practitioners have increasingly come to be interested and involved in the policymaking process, and groups policy-oriented legal approaches into three main schools, examining the rationale and limits of each approach.

Part Two focuses on the nature of policy analysis conducted within Japanese government. Policy analysis was once a craft exclusively reserved for central government bureaucrats. In general, policies formulated and sanctioned at this level, in bureaucrat-led closed policy networks, were approved and implemented with only minor, if any, changes. In Chapter Six, Jun Iio carefully examines why such a bureaucrat-led policy process, which made a tremendous contribution to Japan's rapid economic recovery and development, has failed to function effectively since the late 1980s. One of the unique features of Japanese public administration is that all of the ministries, except the Ministry of Foreign Affairs, have their own research institutes. This is undoubtedly one of the factors that have prevented independent think tanks from developing in Japan. In Chapter Seven, Hideaki Tanaka uncovers the approach to 'policy analysis' in these research institutes by looking at three institutes in which he has worked, either as a researcher or as an administrator. In Chapter Eight, Jun Makita focuses on governmental organisations designed to support legislators, such as the Investigation Bureau of the two houses (House of Representatives and the House of Councilors), the Cabinet Legislation Bureau and the National Library, and examines their role in the policy process. According to his diagnosis, in most cases, the staff of these organisations have been requested to serve legislators not as policy analysts, but as informants or data processors. In Chapter Nine, Kiyoshi Yamaya looks at the role of advisory councils. In most democracies, whenever the government is planning to introduce a significant policy change, they either set up an ad hoc internal policy advisory council or make use of the standing council to request advice. Yamaya questions whether such advisory councils have successfully transformed themselves into bodies where active and substantial deliberation, based on robust analysis, is made. In Chapter Ten, Toshiyuki Kanai closely reviews the varieties of policy-analytic activities that have been practised within the context of local- and regional-level governments. This analysis is set against the backdrop of the shortages of funds at the local level due to the 'incomplete' implementation of decentralisation, which began in the 1990s. This has seen the central government continue to resist transferring the revenue to local- and regional-level governments, thus making the enhancement of policy analysis at this level all the more important.

Part Three turns to the application of policy analysis in the private and civic sectors, such as political parties, interest groups, non-profit organisations (NPOs) and non-governmental organisations (NGOs), think tanks, and the media. As is now widely acknowledged, the performance of democracy is shaped greatly by the quality of policy analysis practised by non-governmental policy actors. The more evidence-informed policy options presented to policymakers by such groups improve the likelihood of 'good' policies being adopted and implemented effectively. No political party lacking advanced policy analysis can be expected to establish either a coherent platform or an attractive or feasible election manifesto. In Chapter Eleven, Takahiro Suzuki considers the reasons why efforts on the part of the two major political parties in Japan (the Liberal Democratic Party and the Democratic Party) to strengthen their policy analysis capability, recently culminating in a project aiming to establish think tanks within both parties, have repeatedly suffered setbacks. In Chapter Twelve, Takao Akiyoshi examines the nature of policy analysis activities practised in business associations and labour unions, taking the regulatory policies vis-à-vis the taxi industry as an example. In Chapter Thirteen, Takafumi Tanaka emphasises the vital need for NPOs and NGOs to improve their analysis and advocacy skills, due to the fact that a great majority of these organisations are still dependent on national, regional and local governments. In Chapter Fourteen, Mika Shimizu, drawing on her experience of having worked for a number of think tanks in the US, explores the political, economic and cultural factors that have prevented the birth and development of independent think tanks in Japan. Here, a great majority of think tanks are either government-affiliated organisations or research units funded and run by large for-profit enterprises. In Chapter Fifteen, Hirotsugu Koike focuses on the media, and, more specifically, the newspaper industry, which is expected to act as a watchdog over power elites within democracies. Koike has extensive experience working both as a journalist and manager for one of the most influential newspaper publishing companies in Japan before moving into academia. He stresses the vital and urgent need to increase articles and stories based on in-depth analysis given the growing prominence of Internet-based news.

Part Four focuses on the future directions of policy analysis in Japan, being composed of three chapters. In Chapter Sixteen, Koichiro Agata highlights the challenges faced by the professional public policy graduate programmes. These were first established in 2000 following a statement by the National Commission on Educational Reform (NCER) that sought to respond to the needs for training professionals with advanced skills and ability in the fields of public policy. Agata looks at the future directions of these programmes, drawing on his own experience of having played a leading role in establishing one of the eight professional graduate public policy programmes in Japan. In Chapter Seventeen, Satoshi P. Watanabe examines why graduates of public policy programmes do not make use of the skills that they acquire and enter into a career in public policy. Watanabe stresses the urgent need for each of the public, civic and market sectors to create systems of employment where the professional knowledge and skills gained by these graduates is valued and maximised. In the concluding chapter (Chapter Eighteen), Yukio Adachi explores options for enhancing the social and political standing of policy analysis as a profession and promoting its wider application, emphasising the need to seriously reflect on what has been missing or insufficient as part of the policy analysis activities practised in Japan to date. Adachi also briefly touches upon a series of drastic institutional reforms to encourage the government and non-government sectors to incorporate policy analysis in the decision-making process.

What constitutes 'good' policy analysis?

The quality of policy analysis ultimately depends on the quality of the previously mentioned three processes of which policy analysis as an intellectual and practical enterprise is composed (analysis of the problems to be tackled, examination and selection of policy objectives, and conceptualisation and selection of specific prescriptions), that is, to what extent these processes are adequately and systematically carried out. This is why the rest of this introduction is devoted to the in-depth analysis of these processes.

Analysis of the problems that policies are designed to address

Public policy analysis starts with the recognition of a problem that needs to be addressed through a policy package. If there is no problem to be addressed, or there is a problem but nothing can be done about it, there is no need for policy. If a seemingly serious problem exists but is likely to be resolved with the passage of time, acting in haste may cause more harm than good, and it may be more prudent to wait. Furthermore, if there are not just single, but multiple, problems to be addressed, public policy analysts must make a choice as to which one to start with. In such instances, they have no choice but to give priority to more serious and urgent problems. If the resolution of a problem is theoretically possible but extremely difficult from a practical standpoint, owing to political or economic factors, people's lifestyles or mindsets, or the values or worldviews underlying such lifestyles or mindsets, attempts to resolve such a problem would have to be deemed unwise.

The process of recognising a problem that needs to be addressed through policy is not an objective process independent of the subjectivity of the observer or analyst. Rather, it is a highly subjective process where a discrepancy between the existing condition and any desirable future condition can create problems. How the existing condition is perceived and the nature of what a successful policy outcome would look like may differ depending on the observer or analyst, and there are no objective, universal criteria or standards in this regard. This means that, in reality, the problem is whatever the individual observer or analyst believes it to be. Most problems subject to public policy are given life only upon their recognition by an observer or analyst as problems, and may not pre-exist as an objective reality.

In view of the foregoing, it can be said that the core aspect of identifying a problem is to strongly impress upon the public that the existing condition is deplorable and intolerable and that any desirable future condition that a policy is designed to bring about is not only worth pursuing, but actually realisable if the necessary efforts are made.

The next task in policy analysis is to investigate the causes of the problem identified, but it is rarely easy to pinpoint the causes of a problem, and only in very rare cases is a problem caused by a single factor. There are many phenomena and problems whose emergence or unique features can only be explained on the basis of multi-causation. For example:

- several concurrent factors, including random events, produce a given effect ($\alpha + \beta + \gamma \rightarrow A$);
- a chain of factors produces a given effect ($\alpha \rightarrow \beta \rightarrow \gamma \rightarrow A$);
- several factors produce the same effect (α or β or $\gamma \rightarrow A$); or
- the same factor produces several effects ($\alpha \rightarrow A$ or B or C).

In fact, a one-on-one relation between cause and effect is the exception. It can be easily understood that this is the case by considering how difficult it is for a physician to arrive at a definitive diagnosis and find an effective treatment.

How deeply must one investigate the causes of a problem? How many resources, including time, should be allocated to the task? If careful analysis of the history and background of the problem is not made and action is taken in haste, it is very easy to overlook key contributory factors, and, as a result, the situation is unlikely to improve and may even be aggravated, making it more difficult to solve the problem. That said, if too much time is given to analysis and investigation, and nothing is decided on or carried out until a fail-safe solution has been found, a prime opportunity to improve the situation may be lost; eventually, the problem itself may get worse or change, making all the effort already expended a waste of time and resources. The correct answer as to when to stop looking for causes lies at a point midway between these two extremes. Unfortunately, there is no definitive guideline for determining where that midpoint should be, and it must be determined separately for each individual case.

The most important task in the process of problem analysis is to examine whether government 'behaviour' has contributed to, or is involved in creating, intensifying or prolonging, problems and to what degree. From here, it is then necessary to examine any government 'behaviour' that may at least be partly responsible for creating, aggravating or prolonging a specific problem. This task is a process of critical importance, one that enables analysis of the existing condition to provide a foundation for change and improvement.

The term government 'behaviour' is used here to highlight the fact that government action, along with its inaction, could be equally responsible for the emergence or proliferation of a particular problem. Failing to act, therefore, can be just as influential as not acting at all.

In cases where a government's action contributes to the generation, aggravation or prolongation of a problem, two possible scenarios can apply. One is where the problem is caused, primarily or partly, by government action to begin with. The other is where the problem is not caused by government action, but shows no improvement or even worsens owing to the government's inappropriate approach to addressing the problem. A representative example of this would be an intervention by the government to address market failure (ie when the market fails to deliver an efficient allocation of resources) that results in furthering the inefficient allocation of resources. Diverse types of government behaviour not directly aimed at achieving the more efficient allocation of resources can also produce similar results. For example, reforms introduced to prevent the national pension programme from going bankrupt may hasten the bankruptcy, or a programme intended to improve the quality of civil service employees may lead to further deterioration. If a government takes no initiative to prevent or address a problem in a situation where prompt intervention could have prevented it from arising or worsening, or if it loses the opportunity to intervene by postponing its decision due to not knowing what action to take, the government cannot evade responsibility for creating, worsening or prolonging the problem or, at the very least, for failing to act, just as it can be held responsible when its activity was the main cause of the emergence, aggravation or prolongation of a problem.

Following the preliminary process of identifying and analysing the problem, investigating the factors behind it, and examining the behaviour of government in relation to it, the process of 'searching for a solution' (formulating government action aimed at breaking a deadlock or improving a situation) begins. The quality of the 'solution' is critically dependent on how well the initial process of identifying and reviewing the problem is carried out.

If government action is the main cause or one of the causes of a problem, the government should remove itself promptly from the field in question, or shift its policy to one that is benign, or at least less harmful, to the situation. If government action itself is not the main cause of a problem, but a government policy implemented to address the problem is inappropriate and unlikely to produce the intended effect, the government should search for a more effective policy. If government action worsens a problem rather than solving it, the best option for the government is to discover and implement a policy capable of ameliorating or resolving the problem. If the chance of formulating such a policy is virtually non-existent, the government has no option but to shift to a policy that will not worsen the situation or completely refrain from implementing any policy. If the government's failure to act leads to the generation, exacerbation or prolongation of a problem, the government may be required to explore and formulate effective and appropriate actions to deal with the problem.

Examination and selection of policy objectives

The enterprise of policy analysis includes, and draws heavily upon, cause-and-effect reasoning. In addition, effective policy analysis requires the ability to be able to imagine a sophisticated conceptual road map for change. The ability to communicate effectively is also important, especially given the need to be able to persuasively describe the benefits that will accrue from a new policy direction.

Once the problem has been identified and reviewed and a direction has been established for new government policy, the remaining task is to flesh out the specific character of the new policy. This process consists of two phases that follow on from one another: (1) establishing the policy objective and the desired changes that it will support; and (2) selecting and presenting the specific means by which the policy objective will be achieved.

There are four levels of government activity involved when developing new policies. These form a closely linked hierarchy, as follows: define the specific elements of the policy; plan; develop a programme for its implementation; and carry out the implementation project in order to begin working towards the policy objective.

Overarching policy objectives (purpose) tend to be quite broad and it is not until the implementation phase, when these are broken down into a number of component parts or specific policy-related objectives (goals), that it is possible to effectively measure progress. This is because, at this stage, the actions that support the overarching objective have been broken down into a set of supporting policy objectives, which are more easily measured. Overarching policy objectives focus on the public value pertaining to a particular intervention (ie social impact). Public values are those that are generally perceived to be important by most sections of society. Examples include freedom, equality, economic growth, social welfare, environmental protection and public safety and security.

As with policies and policy objectives, public values have different levels of abstraction and generality. For example, an overarching objective may be environmental protection, while at the level below, supporting objectives may include CO_2 emissions reduction, water purification and biodiversity conservation. These objectives would support the attainment of the overarching objective (ie environmental protection). However, in the realm of biodiversity conservation, public values to be achieved or enhanced through policy can be formulated in a variety of different ways depending on the target region and species to be protected.

In general, public values at this second level or below in the public values hierarchy are the focus of public policy. For a public value to be fully functional as a yardstick for evaluating government activity, it must be specific, measurable, attainable and time-bound, only then is a judgement as to whether the public value in question was attained, and to what degree, possible. For example, it is not enough simply to establish CO_2 reduction as the objective. It is necessary to specify how much CO_2 is to be reduced and by when.[1]

Thus, in essence, the core task of establishing the objective of a public policy is to define what kind of public value is to be achieved, to what degree and by when.

However, such a definition is not easy, primarily because there are multiple public values to be considered when designing public policies and determining, implementing and/or evaluating them. Furthermore, different public values that are in themselves socially justified can lead to policy decisions that are in conflict with each other.

The following is an example of this. Over the past few decades, Japan has been working on criminal law reform, and one of the biggest points of contention yet to be resolved pertains to restriction orders.[2] A restriction order system may be warranted from the standpoint of ensuring public safety and security. However, if the treatment of mental patients and alcohol and drug abusers may in fact have a better chance of success under an open system in which the patient is allowed a certain level of contact with the outside world, then the alternative closed system, which sees mentally disordered or alcohol/drug-addicted people who have committed serious crimes locked up in high-security treatment centres, may be in conflict with a number of public values, including personal liberty and well-being.

If surveillance cameras are placed all over towns, as in London, or if people are encouraged or required to report to the authorities if they notice any suspicious characters, as in Nazi Germany or Japan immediately before and during the Second World War, it may be possible to reduce 'crime' and increase public safety and security. However, such actions come with a high price in the form of privacy invasion and a weakening of basic trust within a community. Other public values that are typically in conflict with each other include equality (correction of economic disparity) versus economic growth, and environmental protection versus economic growth.

As the foregoing examples indicate, the public desirability of a policy aimed at contributing to the attainment of a given public value can only be guaranteed conditionally. In other words, desirability can only be guaranteed in the short term and while conditions are favourable.

This view concerning public value roughly corresponds to Ronald Dworkin's understanding of a principle. Dworkin (1977: 26) states:

> A principle like no man may profit from his own wrong does not even purport to set out conditions that make its application necessary. Rather, it states a reason that argues in one direction, but does not necessitate a particular decision.... There may be other principles or policies arguing in the other direction.... If so, our principle may not prevail, but that does not mean that it is not a principle of our legal system, because in the next case, when these contravening considerations are absent or less weighty, the principle may be decisive.

Thus, conflict with other public values increases as the level of the public value targeted by a policy rises or the strength of commitment towards achieving or enhancing a given value increases. For example, once the level of public safety and security passes a threshold value, serious infringement of personal liberty and privacy can result. The higher the targeted level of safety and security, the greater the negative effects will be. Conversely, if freedom and privacy are considered inviolable under any circumstances, it can have the highly detrimental effect of undermining public safety and security.

The same can be said about time frame. A shorter time frame for achieving the policy objective can make satisfying the demands for other public values more difficult.

Conversely, a longer time frame tends to make it easier to achieve adjustment and coordination among values.

There are no universal guidelines for determining how high to set a policy objective or what timetable to establish for achieving that objective. Judgements must be made on a case-by-case basis in line with conditions specific to the situation, and responsibility for the consequences must be accepted. There may be times when analysts are forced to set the policy objective at a much lower level than theoretically or technically possible or establish a long time frame owing to an overriding need to achieve social integration and gain consensus. On the other hand, there may be times when immediate efforts to realise the highest possible level of a given public value are allowed or demanded, such as when radical reforms of a revolutionary nature are being courageously implemented. A different set of considerations is required when faced with two opposing public values that cannot be easily reconciled.

Conceptualisation and selection of specific prescriptions

Any notion that designing a policy is a systematic two-step process – consisting of, first, establishing the policy objective, based on a careful analysis of the problem, and then, second, finding the best means of achieving that objective – is a misperception. The exploration of means cannot be performed without some idea of the objective to work towards, and, in general, it is not easy to discover and establish an appropriate policy objective at the early stages of policy analysis. In reality, the analyst follows a zigzagging process consisting of an initial cycle of problem analysis, identification of policy objective and exploration of specific measures, followed by additional cycles of problem reanalysis, adjustment of policy objective and adjustment of specific measures. Finally, at the end of all these repeated cycles, the analyst is able to determine the policy objective and the means for achieving that objective, both at the same time.

The activity of formulating a specific prescription, therefore, is not a uni-linear, instrumentally rational process consisting of exploring and finding the most effective means for achieving a clearly defined policy objective. Rather, it is a process consisting of conceptualising or thinking up as many objectives–means combinations as possible, predicting what social consequences (costs and benefits) are likely to arise and to what degree of probability, and selecting the one that is expected to produce the best, or most preferable, consequences for society as a whole.

The task of conceptualising and selecting a specific prescription is never easy, and is just as difficult as the other two tasks. The high-level ability to do so is not achieved overnight. It requires years of practical experience working with policies, and only those who have gained penetrating insight and keen instincts can become a master of the prescription-conceptualising process. Unfortunately, the expertise of such masters cannot be described in logical steps or compiled into a how-to manual.

Problems that may be addressed by public policies are enormously diverse, and no two problems are entirely the same in real life. Because of this, ultimately, the task of conceptualising a specific prescription that is the means to achieve a given objective is essentially a unique, one-time endeavour, one that requires flexible thinking adapted to the situation at hand, as well as the capacity to make sound judgements.

However, this does not mean that there is no tool to assist this difficult task. It is possible to find several generic policies, or stock strategies, that have been proven, through past successes and failures in policy implementation, to have a certain level of effectiveness as prescriptions against similar problems occurring under similar conditions. Weimer and Vining (1989) classify generic policies into the following five categories:

- freeing, facilitating and stimulating markets;
- subsidies and taxes used to alter incentives;
- establishing rules;
- supplying goods through non-market mechanisms; and
- providing insurance and cushions (economic protection).

When conceptualising a prescription, it would be highly useful to consider if one of the generic policies that vary greatly in the degree and form of government involvement can be utilised, or if it is possible to increase effectiveness by combining some of them.

Of course, there may be times when none of the generic policies appear useful, and therefore original thinking is called for. It is also important to avoid the trap of relying excessively on them to the extent of losing the ability to make necessary changes or adjustments. Provided that this point is kept in mind, it makes good sense to start the design process with one or two generic policies. We must not dismiss the wisdom and practical and experiential knowledge of our predecessors, as there is more to be learned from them than is usually assumed.[3]

Once the basic form has been determined, the remaining task is to decide the specifics. This task could be successfully performed by comparing widely shared criteria and ranking the multitude of similar prescriptions that are available. This would result in a process that compares cost-effectiveness, feasibility, preparedness for uncertainties and complexities, and the ethical justifiability of different prescriptions. Nevertheless, this is a complex process that will likely face enormous difficulties.

Notes

[1] Quantification is not necessarily required to achieve the controllability of a policy objective. While quantification offers great advantages, it can turn into the be-all and end-all of policy implementation if not handled carefully. First, the numerical target must, above all, be realisable, with a certain amount of leeway built into it. An inappropriate and unrealistic figure is liable to discourage rather than motivate policy implementers. Second, it is also essential to avoid the trap of focusing only on the quantifiable portion of a policy objective and losing sight of the non-quantifiable portion.

[2] When a person who has committed a crime punishable by imprisonment or death, such as murder or arson, is found not guilty or given a light sentence by reason of insanity or diminished capacity due to alcohol or drug abuse, and deemed by the court to be highly likely to reoffend unless treated for the mental disorder or addiction, that person may be placed in a newly created high-security treatment centre, different from a normal psychiatric hospital, under the jurisdiction of the Ministry of Justice. Restriction orders consist of treatment orders applicable to those with mental disorders and confinement orders applicable to alcohol or drug abusers.

[3] Research on stock strategies or generic policies long remained at the nascent stage, with a few pioneering works by Weimer and Vining (1989), Carabresi and Bobbitt (1978),

---

Hood (1983) and Lowi (1979). However, research on them has drastically increased in number and quality over the last decade or so, the most epoch-making of which is that by Michael Howlett (2011).

References

Adachi, Y. (2009) *Kokyo-seisaku-gaku towa nanika?* [*What Is Policy Studies as a Discipline?*], Kyoto: Minerva Publishing Company.

Bardach, E. (2012) *A Practical Guide for Policy Analysis: The Eightfold Path to More Effective Problem Solving* (4th edn), Washington, DC: CQ Press.

Carabresi, G. and Bobbitt, P. (1978) *Tragic Choices*, New York, NY: W.W. Norton.

Dobzinskis, L., Howlettt, M. and Laycock, D. (eds) (2007) *Policy Analysis in Canada*, Toronto: University of Toronto Press.

Dunn, W. (2011) *Public Policy Analysis: An Introduction* (5th edn), Englewood Cliffs, NJ: Prentice Hall.

Dworkin, R. (1977) *Taking Rights Seriously*, Cambridge, MA: Harvard University Press.

Fischer, F. (2003) *Reframing Public Policy*, Oxford: Oxford University Press.

Geva-May, I. (ed) (2005) *Thinking Like a Policy Analyst: Policy Analysis as a Clinical Profession*, New York, NY: Palgrave Macmillan.

Heineman, R., Bluhm, W., Peterson, S. and Kearny, E. (eds) (2001) *The World of the Policy Analyst*, New York, NY: Chatham House Publishers.

Hood, C. (1983) *The Tools of Government*, London: Macmillan.

Howlett, M. (2011) *Designing Public Policies: Principles and Instruments*, London and New York, NY: Routledge.

Lejano, R. (2006) *Frameworks for Policy Analysis: Merging Text and Context*, New York, NY: Routledge.

Lowi, T. (1979) *The End of Liberalism: The Second Republic of the United States*, New York, NY: W.W. Norton.

MacRae, D. and Wilde, J. (1985) *Policy Analysis for Public Decisions*, Lanham, MD: University Press of America.

Patton, C. and Sawicki, D. (1993) *Basic Methods of Policy Analysis and Planning* (2nd edn), Englewood Cliffs, NJ: Prentice Hall.

Radin, B. (2000) *Beyond Machiavelli: Policy Analysis Comes of Age*, Washington, DC: Georgetown University Press.

Stokey, E. and Zeckhauser, R. (1978) *A Primer for Policy Analysis*, New York, NY: W.W. Norton.

Weimer, D. and Vining, A. (1989) *Policy Analysis: Concepts and Practice*, Englewood Cliffs, NJ: Prentice-Hall.

PART ONE
STYLES AND METHODS OF POLICY ANALYSIS IN JAPAN

ONE

Historical background of policy analysis in Japan

Jun Iio

Introduction

This chapter illustrates the background history of the development of policy-related studies in Japan. As, in the strict sense, policy analysis has still not taken root in Japan, if we concentrate solely on the discipline of policy analysis, we would only pick up sporadic and specific examples of the policy process. Therefore, we need to trace the various related research activities that have been conducted for many years. Such research developments in various policy areas, for example, the education system, government structure and so on, have formulated the current state of policy analysis in Japan.

Japanese modernisation and policy-related analysis

It is widely acknowledged that the present political regime in Japan began at the end of the Second World War with the new constitution. This book, including this chapter, will focus on this period, especially the past 20 years. Even before this period, there were many government and non-government activities related to policy and policy research throughout the course of modernisation. Japanese modernisation began around the middle of the 19th century, at the time of the 'Meiji Restoration'. During this period, Japan opened itself to Western countries, importing innovative technologies and academic studies in order to strengthen the nation against colonisation. Even though many aspects of intellectual heritage and cultural tradition were affected before that time, there is a clear discontinuity between the pre-modern and modern eras.

In the Meiji period, top leaders began to study sciences and theories from Western countries. The government's principle for policy selection is reflected in the slogan *Fukoku-Kyohei*, meaning 'Wealthy nation and strong military power'. Under this principle, the Meiji government aimed to secure national independence from colonial powers by strengthening its military power through imported technology, Westernised industry and expanding the export sector to increase the circulation of foreign currency and cover the expenses of importing goods. For this purpose, the introduction of Western science, technology and academic investigation became a very important government pursuit. Among the sciences, government leaders had a preference for the engineering and military sciences. For example, the Ministry of Engineering established their own college of engineering, which later became a part of the University of Tokyo, to introduce state-of-the-art civil engineering, mechanical engineering and metallurgy, among others. The high status given to departments of engineering has been one of the characteristics of Japanese universities. The Japanese army began imitating the French style at first, but later shifted to the new German army system after the triumph of Prussia against France. The imperial navy learned mainly from the British navy, and partly from the US navy. Both the army and navy sent officers to those countries, invited foreign trainers and established their own military colleges and various schools for the research of and education in military technologies and strategic studies.

In the early Meiji period, government leaders consisted of revolutionaries and warriors, but they later tried to instruct their successors through the formal educational system. The University of Tokyo (then Tokyo Imperial University) was established as the first Western-style higher educational institution, including many departments such as law, medicine, engineering, science, literature and agriculture. As a starting point, the government invited many professors from European countries, offering them relatively high salaries in exchange, with Japanese scholars later taking their place and giving lectures in Japanese. Among its departments, the faculty of law at the Imperial University was expected to be a higher training organisation for government officials. That is why Japanese departments of law, the curricula for which extend beyond the realm of jurisprudence, are not strictly training organisations for the legal profession, as are their European counterparts. As a result, most high officials in Japanese government obtained a Bachelor of Arts in Law, and many policy specialists had a background in jurisprudence. It is likely that the Meiji government regarded legal training so highly because adopting the Western legal system was a relatively easy way to modernise Japanese government and society. Japanese leaders knew that many Western countries had tried to establish their own comprehensive legal systems in the late 19th century. The fact that Western countries urged the Japanese government to accept the Western legal system in order to promote Japanese independence would also have been a motivating factor in promoting legal education.

At the turn of the century, another imperial university, Kyoto University, was established, and some private educational institutions were accredited as universities as well, such as Keio University and Waseda University. These universities, which did not aim to train future public officials, offered a different kind of subject than the University of Tokyo in order to enrich policy-related research.

At this stage, policy-related academic societies were gradually organised, such as *Kokka-gakkai* (Society for State Science), which was organised mainly by the faculty of law at Tokyo Imperial University and developed forums for various policy-related research activities not limited to jurisprudence. Later, the Japan Society for Social Policy Studies was founded in response to a period of social unrest. Among related studies, policy administration treated a wide range of social problems, and required of scholars some degree of policy analysis. From the 1920s, Marxism also penetrated Japan and some social problem-oriented scholars were considerably influenced by its ideas, resulting in the development of related studies.

As Japan had colonised Korea and Taiwan, and gained special interests in the north-east of China, studies related to colonial policy were founded in Japan. This field produced various scholars who were strongly interested in policy problems. *Mantetsu-chosabu* (the research section of the southern Manchuria Railway Company) was one of the earlier think tanks to conduct policy-related research. As Japan entered into war with China and the Second World War, general mobilisation required planning in cooperation with policy-related research.

Post-war reform and institutional change

After Japan's defeat in 1945, occupying forces mainly from the US reorganised the Japanese government and social system for the purpose of demilitarising Japan and introducing democratic institutions. Administrative institutions took one of two directions: one was continuation even through occupation; the other was extinction between the pre-war and post-war era. For example, occupying forces abolished the army and navy in Japan, dismantled the Ministry of Interior, and purged military leaders, police officers and right-wing activists, while other ministries were permitted to operate as they had before the war.

One major change to the social and economic systems under the occupation was the reallocation of agricultural landownership (*Nochi-Kaihou*), which prohibited large landownership for agriculture and reallocated farmlands to small farmers. Although it was a revolutionary reform that drastically changed the economic structure, the implementation of the policy was relatively smooth because the Japanese Ministry of Agriculture and Forestry had already prepared the basic idea behind the reform during the war, based on an in-depth survey of rural areas.

Occupying forces also introduced many new institutions, such as the new Japanese constitution, the administrative committee system that was popular in the US, freedom of speech and other ideas on policy. For example, the US sent an advisory group of scholars to discuss taxation, and this group proposed a new tax system that has mostly been maintained to this day. From this time, the influence of US social sciences would increase, gradually replacing what had previously been a mainly continental European influence.

At that time, new ministries were established, such as the Ministry of Welfare, the Ministry of Labor, the Ministry of Construction, the Ministry of Post and Telecommunication and the Ministry of Transportation. These new ministries would emphasise their specialties and try to learn policy-related academic achievements. In addition, the newly established Headquarters of Economic Stabilization (which later became the Economic Planning Agency) regarded economic analysis as its main task, and trained many economic bureaucrats who would introduce various policy analysis methods to Japan. Economic bureaucrats and scholars of economics cooperated. One example of such cooperation is the priority production system (*Keisha Seisan Hoshiki*), which was an early strategy for post-war reconstruction. Inside the ministries, many old bureaucrats resigned and relatively young bureaucrats drafted new policies introducing foreign knowledge in order to build up a new policy system. The standard method was a comparison of several Western countries' experiences and policy solutions. Such imports from abroad, based on comparative institutional studies, eventually became a mainstay of Japanese policy formulation.

Expansions of policies under high economic growth and policy analysis

Even after the end of the occupation, the basic structure and administrative framework has continued. Since the Liberal Democratic Party (LDP) was formed in 1955, it has controlled the administration and legislature (Diet) continuously except between 1993 and 1994 and 2009 and 2012. Under the long-lasting control of the LDP, the

Japanese political system has enjoyed considerable stability. As a result, each ministry has kept relative autonomy within its own policy domain, and the way of thinking on policy matters has been relatively fixed.

A typical policy area of the time was the Ministry of International Trade and Industry's industrial growth policy, which supported high economic growth. Today, there are two different evaluations of Japan's industrial policy: one that stresses the role of government in economic growth; and the other that considers the role of government to be limited. At the time, however, the notion that the government should intervene in the economy to promote its growth was relatively novel, and had a strong influence on other Asian countries.

Each ministry formed a way of drafting new policy by using *Shingi-kai* (advisory councils), which consist of scholars and specialists from related sectors and are managed by ministerial bureaucrats. These advisory councils provided opportunities for coordination among interest groups, the exchange of opinions among scholars and bureaucrats, and, as a result, the setting up of policy communities. Although some scholars predicted that this system would become the centre of policy coordination, many academics gleaned policy information and original data from it. As members of the advisory council were numerous within both central and local authorities, many scholars became involved in this system and devoted considerable attention to policy matters.

Of course, the degree of policy orientation varied among disciplines. Many scholars criticised the government and refused to participate in policymaking. For example, in the area of international relations, many scholars had an anti-government stance because of the opposition to the revision of the US–Japan Security Treaty in 1960, and only a limited number of scholars had close relations with the government for a long time. Consequently, the size of the policy community on diplomacy and national security was very small in Japan until the early 1990s. In some novel spheres, independent research activity from the government had some very important contributions. For example, environmental pollution was a very important issue because the government could not cope with the problem quickly due to its pro-industry bias.

The pattern according to which government bureaucrats tended to discuss and formulate policies had been formed during high-growth days because the continuation of one-party predominance compelled most politicians to concentrate on interest intermediation and power struggles, thus leaving to the bureaucracy most policy-related decisions, including the direction of the macroeconomy. Under these conditions, Japanese bureaucrats were confident, and almost dominated the policy formulation stage. Many people took it for granted that each ministry was a kind of think tank in the Japanese context. However, there was some bias in bureaucratic policy research. Most of the high officials had a law background: over 90% of those in the highest positions were law graduates. They were very knowledgeable regarding political coordination and logical consistency in policy formulation, but not at field research, statistics or model analysis. As this type of bureaucrat formed mainstream behaviour, a policy analysis orientation remained a relatively minor movement (Hayakawa, 2004).

Oil shock and the switchover from the developmental state

Even though the role of the bureaucracy in the policy process did not essentially change after the oil crisis of the early 1970s, the power of LDP politicians gradually increased as the idea of democracy took root in society. Many politicians gained detailed knowledge in policy matters, even if they were only interested in the politically sensitive aspects of them, as they had accumulated experience through intervening in the policymaking process. In addition, policymaking became mainly a matter of coordination among various vested interests because the policy space became clouded, so bureaucrats had to rely on the democratic authority of party politicians. As a result, politicians and public officials shared a basic policy framework and devoted themselves to interest adjustment. Under these circumstances, very few officials were interested in policy analysis because many of them believed that things were decided by compromise not by rightness. Normally, a situation such as the oil shock, under which economic conditions had changed drastically, would have required strict analysis, but there were few attempts to analyse and formulate new policy proposals.

Exceptional cases included an attempt to introduce the US idea of the Planning–Programming–Budgeting System (PPBS) in the late 1960s. The government sent young officials to learn the system and, though the attempts to import PPBS were soon abandoned, some of these officials learned new methods in public management and policy analysis, and they taught many of these new skills in universities. They introduced the idea of policy sciences to Japan and prepared for its future development (Miyakawa, 2002).

There were also some noteworthy trends in the advisory council system. Until that time, economics scholars who were interested in policy matters usually had a background in Marxist economics. They tended to rely on their theoretical framework, not on detailed research of markets or on model analysis. During this period, many modern economists who had been studying in the US entered into the advisory council system. They introduced various economics methods of policy analysis and gradually became influential. In addition, after the Japanese government enlarged its welfare programme during the 1970s, social security-related policy research was conducted. Many study groups were organised around the traditional advisory councils and many social scientists were involved. Furthermore, non-governmental research activities in relation to environmental pollution had begun to influence policy decisions and the government established the Environmental Agency.

Policy study movements in local government

The frontier in the field of policy-related research was opened at the local level after the period of high economic growth (Matsushita, 2006). Japanese local governments were authorised as independent governing bodies and democratised through post-war reforms. Direct election by local residents was launched for both heads and assembly members of local governments. Even under the new local system, most central government policies were implemented through local governments. As local leaders broadened their experience, they also developed their own policy preferences. In addition, an increase in various public services that were delivered through municipalities compelled them to develop the ability to treat policy matters, despite the fact that central ministries considered local authorities as instruments for their own devices.

From the late 1960s, the Left gradually began to win mayoral and gubernatorial elections in some urban cities and prefectures because urban residents had grown discontented with the LDP's pork-barrel policies, which mainly benefitted rural residents. 'Progressive local authorities' with leftist heads had tried to start new programmes relating to social welfare and environmental problems that were more advanced than central government policies. In local governments, progressive scholars who were independent from the advisory council system of central ministries had decisive influence on the policy formulation process, and enlarged the scope of the Japanese policy system. Such developments made the LDP sensitive to welfare and urban problems, and the LDP government introduced welfare policies that rapidly developed during the 1970s. The increase in welfare policies also enhanced the role of local governments as the implementing organisations.

In these circumstances, many local authorities established training institutions to enhance local public officials' policy formulation abilities. This meant that local governments were considered independent policy formulators. For example, the introduction of comprehensive local administrative plans required the setting up of a planning section and the hiring of officials who had analytical abilities. These changes gradually spread nationwide. Some local training institutions established research divisions based on such changes, and these divisions would later develop their own ideas on policy matters.

In the 1980s, the average educational background of local officials increased and caught up with the background of central ministerial bureaucrats in some big cities and prefectures, and the number of capable local officials increased. Among them, some local officials established academic societies on local legal practices with related jurisprudence professors. These movements aimed to influence local governments to compete with the central government by enacting their own local ordinances, which, in turn, led to the concentration on some local frontier problems. This is also a reflection of the image that jurisprudence is key to formulating policies in central government.

After the 1990s, decentralisation encouraged local administrators to formulate new policies. One such initiative was the introduction of a national nursing care insurance system, which was formulated by the Ministry of Welfare and based on the advice of local specialists in the mid-1990s. At that time, the Ministry of Welfare relied on hearings from local practitioners because the ministry did not have adequate knowledge of local situations. This was a new means of policy formulation in Japanese government and similar practices would increase thereafter. At the same time, the voices of local political leaders gained in influence because some heads of local governments were successful in their attempts to promote local administrative reform above the central government. Many local governments tried to introduce new methods in public management, primarily the imported 'New Public Management' policy, which included measures such as performance measurement, programme evaluation, compulsory competitive tendering and the establishment of agencies. Some local officials set up networks on research activities related to public management reform, which circulated pertinent information and analytical tools among local government officials. Some local officials were enthusiastic about their research, became scholars of administrative studies and developed local public management research domains in the colleges.

Up until this time, local public officials mainly conducted policy-related research, but the situation gradually changed as local politicians grew interested in policy analysis, which seemed to be a tool for changing the present system. After the 2000s, the 'manifesto' movement – which insisted that candidates for local head elections should express concrete and comprehensive reform plans – became popular and many local politicians had to settle their policy plans based on some analysis. Local assemblies from relatively rural areas awoke after the famous collapse of one rural city instilled distrust of the government's financial sustainability. Such assembly members began to study networking research with other local politicians.

The promotion of public–private partnerships increased contact between local officials and non-profit organisation (NPO) members, and enhanced the opportunities for local governments to absorb the new ideas and knowledge from the NPOs. Emerging independent policy advocacy groups often targeted local governments, which they could easily access.

The age of administrative reform

By overcoming two oil crises, the Japanese economy launched an era of stable growth. The 'Japan model' attracted a wide range of interest from around the world because Japanese growth was relatively high compared to other Western countries, even though it was much lower than it was during the era of high economic growth in Japan. The transition of the government system required by economic change was noticed but was not easily achieved. During this time, two policy research attempts in Japanese government deserve special attention as they formed the pinnacle of the Japanese advisory council system.

One of these research attempts was 'Prime Minister Ohira's study group', which was established to research the policy agenda and solutions broadly related to the changing Japan. The group consisted of various kinds of scholars, business leaders and bureaucrats, and was divided into eight sections. Such research, which covered government-wide problems, was relatively rare and furnished a good opportunity for the work of related ministries and scholars. Although the research activity of this group was halted after Prime Minister Ohira's sudden death, the report and its human network were very influential in later policy formulations.

The other research project was the *Dai-ni Rincho* (Second Provisional Administrative Reform Council), which was held by the cabinet for the purpose of reviewing and restructuring government activities. In spite of maintaining relatively good economic performance, the Japanese government had accumulated a huge deficit for the first time in the post-war era and failed to introduce new tax revenue to make up for it. As a result, LDP political leaders were pressed to decrease expenditures before proposing tax increases, but they were only familiar with logrolling and requesting finance from the ministerial bureaucrats and so were not able to cut spending on their own. The government and ruling party asked the council to review the policy and adjust the situation. The council consisted of business leaders, labour leaders, former high officials from most ministries and university professors from various backgrounds. The distinctive feature of this council was the leadership of the council members. Usually, the secretariat of the committee drives the direction of the discussion and drafts the report, but in case of *Dai-ni Rincho*, members were eager to do the work themselves and the secretariat was independent from the ministries. As the ministries mainly formulated Japanese policies, administrative reform affecting the organisational settings inside government was the one focal point that changed policy matters. This discussion style within the cabinet was frequently introduced in cases of larger governmental reforms after this time. In several reports, *Dai-ni Rincho* proposed various kinds of administrative reorganisation, policy reform and the leading ideas of governments, including privatisation, deregulation and simplification of procedures.

The introduction of neoliberal economic policy was a key characteristic of this era. With the salience of active economists in administrative reform, active outsiders with policy-related knowledge found that they could participate in the governmental process by way of *Rincho*-style committees. Under the ordinary advisory council system, iron triangles had been so strong that drastic new ideas were not easily introduced. Nevertheless, under the title of administrative reform, which introduced deregulation as a measure of changing the governmental role, neoliberal ideas were able to enter the arena and affect some policies.

In the field of international relations, some scholars insisted on strengthening military power to enhance the Japan–US alliance and proposed some related policy changes that would affect government–academic relations in this field, and discursive forums addressing this problem were widened. A few research institutions on international relations and strategic studies were established in this period, and began to exchange opinions with foreign counterparts. Similarly, it had previously been difficult to discuss educational policy due to ideological rivalry among scholars. The government induced scholars to participate in the reform discussion via *Rincho*-type councils and this exchange also vitalised educational policy discussions in Japan.

With the introduction of the consumption tax system to Japan in the late 1980s, many professors of economics participated in the policy discussion, which attracted the attention of the public. At the same time, various simulations and calculations were published and many experts became interested in policy analysis through political debates and were aware of the political role that analysis played. The 1980s was also an era of trade friction with the US, and related studies were encouraged. Among these studies, the *Maekawa Report*, which proposed an active role for Japan in offering international common goods, was a typical example of contemporary proposals based, to some extent, on policy analysis. Through such interactions, government officials acknowledged the importance of policy-related analysis, especially related to economics, and endeavoured to utilise such analysis. Some ministries started a training programme in economics for bureaucrats with law degrees.

The breakdown of the bubble economy and the end of the Cold War

After the breakdown of the bubble economy in the early 1990s, the Japanese economic slump continued and the dysfunction of the Japanese social system was recognised. The prestige of the Japanese bureaucracy – especially of economic ministries like the Ministry of Finance, the Ministry of International Trade and Industry and the Bank of Japan – was lost due to economic policy mismanagement. At the same time, the end of the Cold War changed the basic conditions for Japanese international relations, and the LDP lost its status as sole guardian of Western free trade countries. The political reform movement, led by political scientists, business leaders, labour leaders and journalists, had strong influence, and it promoted electoral reform proposals and other institutional reforms. Under these circumstances, successive political scandals damaged the LDP's reputation, and it lost control after its split in 1993. Enduring one-party predominance in the party system ended, providing a new opportunity for political change and the policy framework (Iio, 2008).

Deregulation, which had been proposed but not widely enacted, grew in popularity and was eventually carried out as political obstacles weakened and the US government required deregulation in Japan. For example, the Leased Land and House Lease Law was amended, introducing new lease rights based on the proposals of law and economics scholars, who persuasively made their case through the use of data and simulations. In decentralisation reform, professors of administrative law and public administration took part in *Rincho*-type committees, and promoted radical decentralisation through negotiations with the bureaucracy. This is another example of policy analysts' initiatives. When AIDS contracted from contaminated blood products became a political issue, the Minister of Welfare ordered the disclosure of information about the deliberative council, and this record indicates the responsibility of closed policy communities. After this incident, the nature of advisory councils became more open.

In the late 1990s, many policy problems – such as the Asian financial crisis, the rising tax rate and educational reforms – attracted a great deal of public attention, and many policy experts and scholars engaged in debates in the mass media. This indicates that policy disputes flowed out of the closed advisory council system, and the discussion about the role of public intellectuals grew in popularity. Some policy experts became popular public intellectuals in this period.

Emergence of alternative policy analysis

As a result of public awareness of policy analysis, many people, including Diet members, journalists and business leaders, insisted on the necessity of large-scale think tanks that could propose various policy alternatives from the mid-1990s, in comparison with the US situation, where many think tanks and foundations play important roles. Even though there had been organisations that regarded themselves as think tanks, most of these were profit-making corporations that sold their analytical services or conference management services. The National Institute for Research Advancement (NIRA), a public corporation established by the Japanese government in the mid-1970s, was expected to be a model for think tanks in Japan. Although it had the potential to be an information hub among social research organisations in Japan, it did not prove to be an excellent think tank or incubation centre for future think tanks. In the late 1990s, the government implemented the reorganisation and downgrading of NIRA.

New organisations, such as the Tokyo Foundation, started policy advocacy, and some newly established NPOs became famous for their advocacy activities, such as the Japan Initiative. These activities occasionally influenced the policymaking process. Many people became interested in policy dispute. Both the LDP and the Democratic Party of Japan (DPJ), which was newly organised as a rival party to the LDP in the late 1990s, were interested in founding their own think tanks in the early 2000s, but neither was able to launch any successfully.

When many Japanese universities restructured their faculties and departments in the 1990s, some of them established undergraduate departments related to policy analysis, such as the Department of Policy Management of Keio University, the Department of Policy Sciences of Chuo University and the Department of Policy Science of Ritsumeikan University. Many universities followed suit, developing up to 80 departments or majors. These universities would later develop respective graduate programmes as well. The National Graduate Institute of Policy Studies (GRIPS) was established in the late 1990s by the Japanese government for the recurrent education of public officials, both in and out of Japan. In addition, major Japanese national universities such as the University of Tokyo, Kyoto University, Tohoku University and Hokkaido University, as well as influential private universities like Waseda University and Meiji University, established policy analysis or policy management graduate schools in the early 2000s. As a result, there are now many faculties and educational programmes in policy studies at both undergraduate and graduate levels in Japan. However, there has not yet been an open and established labour market for policy analysis professionals who have graduated from these schools. Most cannot find policy analysis jobs in the public sector, which generally still looks for recruits among jurisprudence graduates. Thus, there is a gap between the supply and demand of policy analysts.

As the importance of policy analysis and policy studies was recognised to some extent from the mid-1990s, the Public Policy Studies Association, Japan, was founded in the late 1990s, and other specialised academic societies for policy analysis have been established since then. In addition, some local governments and local policy research organisations are forging connections and setting up networks that offer new training programmes and research projects. The appointment of Professor Heizo Takenaka, who was one of the most famous public intellectuals, as the minister for economic planning of the Koizumi cabinet in 2001 made a strong impression about policy analysts among the public.

Dysfunction of the Japanese bureaucracy following political change

The general mistrust of the Japanese ministerial bureaucracy has been prolonged because poor economic conditions have not changed for a long time and the effect of economic policies drafted by the government is doubtful. Conversely, people have increasingly expected politicians to play an active role. Traditionally, Japanese politicians have been interested in micro-interest intermediation, not in macro-policy coordination. Paradoxically, with politicians' initiatives, the burden on bureaucrats – who should coordinate policy consensus among ruling party politicians – has become heavier than before because politicians do not entrust public officials with policy matters. This is completely different to the situation prior to the 2000s. Under these circumstances, bureaucrats are fully occupied with political coordination and have little time to analyse policy content. The total amount of policy analysis activity on the part of the Japanese government has seemingly decreased over the last 10 years, even though the general perception of the importance of policy analysis has been increasing.

Japanese central ministries were drastically restructured in the early 2000s. Many ministries merged into larger entities, the core executive was strengthened and decentralisation to local governments was promoted. Among these changes, the creation of the Economic and Financial Advisory Commission became the focus of public attention under the Koizumi cabinet because economic policy debates inside the government were widely reported through mass media coverage. The centripetal tendencies of the cabinet and prime minister made many officials hope to work at the cabinet secretariat. These new trends have encouraged policy analysts who had not previously had any relationship with the ministries to participate in the policy formulation process through cabinet office or related committees, and the government to improve policy analysis capability.

The change in governing parties in 2009 gave the Japanese government a chance to reorganise policy networks. On the one hand, the DPJ government had demonstrated its inability to manage governmental organisation or to draft consistent policies. On the other hand, it provided an opportunity to re-examine established policies and encouraged new NPOs and intellectuals to cooperate with the government. It enlarged the scope of policy networks in Japanese government.

Under the Abe cabinet since 2012, the LDP regained control, but the policy system changed. Prime Minister Abe tried to utilise this change and introduce a new policy programme that was not the result of inter-ministerial coordination, but based on the will of the prime minister himself, in consultation with his personal advisers. It showed the importance of advice. The result of such policy will directly link with the effectiveness of policy analysis.

As the established pattern of policy formation has been destroyed by political change, the possibility for introducing policy analysis methods into the policy process has increased. At this moment, the pattern of diffusion of policy-related knowledge is unclear because it is just beginning. People gradually became aware of the necessity of policy analysis through the debate on, for example, deflation, nuclear energy and the tax system.

Policy analysis in Japan has gradually developed over a long period, but it has not yet reached its full potential. The number of policy analysts, however, has been steadily increasing and both the government structure and general perception have begun to recognise the necessity of policy analysis. Consequently, the role of policy analysis will increase.

References

Hayakawa, Y. (ed) (2004) *Seisaku Katei Ron* [*Policy Process*], Gakuyo Shobo.

Iio, J. (2008) *Seikyoku kara Seisaku e* [*From Political Struggles to Policy Competitions*], NTT Shuppan.

Matsushita, K. (2006) *Gendai Seiji: Hasso to Kaiso* [*Contemporary Politics: Idea and Memoir*], Hosei University Press.

Miyakawa, T. (2002) *Seisaku Kagaku Nyumon* [*An Introduction to Policy Sciences*] (2nd edn), Toyo Keizai Shin Sha.

TWO

Beyond a formal approach? Seeking adequate policy analysis in Japan

Sukehiro Hosono

Introduction

Policy analysis is a tool for public policy evaluation, with the aim of improving decision-making and implementation. Therefore, policy analysis is useful when policymakers seek to improve efficiency and equity in allocating public goods. Despite these potential benefits, policy analysis generally exerts only a marginal influence on policy formation and decision-making across all government levels. This chapter discusses the fundamental reasons why policy analysis performs only a peripheral role in policy formation.

Japan offers a particularly narrow role for policy analysis compared with other developed countries for two reasons: first, Japan emphasises coordination and compromise between social organisations regarding rationalised policy formation and decision-making; and, second, Japan's immense public debt clearly attests to the nation's inadequate formal approach to rational policy analysis, which should be performed after explicit or implicit political interventions.

To an outsider, Japan appears to be a centralised bureaucratic country based on democracy. Indeed, while Japan does not advocate a planned economy, a 'somewhat restricted' atmosphere nevertheless pervades Japanese society, wherein individuals must be sensitive to the bureaucratic stiffness without any reason. Japanese society thus appears to prefer a 'tepid or lukewarm society' filled with vested interests served by the government.

However, the cumulative government debt needed to maintain this paternalistic society at a high level of welfare is obviously not a rational long-term policy. Moreover, no sober policy analysis has been conducted to provide a solution to this situation. Instead, the greater part of governmental problems has been addressed on a case-by-case basis, without a clear, systematic national policy vision and design.

In 2012, the Japanese public elected a Liberal Democratic Party-led coalition government, which appeared to be *relatively better* at political governance than other parties. This victory was a consequence of disappointment with the Democratic Party governance, which had attempted but failed to completely change the budget under the slogan 'From concrete to people'. The prime minister must understand the utility of policy analysis and apply it when he/she becomes a policy leader. If policy analysis were given a more prominent role in the policymaking process, Japan could recover from its critical fiscal condition. In addition, the global dissemination of more concrete and clarified policy analysis (such as macroeconomic planning for fiscal reconstruction) would provide foreign countries with a framework for properly understanding Japanese policymaking. It is generally expected that the formal approach towards policy analysis promotes the exchange and discussion of ideas between scholars and practitioners, departing from political intervention regarding national policy and international macroeconomic coordination with logical and analytical tools.

Therefore, first, this chapter determines why Japanese society disregards policy analysis. Second, it establishes the need for a formal approach towards policy analysis to accelerate the evolution of the policymaking process. The chapter contains five sections: the first section discusses the general characteristics of the formal approach; the second section explains Japan's unique underemphasis of formal policy analysis; the third section focuses on macroeconomic modelling, the universality of the formal approach and global trends in policy analysis; the fourth section examines the role of policy analysis and the importance of constructing a 'grand design' in Japan; and the fifth section provides a conclusion.

General discussion on the formal approach

Policy analysis is classified into two approaches: the formal and historic. The formal approach focuses on logical and qualitative or quantitative modelling based on analysing relationships and causal connections between key elements. This approach facilitates not only identification of causal inferences, but also exploration of derivational activities, such as predictions, by deducing conclusions from a hypothesis.

Conversely, the historic approach employs an object's uniqueness and peculiarities to conduct an analysis based on the axes of geography and time. Reference, not prediction, is the primary objective of the historic approach as it is based on the perspective that events occur only once; it tries to discern a moral or a lesson (Acemoglu and Robinson, 2012). This chapter concentrates on examining the formal approach, which gradually adds individual specificity to determine a policy agenda's validity, while also considering the universality of the policy analysis approach. The differences between the historic and formal approaches are not significant; they raise the question as to which explanation concerning policy studies is more important: the plausible or substantive (Ramseyer and Rosenbluth, 1995).

Formal policy analysis can be divided into two main approaches: the first is cost–benefit analysis based on the welfare economic paradigm or the normative framework of economics: and the second is model building and simulation of macroeconomic dynamics using real data. The formal approach is more impersonal, universal and neutral as to policy constraints and their pressures than the historic approach, because explanation in the formal approach is relatively and logically more persuasive, with causality or relations between policy variables (Hacking, 1990; Porter, 1995). Nevertheless, as all approaches are expected to be biased and interrupted by political forces, including interested stakeholders, their supporting politicians and organising pressure groups, so, too, can the formal approach be biased or captured by corrupting political and economic factions in the research and publication process (Persson and Tabellini, 2002). One typical and important example of such political intervention is the manipulation of basic economic policy indicators, for example, gross domestic product (GDP) and its growth rate, price indices, public deficit, balance of payments, and so on. These indicators are important and reflect upon the managerial performance of the cabinet and incumbent parties. As a result, the manipulation of these indicators offers political weapons to opposing parties. Therefore, this scenario suggests that the formal approach in policy analysis can represent a double-edged sword.

Hereafter, I focus the present discussion on macroeconomic modelling and simulation. Although cost–benefit analysis is more popular in specific or domestic policy analysis compared with macroeconomic modelling and simulation, the latter plays a more influential and potential role in public policy formation. Moreover, the current formal approach is heavily dependent on cost–benefit analysis rather than macroeconomic modelling and simulation as policy analysis plays a limited role in policy formation. Cost–benefit analysis can be effective in objectively and quantitatively evaluating the functions of political biases and interventions (Adler and Posner, 2001). All Japanese ministries commonly perform cost–benefit analysis to evaluate each policy's implementation, free from special interests. Nevertheless, it is difficult to deny that cost–benefit analysis tends to be biased by the motivations of inner circles, which can emerge with the tacit and/or explicit understanding and approval among their colleagues (Fisher and Forester, 1993). When discussing policy analysis, questions such as 'Was a policy analysis conducted?' and 'Was the policy analysis applied to the actual policymaking process?' should be clearly differentiated. The formal approach ensures this distinction via three processes: first, analysis of the situation to predict the future outcome; second, objective evaluation of the process; and, third, clearer communication to support policy agreements.

Many texts on policy analysis generalise the policymaking process, while some illustrate how policy analysis itself was addressed in the policymaking process (Stokey and Zeckhauser, 1978; Jenkins-Smith, 1990; Weimer and Vining, 2011; Dunn, 2012). The seminal text by Stokey and Zeckhauser (1978) is an example of the formal approach, while Jenkins-Smith (1990) discussed the policy analysis function within the democratic process. Dunn (2012) and Weimer and Vining (2011) provide policy analysis standards in their studies, which increased in thickness at each reprinting. The Japanese researchers Noguchi (1982), Yakushiji (1989) and Hosono (1995) presented the economic-oriented characteristics of policies. These texts highlighted that the idea that the 'welfare of individuals is the supreme goal of public policy' is universal in policy analysis. Simultaneously, 'market failure' and 'government failure' can be ranked as the two most frequent hindrances to achieving this goal. In microeconomics, market failures are discussed in terms of monopolies, uncertainties and externalities, while in macroeconomics, they are discussed in terms of the impact of government intervention on unemployment, commodity prices and international trade friction (Salanie, 2000). On the other hand, government failures are discussed as the outcomes of lax and irresponsible governmental attitudes, as well as inadequate budgetary discipline due to the influence of pressure groups, politicians and bureaucrats (Persson and Tabellini, 2002).

Stokey and Zeckhauser (1978) point out choice-based microeconomics. They include analytical methods (economics, mathematics, operations research and systems analysis) and conclude by explaining the role of choice and decision in policymaking. Stokey and Zeckhauser did not transcend microeconomics; rather, they declared themselves 'neutral' from politics and economics, limiting their argument to 'predict only the consequences', writing about 'goals and means' at the end, despite this being a natural topic to discuss at the beginning. We must ask as to the appropriateness of such an approach. Policy analysis exists to decelerate the collapse before and after government failure, as well as to improve policies, whether a formal or other approach – or a mixture – is pursued; this is the essence of policy analysis (Lindblom and Woodhouse, 1993).

Recently, microeconomics has emerged from simple rationality axioms of fictitious players to include bounded rationality and anomalies; however, it remains vulnerable to unpredictable consequences, which can result from many actors participating in policy spaces. This means that transaction and social costs in the political arena are significantly higher than those in the economic sphere, leading to an increase in non-cooperative or opportunistic behaviours among actors in an uncertain 'prisoner's dilemma-like' situation. Therefore, the previously mentioned factors prevent rational and apt judgements in the policymaking process and reduce governance (Williamson, 1996; Dixit, 1997). Accordingly, the main subject or focal point of public policy analysis has shifted from the market to government failure.

Japan's unique situation regarding the formal approach

Policy analysis is meaningless without prescriptions relating to a policy agenda. For example, despite being a brilliant, formal model offering rigorous mathematical descriptions to explain a balance between falling birth rates and increasing family income, the Becker and Lewis model (Becker, 1981) neither rectifies the declining birth rate nor estimates future population levels. Furthermore, Japan has a unique perspective on this topic. Although sufficient analyses of the current situation, as well as policy predictions, have been made by government institutions, the results have not been seriously considered during the policymaking process by the Ministry of Welfare (now the Ministry of Health, Labour and Welfare).

In the 1960s, the problem of Japan's ageing population was already foreseen, with a demographic analysis concluding that the end of the baby boom after the Second World War would lead to a precipitous decline in the birth rate and the population in the 1980s. At that time, some academics insisted that the population needed 80 more years to stabilise; therefore, careful observation, as well as patient and effective effort, was all that was required (Kono, 2007). Unfortunately, following this recommendation was prevented by the hierarchical structure of the Japanese bureaucratic organ, the so-called Kasumigaseki (the area in which the Japanese central bureaus' offices are located). As higher-ranked bureaus' negligent treatment of the population problem took precedence over lower-ranked ones, Japan missed an opportunity to tackle the problem at an early stage, leading to a slow but large demographic change that is shifting the structure of the entire nation.

This example also reveals the gap between 'knowing' facts from a policy analysis and 'taking advantage of' these facts. This gap occurs in four situations: (1) when one is unaware of the existence of an adequate policy analysis; (2) when one has information as a result of a policy analysis but avoids using it because the result is undetermined; (3) when one has confidence in the results of policy analysis but there is no intermediary; and (4) when one cannot apply the results of policy analysis to a situation. Filling this gap is required to achieve the implementation of policy analysis in Japan.

In terms of the 'reliability' issue, I consider why policy analysis, especially the formal model, is not correctly employed in Japan. A representative example of policy analysis based on the formal approach is the macroeconomic model that was implemented to draw up Japan's economic plan after the Second World War (Hayashi, 1997). Its high level of analysis offered sufficient and statistically refined data compared with its implementation in other countries. Nevertheless, the Japanese government's macroeconomic model was not widely recognised by experts as it lacked accuracy compared with those of the private sector (Suzuki, 1995). With such low reliability, there was little opportunity to 'employ' the model and attract the attention of the public.

So, why was the reliability low? Why does the government's data 'lose touch with reality in the real world', and why was the government unable to fill this gap? The statistical data used in the prediction model were reliable, and the suggested policy measures (such as the monetary and fiscal policies and chosen and used policies) were diverse. In the 1960s and 1970s, the national economy was not as globalised as today and most governments, including that of Japan, could enjoy the public's trust regarding macroeconomic policy. In one typical instance, a distinguished expert from the Bank of Japan stated that 'Japan's money supply is controllable at an accuracy of only 1%' (Hosono, 2009). Despite such a favourable condition, the government's prediction model performed poorly from the outset, as did the medium-term macroeconomic model built in 1965. Paradoxically, despite many efforts to incorporate recent information, the model's accuracy barely improved.

This inadequate improvement can be attributed to the fact that the Japanese government's model contains more exogenous variables than necessary. In the absence of a commanding or strategic office, ministries have significant discretion, which, in turn, hampers the prediction's performance by tying up the model with exogenous variables. Exogenous variables are 'speculative' data emerging from non-coordinated policy scenarios reflecting the ministries' sectionalism. The validity of an assumed exogenous variable prescribes the prediction's accuracy, and its value is determined by the policy scenario. If the expertise from all the concerned governmental departments is combined to formulate a policy scenario, its predictions can be expected to be more precise. However, scenarios drawn by members who lack awareness of the benefits of policy analysis and abuse their discretionary power to incorporate exogenous variables lead to unreliable predictions. These members do not even attempt to improve the model. The French mathematician Laplace accurately stated that 'the right and wrong of social decisions depend largely on the quality of the decision-maker rather than on the decision-making approach, such as the majority vote' (Laplace, 1814).

Furthermore, the assumption that 'the result has already been decided' hampers the model's performance, making it incapable of calculating government-fixed capital formation, for example, or budget allocations for public works projects. As an example, 'Kasumigaseki's bureaucratic dynamics' influenced macroeconomic predictions. During Prime Minister Hashimoto's administrative reform, an extremely popular ditty called 'Metrics by Rule of Thumb' mocked the 'stingy' Ministry of Finance, the 'extravagant' Ministry of International Trade and Industry (now the Ministry of Economy, Trade and Industry) and the 'chaotic' Economic Planning Agency (now merged into the Cabinet Office). Although such ditties do not exist anymore, do these accusations remain accurate despite changing the names of the agencies and ministries involved? Without verification, the predictive performance of Japan's macroeconomic models cannot be improved.

Globalisation has increased the circulation of currency in foreign countries. Therefore, the factor of income from abroad, such as dividend and interest, cannot be ignored. Globalisation complicates policy analysis by making global interactions more chaotic (Schoppa, 1996). Without this understanding, 'the failure in prediction' will lead Japan to suffer from a 'failure at the helm', as was the failure in financial administration after the bubble burst in the 1990s. However, 'Kasumigaseki's jargon or rhetoric', which provides a monthly assessment of the economy, does not reflect responsibility or crisis. What does the statement: 'Japan's economy moderately slows down but continues to expand' mean? Only three simple expressions should be needed in government economic discussions: recovery, uptrend and downtrend (Suzuki, 1995). Pursuing micro-rationality to benefit ministries and agencies does not necessarily ensure macro-rationality, which would benefit the entire country.

Macroeconomic modelling as a typical formal approach

Macroeconomic prediction and planning based on the formal approach is one of the most popular and effective ways to decrease transaction costs in real politics. However, such an approach is not always welcomed, especially in Japan (Hayashi, 1997). This rejection can be traced to the ideological confusion between the 'planned economy in socialist countries' and 'economic planning in capitalist countries' among the politicians and businesspeople who possessed the social power to lead Japan's economy in the post-Second World War era. However, this misunderstanding does not only afflict Japan; it is universal. I present a brief history of the aforementioned reluctance in using the formal approach or planning behaviour. Keynesian macroeconomics can be considered a representative formal approach that is welcomed not only in academia, but also in real politics because of popular distrust in the functioning of real and monetary markets. Economic fluctuations frequently and cyclically cause vicious factors such as suffering, destroying lives and leading to global disorder, which have also triggered worldwide conflicts. Keynesian economic policy endorses an enlarged sphere of government activities in conjunction with policy analysis to prevent excessive accrual of governmental power. However, developed countries' governments at the time believed that Keynesian macroeconomics would support the expansion of governmental power without adopting the idea of additional checks on power via policy analysis.

I now provide a brief history of the macroeconomic prediction model to offer a deeper understanding of its genesis and development. Most econometricians seem to think that macroeconomic models do not represent pure science, but are situated somewhere between art and science, with the models' predictions still expected to be accurate, precise and concrete (Tinberge, 1952; Klein, 1971).

Further, we explain macroeconomic or econometric models as examples of the typical formal approach in policy analysis. Macroeconomic or econometric models commonly identify reciprocal or causal relationships between political and/or socio-economic factors, variables, and phenomena relevant to policy subjects. These causal entities or variables are strictly divided into two categories: the policy targets (or policy ends); and policy instruments (or policy means). The policy instruments are classified into external or exogenous variables and policy targets are internally determined endogenous ones in a formal equation system constructed by policy analysts and econometricians. The work of classification intrinsically depends on the scope, frame, academic discipline and skill of analytic experts and specialists, including economists, sociologists and political scientists (Fisher and Forester, 1993). Moreover, it is similarly important to consider the narrow and local motivations or special interests of these experts and their links to the state and political parties

(Ramseyer and Rosenbluth, 1993; Drazen, 2000; Besley, 2006). Therefore, it is noted that the critical study of classification is crucially important when a team of policy analysts or experts develop an econometric model because it will decide the model's predictive performance. In addition, the classification of variables and empirical data must determine the forecasting performance of macroeconomic models. All endogenous variables are reduced by predetermined endogenous and exogenous variables. These predetermined variables are partly assigned as controlled variables, political messages and end values of cabinet policy, that is, unemployment rate, GDP gap, discretionary fiscal expenditure and money supply, social welfare expenditures, and so on. Moreover, all the international factors are obviously exogenous variables, that is, the global interest rate, global GDP growth rate and so on (Kitaura, 2009).

A formal model using empirical data was developed and employed mainly by Jan Tinbergen at the League of Nations in 1939. However, this approach faced widespread scepticism. One leading critic was J.M. Keynes, who severely criticised Tinbergen's macroeconomic model in the *Economic Journal* (Sutton, 2000). His questions focused on the data set accuracy and theoretical grounding of Tinbergen's multiple causal relationships. Keynes posed questions such as 'Are economic variables measurable?' and 'Are they intrinsically non-stationary?', as well as discussed the correlation matrix of economic variables selected and calculated by Tinbergen. The prolonged discourse between Keynes and Tinbergen enhanced the effectiveness of econometrics, which, in turn, allowed the macroeconomic formal approach to become widely accepted and, thus, utilised in policy formation in developed countries. Econometric studies based on Keynesian macroeconomics gradually gained popularity, with high-performing forecasting and the resulting policy suggestions adopted by political leaders in the developed Western world (Morgan, 1990).

In 1950, an econometric model with 10 variables (six endogenous and four exogenous variables) was developed by L.R. Klein to: (1) predict the macro-behaviour of national economies in quantitative aggregate terms; and (2) evaluate and compare the model with the necessary policy measures and their impact on managing the national economy. Following the predictive success of this model, the Klein–Goldberger model was developed in 1955 to include 21 variables (Klein, 1962, 1971), offering enhanced predictive performance. In 1965, Japanese policymakers developed a medium-term macroeconomic model containing 62 variables (43 endogenous and 19 exogenous variables), which would become the basis of medium-term economic planning (Hirai, 1981).

However, Keynesian macroeconomics lost its influence as stagflation developed after the 1970s' oil crisis and Western governments' faith in robust multiple causal relationships among domestic variables, like the Phillips's Curve, weakened. Ironically, Keynes had already predicted the possibility of causality between controlling and controlled variables vanishing during the aforementioned dispute in 1939. Consequently, alternative models, such as the rational expectations model and time-series analysis, including autoregressive models, gained prominence in academic and practical fields. As a result, market fundamentalism and neoclassical monetarism gained in popularity, leading its followers to declare 'the death of Keynesian economics' and to proclaim 'small government' as the solution to government failure or 'disability of government control'. However, monetarist and market fundamentalist approaches have also gradually lost respect following their failures of policy prescriptions at the end of the Reagan and Thatcher eras. Moreover, innovative macroeconomic models are now being adopted, some of which are severely critical of the older paradigms.

Currently, with developed countries suffering from financial stringency and low growth, some are attempting to resurrect Keynesian models. One such model, the so-called simulating model for financial reconstruction and a sustainable viable economy, is a large-scale model with more than 3,200 equations, and the data are updated and refined annually, quarterly or monthly, as needed, to yield high-performance forecasting and control.

The 'flat economy' concept that emerged from globalisation due to technological and informational innovations has drastically changed the environment surrounding states' policy analyses. Moreover, this concept expands the policy analysis market, but, simultaneously, the supply of policy analysts remains small. Therefore, universities are forced to produce more competent policy professionals and experts. We discuss the education system of the public policy school in Japan in several chapters of this book.

Reasons why the formal model failed to play an important role in Japan

Neither quantitative nor systemic analysis has played a central role in the policymaking process in developed countries, a phenomenon that can be explained by three factors in the context of Japan. The first is the intrinsic structure of the bureaucratic organisations. No effective flow of information existed between the line departments that made decisions and those that implemented policies, or even those that analysed special matters. Staff departments rarely obtained consent from decision-makers compared with line departments, and often lacked the organisational capacity for optimisation and organisational consistency. In addition, policy analysis itself was disallowed or shelved owing to strong resistance from policymakers, who were frightened at the potential damage resulting from publishing facts. The Ministry of Finance has been one such offender despite its departments having a research institute with staff and experts. Although line departments fear facing unexpected obstacles or making trade-offs in policy formation and implementation, their superiority in every ministry makes such conduct frequently permissible. The Japanese rarely blame bureaucratic sectionalism, but instead attribute policy malfunctions to the narrow sectionalism maintained by ministry-specific interests. Typical evidence for such political failure is Japan's infamous and sizeable public debt. While the Japanese government has attempted to correct fiscal anomalies by increasing the consumption tax rate (Kitaura, 2009), it has not attempted to persuade the public or gain their understanding and support regarding public debt reduction using formal policy analysis. On the other hand, the Western world traditionally employs the macroeconomic simulation model to predict the expected results of a particular national economic policy (Suzuki, 1995).

The second reason for the failure to employ quantitative or systemic analysis concerns the validity of both the data and methods. When restrictions exist on data accuracy or a time lag occurs in the data-gathering process, both of which can appear with surprising frequency (especially in international case models), the validity and performance of policy analysis tend to be lower than expected by global society. Even in a national case model, the same result frequently occurs. In Japan, several reasons may explain the lower performance of policy analysis using the formal approach: ministries use different definitions of figures in pursuit of their specific policy objectives, or data are not provided because of tacit or overt factionalism. However, such an outcome can also result from inadequately developed models and/or lack of transparency about model information (Ichimura and Klein, 2011). In such cases, political disputes may be exacerbated by each party using conflicting presumptions derived from partisan objectives, concerns and interests (Morton, 1999; Radin, 2000).

The third reason for the failure to employ quantitative or systemic analysis is the incompatibility between models. Even if sufficient data are provided, many models can be developed to explain the movement of an event under consideration by breaking down the data and underlying theoretical or logical structure. Both theory without refined measurement and measurement without adequate and updated theory are weak in the real political arena, and neither can be used to solve political problems (Koopmans, 1975). Therefore, some advocate 'letting the data speak for themselves' rather than using low-validity models based on limited theoretical or empirical investigations and information (Granger, 1999). This confrontation does not cause any problems in academia, but it is better avoided in the policymaking process in which many actors intensely and keenly compete with political rivals and the winner is determined through social and political selection with a series of coincidences.

This chapter is written hoping that the formal approach becomes more common and respectable in Japan, as I believe that it improves the quality of both policy and political discourse. Hereafter, the discussion focuses on the macroeconomic simulation model as a typical formal analysis to reveal Japanese characteristics in policy analysis and clarify the status of policy analysis in Japan. Japan is the most intolerant among all developed countries in terms of forecasting performance via macroeconomic policy analysis. In Japan, a high level of precision in both analyses and figures – a requisite level that may be significantly higher than that expected in academia – is required, especially from the media, other policymakers, political parties and public opinion leaders. Therefore, to avoid confrontation, policy analysis failing to meet this stringent standard is given limited application. However, an adequate response to the declining birth rate and ageing of society in the context of financial stringency requires a more advanced policy analysis. Policy analysis must not be limited to simple evaluations, but utilised during the policymaking process (Hosono, 2005; Yamaya, 2012).

In Japan, 'policies that are contestable at the elections' have governed analyses' outcomes in administration and politics. The time has come to eradicate the formulation of budgets with no strategic foresight or political consistency and systematise the budget process with a macroeconomic model (Suzuki, 1995). In Japan, the forecasting performance of the Japanese government's macroeconomic model may have been below that of not only models used by private research companies, but also those used in Western countries. Such a low status can be primarily attributed to the inclusion of exogenous variables predetermined by government agencies and restricted by the concerns of particular political groups, as illustrated earlier.

Many political scientists interested in Japan believe that Japan's main decision-making body is not the incumbent party, but rather the bureaucratic body. However, this belief is completely incorrect: the bureaucratic body is effectively and tacitly controlled by the incumbent party, and thus its freedom and neutrality regarding decision-making are restricted (Ramseyer and Rosenbluth, 1993). Evidence of restricted freedom is provided by the predetermined set of exogenous variables included in the forecasting and predicting simulation model, which follows formal and informal discussions in the political inner circle, including those of high-level bureaucrats, special-interest politicians and party leaders. Therefore, we can certainly expect such a model to result in poor performance and yield an implausible output. However, the government also possesses policy instruments and devices, that is, fiscal policy, monetary policy and combinations of the two, to fine-tune economic fluctuations. Hence, from the perspective of data accessibility and control measures, the government's model must attain a higher forecasting ability than other research institutions. However, the reverse is also true (Suzuki, 1995). The incentive to devise a high-performing model that offers accurate predictions is a low priority for the government. Generally, politics is stronger than analytics (Radin, 2000). The Japanese government must honestly and immediately explain the plan to resolve its sizeable public debt, which must be rational, logical and divorced from the political biases of special-interest groups. Therefore, the government should use a standardised macroeconomic model based on an appropriate analysis to yield an accurate solution and policy and rally public opinion around it.

Further, we discuss other aspects of adopting a formal policy analysis approach in Japan to obtain high-quality policy programmes. First, business administrators concerned about the public good and having more 'alternatives' in policy analysis are sorely needed in a globalised world (Hosono, 2010). The importance of alternatives is demonstrated in the US, where think tanks influence policies. A similar policy analysis market must be constructed in Japan to attract and foster the concentration of human resources, which will improve the quality of policy analysis. Second, an advisory panel is a distinctive characteristic of Japan's policymaking process. However, the advisory body members are not always chosen for their high degree of professionalism and expertise; these posts are honorary, providing a convenient shield for bureaucratic intent. However, mature policy discussion is impossible without proper professionals and experts. In particular, when discussing regulatory frameworks, the members may be required to analyse the policy, including alternatives, as independent experts.

Third, 'meta-analyses' combining and testing several policy studies and analyses is required to improve policy analysis. Performance evaluation of policy analysis requires further insights into the ethics, morality and philosophy of the analysis and its context (Goodin and Tilly, 2006). In addition, the most effective style for communicating the result must be determined. A policy is only effective when it is persuasive and responsive. The low predictive performance of the macroeconomic model discussed earlier and its concomitant unpopularity are unique Japanese characteristics that decrease the possibility of worldwide public policy coordination. To overcome these obstacles, we must not limit actors to only subjects involved in administration, but include subjects free from politics, such as those in the private sector, universities and associations of academies, as well as to analyse the cooperation between these organisations (Hosono, 2010). As 'the potential or latent clients' of policy analysis already exist outside the government, Japan is ripe for the construction of a policy market. The final remaining task is constructing a recruiting system to enable the education and cultivation of those engaging in such policy analysis.

Conclusion

Policy analysts often try to please their client by giving the advice that the patron wants to hear instead of proposing the policy that their expertise indicates is optimal.

It is a common scene around the world, but especially in Japan, where public policy has a weak influence on politics, and where, in turn, the influence of politics on policy lacks any long-term vision and simply reveals the raw politics. Moreover, in such situations, policy analysis can rarely provide a radical change of ideas, but it does effectively evaluate the subjects, issues and problems within a specific political field. This limitation has led some to accuse policy analysis of suffering from inherent flaws.

However, I will voice suspicions as to why there are no scholarly voices advocating the need for discussion of policy analysis. Although the formal approach towards policy analysis deserves criticism, a detail-oriented cost–benefit analysis still remains in the mainstream of the formal approach. Considering the current situation of developed countries as lacking political and economic stability, it is time to consider applying the formal approach towards policy analysis in a positive manner to the 'decision of national basic and fundamental policy'. It is for this reason that I narrowed the point of this chapter to a macroeconomic model but not cost–benefit analysis, which is the typical model of the formal approach in microeconomics.

Greater transparency is required not only to improve domestic policies, but also to persuade foreign countries when addressing the need for international policy coordination within a globalised society, especially through simulations based on globally linked open macroeconomic models. While Japan is recognised as a country having refined and comprehensive statistical data, a gap remains between its strictness and performance. This paradoxical phenomenon can be traced to the inadequate effective communication and coordination among ministries and politicians. Occasionally, the Japanese government has no incentive to clearly demonstrate its conduct or the rationale behind its policies; however, democracy exists in the collective consciousness and through social agreement. Japan must immediately construct a new design that follows 'the balanced development of regional economies' to include effective discourse and cooperation with the Japanese people, as well as to show a strong presence within international society. This new design must be initiated and delivered with a bold and sensitive policy analysis. To this end, the formal approach represents the first step towards meeting the minimum expectations for policy analysis in Japan; only then can we exceed those expectations.

References
Acemoglu, D. and Robinson, J.A. (2012) *Why Nations Fail*, New York, NY: Crown Business.
Adler, M.D. and Posner, E.A. (2001) *Cost–Benefit Analysis*, Chicago: University of Chicago Press.
Becker, G.S. (1981) *A Treatise on the Family*, Cambridge, MA: Harvard University Press.
Besley, T. (2006) *Principled Agents?*, Oxford: Oxford University Press.
Dixit, A.K. (1997) *The Making of Economic Policy*, Cambridge, MA: The MIT Press.
Drazen, A. (2000) *Political Economy in Macroeconomics*, Princeton, NJ: Princeton University Press.
Dunn, W.N. (2012) *Public Policy Analysis* (5 edn), Boston, MA: Pearson Education Inc.

Fisher, F. and Forrester, J. (eds) (1993) *The Argumentative Turn in Policy Analysis and Planning*, Durham, NC: Duke University Press.

Goodin, R.E. and Tilly, E. (eds) (2006) *The Oxford Handbook of Contextual Political Analysis*, Oxford: Oxford University Press.

Granger, C.W.J. (1999) *Empirical Modeling in Economics*, Cambridge: Cambridge University Press.

Hacking, I. (1990) *The Taming of Chance*, Cambridge: Cambridge University Press.

Hayashi, Y. (ed) (1997) *Shinpan Nihon no Keizaikeikaku* [*Economic Planning in Japan*] (new edn), Tokyo: Nihon Keizai Hyoronsha.

Hirai, S. (1981) *Nihon Keizai no Simyureishon Bunseki* [*Simulation Analysis of Japanese Economy*], Tokyo: Sobun Sha.

Hosono, S. (1995) *Gendai Shakai no Seisaku Bunseki* [*A Policy Analysis in Modern Society*], Tokyo: Keiso Shobo.

Hosono, S. (2005) *Seisaku Toukei* [*A Tool Box of Policy Analysis*], Tokyo: Chuo University Press.

Hosono, S. (2010) *Komyuniti no Seisaku Dezain* [*Policy Design for Japanese Community*], Tokyo: Chuo University Press.

Ichimura, S. and Klein, L.R. (2011) *Nihonkeizai no Makurokeiryou Bunseki* [*Macroeconometric Analysis of Japan*], Tokyo: Nihon Keizai Shinbun Shuppann.

Jenkins-Smith, H.C. (1990) *Democratic Politics and Policy Analysis*, California, CA: Brooks/Cole.

Kitaura, N. (2009) *Makuro-keizai no Simyureishon Bunseki* [*Macroeconomic Simulation Analysis*], Kyoto: University of Kyoto Press.

Klein, L.R. (1962) *An Introduction to Econometrics*, Englewood Cliffs, NJ: Prentice-Hall.

Klein, L.R. (1971) *An Essay on the Theory of Economic Prediction*, Chicago, IL: Markham Publishing Co.

Kono, S. (2007) *Jinkogaku he no Shoutai* [*A Primer for Demography*], Tokyo: Chuo Koron Sha.

Koopmans, T. (1975) *The Collected Scientific Papers of T. C. Koopmans*, Berlin: Springer-Verlag.

Lindblom, C. and Woodhouse, E. (1993) *The Policy-Making Process*, Englewood Cliffs, NJ: Prentice-Hall.

Morgan, M.S. (1990) *The History of Econometric Ideas*, Cambridge: Cambridge University Press.

Morton, R.B. (1999) *Methods and Models*, Cambridge: Cambridge University Press.

Noguchi, Y. (1982) *Koukyou Seisaku* [*Public Policy*], Tokyo: Iwanami Shoten.

Persson, T. and Tabellini, G. (2002) *Political Economics*, Cambridge, MA: The MIT Press.

Porter, T.M. (1995) *Trust in Numbers*, New Jersey, NJ: Princeton University Press.

Radin, B.A. (2000) *Beyond Machiavelli: Policy Analysis Comes of Age*, Washington, DC: Georgetown University Press.

Ramseyer, J.M. and Rosenbluth, F.M. (1993) *Japan's Political Market Place*, Cambridge, MA: Harvard University Press.

Ramseyer, J.M. and Rosenbluth, F.M. (1995) *The Politics of Oligarchy*, Cambridge: Cambridge University Press.

Salanie, B. (2000) *The Microeconomics of Market Failures*, Cambridge, MA: The MIT Press.

Schoppa, L. (1996) *Bargaining with Japan*, New York, NY: Columbia University Press.

Stokey, E. and Zeckhauser, R. (1978) *A Primer for Policy Analysis*, New York, NY: W. W. Norton.

Sutton, J. (2000) *Marshall's Tendencies*, Cambridge, MA: The MIT Press.

Suzuki, M. (1995) *Keizai Yosoku* [*Economic Forecasting*], Tokyo: Iwanami Shoten.

Tinbergen, J. (1952) *On the Theory of Economic Policy*, Amsterdam: North-Holland.

Weimer, D.L. and Vining, A.R. (2011) *Policy Analysis* (5 edn), Boston, MA: Longman.

Williamson, O. (1996) *The Mechanisms of Governance*, Oxford: Oxford University Press.

Yakushiji, T. (1989) *Koukyou Seisaku* [*Public Policy*], Tokyo: University of Tokyo Press.

Yamaya, K. (2012) *Seisaku Hyouka* [*Policy Evaluation*], Kyoto: Minerva Shobo.

THREE

Policy research movements in local governments

Kimie Tsuchiyama

Local authority policy research

Policy research as a necessity

Local authority policy research was originally initiated by local authority officers facing a pressing need to address specific problems. For a long time, policy research was not recognised as an activity within Japanese local authorities' jurisdiction. Even as late as the 1980s, the ability to address policy issues was thought to be required only by the high-ranking officers of large local authorities (Nishio and Matsushita, 1987: 270–2). The post-war constitution describes local authorities as *chiho kokyo dantai* ('local public entities'); however, this Japanese expression does not convey a sense of true authority or self-government. The guarantee of local autonomy, the new principle of the post-war constitution, was not reflected in the chosen expression. As in the pre-war constitution, local authorities were regarded as lower bodies in a hierarchical or master–servant relationship (Chihobunken Suishin Honbu, 2000: 3), and restrictions were imposed by national government. Although the term '*jichi-tai*' (literally, 'a self-governing body', as prefectures and municipalities) increased in popularity over time, even today, such entities are still officially referred to as *chiho kokyo dantai*, or 'local public entities'.

Nevertheless, due to the social changes resulting from Japan's post-war high-growth period, local authorities conducted policy research and studies to deal with regional issues, became agents in the creation of policies and systems, and pushed forward the 'governmentalisation of local authorities' (Tsuchiyama, 2007). The entities had become *jichi-tai*, and would later be able to be called governments, especially after decentralisation reforms of 2000. This may all be seen as the result of the pressing need for the officers working at the then 3,300[1] local authorities to address the emergence of a wide range of novel challenges.

Policy research and studies in local authorities

The scope of policy research and studies is wide. Working from the assumption that the overall concept or design of a given policy is itself 'always a policy respecting a specific individual area', Adachi (2009: 12–16) roughly divides policy studies into 'studies of individual policies and policy areas' and 'interdisciplinary policy studies'. Interdisciplinary policy studies are further divided into studies on 'policy knowledge', concerning general theory and policy types, and studies on 'policy-related knowledge', concerning knowledge that has emerged from various scientific disciplines that contributes to policy conception and improving the policymaking process.

Some claim, however, that surveys conducted and/or policies drafted in relation to a specific job assignment by the offices of a given local authority are not properly considered policy research and studies (Mori, 1992: 4–5). However, activities performed in relation to a given policy issue, such as information gathering, conducting surveys and analysis, and the drafting of a given policy, may all be regarded as forms of policy research and study activity.

Consequently, here, local authority policy research is defined as surveys, analyses and/or studies of possible measures that may be applied to solving policy issues, as well as training in these matters, conducted by local authority officers or by a local authority in general.

Local authority policy research (as well as the related occasions for initiating such research) may be divided into: those conducted by local authority officers in addressing local policy issues; those conducted by an organisation established by local authorities or individual organisations with an interest in local authority policy; and self-study sessions, societies or local authority job training programmes, which increased sharply after 1980 as venues for policy research by local authority officers.

For the purposes of the discussion, using the above three divisions, the time span between around 1960 and the 2000s will be divided into the following four periods in order to better examine the evolution of local authority policy research.

The first period is the 1960s, when social changes associated with the high-growth period began to demand political solutions to regional issues, progressive local authorities proliferated and policy research was initiated in the search for measures to solve local authority issues. The second period is the 1970s, when such progressive local authorities became pioneers in developing and implementing various new policies, and the function of local authorities as policymaking bodies began to be gradually acknowledged. The third period is between the 1980s and the early 1990s, when the slogan 'the age of regionalism' was commonly invoked, and various local authorities developed and enforced a wide range of policies. The fourth period stretches from the mid-1990s to the 2000s, from when the political resources of local authorities became ever-more scarce due to the deepening financial crisis, and to the decentralisation reforms in 2000 and their aftermath.

The high-growth period and emergence of progressive local authorities: the 1960s to the 1970s

Social change and the beginning of local authority policymaking: the 1960s

The high-growth period and local authorities

Since the Meiji Era in Japan, both the construction of a system of national governance and economic development had traditionally been pursued under the aegis of strong centralised power, or, more precisely, of the absolute and unquestioned authority of a centralised administration. The primary national policy concerns had been national prosperity and defence in the pre-war period, and reconstruction and economic growth in the post-war period; thus, policies and systems for supporting the foundation of civic life were weak.

However, modernisation, consisting of industrialisation and democratisation, greatly altered the social structure during the post-war high-growth period. The large-scale migration of population brought about rapid urbanisation and changes in the industrial structure, resulting in alterations in people's lifestyles and the weakening of the traditional local community. The young workers moving into cities formed an increasingly large part of the municipal demographic, and the concentration of population, combined with the weak foundation for civic life, resulted in public problems connected to everyday life, known as urban issues, which rapidly intensified.

Such public issues, intertwined with civic life, typically reflected the context, characteristics and personality of each region, and context-specific measures to solve these problems, through policies and systems, were required. In these circumstances, municipalities naturally emerged as the institutionalised policymaking bodies most intimately connected to their citizens, and this led to the expectation that such local authorities would act as the policymaking bodies in tackling regional public problems. Citizens' movements for environmental and urban issues spread widely (Krauss and Simcock, 1980), almost for the first time in Japan, and supported new types of local authorities to break the ancien régime.

Progressive local authorities and the beginning of policy research

In the 1963 nationwide local elections,[2] a large number of candidates connected to progressive parties, who pledged to deal with urban issues, were elected as the heads of local authorities, mainly in urban centres such as Yokohama City, and these local authorities became known as 'progressive local authorities'.[3] Those who were members of or were supported by progressive parties had been elected as heads of local authorities in the past,[4] but these local authorities were intrinsically different in several ways. Their most important mission was to solve the issues created by social changes during the high-growth era, setting their priority on civic life more than on economic growth, based on the post-war constitution. A considerable number of such progressive authorities emerged from the late 1960s to the 1970s. Their issues made them face the need for policy development, and it was the start of the innovation of local authorities and autonomy.

These stances of progressive local authorities were typically in direct confrontation with the central government's notion that local authorities were subordinate offices of the central government, and with the government's long-standing policy objective since the Meiji Era, economic growth. Japanese central government is based on the deep and long relationship between the conservative party (the Liberal Democratic Party) and bureaucrats. Progressive local authorities' principles and policies were in conflict with both of them. As epitomised by the so-called 'economic harmony article'[5] of the Environmental Pollution Prevention Act 1967, the government was extremely reluctant to restrict economic activity, and thus very slow to establish social welfare policies that did not directly increase national wealth; when such policies were proposed, they were usually a mere reward for economic growth. Tamura (1983, 112) mentioned about the repulsion from central government officers for the regulatory measures introduced by Yokohama City, then a famous progressive local authority, of its own initiative. Although the innovative meaning of progressive local authorities had not been understood by progressive parties – both the Japan Communist Party and the Social Democratic Party Japan, whose focus was on national-level politics

(Szajkowski, 1986: 4), local autonomy and authorities' innovation were begun by progressive mayors and governors.

The number of progressive local authorities continued to increase through several subsequent nationwide local elections, and this ultimately led to profound changes in the shape of local autonomy in Japan. Fully fledged policy research, conducted out of necessity when drawing up policies for addressing the numerous emerging urban issues, originated during this time. Such efforts by progressive local authorities soon began to transform the image of the local authority into that of a political and administrative policymaking body responsible for regional policy issues, according to the principles of autonomy and decentralisation, and the standards of citizens' participation and freedom of information (Tsuchiyama, 2007: 149–94).

The progressiveness shown by these progressive local authorities became increasingly accepted throughout the 1960s and the 1970s,[6] and this diminished the level of confrontation between the conservatives and progressives with respect to local autonomy, which had been initially caused by the progressive local authorities. Whether one was conservative or progressive in outlook, local authorities could be seen as policymaking bodies with respect to regional issues, developing and executing related policies, as well as autonomous entities conforming to the emerging standards of citizen participation and freedom of information.[7] The idea of *machizukuri* – citizens' partnership and participation in city planning – began to be shared at this time (Watanabe, 2009). The number of such progressive local authorities began to decline in the 1980s, and local authorities that developed excellent policies or systems for addressing regional issues began to be referred to as 'pioneering local authorities' (Tsuchiyama, 2007: 79–83).

Policy research for addressing issues in the 1960s

Many progressive local authorities emerged in urban areas as a result of the elections in 1963 and 1967 (Steiner 1980: 322–6), and developed policies specifically dealing with urban issues, and these pioneering policies and their informing methods began to be shared among local authorities faced with similar problems connected to rapid urbanisation. Gradually, the developed methods spread to a still broader range of local authorities, regardless of whether they were progressive local authorities or not.

The guidelines for residential land development, pollution control agreements and so on, which later evolved into an integrated method known as 'guideline administration', provide one such example. At the time, local authorities could not impose regulations stricter than the national standards. However, with the mounting pressure of social criticism directed at companies involved in uncontrolled residential land development, air pollution and so on, and with the local authorities' right to grant zoning approval in the background, local authorities steered policy towards cooperation. Among these efforts, the 'Yokohama-style' pollution control agreement was highly praised. In this agreement, individual plants promised Yokohama City that their plants would have higher level regulations than legal standards, and would accept on-the-spot inspection by Yokohama City in particular circumstances. Due to the power of the central government, careful research and study is needed to put local authorities' original policies and standards into action, especially for early cases.

Owing to the efforts of these progressive local authorities, the release of comprehensive plans setting out policy issues and their related measures, such as the

Tokyo Metropolitan Government's 1968 mid-term plan, and the publication of White Papers on policy issues based on individual local authorities' independent research, such as Yokohama City's 1964 White Paper on housing complexes, began to multiply.

Policy research organisations and policy research as training/study opportunities in the 1960s

By the 1970s, a job training system for local authority officers had existed for some time; however, it did not include policy research. For example, the Local Autonomy College was established in 1953 by the Act for the Establishment of the Local Autonomy College, enacted in response to the Local Public Service Act, promulgated in 1950; however, a policy research curriculum component was only established in the college after the 1980s. The Japan Center for Cities was established in 1959, but full-scale policy research only began around 1970.

Nonetheless, opportunities for policy research under the aegis of local authorities, as well as local authority policy research organisations, first began appearing in the late 1950s. One such example is the national conferences held by local authority workers' unions as part of their union activities. The All-Japan Prefectural and Municipal Workers' Union (*Jichiro*) began to hold conferences regarding local authority research, conducted on an individual union basis, in 1957, and gradually began to include urban issues and policy issues in the meetings. Additionally, those connected to the Japanese Communist Party formed the Japan Federation of Prefectural and Municipal Workers' Unions (*Jichiroren*), which began holding national meetings collectively referred to as the Local Authority School in 1964.

In terms of research organisations concerned with local authority policies, the Tokyo Institute for Municipal Research was already established in 1922. However, research centres connected to workers' unions, whose stated purpose was policy research, began to be established by individual local authority workers' unions only around the 1960s; these were the Local Government Research Center, connected to *Jichiro*, and the Japan Institute of Local Government, connected to *Jichiroren*.

The Local Autonomy Center, founded in 1965, was an independent organisation unconnected to existing organisations, whose aims were to establish cooperation among progressive local authorities and conduct policy research. It published the bulletin, *Chiho jichi tsu shin* (*Local Autonomy Report*), which covered the pioneering policies and movements of local authorities until the end of the 1980s.

The progressive local authorities and developments in policy research: centring on the 1970s

Reform and popularisation of local autonomy

The 1971 Tokyo gubernatorial election was an intense battle between incumbent Ryokichi Minobe, the progressive governor of Tokyo, and Akira Hatano, who was strongly supported by the Liberal Democratic Party and the Japanese government (Stainer, 1980: 330–1). It was a struggle between those calling for civic welfare and a direct connection with the citizens on the one hand, and economic development and a direct connection with the central government on the other. The result was a landslide victory for the progressive governor. The battle between the two opposing positions with respect to local autonomy, and its dramatic result, became the decisive moment in the popularisation of the reforms spearheaded by the progressive local authorities, whose numbers only increased in the nationwide local elections of 1971 and 1975. The slogans and defining notions characteristic of these progressive local authorities began to transcend political party and regional differences, until the image of the local authority as a policymaking body began to be widely accepted. Under these circumstances, policy development at progressive and other local authorities, as well as the policy research supporting it, proliferated.

Policy research for addressing issues in the 1970s

This was the period in which: many pioneering policies were established, primarily by the progressive local authorities; the necessity for related policy research was beginning to be widely acknowledged; and the pioneering methods of the earlier period were being widely shared. Furthermore, the clarification of policy issues and the formulation of comprehensive plans led to the creation of White Papers, local statistics and indexes, benchmarks, and so on, and these, in turn, led to greater civic participation in the policy process and greater freedom of information.

Some of the policy research of this period was conducted by local authority teams who examined a given policy issue (or issues) for several years. For example, the Tokyo Metropolitan Government and Kanagawa Prefecture jointly examined the management and disclosure of documents containing administrative information (Chihojichi Center Shiryo Hensyu Iinkai, 1998: 269–75), and this led to the enactment of the Freedom of Information Ordinance in the 1980s.

Policy development through local authority cooperation was also observed. For example, the cities of Yokohama and Kawasaki, which were both progressive local authorities, began a joint survey along with Kanagawa Prefecture in 1973, and organised the Conference on Environmental Pollution Control, focusing on Tokyo Bay and on the Tama River. In 1976, at the Meeting of the Heads of Progressive Local Authorities in the Metropolitan Area, they agreed on the joint construction of the Pollution Health Center and on joint research into an environmental assessment system. In addition, through cooperation between progressive local authorities such as the Progressive City Mayors Association, proposals for individual issues and the autonomy system were drawn up.[8] Some of their proposals at this time were implemented in the decentralisation reform of 2000. The association of Progressive City Mayors Association, in this respect, makes a good contrast with the Japan Association of City Mayors and the National Governors Association, that have generally played the role of interest groups (Reed, 1986:40) but not policymaking groups.

Policy research organisations in the 1970s

Meanwhile, the establishment of research organisations and activities focused on local authority policies began to be more actively pursued. At the Japan Center for Cities, independent research, joint research with the Japan Association of City Mayors and contract research from local authorities all sharply increased after 1970 (Nihon Toshi Center, 1976). In 1974, the Japan Research Institute for Local Government was established by *Jichiro*, with a stated purpose of contributing to the 'development of empirical and theoretical research on local autonomy', promoting research exchange and training researchers.[9] Since then, the institute has developed into a fully fledged research institution.

Also during this period, some prefectures began to establish incorporated foundations for conducting policy research (Makise, 2009: 73). A famous example of such a policy research organisation created under the aegis of a local authority was the Kanagawa Institute for Local Autonomy (KILA). First elected in 1975, Kazuji Nagasu, the progressive governor of Kanagawa Prefecture, created a research division within the existing training organisation in 1977, which was to bear the burden of creating the foundation for policy formulation, and then established the aforementioned institute in 1980 (KILA, 2008, 48).

Policy research as training/self study in the 1970s

Reflecting these trends, the spread of policy training as part of local authority officer training and self-improvement began to be seen. Beginning in the late 1970s, an increasing number of local authority officers began to form study groups in their workplaces, sometimes with neighbouring local authorities, and these were termed 'voluntary study groups'.[10] Meanwhile, in 1981, the Rule of the National Personnel Authority was amended, making it possible to consider an officer's voluntary participation in activities held outside work hours as job training, and this supported the popularisation of such voluntary study groups. In 1983, the Study Group for Energizing Local Autonomy was established as a national liaison organisation for these voluntary study groups, and for personnel in charge of local authority job training. According to a survey conducted at the time of its founding, close to 600 voluntary study groups already existed at that time (Chihojichitai Kasseika Kenkyukai, 1984).

Expansion of local authority policy studies

Policy research in the age of regionalism: from the 1980s to the early 1990s

The notion of the 'age of regionalism', proposed in 1978 by Kazuji Nagasu, governor of Kanagawa Prefecture, which served as a buzzword for participation-type decentralisation, gained wide popularity from the 1980s to the 1990s (Kubo, 2006). Although the number of progressive local authorities was decreasing, the image of the local authority as inherently connected with participation and freedom of information, and as an autonomous body regarding regional issues, became widely accepted. As a result, a wide range of activities were conducted by local authorities as policymaking bodies.

This was the period in which the importance of policy research was fully recognised, and the environment for policy research was more fully organised, in terms both of officer training and voluntary research activity. However, it was also a period in which the quality of policy research was coming into question in a number of respects. The stable growth of the 1980s was heating up into the economic bubble, spending by local authorities was increasing, large-scale projects were planned and policies drawn up by planning offices were increasingly criticised as mere rhetoric.

Policy research for addressing issues from the 1980s to the early 1990s

Around 1980, the freedom of information system that the Tokyo Metropolitan Government and Kanagawa Prefecture had been examining began to be enacted as the Freedom of Information Ordinance and spread in this form to some other local authorities. The first Ordinance of Freedom of Information was enacted in Kaneyama Town in 1982, and then in Kanagawa Prefecture and Saitama Prefecture in 1983. The spread of the Freedom of Information Ordinance, in turn, led to the enactment of national legislation, the Act on Access to Information Held by Administrative Organs, also known as the Freedom of Information Act 1999. At that time, about 200 local authorities had the ordinance, and until 2010, almost all local authorities enacted it. This provides an symbolic example of policy transmission in which an ordinance that was the product of pioneering local authorities' policy research spread to other local authorities not merely directly, through horizontal transmission, but from such pioneering local authorities to the national government, and then (vertically) to other local authorities who adopted it later on.

The dynamic relationship between the Freedom of Information Act and the Freedom of Information Ordinance established an important precedent in which a policy or system created as a result of local authority policy research spread from pioneering local authorities to the national government, and then from the national government to the local authorities that had yet to develop such a policy or system, a cyclic process of transmission first noted in 1987 by Keiichi Matsushita (1989: 26), and repeated, for example, in the introduction of the sun-shadow regulation into the Building Standards Act in 1976, and in the Landscapes Act, which was fully enforced in 2005. In addition, the complementary cycle involving policy quality improvement as the concomitant result of the transmission of such policies and systems has also been confirmed (Ito, 2006: 97–9).

Policy research organisations from the 1980s to the early 1990s

At the same time as local authority policy research was becoming widespread, criticisms were emerging regarding the practice of the local authority policy planning sections, which were responsible for drawing up comprehensive plans. The criticisms focused on such sections' perceived detachment from the actual ongoing problems before them, and suggested that the results of the related research often amounted to nothing more than rhetorical reports. By around 1990, critics were calling for a policy and legislative affairs component to be incorporated into the workings of local authorities to improve their legislative techniques. Accordingly, the number of local authorities establishing a legislative affairs department (eg through reorganisation of their document management department) and/or offering related training increased gradually. At the same time (in the late 1970s), private think tanks were increasingly entrusted with the policymaking activities of local authorities, which ultimately led to the creation of the Council of Local Think Tanks in 1985.

Policy research as training/self study from the 1980s to the early 1990s

In the 1980s, increased understanding of the necessity for local authority policy research, and of the need for local authority officers to possess such ability, helped to expand the opportunities for studying policy.

An organisational meeting to establish the Japan Association of Local Government Policy Studies was held in 1986. Emerging from a series of exchange meetings on policy research that began in 1984, the organisation was dedicated to conducting practical region-based research from a citizen's perspective.[11] The establishment of a nationwide policy research organisation, welcoming the voluntary participation of local authority officers, was an epoch-making event. Anchored by such local authority officers, the Association rapidly gained a wide-ranging membership, including citizens, researchers and elected councillors, having 2,000 members by the 1990s.

The Japan Association of Local Government Policy Studies was not registered as an academic society until the 2000s, but its founding marked the beginning of the creation of an increasing number of societies, including academic societies, related to local authority policy research, including the Nippon Urban Management and Local Government Research Association, and the Japan Association for the Study of Local Government, both established in the latter half of the 1980s, followed by the establishment of the Public Policy Studies Association, Japan, in 1996, and the Japan Local Autonomy Association in 2000.

Although the opportunities for education in policy research under the aegis of local authorities, through job training or voluntary study groups, had increased, and activities related to policy studies by pioneering local authorities and local authority officers had expanded, national-level recognition, and even the acknowledgement of other local authorities, was often lacking. In addition, skills related to policymaking were typically still not perceived by non-progressive local authorities as relevant to the work of local authority officers (Mori, 1992: 53).[12]

Even in the latter half of the 1980s, at the Local Autonomy College established by the former Ministry of Home Affairs, and at the Japan Academy for Municipal Personnel (JAMP), established in 1987 by the Japan Association of City Mayors and others, the training programmes for policy research were restricted to manager-class officers of prefectures or large cities (Nishio and Matsushita, 1987: 279–80). Nevertheless, while limited to only managers and wide-area local authorities, training in policy research and policy formulation was beginning to spread even into organisations established by the national government.

From a local authority to a regional government: from the mid-1990s to the 2000s

Two significant changes with respect to policy research arose in the latter half of the 1990s. One was the movement towards decentralisation reform, and the other was the decrease in local authority resources due to the financial crisis.

The decentralisation reforms in 2000 involved the Act on Arrangement of Relevant Acts for Promotion of Decentralisation of Authority, which delegated various functions to local authorities, as well as a significant amendment of the Local Autonomy Act, which profoundly altered the relationship between the national government and local authorities from that of lower and higher bodies in a hierarchical or master–servant relationship to that of an equal and cooperative relationship. In addition, as part of a national system, the range of local authority policy activities was greatly expanded: the assigned functions of local authorities, wherein such authorities acted as subordinate offices of the national government, were abolished; notifications that limited interpretations of laws and regulations were invalidated; and unrestricted interpretations of national law were made possible. In addition, the right to enact ordinances was strengthened, and the Central and Local Government Dispute Management Council was established to deal with disagreements between the national government and local authorities regarding the interpretation of laws or regulations. On the other hand, mergers between local authorities progressed rapidly due to the proactive stance of the Ministry of Internal Affairs and Communications, in keeping with the decentralisation reforms.

At that time, the financial crisis involving both the national government and local authorities intensified. Wasteful expenditures on policies and public works from the time of increasing local authority budgets were increasingly scrutinised. Administrative reforms and cuts in the number of legislators were sought in order to reduce costs, resources for job training and policy research were becoming scarce, and the time allocated to such activities was becoming limited. Such trends were common to Japanese society as a whole, but local authority officers in their 50s were the largest age group, while those under 30 comprised only about 10% of the total number. However, when policy resources are insufficient, there is even greater need for policy research in order to optimise efficiency in solving related problems.

Policy research for addressing issues from the mid 1990s to the 2000s

After the decentralisation reforms of 2000, governmental policy was increasingly defined in terms of local authorities, and among the most common measures to emerge were ordinances such as the local authority basic ordinance, also referred to as a local authority constitution, which was not intended to address a specific problem, but instead to provide a general regulatory framework. Another characteristic of this period was a trend towards policy research more deeply rooted in their local areas. If regional research may be regarded as policy research, then the growth of *jimotogaku* epitomises this trend. With this notion, Tetsuro Yoshimoto, then an officer of the Minamata City local authority, proposed the rediscovery and creative utilisation of regional resources within the living cultural context of a given region, instead of importing what the region lacked, as well as the sharing of these resources, in order to vitalise the region. His proposal positioned not only local authority officers, but also citizens, as primary actors, and had a great influence on regional policy research.

Although policy development based on multi-sector partnerships, which reflected the diversification of policymaking bodies, has been criticised as merely an inexpensive commission for the civil sector, it has nonetheless gained strength as a novel form of policy formulation.

Policy research organisations from the mid 1990s to the 2000s

Beginning in the later years of the 1990s, the creation of policy research organisations within local authorities, in this case, local authority think tanks, once again became the object of attention (Makise, 2009). The incorporated foundation–type policy research organisations emerging in the latter half of the 1970s had been reorganised and reduced; however, this time around, local authority think tanks were established as practical organisations seeking greater effectiveness through cooperation with the section that has real policy issues, and, as such, received considerable attention. Such think tanks were said to be influenced by the aforementioned Kanagawa Institute for Local Autonomy (now Kanagawa Policy Studies Center) and modelled on the Joetsu City Policy Research Unit established in 1998 (Makise, 2009: 101–10). Although these organisations were sometimes established in response to the strong wishes of individual heads of local authorities, and it is too early to make an overall evaluation, they clearly testify to a need for practical policy research.

Policy research as training/self study from the mid 1990s to the 2000s

Although the internal resources available for the policy studies training of local authority officers were, at this time, becoming increasingly limited due to the intensification of the financial crisis, the opportunities for policy research actually increased as the subject became a common feature of the programmes offered by the Local Autonomy College, JAMP, the Japan Intercultural Academy of Local Authorities (JIAM) and so on.

Graduate schools in the field of policy research

With Saitama University's Graduate School of Policy Science, established in 1977 (later separating from Saitama University to become the National Graduate Institute for Policy Studies in 1997), as a model, the Doshisha University Graduate School of Policy and Management, along with a host of other policy studies graduate schools welcoming members of society at large, were established in the 1990s. In 2003, public policy (public administration) was formally introduced into the professional graduate school system, and a professional graduate school in the field of public policy was established. By around 2005, approximately 80 non-professional graduate schools in the field of public policy had been established, and as of 2007, there were eight professional graduate schools (Tamura, 2008: 38–9).

Trans-regional research exchange activities involving local authority officers

As was evident in the case of the voluntary study groups, research exchange activities among interested local authority officers, which go beyond the scope of traditional job training, have become increasingly popular. For example, an open lecture series targeting local authority officers, called the Hokkaido Saturday Lectures on Local Autonomy, jointly held by the Hokkaido Association of Towns and Villages and Hokkaido University, has been offered for 16 years since 1995. As a result of the connections developed through these lectures, the group that planned the Niseko Town *Machizukuri* (district enhancement) Basic Ordinance, said to be Japan's first local autonomy basic ordinance, was born.[13] Another example may be seen in the Society for Interested Municipal Officers, a nationwide group that corresponded mainly via a mailing list, or in the Kinki-area Platform for Creating Autonomy Kyoto

Moyainaoshi Society, a non-profit organisation created by a group of local authority officers to pursue policy research and provide practical assistance.

Policy research and 'governmentalisation' of local authorities

In response to high-growth era societal pressures, local authorities in Japan evolved from the relatively powerless 'local public entities' to true local authorities, and then to comparative equals to the national government after the decentralisation reforms of 2000. In this process, they were gradually transformed into the governmental entities more/most intimately connected with their citizens, and were increasingly entrusted with policy issues and policy resources by their citizens. This change may be seen as the 'governmentalisation' of local authorities. In this chapter, the evolution of policy research was conceived as arising from the fundamental need for local authorities to become such self-governing bodies in order to address regional issues through policies tailored to their respective regions. The chapter also noted the widespread phenomenon whereby the fruits of the efforts of pioneering local authorities were shared with the national government, and then, through the latter's activity, passed on to other local authorities.

As a result, the nation's overall policymaking has been diversified, and collaboration and cooperation (as well as strain and competition) between citizens and corporations, as bearers of regional policy, are becoming more vital than ever. In addition, various forms of collaboration between local communities and college departments, graduate schools and research institutions in the field of policy research are becoming widespread.

It has been argued that the transformation of local authorities into governmental bodies, as well as local authority policy development, is certain to be restricted by the centralised national government. However, institutionally, decentralisation has undeniably been accomplished to a certain extent. On the other hand, the environment surrounding local authority policy research and policy development has clearly been affected by the financial crisis and reductions in administrative activities. In addition, restrictions on policy resources are intensifying due to the long-term evolution of the social structure caused by the low birth rate, increasing longevity and challenging economic environment in Japan.

Nevertheless, if local authority policy research is indeed necessary for addressing regional issues, what is truly required is policy research founded upon the effective utilisation of limited resources. As the governmental entities most intimately connected with their citizens in dealing with regional issues, local authorities are expected to take advantage of the institutional changes resulting from the decentralisation reforms, and to strengthen and refine their policy research capabilities.

Notes

[1] Japanese local government is a two-tier system. There are 47 prefectures, and in the 1970s, there were approximately 3,300 municipalities. Due to the great Heisei mergers of the 2000s, the number of basic local authorities has been reduced to roughly 1,700.

[2] After the war, a new constitution and the Local Autonomy Act were enacted, and in 1947, elections were held in all the local authorities. From that time onwards, elections

of the heads and legislators of local authorities, and elections for local authorities that have seen no mid-term resignations or dissolution, have been held at the same time, every four years, and are referred to as nationwide local elections.

[3] The number of cities (thus excluding prefectures, towns and villages) considered progressive local authorities was 84 after the 1963 nationwide local elections, 92 in 1967, 114 in 1971, 122 in 1975 and 103 in 1979 (data from Zenkoku Kakushin Shichokai and Chihojichi Center, 1990: 549–58). The total number of cities in Japan was 560 in 1965, and 643 in 1975. Thus, approximately 20% of the cities in Japan were progressive local authorities.

[4] Ninagawa Trazo was a famous Kyoto prefecture governor in office from 1950 to 1978. Krauss and Simcock (1980) pointed out that the Ninagawa regime manifested itself more in distributive and regulatory policies than in redistributive ones. He held strong charismatic power for many years. After his time, progressive party candidates have not won the elections.

[5] Article 1, Paragraph 1 of Environmental Pollution Prevention Act 1967 states that the Law's 'purpose is to protect the health of the people and preserve their living environment'. However, Paragraph 2 states that 'the preservation of the living environment prescribed in the preceding paragraph shall be in harmony with sound economic development'. This statement was subjected to severe criticism, and as part of a major amendment of the Environmental Pollution Prevention Act, in 1970, when pollution problems had become the focus of increasingly serious disputes, this 'economic harmony article' was deleted.

[6] For example, in 1975, the then mayor of Yokohama City, Ichio Asukata, said that:

> During the nationwide local elections, almost all progressive policies were copied by the conservatives … it became difficult to distinguish between the conservatives and the progressives; and even when there was a difference, the general perception taking hold among the citizens was that it was merely a difference in number. (Zenkoku Kakushin Shichokai and Chihojichi Center, 1990: 11)

[7] The progressive local authorities were not the only local authorities engaged in policy development. The first local authority to establish guidelines for residential land development, so as to establish some level of restriction on indiscriminate land and other development, under the name of Development Standards for Housing Complexes, Etc., was Kawasaki City in 1965, which was at that time not a progressive local authority (Tsuchiyama, 2006: 53–7). This chapter positions progressive local authorities at the inception of policy studies in Japan because: (a) they were founded on the premises of the principle of autonomy and the transformation of the image of local authorities; (b) the policy studies by such progressive local authorities were conducted not merely as means of addressing individual issues, but in the manner of a fully fledged policymaking body; and (c) their movement changed the fundamental approach to policy studies nationwide.

[8] For example: 'A Study on European Progressive Municipalities', which aimed to compare, survey and identify issues involving progressive local authorities in Japan and Europe (1968); a survey on the issue of the excess burden of nursery school costs and so on

(1973); a study on the regulation of exhaust gas from motor vehicles by progressive local authorities in the greater metropolitan areas (1974); and 'Recommendations on Regional Administrative and Financial Reforms for Establishing Local Autonomy' (1978; see also Zenkoku Kakushiin Shichokai and Chihojichi Center, 1990: 168–86). In addition, it is said that, at the time, Saburo Ito, Mayor of Kawasaki City, was considering a joint proposal with Yokohama City for an environmental assessment system (Ito, 1982: 151).

[9] See the webpage of the Japan Research Institute for Local Government, 'About us'. Available at: www.jichisoken.jp (accessed 10 January 2013). The institute became an incorporated association in December 1994, and a public interest incorporated foundation in March 2010.

[10] See Chihojichitai Kasseika Kenkyukai (1984: 322); however, the exact expression as to the timing in the original document was 'between around 1970 and 1975'.

[11] Article 2 of the Rules of the Japan Association of Local Government Policy Studies.

[12] When involved in the planning of the Japan Association of Local Government Policy Studies, Mori recounts being told that 'It may not be prudent for such a local public body to engage in policy-making, since Kanagawa Prefecture may well be perceived as presumptuous' (Mori, 2006: 56, 60).

[13] In the 1970s and 1980s, some local authorities considered enacting a local authority constitution nearer in form to a home rule charter. Among these were the cities of Kawasaki and Zushi. However, none were able to gain the approval of their respective assemblies required for such an enactment.

References

Adachi, Y. (2009) *Kokyo Seisakkugaku towa Nanika* [*What is Public Policy Studies?*], Minervashobo.

Chihobunken Suishin Honbu (2000) 'Start! Chihobunken' ['Start! Decentralization'], Headquarters for the Promotion of Decentralization HP. Available at: http://www.bunken.nga.gr.jp/data/link/start.pdf (accessed 1 February 2013).

Chihojichi Center Shiryo Hensyu Iinkai (1998) *Shiryo Kakushinjichitai (zoku)* [*The Material Collection of Progressive Local Authorities(2)*], Nihonhyoronsha.

Chihojichitai Kasseika Kenkyukai (1984) *Jishukenkyu Jissen Handbook* [*The Handbook for Practical Voluntary Studies*], Sogorodokenkyuzyo.

Ito, S. (1982) *Nomi to Kanadzuchi* [*The Chisel and the Hammer*], Bokutakusya.

Ito, S. (2006) *Jichitai Hatsu no Seisakukakushin* [*Policy Innovation from the Local Authorities*], Bokutakusya.

KILA (Kanagawaken Jichi Sogo Kenkyu Senter) (2008) *Chihojichitai ni okeru Seisakukenkyu no Ayumito Kongono Tenbo* [*The Progress and the Vision of the Policy Studies in Local Authority*], KILA.

Krauss, E. and Simcock, L. (1980) 'Citizens' Movements: The Growth and Impact of Environmental Protest in Japan', in K. Steiner, E. Krauss and S. Flanagan (eds) *Political Opposition and Local Politics in Japan*, Princeton University Press.

Kubo, T. (2006) *Chiji to Hosakan* [*The Prefectural Governor and the Aides*], Keibundo.

Makise, M. (2009) *Seisakukeisei no Senryaku to Tenkai : Jichitai Thinktank Josetsu* [*The Strategy and Development for Policy Making: An Introduction to the Local Authority Thinktank*], Tokyo Horei Syuppan.

Matsushita, K. (1989) *Toshigatasyakai no Jichi* [*The Autonomy of the Urban Type Society*], Nihonhyoronsya.

Mori, K. (1992) *Jichitai no Seisakukenkyu* [*The Policy Study of Local Authority*], Kojinnotomosya.

Mori, K (2006) *Jichitaigaku no 20 nen* [*The 20 years of the study of local authority*], Kojinnotomosya.

Nihon Toshi Center (1976) *Nihon Toshi Center: Sono 15nen no Ayumi* [*The Japan Centre for Cities: 15 years' History*], Nihon Toshi Center.

Nishio, M. and Matsushita, K. (1987) 'The Dialogue, from Public Official Training to Autonomous Studies', *Chihojichi Tsushin*, 206:1–4, Chijojichi Center.

Reed, S.R. (1986) *Japanese Prefectures and Policy Making*, University of Pittsburgh Press.

Steiner, K. (1980) 'Progressive Local Administrations: Local Public Policy and Local–National Relations', in K. Steiner, E. Krauss and S. Flanagan (eds) *Political Opposition and Local Politics in Japan*, Princeton University Press.

Szajkowski, B. (ed) (1986) *Marxist Local Governments in West Europe and Japan*, L. Rienner Publishers.

Tamura, A. (1983) *Toshi Yokohama wo Tsukuru* [*Building the Urban City Yokohama*], Chukoshinsyo.

Tamura, H. (2008) 'Recent Researches of Higher Education of Public Policy: 1 The Education of Graduated Course and the Graduated School of Public Policy' (in Japanese), in K. Tsuchiyama and O. Oyano (eds) *Chiikikokyoseisaku wo ninau Jinzaiikusei* [*Human Resource Development for Local Public Policy*], Nihonhyorohnsya, pp 27–48.

Tsuchiyama, K. (2006) 'The Historical Position of Kawasaki City as the Pioneering Local Authority' (in Japanese), in A. Uchikoshi and M. Uchiumi (eds) *Kawasaki Shisei no Kenkyu* [*The Study of Government of Kawasaki City*], Keibundo.

Tsuchiyama, K. (2007) *Kodoseichoki Toshiseisaku no Seijikatei* [*The Political Processes of Urban Policies of Japan during High-Growth Era*], Nihonhyoronsya.

Watanabe, S. (2009) 'Machizukuri in Japan: A Historical Perspective on Participatory Community-Building Initiatives', in C. Hein and P. Pelletier (eds) *Cities, Autonomy, and Decentralization in Japan*, Routledge.

Zenkoku Kakushin Shichokai and Chihojichi Center (eds) (1990) *Shiryo Kakushinjichitai (zoku)* [*The Material Collection of Progressive Local Authorities (Continued)*] , Nihonhyoronsha.

FOUR

Policy analysis and normative theory: with a focus on social security policies

Wataru Sano

Introduction

It has long been noted that public policy in Japan is ad hoc in nature, unsystematic and inconsistent. Why has this situation persisted for so long? Much debate has already been devoted to this very question. Causes that have often been cited include the existence of vertical divisions in hierarchical administrative organisations and the inability by the ruling cabinets and political parties to integrate those divisions.

Of course, these observations are, for the most part, valid. In addition to such factors, however, I identify deficiencies of policy analysis, particularly of analyses involving values and norms. In reality, a single policy is formed through a complex interaction among many factors: an array of laws, codes, governmental and ministerial ordinances, notices, much administrative work, budgets, and a host of administrative organisations involved in the policy's implementation. Unless these elements are integrated to realise a specific goal, it is difficult to achieve that goal effectively. To accomplish this kind of integration, it is necessary to clarify the values and norms that form the rationale for that policy. In my view, the absence of such analysis has contributed to the inconsistent nature of policy in Japan.

As an example, I take up social security policies and confirm that they are deficient in terms of consistency, and explore the factors behind that deficiency.

The state and characteristics of social security policies in Japan

To begin with, I present an overview of Japan's social security policies, and go on to discuss whether they can be characterised as truly inconsistent, and, if so, in what sense.

History and the present

As is the case with many developed nations, poverty relief policies in Japan were first put in place in the late 19th century in response to the swelling numbers of the poor associated with the expansion of the market economy, industrialisation and urbanisation. The government's stance was consistently that the burden of providing assistance to the needy should be shouldered by their families and their local communities. However, to deal with frequent serious economic recessions and the ensuing social unrest, the government began to devise new measures. As a result, by the outbreak of the Second World War, Japan had in place social security policies that were aimed at single-mother households, the elderly and especially disabled veterans and the families of dead soldiers. Furthermore, to maintain the power of the army, a national health insurance law and employee pension insurance law were enacted during the war.

To accommodate the vast numbers of people who became poor and needy as a consequence of Japan's subsequent defeat, the poverty relief schemes that had existed were consolidated and the Public Assistance Act was established. This new law not only resolved the complexities stemming from numerous overlapping schemes, but was developed in the spirit of the new constitution; hence, it eliminated the mechanisms by which military personnel were given priority and focused on treating all needy persons the same. Later, in 1950, for the purposes of explicitly recognising the right of all Japanese citizens to receive public assistance and removing disqualification clauses, the Public Assistance Act was revised. Around the same time, to address problems that could not be dealt with under the Public Assistance Act alone, the Child Welfare Act 1947 and the Act on Welfare of Physically Disabled Persons 1949 were enacted. Furthermore, around 1960, a series of laws were passed to provide assistance to people with intellectual disabilities, the elderly and single-mother households. In addition to the system, schemes for universal national pensions and universal health-care insurance were established as well.

The late 1960s saw the emergence of the 'progressive local governments' (*kakushin jichitai*) throughout Japan. These were local governments in which the leaders were backed by progressive parties. As they pursued welfare policies independently of the central government, around 1970, the central government began to move ahead with more progressive welfare policies. For example, people 70 years or older became exempt from paying medical expenses, and pension payments were raised considerably. This trend, however, did not last long. Once the 1973 oil crisis hit, the shift towards greater fiscal soundness gained momentum. In the latter half of the 1970s, the number of progressive local governments began to decline, and people began calling for cuts to welfare budgets at the national level as well. The government laid out its vision for a 'Japanese-style welfare society' that emphasised mutual assistance within families and mutual support within local communities. This initiative was critical of more generous welfare policies, saying that they would increase people's dependence on the government and invite the 'British disease' (cf Shinkawa, 1993).

At the same time, however, the social security budget continued to consistently grow throughout and after the 1970s. In part because of Japan's rapidly declining birth rate and aging population, social security benefit expenses have ballooned sharply in recent years. Moreover, around the year 2000, a nursing care insurance scheme was adopted and child benefits were increased, which is indicative that the government has not necessarily sought only to curtail welfare spending.

Like other developed nations, Japan has implemented most of the basic policies, though it has taken a zigzag path in doing so. In terms of Esping-Andersen's typology, Japan has elements of both conservative and liberal regimes, in that livelihoods are maintained through reliance on employment and family, while risks to livelihoods posed by illness or accidents are covered by insurance schemes. For people who have become unable to maintain their livelihoods even with these insurance schemes, the central government offers selective support through its public assistance. Although Japan's social security-related budget takes up more than a small portion of the government's total budget, as a percentage of gross domestic product (GDP), it is about as low as that of the US (Esping-Andersen, 1990). What is more, Japan's social security policies have several characteristics not seen in other developed countries.

First, the elderly enjoy a particularly generous portion of the country's redistributed wealth, but government assistance to other age groups and other recipients is meagre. For this reason, Japan's social security policies do not sufficiently contribute to the alleviation of economic disparities. Second, compared with other countries, the benefits are substantial, but the number of people receiving assistance is extremely small (Uzuhashi, 1999). Third, the government of Japan has placed a high priority on having its citizens maintain their livelihoods through employment rather than through reliance on welfare benefits and public insurance, yet these ideals have been realised not as a result of affirmative programmes to provide re-employment assistance or job training, but as a by-product of efforts to protect corporations through public works projects and regulations (Miyamoto, 2008). The last characteristic is one common to many Japanese laws, but it is especially true of laws relating to social security policies: the provisions of the articles are vague and subject to broad interpretation (cf Ohashi, 1989).

Inconsistency

The sketch I have drawn hints at the fact that, compared with the social security policies of other countries, the guiding principles behind Japan's policies are ambiguous and lack consistency. A broad spectrum of principles, philosophies and ideals has been put forth regarding social security. Nevertheless, the actual policies currently in place lack any consistency.

First, the links among the various schemes operated under Japan's social security policies are weak. For example, the minimum standard of living established according to the Public Assistance Act is supposed to be used not only as a criterion for determining whether to grant public assistance, but also in the determination of the minimum wage and pension payments. In reality, however, these are not always consistent with one another. For example, it is common for people working at a job that pays the legal minimum hourly wage to make less than what they would receive if they were on public assistance.

Second, the issue of compatibility with policies adjacent to social security policies is not sufficiently taken into account. For example, it should be essential to take into account links to employment and education when considering the issue of social security, but not even that is done adequately. In fact, there have been no substantial reforms of the kind seen in many other countries, for example, the coupling of unemployment benefits and public assistance (cf Tsuru, 2000; Tabata, 2011).

Third, the provisions of the relevant laws remain abstract and vague, and implementation is often left up to local governments, so the substance of many social security policies tends to vary from one local government to the next. Moreover, the way in which the policies are implemented tends to depend on the socio-economic situation and social climate, not on any value or principle. As for public assistance, it becomes clear that, although the scheme is supposed to be implemented uniformly throughout the country for the purpose of guaranteeing a minimum standard of living, there exist large variations in how it is administered from local government to local government. Of course, one might be tempted to think that the government has deliberately allowed such variations, but given that the Ministry of Health and

Welfare frequently issued firm directives to local governments in the past, based on at least a consistent line of thinking, it is difficult to conclude that the government intentionally tolerated these variations. The truth is rather that whenever the mass media has brought attention to problems and public opinion has begun to shift, the government has responded frantically by issuing official notices. Conversely, to the extent that it does not garner the public's attention, the central government has continued to leave the administration of the scheme completely in the hands of individual local governments. For example, the scope of eligibility for public assistance has been (arbitrarily) widened and narrowed based on notices from the government and on the discretion of the individual local governments (cf Fukawa, 2009).

Fourth, Japan's social security policies are not merely fragmented; they are often changed haphazardly. It is, of course, sometimes necessary to revise policies as the situation demands, but before doing so, there should be adequate consideration and discussion as to whether changes should be made in light of the policies' initial guiding principles, or, alternatively, whether the guiding principles themselves should be changed. There have, in fact, been major reorganisations of social security policies in many countries in recent years, but in all of those instances, the changes to the principles (or the changes to the interpretations of the principles) were made clear. In comparison, in Japan, partly because of the ambiguities in the laws' provisions, in many cases, substantive changes to policy principles are made due to changes in interpretations of laws guided by government notices and such without adequate discussion of those principles.

For example, from 1948 to 1960, for the purpose of eliminating absolute poverty, the public assistance payment amounts were calculated using a market basket method. In the turbulent years following the war, the objective present in the minds of the people involved in the enactment of the Public Assistance Act was to give every citizen the ability to maintain a minimum standard of living, and they attempted to estimate the necessary amount using necessary consumer goods. However, as the country's economic growth accelerated, with this calculation method, the government became unable to justify increases in payment amounts commensurate with the rising standard of living of ordinary citizens. Therefore, in 1961, on the authority of the minister of health and welfare, a method using Engel's coefficient replaced the market basket method for calculating payment amounts. This method used as a point of reference the ratio of food expenses to the total expenses of low-income households to determine the public assistance payment amounts. The intent of this method was to guarantee a standard of living relative to the entire population. To put it differently, a scheme designed for the purpose of guaranteeing the minimum level of economic security to survive in the chaotic post-war years was transformed through changes to payment calculation methods into a scheme whose purpose was to narrow economic gaps (cf Iwanaga, 2011). If we look only at the amounts, we see that they have merely grown to levels higher than in the past, but behind that increase, there was clearly a change made to a policy principle, and the problem lies in the fact that the government altered the guiding principle of the policy without explicitly indicating that it was doing so. Furthermore, while some justification has always been provided, the effect of those repeated changes has been to cause the purpose and guiding principle of the scheme itself to become increasingly opaque.[1]

The causes of inconsistency

The diffusion of political and administrative power

So, what is the cause of the inconsistent nature of social security policy? Generally speaking, the greatest factor is the diffusion of political and administrative power.

It should first be noted that the Liberal Democratic Party (LDP), which has long been the ruling party, was not born out of a clear set of shared principles. Rather, it began as a melange of politicians from different parties that came together as an opposition force in response to the merger of the leftist and rightist camps of the Social Democratic Party of Japan (SDPJ). Moreover, because the single non-transferable vote system (which existed until 1994) made it nearly impossible to enforce greater party discipline, the differences in policy preferences among the different political cliques and among different Diet members within the party were quite large. It was thought that dealing pragmatically with policy issues was the proper stance for a conservative political party to take. There were considerable differences in philosophy within the LDP with regard to social security policies as well (Tanabu, 2011), but those differences rarely compelled them to have discussions with the aim of sharing common principles. From the 1970s onward, Diet members commonly referred to as 'special interest legislators' (*zoku-giin*) emerged, and a sturdy 'sub-government' involving politicians, bureaucrats and interest groups evolved. As a result, the ability of cabinets and of the LDP to integrate declined even further. This decline, together with the vertical divisions, meant that many policy arenas became increasingly exclusive. As these policy arena memberships became more and more static and their members came to possess a kind of 'extraterritorial' status, policymaking increasingly turned into an unmitigated process of reconciling different interests (Inoguchi and Iwai, 1987).

Regarding social security policies, from 1949 until 2001, the Advisory Council on Social Security was an authoritative organisation, with the power to research, deliberate and issue advice on all matters related to social security policies. It was expected that this advisory body would have discussions on guiding principles and visions for social security policy as a whole and then develop policies in a systematic manner, but, in reality, it did not adequately fulfil the role. Based on recommendations in the Wandel Report, the Advisory Council on Social Security was established as an advisory organisation to the prime minister. It was made up of Diet members, bureaucrats, academics and representatives from industry and labour unions. As its membership numbered all of 40 people, it may have been difficult to have substantive discussions from its very inception (cf Murakami, 2000). In addition to the Council, there existed many other advisory councils and study groups within the Ministry of Health and Welfare, such as the Central Social Welfare Council. With the 2001 reorganisation of ministries and agencies, many of these advisory bodies were consolidated, but many still exist. For example, as for advisory boards related to public assistance issues, under the Social Security Council, there is a welfare working group, a public assistance criteria working group and a special committee for exploring modes of assistance to the poor. Furthermore, under the welfare working group is a panel of experts dedicated to examining the ideal roles that public assistance should fulfil. There also exist many unofficial study groups and committees. While it is not that uncommon for these organisations to consult informally with one another – partly because the memberships in them overlap to a certain degree – for the most part, the discussions by these councils and study group organisations are held with the aim not of actively developing a coherent system of policies guided by a consistent set of principles, but rather to discuss issues individually on a per-topic basis.

Of course, even under this kind of system, there have been conflicts and disputes among sub-governments. In most cases, they have either been resolved through an 'add and halve' style of reconciliation, or have resulted in deadlocks because of 'postponed' discussions. Very little effort has been exerted on the part of politicians and bureaucrats to return to policy principles and, through open debate, to follow through with their positions in a logical manner. This is likely due to the absence of a power base capable of achieving that kind of consistency, and the fact that neither politicians nor bureaucrats have shown the desire and willingness to try to bring about such consistency.

The diffusion of political and administrative power also occurred between the central government and local governments. More so than in other countries, the provisions of Japanese laws are quite ambiguous and there is a great deal of room for discretion in interpreting them. As a result, their application is largely dependent upon individual decisions made when and where they have to be applied. Even if the policy is a national one, its implementation is often delegated to local governments (cf Hatakeyama, 1989). In cases involving social security policies in particular, it was not uncommon for local governments, welfare offices and caseworkers to arrive at different decisions, a reality that caused the guiding principles behind the social security schemes to become even more ambiguous.

Deficient analyses

The diffusion of political and administrative power has so far been put forth as the most widely accepted factor underlying the inconsistent nature of policy, and I do not intend to refute that argument. I would nevertheless like to further note not only that this diffusion of power directly has given rise to inconsistency, but also that the fragmentation of the policy process has made any discussion of principles and values extremely difficult, and this might have further exacerbated the inconsistency of policies. Furthermore, I wish to point out that even if the diffused state of political and administrative power were somehow reversed, that alone would not likely lead to consistency in policies. I focus on and discuss deficiencies in policy analysis as an additional factor impeding the consistency of policies. To that end, I place policy analyses into one of two types: empirical analysis involving the recognition of current realities and the elucidation of causality; and analysis involving values and norms.

To begin with, any analysis requires a certain level of knowledge of the contemporaneous situations. Of particular note is the staggering amount of research that was done on the lives of the impoverished for the purposes of establishing public assistance criteria, research that was utilised during policy design phases. In fact, even before the war, many scholars in the field of social policy, inspired by the work of Rowntree, had already begun building on research into the lives of the poorer segments of society. Likewise, a number of labour unions conducted studies to accumulate data to justify their demands for higher wages. The Ministry of Health and Welfare was not only more than eager to utilise the findings of these research efforts, but also conducted various studies of its own. For example, for some years after the war, around the time that the market basket method was adopted for calculating public assistance criteria, a series of detailed studies was conducted concerning consumer behaviour in poor households, the findings of which led to considerations of everything from how people ate fish to how many pairs of underwear they needed. Even after the switchovers to the Engel method and the parity method, careful studies were conducted of the spending habits and day-to-day lifestyles of ordinary households, with detailed data collected on the differences in lifestyles among each income strata (Soeda, 1995; Iwanaga, 2011).

That said, the forecasts and analyses of the causes of poverty conducted by the government were not always sufficient. With regard to public assistance, for some time after war, the existence of poverty was viewed as unavoidable. Little attempt was made to analyse the underlying causes. The forecasts that were made never rose above conjectures based on the individual official's experience and intuition. Few, if any, analysis was performed, and as a consequence, unanticipated developments were common. In the 1950s, for example, large numbers of tuberculosis sufferers became public assistance recipients. This was because drugs to treat tuberculosis had become widely available before there was a national health insurance scheme covering the whole population, a scenario that the Ministry of Health and Welfare had not foreseen (Takechi, 1996). This lack of foresight is not just evident in the area of public assistance. Many social security policies not only strove to guarantee human rights, but also had the (implicit) objectives of maintaining a healthy workforce, preventing crime, improving the economy and so on, but there is very little evidence that the government made empirical predictions from these perspectives. For example, it was only in the 1980s that serious research into the macroeconomic effects of social security policies commenced in Japan.

In the preceding examination, I have attempted to demonstrate deficiencies in analyses involving the understanding of current realities and causal relationships. In the same vein, there have also been similar inadequacies in analyses regarding values and norms. Needless to say, the issue of values and norms is a critically important one in the field of social security policy. The issue has been the topic of many debates in a broad range of academic fields. Despite this, values and norms have unfortunately not been given adequate consideration in the actual design of policies.

First, even though diverse sets of values are especially relevant to social security policies, in many cases, the focus of social security debates has been exclusively on human rights guarantees, with little consideration given to how they relate to other values or the prioritisation thereof. Generally speaking, many different values and norms are closely tied to social security policies, including matters of rights, fairness, efficiency, public order, autonomy, solidarity, social inclusion and many more. Surprisingly, however, the prioritisation of these values is rarely discussed outright when policies are actually made. Even if we just limit our scope of examination to that of public assistance, it becomes clear that even the most basic questions have rarely been subject to debate, questions such as: 'Just what constitutes the minimum standard of living that the policy aims to achieve?'; 'How should we think about the personal responsibility of the recipients?'; 'How should values of autonomy be taken into account?'; and 'What kind of stances should be taken on the issue of the balance between the merits of public assistance and its costs?'.

Another observation worthy of making in relation to this point is that even when two or more policies share similar objectives, if the field or targets of those policies differ, they tend to be designed in accordance with different standards. In fact, the issue of compatibility with the standards used in other policy fields is not even brought up for debate. For example, when people advocate for the protection of small- and medium-sized enterprises, the protection of small farmers, or the revitalisation of depopulated communities, they frequently base their arguments on the need to 'protect the weak' and invoke the idea of a national minimum, yet there is rarely any debate over the consistency of the values and principles that they have cited with the values and ideals pertinent to 'protecting the weak' in the context of social security policy.

In my opinion, the deficiencies in empirical policy analysis and in analysis concerning norms and values may have contributed in no small part to the lack of consistency in Japan's social security policies. Why, then, has there not been adequate discussion and analysis regarding values and norms?

Reasons for the absence of value analysis

I think that there are five reasons for the paucity of discussion and analysis in Japan concerning values, norms, guiding principles and ideals, particularly as this issue relates to the inconsistency of policies, which I set out in the following.

The socio-economic context

First, we can cite Japan's unique socio-economic circumstances in the aftermath of the war. For a certain period of time in the post-war years, the government was able to serve its purpose just by concentrating on resurrecting the areas that had been reduced to ruins during the war, rebuilding a collapsed infrastructure and passing the minimum required legislation. There was little need to weigh up the priorities of different policies. It only had to fill in its *tabula rasa* with the necessary systems in each individual field. These circumstances not only rendered discussions of values and principles unnecessary, but also made such considerations superfluous with regard to the consistency of policies. On top of that, because economic development continued for many years after the government finished putting in place the minimum necessary infrastructure, it was able to continue to provide generous handouts, and was not therefore faced with the necessity of prioritising the objectives of multiple policies or thinking about the consistency of different policies.

Going back even further into the country's history, Japan had continuously been playing catch-up on its path to modernisation ever since the Meiji Restoration. As a result, the country had very little experience in devising and applying solutions to problems that it alone faced. Nearly all of Japan's policies – including its social security policies – were modelled on advanced policies already in place in the West, so a great deal of energy was spent on figuring out how best to adapt those model Western systems to suit the realities of Japan. The Japanese government was so occupied with studying and mastering the schemes of other countries that it did not pay much attention to the values, principles or philosophies underlying those schemes. As a latecomer to the club of industrialised nations, Japan had the opportunity to 'pick and choose' from a broad range of systems in place in various countries, which made it even easier to neglect the consistency and principles underlying those policies. It is certainly not wrong for a country to learn from more advanced examples, but when that learning process continues for too long and the country suddenly faces a unique problem for which the role model does not have an answer, that country will find

---

it difficult to come up with a proper solution. Furthermore, because the Japanese government did not engage in continual discussion concerning the principles and values at the root of its policies, whenever circumstances changed to the point that conventional policies no longer served their intended purpose, the government tended to favour ad hoc and stopgap responses.

The political context

Second, for many years after the Second World War, Japan was home to conflicts between groups of conflicting ideologies that ran deeper than in other developed nations, and as a consequence, an atmosphere unfavourable to constructive policy debate was born. As stated earlier, the LDP was a collection of Diet members with disparate value systems. Meanwhile, the SDPJ, which was the largest opposition party for a long period of post-war history, took radical, ideologically driven stances against the LDP. This was partly because the left wing of the SDPJ wielded significant internal influence for a long time. For several years following the conclusion of the war, Diet members belonging to the leftist camp of the SDPJ were particularly critical of the government's social security policies, dismissing them as 'revisionist' and designed to extend the life of capitalism. However, once these policies gained wide acceptance among the public, the SDPJ came to support them as well, though with no clear explanation. As a result, it was not just the LDP, but the SDPJ as well, that gave in to forces within the party and bowed to public opinion in accepting these policies with mere ad hoc discussions and without presenting viable alternatives grounded in widely held values and principles.

Since the Cold War ended, the LDP relinquished its reins on the government, the SDPJ dissolved and the Democratic Party of Japan came into being, a two-party political system was established in Japan, though it was only temporary. Elections grounded in the parties' manifestos were called for, and there were hopes that substantive policy debates might become possible, but as it stands now, those hopes have not been fully realised. Most of these manifestos and platforms consisted merely of either abstract rhetoric or a patchwork of claptrap policies. None of them presented any grand vision on prudential grounds.[2]

Policymaking styles

Next, I will make several observations concerning Japanese styles of policymaking. First, as a consequence of the diffusion of power, the policy process became fragmented and policies came to be made incrementally. The effect of this was that the content of policies tended to become fragmented, and the principles and values guiding the policies became less of an issue. Naturally, there is a certain rationality behind incremental policy development, a practice that is seen in all countries. Nonetheless, Japan exhibits a stronger tendency towards incrementalism than other countries. In addition, bold steps to restructure the country's systems based on alternative visions or principles are rare. As one example, Japan's pension scheme has undergone numerous haphazard revisions to postpone the resolution of inherent contradictions, but because of this process, the scheme has become much more complex and elusive than those of other countries.

Second, the 'killing two birds with one stone' style of policymaking is another factor. By 'killing two birds with one stone', I am specifically referring to a policymaking style in which one attempts to achieve multiple objectives with a single policy. If we use the example of dam construction, this style would not entail just flood control, but might include among its objectives water utilisation, sightseeing and job creation. Policies are supposed to be designed as a means to solve specific problems, but, in reality, a single policy is often designed to achieve multiple objectives in order to satisfy, accommodate or persuade budget controllers, politicians and public opinion. The consequence of justifying policies made in this manner is that the original purpose of such policies is easily obscured. Unless the various objectives are clearly prioritised, it becomes difficult to determine which objective to implement improvements to first in the event that circumstances change and a policy needs to be improved. As policies in Japan are often designed in this manner, as well as according to the incremental style, their original objectives tend to be gradually forgotten, leaving them vulnerable to appropriation for entirely different purposes before anyone takes notice.

In relation to this point, it should also be noted that the Ministry of Finance's budget review process has also distorted discussions on the values and principles underlying policies. The ministries engage in discussions for the purpose of justifying and having their budgets approved by the Ministry of Finance, and in the process, they offer all sorts of rationales, from pertinent data to the values and principles that serve as the grounds for their policy proposals. As a result, it is easy for a policy to take on multiple objectives, and for the very nature of the policy to become obscured. In addition, the ministries tend to present the kinds of values and principles that are likely to meet with the Ministry of Finance's approval. Consequently, it is not uncommon for principles that are not necessarily consistent with the initial policy objectives to be emphasised. In addition, whenever the Ministry of Finance's budget review process becomes more stringent, ministries sometimes 'tweak' schemes in ways that make their budgets more likely to gain approval. For example, in the 1970s, at a time when the minimum standard of living criteria had been capped at low levels, the Ministry of Health and Welfare tried to raise the payment amounts as much as possible by establishing mechanisms for household separations and deductions and by creating an 'addition system' (Soeda, 1995). Although these attempts were desirable in that they were intended to improve the standards of living of households receiving public assistance, they also had the effect of making the nature of public assistance even more muddled.

Problems attributable to scholars

Fourth, several points should be made regarding scholars, who should ideally fulfil a crucial role in analyses involving policy values and principles. One of the reasons that analyses of values and principles in Japan's policy process have been inadequate is that scholars in the field of normative theory have not sufficiently addressed practical problems, and, at the same time, scholars who deal with real-world policy issues have not devoted ample attention to values and norms because they have been too focused on practical implementation. Problems such as these on the part of scholars do not directly explain the inconsistency of policies, but, at the very least, it is reasonable to conclude that they have been less than helpful in bringing about the conditions necessary for consistency in policies. To achieve consistency in policies, well-designed visions are necessary, and scholars (and communities of scholars) are the ones best suited to provide and create those visions and values.

In Japan, scholars whose interests include normative theory are spread out across a broad range of academic disciplines, but there has been little academic exchange with one another. There are also no forums like *Social Philosophy and Policy* or *Philosophy and Public Affairs* in which scholars from different disciplines can present discussions that connect normative theory and public policies. Most of the scholars of normative theory have approached the field from the perspective of intellectual history. Discussion of actual policy by such scholars has rarely risen above the level of a side pursuit. For example, scholars of Rawls have presented very detailed arguments concerning Rawls's ideas, but, until recently, there have been few attempts to apply those arguments to Japan's social security policies and conceive of better policies.

On the other end of the spectrum, studies done by scholars in individual policy fields have had a strong tendency to be empirical and focus on the minutiae of schemes and contemporary conditions. When making normative arguments, such scholars have almost always offered up political assertions predicated on the circumstances at that particular point in time, rather than academic examinations. For example, it has been common practice for scholars, on the one hand, to conduct meticulous historical studies, but, on the other hand, to make public their personal views on specific policy issues not as academics, but as citizens in a 'political movement' rooted in specific ideologies. At the same time, such scholars make only superficial mention of the principles and values that are supposed to be at the foundations of policies.

That said, to at least some degree, many social security scholars within the Ministry of Health and Welfare have been conscious of the poor quality of discussion about principles and values, especially with regard to social security policies, and attempts to remedy this situation are not without precedent. However, to be frank, those efforts do not seem to have been enough to raise the level of discussion. As a matter of course, all ministries and agencies 'arm' themselves with theoretical justifications for the policies that they are trying to advance. This is because when they make budget requests, they all need 'weapons' to counter the pressure from politicians. With regard to social security policies in particular, from the latter half of the 1970s, these theoretical weapons became necessary to fight off attacks coming from economists and economic agencies demanding the curtailment of social security (cf Soeda, 1995). One example of an attempt to address and overcome the paucity of academic debate and poor quality of discussions regarding social security policies is a collection of papers titled *Shakai hoshōno atarashíriron wo motomete* (*In Search of New Theories of Social Security*), edited and published in 1991 by Mikio Sumiya, who chaired the Advisory Council on Social Security at the time (Sumiya, 1991). However, most of the papers in this work do not venture beyond discussions of Beveridge, Titmuss and Article 25 of the Constitution of Japan. It reflected little scholarship by political and economic philosophers such as Rawls and Sen, who were already known in Japan at the time. By this time, in fact, the debate on values and norms like equality and fairness, which inevitably come up in any examination of social security policies, had evolved considerably through contributions not just by Rawls and Sen, but also by Dworkin, Nussbaum, Walzer and other thinkers. Yet, in the field of social security policy, serious attempts to build upon these discussions began only after the turn of the millennium. As a result, it has often been the case in the social security policymaking process that those who advocate for improvements to social security in accordance with Article 25 and those who stress personal responsibility and market mechanisms are not able to find enough common ground to engage in meaningful debate.

Of course, divides between theory and practice can be seen in all countries, but it is evident that the gap between the two is extremely wide in Japan. Furthermore, the 'division of labour' regarding the two is distinctly Japanese. For example, most theorists in Western countries do not engage in pure theoretical research exclusively. They often take advantage of opportunities to express their ideas about real-world policy issues, and they do so in a manner that applies the cumulative fruits of their own research. In most cases, they do not argue simply for the mechanical application of theories, but instead offer in-depth discussions that pertain to real-world circumstances. In contrast, theorists in Japan have rarely addressed actual issues, and even when they have, they have either stuck to idealistic arguments with little bearing on actual circumstances or discussed real-world issues in a way in which connections to their theoretical research are tenuous at best.

In addition to the chasm between theory and practice, there are high barriers based on academic affiliations. It is worth noting that these barriers have often followed the same patterns of demarcation as the vertical divisions in hierarchical administrative organisations. For example, with regard to social security policy, we see that, in most cases, they have mostly been filled with scholars in the field of social security policy, plus economists, business representatives and labour union representatives. Members have not included scholars specialising in normative theory. For this reason, until very recently, the findings of normative theory research done in the West have not contributed to discussions in these circles. This situation was not necessarily a product of intention or design. More likely, it was due to the chance confluence of several factors. Members of such advisory councils are often invited from ranks of scholars who are close to bureaucrats or politicians. Alternatively, it is also common for scholars who were once council members to nominate potential successors. As long as this selection process continues, we can expect as a matter of course that advisory council members will continue to be drawn predominantly from certain academic circles. We can also infer from this selection process that most officials in charge of social security policy at the Ministry of Health, Labour and Welfare do not have sufficient knowledge of studies in the area of normative theory, nor do they have close ties with scholars in that field. Furthermore, they are either unaware that studies in this field have made contributions that have very important implications for social security policy, or they are aware but have failed to recognise or utilise findings in this field as 'resources' for policy design.[3]

Other factors include the fact that policy studies in Japan have fallen behind the times and become 'skewed'. In Japan, policy studies have only been recognised as a discrete discipline since the 1990s. Until then, public policy was something that either scholars discussed as a side pursuit or that practitioners discussed as part of their jobs. It was therefore rarely viewed as a distinct discipline. To be sure, techniques for policy analysis were long known to Japanese scholars, and in some exceptional cases, these tools were even used in the design of policies. They were not, however, considered necessary in all allied policy fields. Until recently, scholars in Japan did not view this as a problem.

Furthermore, even after policy studies came to be recognised as a distinct discipline, most policy researchers and scholars still either presented detailed explanations and overviews of specific cases or offered technical analyses. In other words, until recently, the significance of presenting analyses from the perspective of norms and values was not properly acknowledged even among policy scholars.

The political culture

Lastly, the issue of the political culture should be addressed. Although it is difficult to demonstrate, it might also be a cause behind the lack of consistency in Japanese policies.

First, for most Japanese people, values and norms are more or less synonymous with personal tastes and preferences, so any attempt to rationally discuss their relative merits is doomed from the start. In arena of real-world policymaking, this attitude does make it possible to take more pragmatic approaches. This attitude frequently manifests itself in the tendency to put aside difficult and abstract discussions of the principles and values of policies and to discuss the specific details of the schemes at hand. The prevalence of this attitude makes it easier to make concessions regarding the specific content of a policy when disagreements arise in the policymaking process, regardless of whether the parties can agree in terms of principles and values. This helps keep political conflicts in check, contributes to the cutting of costs that stem from them and makes it easier to make policies even in the absence of a clear agreement on their underlying principles and values.

Second, the attitude just described means that there is a tendency to emphasise 'instrumental value'. In point of fact, until quite recently, most people in Japan, regardless of their ideological stances, considered economic growth and technological innovation to be useful insofar as they have been 'instrumental'. If one could design policies from this perspective alone, there would be no need to engage in cumbersome debates over values and norms. Even now, the notion that economic growth will solve all problems persists, but this line of thinking has only served to obviate discussions concerning values and norms.

Third, many Japanese people find it difficult to separate 'public' and 'private'. As a result, the issue of personal morals often makes its way into policy discussions directly. In the area of social security policy in particular, the tendency for public assistance recipients to become victims of envy or prejudice is common to countries throughout the world. In the particular case of Japan, however, there is little discussion of public values such as justice, rights and fairness. These values tend to be accepted as just a matter of superficial reasons, which leads to discussions that are driven more by emotion than reason. Moreover, because politicians and bureaucrats lack the ability to articulate the policy principles necessary to rebut these emotion-driven arguments, the substance of policies is easily swayed by the volatile tide of public opinion. Furthermore, because of the pragmatic intellectual tendencies, and because most Japanese citizens have not had the benefit of an adequate civic education, many Japanese people find it difficult to distance themselves from specific cases for the purpose of considering and discussing issues in an abstract and logical manner. As a result, public opinion in the country is often swayed one way or another by individual events and cases, which may be a factor in the difficulty of developing policies in line with consistent principles.

Conclusion

In the preceding examination, I have argued that Japanese policies – especially social security policies – are far from consistent. One reason is that the values and principles that guide policies have not been subject to adequate discussion. Space constraints made detailed analyses of the content of specific policies impractical, and, in that respect, there are supporting arguments that have yet to be made, but the preceding arguments are sufficient to advance the overall thesis presented here.

That said, in recent years, there have been more and more scholars of normative theory who have attempted to apply the findings in the field to concrete policy issues. In addition, there has been more discussion that builds upon the body of research in normative theory in academic circles dedicated to social policy. These topics warrant further examination.

Notes

[1] Of course, all of the policies in other countries are always more consistent than in Japan. For example the US social welfare system is often said to be awfully inconsistent and incremental. However, in my opinion, the US system is not necessarily inconsistent in broad terms. As Esping-Andersen pointed out, it continues to be a typical case of the Anglo-Saxon model, though it often experiences minor changes. In addition to that, if we admit the inconsistency of the US welfare system, it is not caused by a lack of normative discussion, but by fragmentation of political power.

[2] In addition, political reporting by the mass media has, in effect, worked to sustain this political situation instead of improving it. As others have pointed out, political reporting in Japan tends to focus on political gamesmanship and scandals, without much attention to the substance or guiding principles of policies.

[3] It is nevertheless worth noting that the *Annual Health, Labour and Welfare Report* for the 2012 fiscal year includes a chapter titled 'Principles and Philosophy Associated with Social Security', which describes principles of self-reliance and solidarity. Although it is in the form of a short column, there is also an introduction to Rawls's difference principle and a short outline of libertarianism. These are, however, just brief summaries. The column does not present arguments relating to such principles or philosophies in the context of actual social security policies in Japan. In addition, all sorts of values and principles related to social security policies are not taken up. Of course, there is no discussion about the priorities of those values.

References

Esping-Andersen, G. (1990) *Three Worlds of Welfare Capitalism*, Polity Press.

Fukawa, H. (2009) *Seikatsuhogo no ronten [Issues of Public Assistance System in Japan]*, Yamabuki Syoten.

Hatakeyama, H. (1989) *Kanryosei shihai no nichijo kozo [Daily Life Structure of Bureaucrats' Control]*, San-ichi Publishing.

Inoguchi, T. and Iwai, T. (1987) *Zokugiin no kenkyu [A Study of 'Zokugiin']*, Nikkei Inc.

Iwanaga, R. (2011) *Seikatsuhogo wa saiteiseikatsu wo do koso shitaka?* [*How did the Japanese Public Assistance System Formulated the Concept of Minimum Living Standards?*], Minerva Publishing Company.

Miyamoto, T. (2008) *Hukushi seiji* [*Welfare Politics*], Iwanami Shoten.

Murakami, K. (2000) *Sengo syotokuhosyo seido no kensyo* [*A Study of Postwar Income Compensation System in Japan*], Keiso Shobo Publishers.

Ohashi, Y. (1989) *Gyoseikisoku no hori to jittai* [*Doctrine and Practice of Administrative Regulations*], Yuhikaku Publishing.

Shinkawa, T. (1993) *Nihongatahukushi no seijikeizaigaku* [*Political Economy of Japanese-Style Welfare*], San-ichi Publishing.

Soeda, Y. (1995) *The Social History of Public Assistance System in Japan*, University of Tokyo Press.

Sumiya, M. (1991) *Shakai hoshōno atarashíriron wo motomete* [*In Search of New Theories of Social Security*], University of Tokyo Press.

Tabata, Y. (2011) *Doitsu no saitei seikatsu hosyo* [*Minimum Income Guarantee in Germany*], Gakubunsha.

Takechi, H. (1996) *Gyosei katei no seidobunseki* [*Institutional Analysis of Administrative Process*], Chuo University Press.

Tanabu, Y. (2011) 'Several Currents of Welfare State Theory Among Japanese Conservatives', (in Japanese), *Syakaiseisaku*, vol 2, no 3, pp 67–78.

Tsuru, T. (2000) *Huransu no hinkon to syakaihogo* [*Poverty and Social Protection in France*], Horitsubunka-sha.

Uzuhashi, T. (1999) 'An International Comparative Study on Public Assistance System' (in Japanese), *Kaigaisyakaihosyokenkyu*, vol 127, pp 72–82.

FIVE

Law and public policy in contemporary Japan

Makoto Usami

Introduction

It is conventional wisdom in Japan that public policy is carried out through the law. It is widely recognised that policy goals are achieved by laws, including the constitution, statutes and administrative regulations. For example, the Japanese government pursues the goal of protecting the privacy of citizens by utilising specific provisions in Chapters 2 to 5 of the Protection of Personal Information Act 2003 and other related statutes, as well as some administrative regulations. However, the common wisdom that legal rules and principles work as measures to pursue policy aims leaves half the story untold. They also stipulate the goals of public policy and impose constraints on the policy instruments used to pursue the goals. Article 1 of the act defines the ultimate end of privacy protection policy, and Article 50(1) exempts the press, for the sake of the public's right to access information, from some duties of organisations handling personal information. As these and many other instances illustrate, a more accurate picture of law and public policy may be that their relationship is twofold: policy is conducted through the constitution, statutes and regulations on the one hand; and the law sets forth policy goals and places constraints on policy tools on the other.

Going further from this improved picture, I advance the conception of law as public policy.[1] The system of public policy is multilayered, self-referential and enforceable. It is multilayered in that it ranges from a general level to a more particular one; it is self-referential in that it refers to itself when a superior policy provides a subordinate one with aims and restricts the available measures to attain those aims; and it is enforceable in that many policies can be enforced even if targeted citizens do not want to obey them. These characteristics obviously apply to the system of law. The constitution is more general than statutes and regulations, and a so-called basic law such as the Basic Environmental Act 1993 is more general than specific environmental laws, say, the Environmental Impact Assessment Act 1997. A typical example of legal self-reference is Article 98(1) of the Constitution of Japan, which declares that no law, ordinance or other act of government that is contrary to constitutional provisions shall have legal force. The enforceability of law is illustrated by the Criminal Code, among other things. The overlap of the three characteristics between policy and law indicates that the constitution and statutes are fundamental components of the public policy system. What looks like a bilateral relationship between law and policy is in fact the relationship between legal policies at different levels of generality and superiority.

Given the embeddedness of law in the whole system of public policy, research on the law seems to be an essential part of policy study, and vice versa. In Japan, a great and increasing number of policy theorists and practitioners have engaged in law-related study, and many jurists have got involved in policy-oriented research. There are three major areas of law and public policy: the first field is that of *rippogaku*, which denotes legislative study that covers the legislative process and technical skills used in the process. The second is *seisaku homu*, which means the policy-oriented administration of laws by local government officials. The third is the domain of *ho seisakugaku*, or law and policy, which broadly refers to the branch of knowledge that studies policy design in terms of law. Despite their remarkable development in contemporary Japan, few attempts have been made to review the three areas in the literature in comparative policy analysis in the English-speaking world, much less attempts to examine them in depth. To fill this gap in the literature, this chapter discusses the history, current state and prospect of legislative study, policy-oriented legal administration and law and policy.

In the following, I begin with a look at the development and divisions of legislative study, while sketching the course of enactment in Japan. Next, an overview of the policy-oriented local administration of law and its background is provided. Then, I offer a survey of law and policy, with special reference to a related field – law and economics. Furthermore, I proceed to identify three contemporary features of the areas previously reviewed and to suggest remedies for the weaknesses involved in some of these features. The chapter concludes by pointing out the implications that these domains of Japanese law and public policy might have for other societies.

Legislative study

The question of what legislative study means is susceptible to different interpretations, but it is usually taken as the area of academic research and practical commentary on issues surrounding legislation. This area is particularly significant in the context of the Japanese legal system because the legal system basically falls in the civil law tradition as opposed to the common law culture. After the Tokugawa shogunate collapsed in 1867, the new Meiji government launched a systematic project to introduce Western law into society.[2] Some officials and scholars were sent abroad to study legal codes and institutions in Europe, while foreign law experts were invited to teach in the country. As a result, the Civil Code was enacted on the basis of the structure of the German Civil Code and of many provisions of the French Civil Code; the Penal Code and Commercial Code came from German counterparts. Since a military regime was defeated by the US-led Allies in 1945 and the country was occupied thereafter, Japanese law has been under the strong influence of US law, but its civil law character has been basically sustained. Laws enacted by the legislature are predominant in the civil law tradition, whereas case law is a considerable part of legal sources in the common law culture. This is a reason why legislative study is of great importance in the Japanese context.

To grasp the scope of legislative study, one should note that the course of law-making begins long before the introduction of a bill into the Diet. For bills introduced by the cabinet, low-ranked officials write a first draft of a bill in a ministry or an administrative agency.[3] This draft is submitted to higher-ranked officials and becomes an object of intra-organisational discussion and of inter-organisational negotiation. A revised draft is then examined to adjust conflicting interests by the ruling party's committee in charge of the relevant policy area; it is also checked for accuracy and consistency by the Cabinet Legislation Bureau. The final draft is authorised by the cabinet and introduced into the Diet. For bills introduced by members of the Diet, a draft bill is usually made by a task force in a political party, with the technical assistance of the Cabinet Legislation Bureau. In both cases, the bill is placed under deliberation and brought to a vote in one house of the Diet and then processed in a similar way in the other house. Given such a wide range of activities involved, legislative study covers not merely the course of deliberation and decision within the Diet, but also that of drafting, elaboration and negotiation in the pre-Diet process.

Legislative study has a longer history than any other branches of study on law and public policy. In his seminal article, Izutaro Suehiro (1946) charged that contemporary draft-making relies heavily on the craftsmanship of bureaucrats and suggested the idea of legislation based on scientific research. As the number and scope of new pieces of legislation rapidly expanded in the 1950s and 1960s, a growing number of jurists have emphasised the necessity of established legislative study. A notable work in those days was an anthology of essays written by leading jurists in a variety of areas (Ashibe, 1965). In the 1980s, Ichiro Kato (1981) explored the basic plan of legislative study from the perspective of civil law, and Nobuyoshi Ashibe (1984) did so from that of constitutional law (cf Takami, 1985). Naoki Kobayashi (1984) published a collection of his early papers in which he described the entire enacting process and some notable cases. These papers stemmed from his anxiety that the ideal of democratic legislation had been threatened as conservatives extended their influence in the Diet after Japan's independence from the US-led Allied occupation in 1951.

Since the beginning of the 1990s, legislative study has developed greatly. One jurist sketched a project of the study intended to furnish public officials with techniques in law-making (Yamada, 1994). Some researchers made both general and particular inquiries into the legislative process (Nakamura and Maeda, 1997). Ex-officials who had been involved in the enactment process presented detailed descriptions of the process (Asano, 1997; Nakajima, 2007). A group of academicians and practitioners recently published a comprehensive textbook, which included a description of the legislative process in general, a focused treatment of some noticeable cases, commentary on technicalities and an overview of institutions and processes in some other countries (Omori and Kamata, 2011). An ex-official also offered a concise textbook covering the actual process and necessary skills (Oshima, 2013). These works indicate that legislative study has two major subfields: the first is the empirical study of details of the legislative process; and the second is commentary on professional skills in law-making. Many authors mention legislative policy as a third sub-area, but there are few works therein.

It may be useful to set forth two dimensions involved in legislative study to gain an accurate picture of this area. The first dimension concerns the positive–normative dichotomy that is popular among social scientists. Positive methods, in turn, fall into two subcategories: one is descriptive method, which sets out to rigorously describe a particular aspect of some complex phenomenon; and the other is explanatory method, which seeks to explicate one or more causes of the phenomenon. Most works on the legislative process are descriptive rather than explanatory. On the other hand, one can distinguish two groups of normative studies by referring to a distinction between evaluative and prescriptive sentences. Suppose that someone says 'capital punishment is unjust', and then adds 'so it should be abolished in Japan'. The former sentence is evaluative, while the latter is prescriptive. Commentaries on technical skills to be used in law-making are obviously prescriptive, not evaluative. Another feature of skill-focused works, which is related to their prescriptiveness, is that they are highly technical.

The second dimension of legislative study relates to a general–particular distinction. Take positive research in democracy as an example. A quantitative study that measures the degree of democracy in numerous countries across the world takes a general approach. By contrast, a case study on the dynamic change of democratic degree after the collapse of apartheid in South Africa uses a particular one.[4] Descriptions of the legislative process at large in Japan are general, while case studies focusing on specific enactments are particular. Commentaries on law-making skills are general in nature because they seek to offer law-making techniques, no matter what policy area a possible law falls into. The classification of legislative study based on the two dimensions is shown in Table 5.1.

Table 5.1: Types of legislative study

	Descriptive (positive)	Prescriptive (normative)
General	Study on the legislative process at large	Commentary on technical skills in enactment
Particular	Case study on the process of making a specific law	—

Policy-oriented administration of law

The study of the policy-oriented administration of law is younger than legislative study, but the literature of the former area is today much larger than that of the latter. To understand the motivation and orientation of this field, it seems helpful to briefly look at the history of local ordinances and other forms of local policy in the post-war period. Gross pollution problems caused by rapid industrialisation and urbanisation occurred across the country in the 1960s. The national government responded to the problems by enacting pollution control laws and by strengthening regulations in current laws. Because they found the government's response insufficient, however, some local assemblies issued additional anti-pollution ordinances.[5] In the 1970s, some assemblies developed their pollution control policy by making environmental assessment ordinances. The 1980s observed the emergence of access to information ordinances, which were issued prior to the Access to Information Act 1999. Ordinances on city and town planning and on social welfare services appeared in the 1990s, and so-called basic ordinances came to be popular in the 2000s as basic national laws proliferated. These experiences of a great variety of ordinances have inspired local policy thinkers.

Ordinances are not the sole policy tool by which local governments have acted beyond the national government's intentions. In the 1960s and 1970s, some governments utilised the tool of government–enterprise agreements to achieve more sever pollution control than the legal standard. In the following decade, some municipalities deviated from the national guideline on alien registration. Foreigners living or staying for a long time in the country were obliged to have their fingerprints taken in registration procedures,[6] but some Koreans and other nationals refused in the 1980s. Municipalities were required to make the names of refusers public, and yet some cities did not. More recently, several cities and towns declined to connect to the Basic Resident Registers Network introduced in 2002 because of their anxieties about information spill or misuse, though some of these refusals were turned down by the Supreme Court.

Institutional reforms of decentralisation in the late 1990s and thereafter had a huge impact on the situation of local governments. The first stage of these reforms began when the Committee for Decentralisation was established as a consultant panel for the prime minister in 1995. The committee recommended a wide range of reforms, notably, the abolition of service functions legally assigned to local governments, which was a major backdrop for the national government's control of local governments. The Comprehensive Act for Decentralisation 1999 officially abolished assigned functions and instituted the two categories of local government services: statutorily entrusted functions and self-governing functions. A major reform at the second stage of decentralisation was the so-called trinity reform, which refers to the combination of three financial changes in intergovernmental relationships: reduction of the national government's subsidies; reduction of tax revenue allocated to local governments; and transfer of tax revenue sources to local governments. The trinity reform was intended to enhance the financial independence of local governments from the national government. However, the amount of reduced subsidies and tax revenues exceeded that of transferred tax sources, and thus many local governments encountered fiscal difficulties.

Keiichi Matsushita proposed the independent interpretation of laws by local governments in his book for general readers (Matsushita, 1975). The term 'seisaku homu' was later coined by other authors (Amano et al, 1989), who were inspired by Matsushita's works. Some booklets for local officials appeared in the 1990s (Kisa, 1996; Isozaki, 1999), and a great number of textbooks, anthologies and journal articles were published in the 2000s and thereafter (Kobayakawa, 2000; Yamaguchi, 2002; Isozaki, 2004, 2012; Tanaka and Kisa, 2004; Suzuki, 2007; Kaneko et al, 2008; Koda et al, 2008; Tamura et al, 2009; Kitamura et al, 2011). In addition, some works focused on particular policy areas, notably, environmental policy (Kitamura, 1999, 2008).

Authors diverge on the definition of policy-oriented legal administration, but its three elements are widely recognised. First, this branch of law and public policy focuses on the interpretation, application and enforcement of national laws by members of local assemblies and administrative offices. Second, most theorists and practitioners on the subject have shared the goal of the independent and flexible interpretation of laws within the limits of legality. The intended approach to interpretation is independent in the sense that it differs from the official reading supposed by the national government, and it is flexible so that it can respond to the conditions of a local community and the needs of those living therein. Third, such an attitude towards statutes is founded on the conception of law as the means to policy ends. Since they rely on the instrumentalist conception of law, authors propose that local government officials read a statute flexibly to pursue their own policy goals in a local setting. In short, the policy-oriented administration of law is the theory and practice of the independent and flexible administration of laws by local assemblypersons and administrators, which is founded on the instrumental conception of law.

In the aspect of its practical intention, the policy-oriented administration of law is very different from any traditional discipline that can be identified by the object studied therein or the combination of the object and the method used. For instance, ethics is often defined as the branch of knowledge that deals with the moral principles governing actions of a person or a group of persons. By contrast, some relatively new fields have a characteristically practical intention. It would miss the point to simply say that environmental ethics is the division of ethics that studies moral principles governing the actions of a person or a group in relation to the natural environment. This is because the vast majority of works in this discipline challenge the anthropocentrism embedded in traditional Western ethical thinking. Similar thinking applies to policy-oriented legal administration, which is characteristically oriented towards the independent and flexible interpretation of laws. Such a practical orientation implies that this field is prescriptive in nature.

The policy-oriented administration of law is said to be divided into three sub-areas. The first is so-called legislative administration, which concerns ordinance-making (eg Tanaka, 2010). This is conventionally referred to as legislative because local government officials and researchers on their policy tend to consider a local assembly as a small-scale Diet, although Article 41 of the Constitution explicitly provides that the Diet is the sole law-making organ. The second subfield is executive administration, which deals with the interpretation and application of national laws and local ordinances. The third is evaluative/litigating administration, which covers both evaluating the legislative and executive administration and addressing suits brought by local residents (Murakami, 2010).[7] As these subdivisions have rapidly developed in recent years, becoming increasingly technical. In terms of a general–particular distinction, they range from a general level, at which all policy areas are covered, to a particular level that focuses on specific policy domains.

Law and policy

A field of research that differs both from legislative study and the policy-oriented administration of law is that of law and policy. Law and policy broadly refers to the branch of knowledge that studies policy design in terms of statutes and administrative regulations. There are two founding fathers of this area: Yoshio Hirai (1995) published an influential book in which he applies the tools of decision theory to the system of law. He defines law and policy as a general theoretical framework that is intended to control public problems and to offer legal decision-makers advice on how to solve the problems by refining decision theory from a legal perspective and by connecting the refined version of decision theory with the system of law. He stresses the deference and conflict between the end–means model and the legal decision-making model of thought. According to his view, the former model, which he thinks is the basis of economics, treats persons as means to an end, whereas the latter respects individuals as ends. Based on this dichotomy, he juxtaposes efficiency and justice as general criteria to be used when designing legal institutions. He also distinguishes decision-making types: market-based, authoritative and procedural. By employing the pair of criteria and the tripartite of decision-making forms, he seeks to design a broad range of legal institutions. The other founding father, Yasutaka Abe (1996, 2003) developed the theory of *seisaku hogaku*, or policy and law, which denotes the interpretive and legislative proposals in administrative laws that aim to solve specific social problems. He elaborates a great variety of reform proposals in numerous areas of administrative law. Academic administrative lawyers who studied under Abe explore the possibilities of policy and law (Urabe et al, 2005).[8]

Hirai's project contrasts with Abe's in at least three respects. First of all, his project is deductive because it begins with general evaluative criteria – justice and efficiency – and proceeds to design particular legal institutions. By contrast, Abe's argument is inductive since it proposes many individual reforms and then formulates general principles based on these reforms. Another difference between the two jurists concerns the rationalist–incrementalist division. Hirai is basically rationalist in the sense that he aims to construct institutional plans through cost–benefit analysis and speculation on justice, though he takes existing laws into account; on the other hand, Abe can be said to rely on incrementalism in that he seeks to remedy the drawbacks of current laws. Still another disparity is that Hirai purposes to build a far-reaching theory, while Abe offers reformative proposals within the realm of administrative law.

The second generation of law and policy scholars tends to focus on specific legal fields. Public policy is discussed in the context of civil law (Omura, 2005) and intellectual property law (Tamura, 2008). Moreover, some academic societies and research groups have developed joint research projects. The Japan Association for Environmental Law and Policy, established in 1997, has issued a volume of its journal every year. The Research Group for Law and Policy, a group based at Kobe University, has published a series of anthologies in a great variety of policy areas since 1998. At Hokkaido University, the 21st Century Center of Excellence (COE) programme, 'The Law and Policy of Intellectual Property: Building a New Framework', was launched in 2003 and later developed into a far-reaching Global COE programme, 'New Global Law and Policy for Multi-agential Governance', established in 2008, both of which have issued journals.

Some authors in law and policy have also contributed to the development of law and economics, which originally emerged and developed in the US and then permeated in many other parts of the world. In the 1970s, Koichi Hamada (1977) published a monumental book on the economic analysis of tort law, and Hirai (1980) utilised economic concepts and ideas in his study on damages in car accident cases. Their works were followed by an influential introductory book (Kobayashi and Kanda, 1986).[9] In the 1990s, several jurists and economists published textbooks (Kishida, 1996), monographs (Ramseyer, 1990; Hayashida, 1996) and anthologies (Miwa et al, 1998), while examinations of the discipline were also made (Uchida, 1990; Kawahama, 1993; Shimazu, 1997). Since the turn of the century, further textbooks have been published (Hayashida, 2002; Shishido and Tsuneki, 2004; Fukui, 2007).

The recent literature shows diversity in several aspects: the first is the proliferation of area-focused studies. Some textbooks focus on contracts and corporations (Yanagawa, 2000, 2006). Many efforts have been made to explore corporations and business trade (Hosoe and Ota, 2001; Yano, 2007; Nakamura, 2010), stock markets (Takahashi, 2009), property and leasing (Seshimo and Yamazaki, 2007), compulsory sale by auction (Suzuki et al, 2001), anti-monopoly law (Okada and Hayashi, 2009), intellectual property (Hayashi, 2004), conflict resolution (Miyoshi, 2013), administrative law (Hirata, 2009), international law (Mori, 2010), and social norms (Iida, 2004). Second, some authors have developed new approaches, including evolutionary game theory (Ota, 2000), and others have tried to bridge between this discipline and policy analysis (Tsuneki, 2012). A number of legal philosophers and economic theorists have discussed the significance, limitation and prospect of law and economics (Hasegawa, 2003; Tsuneki, 2008; Usami, 2010). The third aspect of recent diversity is that some economists and academic lawyers have used the tools of economic analysis to advocate deregulation in many policy fields (Fukui, 2001, 2006; Yashiro, 2003; Ohtake et al, 2004; Fukui and Ohtake, 2006; Fukui et al, 2010).

Features and challenges

In the previous sections, three areas of law and public policy – legislative study, the policy-oriented administration of law and law and policy – were briefly reviewed. This review shows that these fields have developed remarkably since the beginning of the 1990s, though legislative study appeared much earlier. The recent literature in these disciplines, or some of it, indicates three noticeable features. The first is practical technicality, which can be observed especially in legislative study and policy-oriented legal administration. The former area's technical characteristic is marked in commentaries on professional skills in law-making, while the latter's technicality can be found in all of its three subfields – legislative, executive and evaluative/litigating administration. Practical technicality is a natural tendency because the enactment and administration of law require highly technical skills; on the other hand, principled thinking also seems necessary in studies on law and public policy, as I argue later.

The second characteristic is what might be called academic patriotism, which denotes that authors tend to be self-sufficient within their domain. This disposition has two components: one component is that writers have a negative attitude towards introducing the methods of and observations in related disciplines into their own realm. For instance, quantitative studies on the Japanese legislative process have developed remarkably in political science during the past two decades, but researchers and educators in legislative study pay scant attention to this development. The underdevelopment of legislative policy research within the field seems to follow partly from the fact that there are few attempts to use techniques of policy analysis. The other part of academic patriotism is the limited interest in the tools of and findings in similar areas in other countries. Few attempts have been made to explore the literature in *Gesetzgebungslehre* in Germany, legislative study in some English-speaking countries, so-called legisprudence or the like.[10] In policy-oriented legal administration, there are few comparative studies on local government policies in other societies. By contrast, some scholars in law and policy have employed methods of law and economics developed in the US and other Western countries.

One factor that lies behind academic patriotism may be the practical technicality previously mentioned. The practice-based technical character of legislative study and policy-oriented legal administration presumably makes writers attend to details of legal practice rather than theoretical methodology and hinders them from paying attention to the literature in related disciplines at home and abroad. Another backdrop seems to be a long-standing and widespread tendency towards fractionalisation of research in law and social sciences. In Japan, many academic lawyers and social scientists have shown a strong inclination to focus on their own field until very recently; moreover, institutional arrangements in universities, academic associations and research funds have reflected and reproduced the inclination. Masao Maruyama calls fractional disposition in Japanese academism the octopus pots of research because fishermen sink traps into the sea so that one octopus is caught in one pot and another in another pot. Still another cause of academic patriotism might be that a great number of ex-officials take part in policy-oriented legal administration and, to a lesser degree, in legislative study. Many of these ex-officials have no experience of systematic education in doctoral courses or of gaining fluency in English and other foreign languages. The insufficiency of their scholarly background and language fluency probably limits their access to the literature in related technical fields and other languages.

The last characteristic of law and public policy that I want to single out is what I call the assumption of exogenous values, which refers to the presumption that public values, such as liberty, equality and efficiency, are established outside the realm of law. This assumption is closely connected with the conventional wisdom that I mentioned at the beginning of this chapter, namely, that the law works as a measure to pursue policy aims. This instrumentalist conception of law is conspicuous in the policy-oriented administration of law, but is evident in commentary on legislative skills within legislative study and in law and policy as well. The proliferation of the literature in law and economics in recent years, in which a law is taken as the means to a policy aim by giving positive or negative incentives to relevant actors, reflects legal instrumentalism coupled with the exogenous value supposition.

The common presumption of exogenous values seems to be rooted in the history of modern Japanese society. Since the Meiji Restoration, political leaders and bureaucrats have been eager to introduce Western legal codes and institutions into society, as briefly described earlier. The transplantation of Western law has been conducted to achieve various and variable purposes. Before the Second World War, the ultimate end of legal and political arrangements was largely the advancement of the nation's economic and military power; after Japan was defeated by the Allies, economic recovery and development became a new national goal. In the 1970s and thereafter, society turned to addressing specific problems, including pollution and environmental degradation, economic depression, fiscal deficits, and the aging society. Throughout the country's modern history, the law has been considered by officials and citizens as what is transplanted and developed to achieve their goals or solve the problems they face.

If I am right in identifying the three features of the current law and public policy – practical technicality, academic patriotism and exogenous value assumption – then this discipline has three challenges to overcome the limitations and drawbacks involved in these features. First, the presumption of exogenous values does not tell the whole story, as I noted at the beginning of this chapter, and thus it should be combined with the recognition of endogenous values in law. The constitution, statutes and administrative regulations provide officials and citizens with legal values that set forth policy ends and place constraints on the means to these ends. As legal values have been analysed and discussed in the philosophy of law and political philosophy, researchers and commentators in law and public policy should arguably collaborate with philosophers. Some policy analysts, notably Yukio Adachi, have indeed explored values within and outside of public policy, while a small number of legal and political philosophers have placed their speculations on values in the context of particular policies (Adachi, 1991, 2005, 2009; Hashidate et al, 1999; Usami, 2008, 2011; Sano, 2010).

The proposed collaboration between policy scientists and social philosophers will in part meet the second challenge, which demands the mitigation of academic patriotism. To meet this challenge thoroughly, however, branches of law and public policy should also seek other possibilities of interdisciplinary and comparative projects. It may be helpful for legislative study to learn from law and policy, as well as law and economics, in order to develop the subdivision of legislative policy. Legislative study will also benefit from *Gesetzgebungslehre*, legislative studies and legisprudence. Writers on the policy-oriented administration of law can learn from observations on local government policies in other societies. The third challenge is to add a principled way of thinking to practical technicality, which will again be met by the collaboration between policy researchers and social philosophers.

Conclusion

The description of and discussion on three areas of Japanese law and public policy in the previous sections were intended to remedy the current state of the comparative policy analysis literature in the English-speaking world, in which the development of these areas has been an unexamined, even unknown, subject. I began by reviewing works in legislative study and identifying empirical studies of the enactment process and commentaries on law-making skills as two major subfields. Next, the extensive literature in the policy-oriented administration of law was reviewed, and its features – a focus on local governments, the orientation to the independent and flexible interpretation of laws, and the instrumental conception of law – were discussed. I also explored the works of founding fathers and succeeding theorists of law and policy, while summarising the growing literature in law and economics. Then, I identified three features of law and public policy at large – practical technicality, academic patriotism and exogenous value assumption – and suggested challenges correlated to these features. The review and examination of Japanese law and public policy presented in this chapter will hopefully plug a gap in the Western literature.

However, I hope for more than that. Today, academic lawyers and policy thinkers in different societies frequently find themselves in similar situations. As the law develops to adjust institutional arrangements to changing social realities, they tend to be eager for practical technicality and to focus on their fractionalised domains. In struggling with social problems or seeking public aims, they are inclined to consider legal rules and principles as means to ends. Given the universal nature of these dispositions in developed systems of law, the experiences of and challenges to Japanese law and public policy might inform Western jurists and policy analysts about how to respond to their own situations.

Acknowledgements

I am grateful to Yukio Adachi, Sukehiro Hosono and Jun Iio, as well as a reviewer for the publisher, for their helpful comments on earlier versions of this chapter. I also thank my secretary, Aki Mishima, for her patient editorial assistance.

Notes

[1] I have addressed the conception of the practice of law in three forms – legislative, judicial and administrative – as that of public policy (Usami, 1999, 2008, 2011).

[2] The project of legal reception stemmed from the Meiji government's challenge of amending the unequal treaties that its predecessor was forced to sign with Western powers, which denied Japan the power to decide tariffs on international trade and granted Westerners the privilege of consular jurisdiction in Japan's territory. To remedy these

one-sided treaties, the government needed to demonstrate that its new legal apparatus was 'civilised' to a compatible degree with Western counterparts.

[3] In some cases, the legislative process seems to start even before the drafting of a bill in a ministry or an administrative agency. Since the beginning of the 1980s, the cabinet, ministries and agencies have instituted numerous councils and advisory commissions. Members of these consulting bodies include researchers, businesspersons and journalists. An inquiry committee proffers to its creator advice or proposals on a particular policy issue, which can suggest the purposes and principles of a possible law or revisions of a current law.

[4] Of course, a distinction between general and particular research is a conceptual one and there can be many borderline cases. A comparative study on democracies in West Africa, for instance, has an in-between approach. However, the existence of borderline cases does not imply that the distinction is impossible.

[5] There are two types of additional ordinance in environmental policy and other policy areas. The first type is *uwanose jorei*, or strengthening ordinance, which imposes more stringent control on the target than laws governing it. The second is *yokodashi jorei*, or widening ordinance, which broadens the range of control to cover other targets.

[6] The system of obligatory fingerprinting with an ink pad for foreigners was gradually eased and finally abolished in 1999, but biometric fingerprinting was introduced in 2007.

[7] The slogan 'Plan, Do, See', which is simpler than 'plan–do–check–act' (PDCA) or the like, is very popular among commentators on and practitioners of public policy, as well as business management in Japan. Legislative, executive and evaluative/litigating administrations are commonly thought to parallel 'Plan', 'Do' and 'See', respectively. However, this parallelism is incorrect. This is because executive administration includes the application of laws, which is planned by the Diet, not a local assembly.

[8] Other early works include a monograph on judicial policy (Matsui, 1987).

[9] Early works in the law and economics literature are reviewed in English by Ota (1991).

[10] A remarkable exception is an exploration of legislative theory and practice in France by Omura (1995).

References

Abe, Y. (1996) *Seisaku hogaku no kihon shishin* [*Basic Principles of Policy and Law*], Kobundo.

Abe, Y. (2003) *Seisaku hogaku koza* [*Lectures on Policy and Law*], Daiichi Hoki.

Adachi, Y. (1991) *Seisaku to kachi: Gendai no seiji tetsugaku* [*Policy and Value: Contemporary Political Philosophy*], Minerva Shobo.

Adachi, Y. (ed) (2005) *Seisakugaku teki shiko towa nanika: Kokyo seisakugaku genron no kokoromi* [*The Modes of Thinking in the Policy Processes: Towards a General Theory of Public Policies*], Keiso Shobo.

Adachi,Y. (2009) *Kokyo seisakugaku towa nanika* [*What Is Public Policy Study?*], Minerva Shobo.

Amano, J., Okada,Y. and Kato,Y. (eds) (1989) *Seisaku homu to jichitai* [*Policy-Oriented Administration of Law and Local Governments*], Nihon Hyoronsha.

Asano, I. (ed) (1997) *Rippo gijutsu nyumon koza, vol 1 Rippo no katei* [*Introductory Lectures on Legislative Techniques, Vol 1 Legislative Process*], Gyosei.

Ashibe, N. (ed) (1965) *Iwanami koza gendai ho 3: Gendai no rippo* [*Iwanami Lectures on Contemporary Law, Vol. 3 Contemporary Legislation*], Iwanami Shoten.

Ashibe, N. (1984) 'A Consideration on Legislation in Japan' (in Japanese), *Jurist*, no 805, pp 10–15.

Fukui, H. (2001) *Toshi saisei no ho to keizaigaku* [*Law and Economics for the Revival of Urban Areas*], Shinzansha.

Fukui, H. (2006) *Shiho seisaku no ho to keizaigaku* [*The Law and Economics of Judicial Policy*], Nihon Hyoronsha.

Fukui, H. (2007) *Kesu kara hajimeyou ho to keizaigaku: Ho no kakureta kino wo shiru* [*Cases in Law and Economics: Learning the Hidden Functions of Law*], Nihon Hyoronsha.

Fukui, H. and Ohtake, F. (eds) (2006) *Datsu kakusha shakai to koyo hosei: Ho to keizaigaku de kangaeru* [*Post-Disparity Society and Employment Law: The Perspective of Law and Economics*], Nihon Hyoronsha.

Fukui, H., Toda, T. and Asami,Y. (eds) (2010) *Kyoiku no shippai: Ho to keizaigaku de kangaeru kyoiku kaikaku* [*The Failure of Education: Educational Reform in the Perspective of Law and Economics*], Nihon Hyoronsha.

Hamada, K. (1977) *Songai baisho no keizai bunseki* [*Economic Analysis of Damages*], University of Tokyo Press.

Hasegawa, K. (2003) 'What Is Legal Justice in the Market?' (in Japanese), *Horitsu jiho* vol 75, no 1, pp 25–9.

Hashidate, T., Hoki, R., Saito, T. and Nakamura,Y. (1999) *Seisaku katei to seisaku kachi* [*Policy Processes and Policy Values*], Sanrei Shobo.

Hayashi, K. (ed) (2004) *Chosakuken no ho to keizaigaku* [*Law and Economics of Copyright*], Keiso Shobo.

Hayashida, S. (1996) '*Ho to keizaigaku*' *no ho-riron* [*The Legal Theory of Law and Economics*], Hokkaido University Press.

Hayashida, S. (2002) *Ho to keizaigaku: Atarashii chiteki territory* [*Law and Economics: A New Intellectual Domain*] (2nd edn), Shinzansha.

Hirai,Y. (1980) *Gendai fuhokoi riron no ichi tenbo* [*A Review of Contemporary Tort Law Theories*], Ichiryusha.

Hirai,Y. (1995) *Ho seisakugaku: Ho seido sekkei no riron to giho* [*Law and Policy: The Theory and Technique of Designing Legal Institutions*] (2nd edn), Yuhikaku.

Hirata, A. (2009) *Gyoseiho no jisshi katei: Kankyo kisei no dotai to riron* [*Enforcement Processes of Administrative Law: Empirical and Economic Analysis on the Dynamics of Environmental Regulation in Japan*], Bokutakusha.

Hosoe, M. and Ota, S. (eds) (2001) *Ho no keizai bunseki: Keiyaku, kigyo, seisaku* [*Economic Analysis of Law: Contract, Enterprises and Policy*], Keiso Shobo.

Iida, T. (2004) '*Ho to keizaigaku*' *no shakai kihanron* [*Social Norms in the Perspective of Law and Economics*], Keiso Shobo.

Isozaki, H. (1999) *Bunken jidai no seisaku homu: Kaikaku no jidai no jichi wo tou* [*Policy-Oriented Administration of Law in the Age of Decentralisation: Self-Government in the Age of Institutional Reform*], Hokkaido Chosonkai.

Isozaki, H. (ed) (2004) *Seisaku homu no shintenkai: Rokaru ruru ga mietekita* [*The New Development of Policy-Oriented Legal Administration: Emerging Local Rules*], Gyosei.

Isozaki, H. (2012) *Jichitai seisaku homu kogi* [*Lectures on the Policy-Oriented Administration of Law by Local Governments*], Daiichi Hoki.

Kaneko, H., Kitamura, Y. and Izuishi, M. (eds) (2008) *Seisaku homu jiten* [*Dictionary of Policy-Oriented Administration of Law*], Gyosei.

Kato, I. (1981) 'Legislative study' (in Japanese), *Horitsu jiho*, vol 53, no 14, pp 6–8.

Kawahama, N. (1993) 'On the Relationship between Law and Economics and Legal Interpretation: A Critical Examination, Parts 1–4' (in Japanese), *Minshoho zasshi*, vol 108, no 6, pp 820–49/vol 109, no 1, pp 1–35/vol 109, no 2, pp 207–34/vol 109, no 3, pp 413–43.

Kisa, S. (1996) *Jichitai homu towa nanika* [*What Is the Local Government Administration of Law?*], Hokkaido Chosonkai.

Kishida, M. (1996) *Ho to keizaigaku* [*Law and Economics*], Shinseisha.

Kitamura, Y. (1999) *Kankyo seisaku homu no jissen* [*The Practice of Policy-Oriented Administration of Environmental Law*], Gyosei.

Kitamura, Y. (2008) *Bunken seisaku homu to kankyo keikan gyosei* [*Decentralized Policy-Oriented Administration of Law and Environmental and Landscape Policy*], Nihon Hyoronsha.

Kitamura, Y., Yamaguchi, M., Izuishi, M. and Isozaki, H. (eds) (2011) *Jichitai seisaku homu: Chiiki tokusei ni tekigoshita hokankyo no sozo* [*The Policy-Oriented Administration of Law by Local Governments: Making Legal Arrangements Suitable to Local Situation*], Yuhikaku.

Kobayakawa, M. (ed) (2000) *Chiho bunken to jichitai homu: Sono chie to chikara* [*Decentralisation and the Local Government Administration of Law: Knowledge and Power*], Gyosei.

Kobayashi, H. and Kanda, H. (1986) *'Ho to keizaigaku' nyumon* [*An Introduction to Law and Economics*], Kobundo.

Kobayashi, N. (1984) *Rippogaku kenkyu: Riron to dotai* [*Legislative Study: Theory and Dynamics*], Sanseido.

Koda, M., Annen, J. and Oinuma, Y. (2008) *Seisaku homu no kiso chishiki: Rippo noryoku, shomu noryoku no kojo ni mukete* [*Basics of Policy-Oriented Administration of Law: Towards the Improvement of Legislative and Litigating Ability*], Daiichi Hoki.

Matsui, Y. (1987) *Shiho seisaku no kihon mondai: Shiho seisaku gaku josetsu* [*Fundamental Issues in Judicial Policy: A Preface to Judicial Policy Study*], Keiso Shobo.

Matsushita, K. (1975) *Shimin jichi no kenpo riron* [*The Constitutional Theory of Civic Self-Government*], Iwanami Shoten.

Miwa, Y., Kanda, H. and Yanagawa, N. (eds) (1998) *Kaishaho no keizaigaku* [*Economics of Corporate Law*], University of Tokyo Press.

Miyoshi, Y. (2013) *Ho to funso kaiketsu no jissho bunseki: Ho to keizaigaku no apurochi* [*Positive Analysis of Law and Conflict Resolution: The Law and Economics Approach*], Osaka University Press.

Mori, D. (2010) *Game riron de yomitoku kokusaiho: Kokusai kanshu ho no kino* [*Game Theory and International Law: The Role of Customary International Law*], Keiso Shobo.

Murakami, J. (2010) *Seisaku homu no jidai to jichitai hogaku* [*The Age of Policy-Oriented Administration of Law and Local Government Jurisprudence*], Keiso Shobo.

Nakajima, M. (2007) *Rippogaku: Joron, rippo kateiron* [*Legislative Study: A Preface and the Legislative Process*] (new edn), Horitsu Bunkasha.

Nakamura, M. and Maeda, H. (eds) (1997) *Rippo katei no kenkyu: Rippo ni okeru seifu no yakuwari* [*A Study on the Legislative Process: The Role of the Government in Legislation*], Shinzansha.

Nakamura, T. (2010) *Ho to keizaigaku: Kigyo soshikiron ni kakaru bunseki shuho no kenkyu: Zaisanken, torihiki kosuto, ejenshi kosuto, Kosu no teiri no kanreisei* [*Law and Economics: A Study on Analytical Tools Concerning Corporate Organisations – Property Right, Transaction Cost, Agency Cost and the Coarse Theorem Interconnected*], Takushoku University.

Ohtake, F., Ouchi, S. and Yamakawa, R. (eds) (2004) *Kaiko hosei wo kangaeru: Hogaku to keizaigaku no shiten* [*A Consideration on Laws Governing the Termination of Employment: The Perspective of Law and Economics*] (revised and enlarged edn), Keiso Shobo.

Okada, Y. and Hayashi, S. (eds) (2009) *Dokusen kinshi ho no keizaigaku: Shinhanketsu no jirei bunseki* [*Economics of Antimonopoly Law: An Analysis of Recent Judicial Decisions*], University of Tokyo Press.

Omori, M. and Kamata, K. (eds) (2011) *Rippogaku kogi* [*Lectures on legislative study*] (enlarged edn), Shojihomu.

Omura, A. (1995) *Hogen, kaishaku, minpogaku: Furansu minpo soron kenkyu* [*Legal Sources, Interpretation and Civil Law Theory: A General Study on French Civil Law*], Yuhikaku.

Omura, A. (2005) *Seikatsu no tameno seido wo tsukuru: Sibiru ro enjiniaringu ni mukete* [*Making Institutions for the Sake of Citizen Life: Towards Civil Law Engineering*], Yuhikaku.

Oshima, T. (2013) *Rippogaku: Riron to jitsumu* [*Legislative Study: Theory and Practice*], Daiich Hoki.

Ota, S. (1991) 'Law and Economics in Japan: Hatching Stage', *International Review of Law and Economics*, vol 11, no 3, pp 301–8.

Ota, S. (2000) *Horitsu* [*Laws*], University of Tokyo Press.

Ramseyer, J.M. (1990) *Ho to keizaigaku: Nihon ho no keizai bunseki* [*Law and Economics: An Economic Analysis of Japanese Law*], Kobundo.

Sano, W. (2010) *Kokyo seisaku kihan* [*Norms of Public Policy*], Minerva Shobo.

Seshimo, H. and Yamazaki, F. (eds) (2007) *Kenri tairitsu no ho to keizaigaku: Shoyuken, taishakuken, teitoken no koritsusei* [*Law and Economics on the Conflict of Rights: The Efficiency of Legal Institutions on Property, Lease and Mortgage*], University of Tokyo Press.

Shimazu, I. (1997) 'Insights of Economics and the Law: A Discussion on Law and Economics' (in Japanese), in M. Iwamura, M. Usui, T. Ebashi, S. Ochiai, K. Kamata, S. Kisugi, M. Kobayakawa, K. Sugeno, K. Takahashi, S. Tanaka, N. Nakayama, N. Nishida, and T. Mogami (eds) *Iwanami koza gendai no ho, 15 Gendai hogaku no shiso to hoho* [*Iwanami Lecture Series on Contemporary Law, Vol 15 The Thoughts on and Methods of Contemporary Law*], Iwanami Shoten, pp 269–303.

Shishido, Z. and Tsuneki, A. (2004) *Ho to keizaigaku: Kigyo kanrenho no mikuro keizaigakuteki kosatsu* [*Law and Economics: A Micro Economic Consideration on Laws Related to Corporation*], Yuhikaku.

Suehiro, I. (1946) 'A Consideration on Legislative Study, with Special Reference to Labour Union Laws' (in Japanese), *Hogaku kyokai zasshi*, vol 64, no 1, pp 14–20.

Suzuki, R., Fukui, H., Yamamoto, K. and Kume, Y. (eds) (2001) *Keibai no ho to keizaigaku* [*Law and Economics on Compulsory Sale by Auction*], Shinzansha.

Suzuki, T. (ed) (2007) *Jichitai homu kaikaku no riron* [*The Theory of Reforms of Local Government Administration of Law*], Keiso Shobo.

Takahashi, M. (2009) *Shokenka no ho to keizaigaku* [*Law and Economics on Stock Market*] (revised and enlarged edn), NTT Shuppan.

Takami, K. (1985) 'Ideal Legislator and Legislation: A Look at Legislative Study' (in Japanese), *Koho kenkyu*, no 6, pp 95–7.

Tamura, Y. (ed) (2008) *Shinsedai chiteki zaisanho seisakugaku no sosei* [*Creating the New Generation of Studies on Intellectual Property Law and Policy*], Yuhikaku.

Tamura, Y., Chiba, M. and Yoshida, T. (2009) *Jichitai seisaku homu* [*The Policy-Oriented Administration of Law by Local Governments*], Yachiyo Shuppan.

Tanaka, T. (2010) *Jorei zukuri no tame no seisaku homu* [*Policy-Oriented Administration of Law Intended to Make Local Governments' Ordinances*], Daiichi Hoki.

Tanaka, T. and Kisa, S. (2004) *Tekisuto bukku jichitai homu* [*A Textbook on the Local Government Administration of Law*], Gyosei.

Tsuneki, A. (2008) *Horigaku to keizaigaku: Kihanteki 'ho to keizaigaku' no saiteii* [*Jurisprudence and Economics*], Keiso Shobo.

Tsuneki, A. (2012) '*Ho to keizaigaku' ni yoru kokyo seisaku bunseki* [*Public Policy Analysis: A Law and Economics Approach*], Iwanami Shoten.

Uchida, T. (1990) *Keiyaku no saisei* [*The Revival of Contract Law*], Kobundo.

Urabe, H., Kitamura, Y. and Kouketsu, H. (eds) (2005) *Kaishaku hogaku to seisaku hogaku* [*The Interpretation of Law and the Study of Policy and Law*], Keiso Shobo.

Usami, M. (1999) 'Law as Public Policy' (in Japanese), in T. Inoue, I. Shimazu and Y. Matsuura (eds) *Ho no rinkai, vol. 3 Ho jissen eno teigen* [*The Law at a Critical Point, Vol. 3 New Visions for Legal Practices*], University of Tokyo Press, pp 143–65.

Usami, M. (2008) 'Law as Public Policy: Combining Justice with Interest', in T. Biernat and M. Zirk-Sadowski (eds) *Politics of Law and Legal Policy: Between Modern and Post-Modern Jurisprudence*, Wolters Kluwer Polska, pp 292–315.

Usami, M. (ed) (2010) *Hogaku to keizaigaku no aida: Kihan to seido wo kangaeru* [*Law and Economics: Exploring the Foundations and Frontiers*], Keiso Shobo.

Usami, M. (2011) 'Justice and Interest: Two cornerstones of law and policy' (in Japanese), *Shinsedai ho-seisakugaku kenkyu*, no 10, pp 15–40.

Yamada, A. (1994) *Rippogaku josetsu: Taikeiron no kokoromi* [*An Introduction to Legislative Study: A Quest for a Systematic Theory*], Yuhikaku.

Yamaguchi, M. (2002) *Seisaku homu nyumon: Bunken jidai no jichitai homu* [*An Introduction to Policy-Oriented Administration of Law: Local Government Administration of Law in the Age of Decentralisation*], Shinzansha.

Yanagawa, N. (2000) *Keiyaku to soshiki no keizaigaku* [*The Economics of Contract and Organisation*], Toyo Keizai Shinposha.

Yanagawa, N. (2006) *Ho to kigyo kodo no keizai bunseki* [*The Economic Analysis of Law and Corporate Actions*], Nihon Keizai Shinbunsha.

Yano, M. (ed) (2007) *Ho to keizaigaku: Shijo no shitsu to nihon keizai* [*Law and Economics: The Quality of Market and Japanese Economy*], University of Tokyo Press.

Yashiro, N. (2003) *Kisei kaikaku: 'Ho to keizaigaku' kara no teigen* [*Reform of Regulation: Proposals from the Perspective of Law and Economics*], Yuhikaku.

PART TWO
POLICY ANALYSIS IN JAPANESE GOVERNMENTS

SIX

Policy analysis and the policy process in Japanese government

Jun Iio

This chapter illustrates an overview of the institutional settings of governmental organisations and the distinctive features of policy processes in Japan. It shows how policy analysis is or is not employed in Japanese government.

Sectionalism in Japanese government and dispersed policy communities

Japan is a unitary state, not federal. Its political system is a constitutional monarchy, where the monarch (Emperor) is the symbol of national unity and has no political power. The Japanese constitution declares that democracy is its basic principle and stipulates to a parliamentary government where the legal sector is independent. The parliament of Japan, which is called the Diet, consists of the House of Representatives (lower house) and the House of Councillors (upper house). Although the lower house supersedes the upper house in premier nomination, treaty ratification and budget setting, their competences are relatively similar. The prime minister, who is nominated by the lower house, appoints ministers and organises the cabinet, which exercises administrative power. The unity of the cabinet is supported by the prime ministerial power of appointment and dismissal of ministers, and the cabinets have a joint responsibility to the Diet. Each minister is in charge of each administrative domain, respectively. The basic structure of the Japanese government under the present constitution has not been changed since its enactment just after the Second World War.

From the viewpoint of public policy, some special features of Japanese parliamentary government are very important (Iio, 2007). The Japanese administrative section under the cabinet has a strong centrifugal tendency in normal working situations, though the constitution gave a significant amount of power to the prime minister and tried to establish a powerful cabinet. For example, the power of the lower house on which the cabinet is based is relatively weak in relation to the upper house. If the government party or parties lose control of the upper house, the cabinet has a difficult time securing its consent. Even if the ruling party secures the majority of both houses, the cabinet does not control the Diet's deliberation; it must still rely on the negotiation among major parties to settle the deliberation schedule. In government, the independence of each ministry is very strong, and it is necessary to seek consensus among the ministries when the cabinet decides anything. In addition, the cabinet does not necessarily control members of the ruling party. Rank-and-file members of the Diet can easily access the bureaucracy. They directly step into daily administration in return for supporting government bills.

Under these conditions, the policymaking process has been controlled mainly by ministerial bureaucrats. Bureaucrats, who are very faithful to their own ministries, have planned and drafted most bills and budgets, which are not often modified or delayed by politicians, including their ministers. Bureaucrats are divided not only by ministries, but also by bureaus and divisions, and they have attempted to draw up detailed policy from an early stage. As a result, both politicians and bureaucrats are not interested in big policy frameworks as a whole.

As the background of these tendencies, there were two conditions: enduring Liberal Democratic Party (LDP) rule and favourable economic and social development. The former gave little motivation for politicians to take the drastic change of policies due to government change seriously. As incremental mutual adjustment among ministries or interest groups was a common way to make policy, rational calculation for selecting policy alternatives was rare under the continuous LDP cabinets. Politicians run their elections by using personal networking not by party organisation, so they could appeal to their constituency with influence peddling. As a result, party pledges at the time of general elections had mixed texts of various requests from interest groups and contained very vague words in order to appeal to a wide range of the electorate. Few people took party pledges seriously. Parties, especially the LDP, were not interested in implementing their original total plan, which included a wide range of policy spheres. Favourable economic and social conditions made it possible to avoid trade-off problems and drastic changes of policies for political parties and governments. It permitted Japan to solve various conflicts in society by subsidising, and helped to maintain policy frameworks by piecemeal modifications.

To some extent, bureaucrats considered policy frameworks based on their organisational interests and legal consistency. They represented social interests through intimate daily contact with interest groups and local governments through the intimate relationship between the state and society in Japan. They were not only mediators of contradictions, but also delegates of social interests in the groups under their jurisdictions. Using this status, Japanese ministries could absorb information on social trends and grasp the composition of interests in society, and then formulate necessary policies. In this sense, bureaucrats substituted for the role of political parties, which usually control policy frameworks in the case of other countries. The general public usually takes bureaucrats as policymakers and relies on them for policy management.

Policy formulation capability of Japanese political parties

Just after the Second World War, various political parties emerged, including left-wing parties that were banned before that time. Until 1955, the government consisted of the right or centre-right parties that belonged to the pre-war major party lineages, apart from several months of a coalition government consisting of left and centre-left parties. The LDP was formed through the merger of the right and centre-right parties in 1955, and would secure the majority of both houses for a long time. The one-party predominance of the party system by the LDP continued until 1993. Although the Socialist Party of Japan once had a big share of Diet seats, and could have been a major rival to the LDP, opposition parties gradually split into several parties that conceded aiming to be the governing party. Therefore, their influence was lost during the days of high economic growth.

The ruling LDP gradually lost its wide range of support in Japanese society because a mature economy and social changes decreased the cohesion of traditional local networks, which were the firm base for a conservative LDP. Even though the LDP seemed to regain its power during the 1980s by reaching out to the centre-left electorate, it lost the government through a split of its own in 1993. The alternative non-LDP government, consisting of eight centre and left parties, vanished within a year, but the fact that the LDP could be an opposition party changed the idea of fixed, one-party predominance. Since that time, the Japanese government has usually functioned as a coalition government. At the same time, the electoral system for the lower house was changed to a new system that introduced single-seat constituencies as its core. The new electoral system has stimulated the merging of opposing parties, resulting in the establishment of, first, Shin-shin-to and, later, the Democratic Party of Japan (DPJ) as competitors to the LDP. A weakened LDP chose one opposition party, *Komei-to*, as a partner in government. As a result, these two parties have maintained a coalition and electoral cooperation since 1999. Under the Koizumi cabinet of the LDP and *Komei* in the early 2000s, the LDP seemed to regain electoral strength, but successive cabinets lost the general public's confidence, and the LDP was defeated in the 2009 general election. The new government led by the DPJ was quite popular at the start, but it showed a lack of government management, and also lost support. In 2012, the LDP and *Komei* won the government back and Abe's cabinet displayed the abilities of both government management and policymaking. Through these two changes in government, the Japanese political system moved away from its old, established style.

Traditionally, the LDP had two main organisational characteristics. One characteristic was that the LDP was the aggregate of individual politicians, and the official organisation was weak or nominal. During election campaigns, most LDP candidates run on their own personal organisation (*Koen-kai*) and mainly their own funding, so that the role of the official party organisation is very limited. As a result, MPs' loyalty to the party is not strong. The other characteristic was the importance of intra-party factions, which have recently, however, been drastically changed. MPs usually belonged to one of the major factions and sought to gain a political position, electoral support and political funds. For this reason, the LDP was composed of the united factions of conservative politicians. The reason behind the strength of the LDP factions was due to the fact that there were usually several LDP candidates in one constituency of the lower house before the 1994 electoral reform. By that time, the factions were de facto parties during the election campaign. Party policy at the time of the general election was not important because multiple LDP candidates, who have different personal pledges, competed. The LDP did not try to compile its policy ideas, even at the elections.

These characteristics made the LDP vulnerable to revolt by its members so that it tried to keep its own unity by logrolling or distributing positions to these members. For this reason, the cabinet was usually reshuffled every year to give the LDP MPs a chance to be cabinet ministers. Almost all lower house MPs of the LDP could be ministers if they experienced over six successful elections. Therefore, many LDP ministers lacked expertise. In order to keep discipline inside the party during Diet votes when the cabinet submitted bills to the Diet, the government was required to deliberate within the LDP beforehand. During such earlier deliberations, at which bureaucrats explained the contents of bills and tried to persuade LDP members, politicians required amendments or concessions to the interests of politicians' constituencies in exchange for passing bills. Politicians and bureaucrats contacted each other daily, and politicians easily utilised the knowledge, networking and official competence of the ministerial bureaucracy. It is natural that the LDP relied on ministries in the respect of policy formulating abilities. The LDP had a relatively big headquarters with a large number of employees, but this was merely the forum of policy coordination based on ministerial preparation. Therefore, the necessity of policy analysis in the LDP has been very limited.

Concerning the rival parties that attempted to become a ruling party instead of the LDP, Shin-shin or the DPJ, the situation has not been so different. They have also been MP-centric parties with hardly any systematic policy compiling mechanisms. These parties usually criticised the LDP or bureaucratic policy management, but have shown few alternatives, usually insisting on changing the government system itself to change policy directions.

As two-party rivalries have become a reality since the 2000s, the situation concerning party policies has changed to some extent. When the general election seemed imminent in 2003, the DPJ, which absorbed the minor Liberal Party, became a plausible challenger to the LDP, announcing the introduction of a 'Manifesto' at the impending general election, which included detailed and concrete pledges of the party. Under Prime Minister Koizumi, the LDP also announced equivalent party pledges and government programmes at that time. These types of campaign promises require political parties to state the number of, and detailed information about, the policies in their pledges, so that they need to examine the conditions of and instruments for their policies, based on cautious analysis. However, parties that had been used to meaningless pledges or to the acceptance of bureaucratic policy coordination did not seriously consider introducing policy analysis measures. When the DPJ got the majority of seats in the lower house at the 2009 general election with its detailed Manifesto, which included various concrete spending items, the general public hoped to see a more transparent and democratic policy process than before. However, the DPJ government could not enact most of the pledges because of financial limitations or other restrictions. The lack of policy analysis capabilities within the DPJ resulted in widespread disappointment. Also, the lack of policy coordination procedures within the DPJ showed that it could not manage to get a policy consensus even among its own members. Therefore, the DPJ split, lost control of the situation and was defeated at the 2012 election.

There are two exceptionally well-organised political parties in Japan, *Komei*, which was strongly supported by one Buddhist group (*Soka-gakkai*), and the Japanese Communist Party. These have many active party members and systematic procedures to set up their own policy lines or election pledges. To form their policies, these parties have their own staff members who gather and analyse information. However, these parties only have limited influence.

Concerning other minor parties, they have been easily formed and easily dissolved by the will of MPs, and they did not usually have enough staff members to perform the functions related to policy analysis. In conclusion, at this time, Japanese political parties do not usually have well-organised policy analysis components or an intention to strengthen their capability for policy analysis.

Policy coordination process by the bureaucracy

When political parties do not compile policies for different policy areas, the government should do it. Although the cabinet or prime minister primarily have to put these policies in order, due to their unstable statuses, neither have enough expertise, time or intention. Usually, a prime minister serves for two years maximum, and often for only one year, and the cabinet is reshuffled every year whether or not the same prime minister remains. For a long time, the bureaucracy settled policy affairs by themselves and was expected to do so by the public. Politicians have relied on bureaucrats to manage public policy well (Kato,1994).

Without cabinet discipline, the Japanese central administration has centrifugal tendencies or sectionalism. The autonomy of each minister has been emphasised in a similar way to that of the ministerial bureaucracy. Under this situation, intra-governmental coordination is the main opportunity for policy formation. Each ministry, bureau and section proposes preferable policy proposals, and they compete and mutually accommodate with each other based on a mutual incremental adjustment process. In this case, total integration is secured by the constellation of ministerial organisations, so that administrative reform becomes a chance to change policy direction as well. For this reason, many policy reforms have been performed under the name of administrative reforms.

Usually, a policy alternative is initiated by some sections or bureaus of ministries, even though the minister sometimes points out the necessity of a new policy, or ruling party members propose it. When an initiative could get the general approval of the ministry, the section in charge tries to receive consent for the concrete policy details from other sections, bureaus and ministries. This process is usually started at the time of the budget compilation and so on, so that the various different initiatives simultaneously compete with each other. Concerning the consent that is required for these policies, the consent from the Ministry of Finance is very important. The Ministry of Finance attempts to adjust items and the cost of the proposed policy in respect of the total budget through the budget assessment process. In addition, legal assessment by the cabinet legal bureau is required. Through these assessments, the Japanese government can consolidate proposed policies as a whole.

At the same time, the section in charge should gain consent from the ruling party, which usually means from LDP politicians. An approval decision of the LDP must be obtained before the final decision of the cabinet for the bill. This is necessary to secure the discipline of LDP members during the Diet session. Bureaucrats try to get a consensus among *Zoku-giin* ('tribe' members), Diet members who usually participate in the exchange with the ministry, as well as consent from their minister or premier. Then, bureaucrats explain their proposals and try to persuade the other members through the pre-legislature examination process of the LDP with the help of tribe members. Bureaucrats visit the personal offices of related politicians daily and persuade or negotiate with them to get their consent. During these interactions between bureaucrats and politicians, there are some logrolling or pork-barrel adjustments. Consequently, due to the autonomous nature of each organisation, this process of getting consent in the government and from ruling party members takes a lot of energy and time of related officials.

After the cabinet's submitting of the bill to the Diet, the focus moves to procedures and timing because bicameralism, the independent session system, the committee system and the lack of government power in the Diet make it difficult for the government to pass bills. Every procedure is on the table for negotiation among parliamentary parties in both houses, and the government has few control measures. Under these conditions, MPs usually concentrate on bargaining over procedure, and do not discuss it article by article. The main system of deliberation is for members to question the government, which is usually not limited to the content of the bill. Drastic amendments are very rare, so there is little need for policy analysis during the Diet session.

Therefore, bureaucrats are the possible consumers of policy analysis, but they usually rely on incremental adjustments. Although they rarely feel the necessity for analysis, this situation has been changing over the last 10 years. Because of an expectation for initiatives from politicians, many politicians have become personally interested in policy matters. This trend should have called attention to policy analysis; however, with the increasing burden of the persuasion of politicians, public officials have become too busy to make use of policy analysis. As a result, both politicians and bureaucrats are pressed into mutual change. Recent developments in the establishment of the leadership of the prime minister or cabinet have created a chance to change the situation and emphasise careful analysis.

Intimate relationship between the state and society in Japan

The ministerial policy formation process is not performed independently of the social context. The Japanese state penetrates society deeply, and the relationship between the state bureaucracy and various social groups is very close. Ministries have converted social interests to policies though mutual interaction with social groups. This is one of the historical inheritances that have led the Japanese state to modernise its economy and society through various intervening means over the past 100 years.

Above all, many business or industrial groups have been very intimate with ministries like the Ministry of Economy, Trade and Industry, owing to a background history in which the ministry guided the merger and unification of separated industrial groups into national industrial groups during the Second World War. The peak associations of the business world, like the Japan Federation of Business and the Japan Chamber of Commerce, have special contact with government officials. For social networking, many industrial groups employ former public officials, and some of them second its employees to ministries as short-term assistants. For example, the intimate relationship between the Ministry of Agriculture, Forestry and Fishery and the Federation of Agricultural Cooperatives and between the Ministry of Welfare and Labor and the Medical Association are famous. In addition, the peak Association of Labour Unions has a special relationship with the Ministry of Welfare and Labor. These groups seem to have a strong influence on the policy process through ministries and related politicians.

These networks can be examined by looking at the coordination type of *Shingi-kai* (advisory councils), which consists of representatives from related interest groups who convey the messages from the groups through official deliberation and unofficial negotiations before the meetings. If there is any difference of interests among related groups, advisory councils become the arena for their mutual adjustment, like the Central Labor Committee, which is the tripartite committee of the labour union, employer group and neutral academics. Related groups also seek to submit proposals, officially or unofficially, to this type of advisory council for inclusion in their concluding reports. In order to prepare the proposals, some peak associations and powerful interest groups have set up their own research institutes.

After introducing neoliberal policy reforms in the 1990s, the relationship between economic ministries and major economic groups or industrial groups has drifted apart. For example, when the Financial Service Agency was separated from the Ministry of Finance, the well-known intimate relationship between the Ministry of Finance and industrial groups of financial business was transformed into a new relationship between the regulating and the regulated.

In some industries or sections, however, intimate relations have been maintained. For example, the Agency for Natural Resources and Energy, which regulates nuclear energy-related industries, has kept intimate connections with the regulated industries, including electric power companies and specialists who work in related research. The cohesive policy communities like the one previously mentioned have a tendency to monopolise policymaking in a closed policy process with the authority of specialised knowledge. This monopoly is also possible because of the general public's indifference. Until the occurrence of unexpected disasters, like the nuclear power plant accident in Fukushima, people were unaware of the problems of this type of policy community.

In the sphere of centre–local relations, ministerial bureaucracy had also been the decisive influence until recent reforms. Until recently, most of the central government policies were carried out by local governments, which functioned as implementing agencies of central ministries that required the obedience of local governments. Under this system, many local governments thought themselves to be faithful, implementing branches of ministries. Decentralisation reforms in the year 2000 enacted various autonomous measures in local governments. Although inertia from the centralised regime of the past has been quite strong, a new direction of centre–local relations has gradually appeared, and the necessity of policy analysis has also increased. Today, some local governments actively propose their ideas to national politicians and enact their own original policy reforms. The demand for policy analysis in local administrations has been increasing.

Basic characteristics of Japanese bureaucracy

Thus far, the importance of public officials in the Japanese policymaking process has been emphasised, so their abilities or analytical competence are next to be examined (Shindo, 2004). By what capabilities do they formulate their policies?

The Japanese bureaucracy has been maintained by permanent officials who usually enter one of the ministries by passing the qualified examination just after graduating from universities or colleges, and are trained on the job. Only limited officials, who are usually in technical positions, have master's or doctoral degrees. Among officials, there are several categories differentiated by the kinds of examination, like bureaucrats of the career to the management level, middle management and ordinary employees. All bureaucrats belong to one of the various groups based on the ministry, examination category and specialty.

Policy formulation or drafting work is usually conducted by candidate management bureaucrats. Among such qualified bureaucrats, the officials who passed a legal specialty or economic specialty are privileged and become candidates for the highest ranks of the ministerial bureaucracy, such as the administrative vice-minister, who is the highest official in a ministry. The other groups, qualified bureaucrats with a civil engineering specialty, medical doctors or other specialties, are less privileged but have their own autonomy of personnel, and a particular specialist group will have exclusive autonomy in some sections or bureaus, like the division responsible for nuclear energy supervision.

Most bureaucrats start their careers at the bottom of the ministerial hierarchy, but qualified bureaucrats are promoted more rapidly than officials of other categories. Promotion is based on the year of entering the ministry and competence or achievements. In the case of qualified bureaucrats with a law specialty, they are usually promoted every two or three years, and most of them become the chief of a particular section, but only promising bureaucrats can obtain an important section position among various sections. After the section chief level, promotion speed is differentiated by evaluations even among same-year members. Until recent years, if one member of the same year group becomes the administrative vice-minister, all other bureaucrats had to resign from ministerial positions. Early-retired bureaucrats could obtain a job outside of the ministry through arrangement with the ministry. This early retirement system is called 'descending from the heavens' (*Amakudari*). This system has become heavily criticised recently and will not be maintained in the future. A bureaucrat may work at another ministry for a short time, but it is always arranged by an original ministry group. Therefore, an official's loyalty to their ministerial group is very strong. However, criticism of *Amakudari* and too much loyalty is transforming the system, so that the promotion system in the Japanese bureaucracy is in transition.

The evaluation of personnel in the bureaucracy is based on a relative assessment among officials of the same entrance year in the same category. Consequently, the evaluation measure tends to be unitary and does not appreciate various different achievements or talents. When intra-administration coordination and political adjustment become important, the officials who are good at negotiation or coordination are inclined to be highly appreciated and promoted to high-ranking positions. Considering this situation, the incentives of bureaucrats to perform well in policy analysis are very limited. Moreover, bureaucrats have been occupied with increasing workloads due to the strictly limited total number of public officials, which was fixed in 1969. Without enough human resources, ministries tend to utilise outside research services, activating networks with researchers and specialists by funding special research and purchasing a consultant service or research reports from policy institutes.

As far as the training programmes for public officials are concerned, the target is usually very general, and programme selection depends on personal choice. Some bureaucrats are enabled to study abroad through public funding, and some participate in special training programmes for a particular purpose. Generally speaking, academic degrees are not appreciated among officials, and there are very few doctors, with only some holding a master's degree in ministries, except for the case of minor technical specialists. Even at the ministerial research institutes, only some institutes require a doctoral degree for their research staff, and many hire ordinary officials who are temporarily seconded from the ministry. Governmental statistics are well-organised and accurate but too rigid to get appropriate information for policymaking.

Above all, a very short time for preparing new policy prevents adequate analysis. Busy bureaucrats usually devote their energies to immediate tasks, resulting in a situation where most policy proposals are drafted in a few months, in time for things such as the budgetary process, for example. The fact that careful research requires money and time makes most officials avoid research activities before policy formulation. Bureaucrats prefer making policies through mutual adjustment or the incremental coordination process. Therefore, in general, ministries pay little attention to policy analysis, though there are exceptional efforts to utilise policy analysis within the government.

When explaining this situation, it is often said by critics who have an economic specialty or other scientific background that mainstream bureaucrats with a legal specialty prevent efficient analysis because of their strong attachment to legal consistency. Admittedly, all policies need to pass a legal assessment but are not required to pass an analytical test. Recently, the new policy movement based on law and economics has been influential, bridging the gap between legal adequateness and analytical validity.

For a more effective use of policy analysis in the Japanese government, a comprehensive reform of its policy process is needed. Concerning the new division of labour between politicians and public officials, the latter should perform more analysis, with long and thorough policy formulation stages that can utilise the analytical method, and with an appropriate evaluation system that appreciates analytical ability.

Policy research activities relating to advisory councils

There are four types of advisory council. First, there are authorisation committees, which are utilised by the ministerial bureaucracy to gain legitimacy for their drafting of policy proposals. Second, there are coordinating committees at which related social interests are adjusted. Third, there are temporal reform committees, which the prime minister or government as a whole requests in order to review and find solutions to a policy or organisation. Finally, there are research committees, by which bureaucrats try to gain knowledge and analyse problems for which they do not have enough knowledge or expertise.

Among these, the last type of advisory council may often require policy analysis skills. They are usually small, temporal and unofficial committees, which are set up by a bureaucratic decision at the bureau director level. Also, sometimes, the ministry organises similar plural research committees due to testing different approaches to the problem. Through deliberation, bureaucrats gain networks with specialists, differentiate preferable researchers from others and learn about the process of treating the problem in the field. They also purchase outside research services with the research committee budget, because it is credible to secure a necessary research budget when setting up a new committee.

However, other types of committees also sometimes require the help of policy analysis. Regarding the coordination type of advisory council, each interest representative sometimes requires factual evidence or estimations based on careful analysis. As far as the temporal reform type of advisory council is concerned, such committees contain a relatively large secretariat and abundant budgets so that they can obtain sufficient research, even though political leaders usually urge reporting promptly in advance, resulting in abbreviated research time.

The chair or president of an advisory council is generally chosen from famous business leaders who have a high position in national business associations and organisational support from their own companies. Such business executives are expected to be neutral mediators among committee members, and manage the deliberation of the committee with the support of the committee secretariats. However, sometimes, the leadership of such business leaders seems to have a pro-business bias, and famous and experienced scholars are requested to occupy the chairs. In those cases, the selection is based not on their specialties, but on their management abilities. Therefore, some business executives or famous professors serve on various different advisory councils.

The methods by which specialists or scholars participate are diverse. Some specialists lead the discussion by their remarks during the meetings. Some experts contribute to the councils by providing their own analysis or data at the time of preparation for the meetings. Many scholars appreciate participating in advisory councils because, on the one hand, it gives them a sense of working for the public good and, on the other, they are provided with various data relating to the policy issues by ministries. The daily interaction between researchers and bureaucrats enhances close networks between them, and forms respective policy communities. In some cases, membership of an important advisory council itself gives social prestige to the professors, such as membership of the tax commission of the cabinet office for public economy professors. The reports or conclusions are not necessarily drafted by specialists; generally, they are drafted and adjusted by secretariat officials, with input from related interests.

Intra-ministerial research activities

As policy and administrative work became more complex and specialised in many fields, beginning in the 1980s, Japanese ministries instituted a planning or policy section, which focussed on intensive planning or analytical work inside these sections. The role of such a section was limited, however, as the basic policy process of the section in charge in drafting and coordinating among various organisations had not changed, and such a policy section remained a junior partner to the ordinary section. As a result, generally speaking, while the general policy section or the equivalent section has edited various reports or White Papers, they have not changed the contents of policy.

Furthermore, there are many intra-research institutes in ministries. The reason for establishing this kind of organisation was due to the perception that the bureaucracy had to be ready for the necessity of policy analysis. Among them, some institutes emphasised basic and academic research, while others emphasised practical or policy-oriented research, and still others stressed the coordination among the ministry and institute. Generally speaking, the strategic use of these ministerial institutes is rare, and the maintenance of the organisation might be the purpose of the activities in some cases, with positions in some institutes operating as a reserve pool of ministry bureaucrats. To improve the situation concerning ministerial institutes, it is necessary to embed the function of the institute into the policy formulation process of the ministry, and to employ skilful research staff members for this purpose.

Ministries are often dependent on the outside research services offered by private research companies, consultants, research foundations and professors of universities because these services are speedy and do not require permanent maintenance. However, these services usually do not include in-depth research methods or careful analysis, though some commissioned research is of high quality and has an impact. This kind of purchased research has decreased recently because of stringent budget assessments, so that commissioning useful and qualified researchers has become difficult.

Emergence of alternative policy inputs to the government

Under the political transition, some bureaucrats lost their loyalty to their own ministries, with some becoming politicians or serving them as personal aides. Some who have cultivated their analytical skills desired to join the field of academics, usually to become public intellectuals. Some attempted to create a new career path as policy consultants or advocacy groups. Based on these activities, former bureaucrats diffused their policy knowledge and expertise throughout society. This trend also raised a reaction from the private sector, and more people have become interested in policy and policy analysis (Policy Analysis Network, 2003).

The number of policy-oriented research institutes, advocacy groups and social groups that are optimistic towards policy proposals has been increasing rapidly, even though traditional or established foundations are unenthusiastic towards policy proposals or analysis. Because non-government organisations that are eager to do policy analysis are generally small and do not have enough funds and human resources, strengthening these organisations and setting up independent policy think tanks are necessary to improve alternative policy analysis in Japan.

In conclusion, we should consider the transformation of the policy process in Japan in order to improve the situation concerning policy analysis. In securing the place of policy analysis in the policy process, the necessity for analysis will automatically be increased. With this movement, various potential resources in Japan will be vitalised.

References

Iio, J. (2007) *Nihon no Tochi Kozo* [*Government Structure in Japan*], Chuo Koron Shin Sha.

Kato, J. (1994) *The Problem of Bureaucratic Rationality*, Princeton University Press.

Policy Analysis Network (ed) (2003) *Seisakugaku Nyumon* [*An Introduction to Policy Sciences*], Toyo Keizai Shinpo Sha.

Shindo, M. (2004) *Gaisetsu Nihon no Kokyo Seisaku* [*An Introduction to Public Policy in Japan*], University of Tokyo Press.

SEVEN

In-house think tanks of ministries: their functions and limitations in policy formulation

Hideaki Tanaka

Introduction

The Kasumigaseki district in downtown Tokyo, where most central government buildings are located, is often referred to as the 'think tank of the Japanese government'. This phrase is testimony to the fact that bureaucracy plays a significant role in the policymaking process in Japan. However, one would wonder why this think tank has an in-house think tank. Rather than directly engaging in scientific or technological research and development, most ministries in Kasumigaseki have within them a think tank or a research body that conducts research on policies. Ministries have internal bureaus or divisions that engage in planning, research and deliberation on policies that fall under their jurisdiction. Research bodies that are separate from such internal bureaus also exist. Other countries that adopt a parliamentary system, like the UK, typically have training institutions or universities intended for civil servants, but research bodies that focus on policies are not so common.[1] However, what roles do such bodies play and what functions do they perform in Japan?

If a think tank is defined as an entity that, while not an organisation charged with drawing up or implementing policies, has the capacity to provide ideas on policies to the greater society from different perspectives to those of such an organisation, and through its activities, makes the process of policy formulation public and adds diversity and competition to such processes (Suzuki, 2007: 108),[2] then research bodies that belong to ministries are clearly not think tanks in this sense. As they are organisations within ministries, they are not purely independent. However, why do ministries have such a think tank? Simply put, many officials in Kasumigaseki are too busy with day-to-day tasks to acquire or accumulate new knowledge or information, and are not able to analyse policies adequately with a medium- to long-term view. Also, the process of policy formulation has tended to be influenced by the logic of the supply side and the interests of specific parties, and has not always worked to optimise social welfare.[3]

Policy research institutes of ministries have often become the target of administrative reform initiatives, but it cannot be said that their roles, functions, limitations and issues have been sufficiently analysed or evaluated. Therefore, in this chapter, I will raise the main research question of whether such research institutes are contributing to the analysis and formulation of policies at ministries, with particular emphasis on whether such institutes are fulfilling sufficient policy analysis functions for policy decisions to be made in a scientific and rational manner. I will then go on to take a close look at their position in the policy process and their function in policy analysis.

This chapter is organised as follows. In the following section, I lay out the basic analytical framework. In the third section, I give an overview of the present research institutes. In the fourth section, I take a close look at specific policy research institutes with a view to analysing their function in the policy process. Finally, I will conclude in the fifth section.

Analytical framework

I will start by defining the research institutes that we discuss here. In this chapter, we will look at research institutes that belong to ministries and mainly engage in research about policies that fall under the charge of such ministries, excluding those that conduct scientific or technological research and development, and will refer to such entities as 'policy research institutes'. As detailed in the next section, as of April 2012, there are 13 such institutes.

I would again like to set forth the main research questions. Policy research institutes can be thought of as an example of trends in political science and the emphasis on policy content in Japan (Miyakawa, 1995), but the key questions are whether such institutes are involved in the policy process at ministries, in what way they are involved, and what roles they play.[4] As examples of resources for policy analysis at ministries, we can think of internal departments (including research divisions), advisory councils and political parties. Do policy research institutes function as another such resource? Answering these questions will be the objective of this chapter.

In order to analyse the function and role of policy research institutes, it is necessary to take a detailed look at the policy process of the Japanese central government. However, this is no easy task and I must make it clear at the outset that this chapter faces some major limitations and constraints.

What we analyse here is the function of policy research institutes or, in other words, the position of policy analysis by such research institutes in the policy process. Generally speaking, the policy process can be broken down into three stages: decision-making, implementation and evaluation. Among these, decision-making is further broken down into four phases or stages: problem finding – agenda setting – comparison of policies – policy selection (Adachi, 2009: 124–5).[5] How each policy research institute becomes involved in each of these steps in the policy process differs from institute to institute, but the main interest of this chapter lies in the early stages of policymaking such as problem finding, analysis and evaluation of reforms and alternatives.

I must also point out that even if we define the scope of this study narrowly, it is no easy task to examine the function and role of policy research institutes in the policy process.[6] Throughout the entire process from problem finding to policy decision-making, a wide array of players come into the picture, including internal bureaus handling policy planning and other advisory bodies, study groups, political parties from both the ruling and opposition blocs, business lobbies, citizen groups, non-profit organisations (NPOs), the media, and academic bodies such as universities. Policies are formed while all these players influence one another. In other words, the policy process is a process where complex interactions and numerous instances of decision-making take place one after another (Hayakawa et al, 2004: 227). While policymaking players, such as bureaucrats who deliberate on the feasibility of each policy alternative, play an important role in the process (Nishio, 2012: 143), engagement by policy research institutes is generally not conducted openly and it is difficult to confirm their involvement. Even in studies by Shiroyama et al (1999) and Shiroyama and Hosono (2002), where analyses of policy processes were carried out for individual ministries, involvement by policy research institutes was not mentioned.

While keeping such analytical limitations in mind, we will take a general overview of the policy research institutes of ministries in the following section, and will go on to focus on and analyse the Economic and Social Research Institute (ESRI) under the Cabinet Office, the Policy Research Institute (PRI) under the Ministry of Finance, and the Research Institute of Economy, Trade and Industry (RIETI) under the Ministry of Economy, Trade and Industry (METI). By taking a look at the characteristics of these respective research institutes, their publications and interviews with researchers and staff of the institutes, we will attempt to clarify the institutes' functions in the policy process. It should be noted, however, that involvement in policy formation occurs in a different way each time, and that it is difficult to generalise about the role that these institutes play in the policy process. In addition to that, their functions may differ between those stipulated in the relevant laws and regulations, those expected by stakeholders, and those actually performed.

Overview of policy research institutes

Some policy research institutes date back to before the Second World War (eg the former National Institute of Population and Social Security Research under the Ministry of Health, Labour and Welfare established in 1939), but most were set up in the 1980s or later (eg the Institute of Fiscal and Monetary Policy under the former Ministry of Finance). Policy research institutes have undergone a series of consolidations over the years and their names have also changed. As of April 2012, there were 13 such institutes (see Table 7.1). Today, there are 12 ministries at the central government. Among them, all but the Ministry of Foreign Affairs have at least one such research institute. The Ministry of Education, Culture, Sports, Science and Technology has two policy research institutes as a result of the merger of the former Ministry of Education, Science, Sports and Culture with the Science and Technology Agency. This chapter looks at institutes that are legally created by ministries. It does not cover entities like *zaidanhojin* or incorporated foundations, even if they are in fact involved in policy formulation or policy analysis at ministries or agencies. Examples of such cases include the National Institute for Research Advancement (NIRA) under the Cabinet Office (formerly under the Economic Planning Agency [EPA]) and the Japan Institute of International Affairs (JIIA) under the Ministry of Foreign Affairs.[7]

Policy research institutes can be classified into two types of legal organisations. One is 'facilities and other organs', which are internal organisations of ministries. 'Facilities and other organs' are defined in Article 8-2 of the National Government Organization Act as 'research and development institutes, inspection and certification institutes, educational and training facilities, medical and rehabilitation facilities, reformatory and internment facilities and work facilities', and their actual scope of operations are set forth in the orders for organisation under the acts for establishment of the respective ministries. The other category is 'incorporated administrative agencies' (IAAs), which were set up in accordance with the independent administrative institution system introduced as part of the central government reform of 2001. IAAs are founded

Table 7.1: Policy research institute under ministries

Ministry	Name of Institute	Legal status	Year of Establishment[1]	Major Functions[2] Research	Statistics	Library	Training	International Cooperation	Others	Remarks
Cabinet Office	Economic and Social Research Institute	Internal organisation	1958/2001	☒	☒					Head: academic
Ministry of Internal Affairs and Communications	Institute for Information and Communications Policy	Internal organisation	1988/2003	☒			☒			Head: civil service
Ministry of Justice	Research and Training Institute of the Ministry of Justice	Internal organisation	1939/1959	☒			☒	☒		Head: civil service
Ministry of Finance	Policy Research Institute	Internal organisation	1985/2001	☒	☒		☒	☒		Head: civil service
Ministry of Education, Culture, Sports, Science and Technology	National Institute for Educational Policy Research	Internal organisation	1949/2001	☒						Head: civil service Advisory committee
	National Institute for Science and Technology Policy	Internal organisation	1988/2001	☒		☒				Head: civil service
Ministry of Health, Labour and Welfare	National Institute of Population and Social Security Research	Internal organisation	1939/1996	☒	☒					Head: academic
	The Japan Institute for Labour Policy and Training	Agency	1969/2003	☒		☒				Head: academic Uniform evaluation system
Ministry of Agriculture, Forestry and Fisheries	Policy Research Institute	Internal organisation	1946/2001	☒						Head: civil service
Ministry of Economy, Trade and Industry	Research Institute of Economy, Trade and Industry	Agency	1987/2001	☒		☒			☒	Head: academic Uniform evaluation system
Ministry of Land, Infrastructure, Transport and Tourism	Policy Research Institute for Land, Infrastructure, Transport and Tourism	Internal organisation	1970/2001	☒						Head: civil service
Ministry of the Environment	National Institute for Environmental Studies	Agency	1974/2001	☒						Head: academic Uniform evaluation system
Ministry of Defence	National Institute for Defense Studies	Internal organization	1952/1985	☒			☒			Head: civil service

[1] Regarding year of establishment, the first number means year when an institute was firstly established and the second number means year when an institution with the current name was established.

[2] Major functions are what are stipulated in laws or government orders.

based on laws established individually for respective institutions pursuant to the Act on the General Rules for Incorporated Administrative Agencies. IAAs are different from facilities and other organs in that they have a separate corporate status and are allowed more flexible budgeting and personnel management. On the other hand, they have an obligation to follow a regulatory framework meant to secure transparency and accountability, such as medium–term goals and plans, annual performance reports, financial statements in accordance with the same accounting standards as those applied to private-sector companies, inspection by independent auditors, and assessment by the ministry's IAA evaluation committee.

The function of policy research institutes is set forth either in the order for organisation or the individual law for the respective IAA. The details are set out in Table 7.1, but the institutes' activities are not purely limited to research and studies. Every institute has its history since foundation or from a merger or consolidation, and is often involved in other activities such as compiling statistics and training employees of the respective ministry.

Another point that could characterise different policy research institutes is the fact that some have installed outside experts and scholars in key positions, such as president or senior researchers, while others mostly promote personnel from inside the ministry. This is an overall observation and it is difficult to draw a clear line, but ESRI, the National Institute of Population and Social Security Research and RIETI fall into the former category. In spite of that, many policy research institutes belong to the latter case. I will shed some light on this point in the next section, but internal promotion could undermine the independence and expertise of research and study activities and this reveals an inherent dilemma that policy research institutes associated with a ministry are faced with.

Role of policy research institutes in the policy process

In this section, we will take a look at ESRI, PRI and RIETI. While these three institutes engage in research activities regarding overall economic and fiscal policies, they are different in several respects, including the way in which they are organised, and present an interesting contrast.

Economic and Social Research Institute under the Cabinet Office

The predecessor of ESRI, the Economic Research Institute (ERI), was established on 1 July 1958 as a facility under the EPA of the former Prime Minister's Office. The ERI was installed in order to integrate survey and research activities on national income and national wealth and to conduct more in-depth theoretical and empirical studies concerning issues such as economic structures and economic cycles.

Later, in January 2001, the ERI was reorganised as a facility of the new Cabinet Office as part of the administrative reform of 2001, and its name was changed to ESRI. ESRI's main function is: to conduct theoretical and empirical studies on topics such as economic activities, economic policies and social activities; to nurture and train research personnel; and to compile statistics based on the system of national accounts.[8] The Cabinet Office is charged with supporting the cabinet with administrative functions concerning important policies (Act for Establishment of the Cabinet Office, Article 3-1), and is positioned as the 'place of wisdom' for deliberating on important issues. In this regard, ESRI works as the Cabinet Office's think tank in linking theories with actual policies.[9] ESRI is composed of the General Administrative Department, the Executive Research Fellow, the Department of Information and Research Cooperation, the Department of Business Statistics, the Department of National Accounts, and the Training Institute of Economics.

ESRI is actively engaged in a variety of survey and research activities in cooperation with outside experts regarding the economy as a whole. Recent topics include the measurement of happiness and social progress and the development and improvement of econometric models and regional economies, with several research projects under way on each of these topics. One characteristic of ESRI is the fact that when performing tasks related to the organisation and function of the Cabinet Office – such as those for the Council on Fiscal and Economic Policy, the publication of white papers on the economy and public finance and of monthly economic reports, and the making of projections of short- and medium-term economic outlooks – the institute conducts surveys and studies based on requests from the Cabinet Office's internal departments. Some of its works include an analysis conducted in the 1990s of policy cooperation among developed countries and studies of the Japanese bubble economy and deflation; as such, many of its survey and research projects are closely related to the government's economic policies. It also engages in large-scale, joint international research projects. These often concern important topics, such as sustainable growth, and are conducted in cooperation with highly expert researchers and universities or research institutes, involving a variety of nationalities. I have participated in several joint international studies myself.[10]

Policy Research Institute under the Ministry of Finance

PRI's predecessor, the Institute of Fiscal and Monetary Policy, was established on 1 May 1985 as a facility of the former Ministry of Finance, absorbing the Finance Training Center in the process.[11] Ryuichiro Tachi, then Professor of Aoyama Gakuin University, served as the institution's first director on a part-time basis. He responded to an interview at the time of foundation by saying that the role of the institute resided in considering the country's fiscal and monetary policies from a holistic, comprehensive and medium- to long-term perspective and in taking an overall view of fiscal and monetary policies against the backdrop of the structural changes in the Japanese economy and society. Specifically, he was reported as saying:

> The institute will be a venue for in-depth deliberation from a medium- to long-term perspective with an eye on both theory and experiment, and will conduct studies in a way that will respond to the issues at hand as required. Research work will also be conducted in cooperation with external sources – scholars both from Japan and abroad. (Tani, 1985: 59)

At the time of foundation, the institute was composed of four departments: the Research Department, the Information System Department, the Training Department and the General Administration Office. In July 1990, the Research Statistics Department was established to take over statistics-related tasks conducted by the ministry's Securities Bureau and Research and Planning Division, and in July 1992, the International Exchange Office was installed as a subdivision of the Research

Department to boost efforts to provide official development aid to developing countries and to promote international research exchanges.

A review was made of PRI in the 1990s, when a spate of corrupt wining and dining cases involving Ministry of Finance officials caused a public outcry, triggering criticism of the organisation as a whole. Specifically, the Advisory Body on the Administration of the Ministry of Finance (presided over by Ryuzo Sejima) issued a report in 1998 which stated that in order for the ministry charged with running the economy to bolster its foundation of policymaking and to formulate policies from a medium- to long-term perspective, it was necessary to reinforce research-oriented departments and bureaus, including the Institute of Fiscal and Monetary Policy. As for the institute, it was proposed that it should beef up practical research activities closely connected with policy formulation, and strengthen ties with ministry departments, as well as outside organisations.[12] Prompted by the report, the institute was reorganised into the present PRI in July 2000, with the aim of enhancing the institute's ability to support the ministry's functions in planning and formulating comprehensive policies.[13]

An overview of PRI's research and study activities are described in the following.[14] While PRI is primarily charged with research and studies, it is part of the Ministry of Finance, and its activities are based on the staff at the Ministry of Finance. The annual personnel reshuffle takes place through June and July, during which a new regime is set for PRI. PRI then starts formulating its research plans for the coming year. Research topics are considered after taking a survey of the ministry's internal departments, as well as taking into account the interest areas of researchers, and are determined through discussions by the PRI management. These are then subject to approval by the ministry's senior officials.

In the early years, PRI was more likely to invite outside experts to hold seminars, but in the last 10 years, there have been more studies conducted by PRI researchers, either on a joint-study basis or individually. The ministry is becoming more inclined to assign people who are interested in research, as well as hiring young researchers from outside (mainly assistant university professors and postdoctoral scholars) for two to three years. For such young researchers, experience at PRI often serves as a stepping stone to a teaching position at a university.

Research Institute of Economy, Trade and Industry under the Ministry of Economy, Trade and Industry

RIETI's predecessor, the Research Institute of International Trade and Industry, was founded on 1 July 1987 as a facility of the Ministry of International Trade and Industry (MITI). The institute conducted research mainly in the fields of trade, industry and companies, but on 1 April 2001, it was reorganised as RIETI, an IAA, which was introduced as part of the administrative reform. IAAs were modelled on the executive agencies in the UK, and have a degree of autonomy in managing their budgets and personnel, while having the obligation to set targets and evaluate performance with a view to result-oriented management. Many research institutes in the field of science and technology were reorganised as IAAs through the administrative reform, but RIETI, the Japan Institute for Labour Policy and Training and the National Institute for Environmental Studies were the only policy research institutes that became IAAs. Unlike conventional government organisations, IAAs have a degree of autonomy, such as receiving subsidies in the form of lump-sum grants with no detailed line-item budget. In this regard, RIETI was re-established as an IAA and did not rely on the civil service; instead, it had more flexibility in hiring personnel and executing budgets with a view to performing its important and indispensable function in policy research concerning public policies in an effective and efficient manner.[15]

RIETI has a legally stipulated objective 'to contribute to the planning of economic and industrial policies'.[16] In addition to research and studies, its functions encompass policy proposals as a matter of law.[17] Unlike ESRI and PRI, RIETI aims to conduct not only research and studies, but also policy planning and proposals and clear communication of such plans and proposals,[18] thereby aspiring to become the 'platform for policy formulation'.[19] For this purpose, the institute retains 'a certain degree of independence from the government, where not only administrative officers but also academic and private-sector experts and researchers from overseas can work in friendly competition'.[20]

In accordance with the Act on the General Rules for IAAs, an IAA is obligated to: set medium-term goals and a medium-term plan to deliver on the goals; prepare an annual business plan and performance report, as well as a project report, with respect to the medium-term plan; review its organisation and overall functions at the completion of the medium-term plan; prepare financial reports; conduct a financial audit; and undergo a third-party evaluation and review by the IAA evaluation committee of the respective ministry, as well as the Assessment Committee of Independent Administrative Organizations under the Ministry of Internal Affairs and Communications. All such activities are documented and are made publicly available, making it possible to gain a detailed understanding of RIETI's research activities. There is also an external advisory board that consists of outside experts from the academic and industrial communities (which currently has seven members), which checks on the appropriateness and progress of RIETI's research projects and evaluates and advises on the way in which the institute communicates and puts its research findings into practice.

In order to reflect its status as a stand-alone corporate entity, RIETI is composed of three divisions: in addition to executive officers such as the chairman and vice chairmen, president and vice president, there are the General Administrative Group, Research Group and International/Public Relations Group. The Research Group is further composed of the Director of Research, Research Coordinator(s), Research Support, Quantitative Analysis and Database, Policy History Group, Full-time Fellow, Faculty Fellow, Consulting Fellow, Visiting Fellow and Research Associate. Characteristically, university personnel are invited as faculty fellows to promote high-level academic research, while officials from ministries (not only METI) are invited as consulting fellows so as to incorporate their practical perspectives in research activities.

Comparison of the three institutes

Now that we have taken a look at the function of the three policy research institutes, I would like to proceed to analyse policy research institutes with respect to their role in policy formulation, and policy research institutes as a resource of policy analysis. First is a brief overview of the characteristics of policy formulation in Japan.

As to the characteristics of policy decision-making in Japan, a number of theories and models have been presented, including Japanese-style pluralism, the political bureaucracy theory and the policy network theory. The details notwithstanding, it can be said that it was special-interest legislators and bureaucrats who wielded great influence on policy decisions under the 1955 political set-up (Uchiyama, 2007: 16–17).[21] Above all, officials of the central ministries played prominent roles, meaning that the administrative part of the government, which actually implements policies, took a lead in bringing up issues, drafting and planning policies, and even in making decisions (Nakamura, 2010: 136).[22] Such a model worked well when Japan was enjoying rapid economic growth, but as the Japanese economy and society matured and grew more complex, it became increasingly difficult to balance conflicting interests and to solve problems. Under such circumstances, in order to present more rational options in policy formulation, it became necessary for an independent entity other than a body with direct involvement in politics, administration or other related parties to study policies (Nakamura, 2010: 135). The move by ministries to set up or make use of policy research institutes can be thought of along these lines. Needless to say, policy research institutes do belong to ministries and there is a limitation to how independent they can be. Still, to a certain extent, they are expected to contribute to conducting policy analysis and formulating more sophisticated policies.

A comparison of the three policy research institutes can be found in Table 7.2. ESRI is the largest institute in terms of its number of employees and budget due to its role in compiling important government statistics, such as the system of national accounts. Meanwhile, RIETI, with numerous experts, produces the largest number of publications.

Table 7.2: Comparison of three policy research institutes

Name of Institute		Economic and Social Research Institute (ESRI)	Policy Research Institute (PRI)	Reserch Institute of Economy, Trade and Industry (RIETI)
Legal status		Internal organization of Cabinet Office	Internal organization of Ministry of Finance	Independent agency under Ministry of Economy, Trade and Industry
Number of staff		139 (FY2011 Budget)	62 (FY2011 Budget)	47 (full time, on 31/3/2012)
Yearly expenditure		2.31 billion yen (FY2011 Budget)	0.61 billion yen (FY2011 Budget)	1.28 billion yen (FY2011 oeprating expense)
O u t p u t	Journals & magazines FY2009/FY2010/FY2011	(J) 3/4/3 total 10	(J) 7/6/4 total 17 (E) 5/3/2 total 10	(no publication)
	Discussion papers & Working papers FY2009/FY2010/FY2011	(J) 28/32/24 total 84 (E) 5/6/5 total 16	(J) 8/8/7 total 23 (E) 3/7/7 total 17	(J) 28/53/46 total 127 (E) 58/22/61 total 141
	Reports by study groups FY2009/FY2010/FY2011	(J) 6/7/8 total 21	(J) 2/3/4 total 7	(no publication)
	Books FY2009/FY2010/FY2011	(J) 7/4/0 total 11 (E) 0/1/0 total 1	(J) 1/1/3 total 5	(J) 3/8/7
	Conferences & symposium FY2009/FY2010/FY2011	(J) 4/4/3 total 11 (E) 5/6/1 total 12	(J) 1/0/0 total 1 (E) 2/0/1 total 3	(J) 6/3/3 total 12 (E) 2/1/3 total 6
	Seminars & workshops FY2009/FY2010/FY2011	(no)	(no)	(J) 45/47/48 total 140 (E) 28/20/19 total 67

[1] Number of staff and yearly expenditure are the figures for the whole of organisation (not only for research activities)
[2] Figures in outputs are what are identified from the homepages of relevant institutions. (J): written in Japanese, (E): written in English
[3] Numbers of conference and seminars are those open to public.
[4] FY = fiscal year, from April to March

The difference between the three institutes goes deeper than budgets, reaching more fundamental levels. PRI and ESRI are chiefly charged with research and studies in terms of their organisational structure, as well as legal standing, but RIETI's stipulated functions encompass not only research and studies, but also contributions to policy formulation and proposals. Legally speaking, the function of PRI and ESRI is to research and study, though they are expected to contribute to policymaking. In other words, they can be excused for not being involved directly in policymaking. On the other hand, RIETI has an organisational mission to work to influence policy formulation, and their actual function should be assessed from the point of view that they contribute to policy formation.

Next, I will analyse the three institutes with respect to their involvement in policy formulation. In terms of engagement in actual policymaking, it can be said that PRI is the least involved. Like the other institutes, PRI receives requests from bureaus and divisions of the Ministry of Finance with a view to contributing to the ministry's policy formulation, but bureaus such as the Budget Bureau and the Tax Bureau have their own dedicated research sections and related advisory panels, which respectively become engaged in policy analysis and deliberation. Cases of PRI's involvement need to be examined on an individual basis, but, generally speaking, the degree of PRI's contribution to or involvement in policy formulation at the ministry is considered to be low.[23]

Whether PRI is to be utilised as a resource for policy analysis tends to depend on the intent of senior officials, including those at the Ministry of Finance and the president of PRI. Some presidents are more understanding of the meaning and importance of research and studies, but others are less inclined to do research work related to the bureaus at the ministry. Put differently, there is a risk that the way in which the institute is run may change significantly depending on the willingness of the president, and there may be occasions where the morale of researchers is undermined. Also, a major problem from the perspective of research and studies is the fact that the institute's president can be appointed or dismissed due to personnel reshuffling at the ministry. In the 27 years from the institute's foundation in July 1985 to July 2012, there have been as many as 24 presidents, meaning that their average term of office is just over one year.[24] The only presidents who were not civil servants were the first president Ryuichiro Tachi (part-time; May 1985 to June 1989) and Masahiro Kawai (former Vice-Minister of Finance; March 2003 to July 2003).

Unlike RIETI and other institutes that take the form of an IAA, PRI is an internal organisation of the Ministry of Finance and is meant to serve the ministry. Naturally, it is difficult for the institute to conduct research and studies far removed from the interests and objectives of the ministry, and there may be cases where the ideal of neutrality and independence is compromised. Even compared to ESRI, also an internal organisation of a ministry, there are fewer cases of participation by outside scholars and experts, and we must say that the level of expertise or independence of PRI's work tend to be low.

The positive side of PRI can be said to be its function as the training ground of ministry employees rather than as a direct contributor to policy planning. When an employee is assigned to PRI, he or she has the opportunity to network with outside experts and university professors, participate in joint studies with researchers working at PRI for a limited term, and attend academic conferences, which can serve as a learning step for individuals who are research-inclined or scientifically minded. As the number of such personnel grows, it is possible that the ministry will be better equipped to formulate policies more rationally in the future.

Overall, even though it was expected to at the beginning, the actual involvement of PRI in policymaking is low because what the Ministry of Finance is doing, say, budgeting and taxation, is politically sensitive and most senior officials do not want intervention from outsiders. There exists an inconsistency between the expectation and the result.

Next, ESRI is mainly engaged in economic and fiscal policies, which encompass a broad range of areas, such as social security. Policy formulation by the Ministry of Finance covers fundamental systems, such as tax laws, and requires political coordination, resulting in research and studies being unlikely to have a direct bearing on law-making. By contrast, ESRI's role has more to do with the actual management of the economy and finance rather than with law-making, and it is not difficult for ESRI to become involved in policy formulation. In fact, in the days of the Council on Fiscal and Economic Policy, ESRI would be requested to conduct research and studies to provide material for deliberation by the council. Even though there are needs and expectations regarding ESRI, in many cases, the institute is asked to turn in immediate results and outputs, and it is likely that ESRI often has difficulty responding to such requests in a swift manner.

Research and study requires time, so in order to respond to requests from the council or other bodies, it is essential to be one step ahead in starting to analyse topics that may be of interest to lawmakers. However, such studies do not always attract outside experts, and work solely by internal researchers tends to lack expertise and neutrality. Either way, the workload has been increasing in recent years for all ministry departments, making it difficult to train a large number of capable individuals who can conduct research and studies and to improve both the quality and quantity of policy analysis.

It is RIETI that has the potential of significantly influencing policy formulation. The institute has made great efforts and devised a number of schemes to become involved in policymaking. The first example is the brainstorming that the institute conducts when a new project is launched, with personnel from ministry divisions actively participating in study meetings and debriefing sessions for discussion papers, and providing venues for an active exchange of opinion between researchers and practitioners. It should be noted, however, that interaction with ministry departments could lead to being influenced by the wishes of such divisions, which could compromise the neutrality and expertise of research. Second, employees of ministries other than METI also participate in research projects as consulting fellows.[25] Third, in a number of topics, such as productivity, labour and corporate governance, studies have been conducted on an ongoing basis to build up expertise as a research institute. METI, the ministry overlooking RIETI, has traditionally spoken openly about policies managed by other ministries and agencies, which is a characteristic that sets it apart from other organisations, such as the Cabinet Office and the Ministry of Finance. This culture may be a factor that has made it easier for RIETI to become involved in policy formulation.

The point in question is whether such efforts really influence actual policy formulation. In accordance with the IAA system, RIETI subjects itself to various evaluations. One example is the performance evaluation report (RIETI, 2012), outlined as follows:

- *Surveys of officials representing the major policy research domains.* RIETI surveys division heads at METI by asking them to look at the results of research projects (theses and other publications) and to reply as to whether such projects reflect the needs of the ministry's departments.[26] Of the respondents, 70% to 100% said that the research results reflect the needs and contribute to policy planning.[27]
- *Questionnaires targeting bureaus of the METI.* These questionnaires allow bureaus to evaluate the degree to which research output meets policy needs on a scale of 1 to 3 (A = 3, B = 2, C = 1) and the level of impact on policy formulation on a scale of 1 to 5 (AA = 5, A = 4, B = 3, C = 2, D = 1) regarding research domains such as the ageing of society, innovation and the world and Asia. Respondents put the degree to which research products meet policy needs at an average of 2.5 to 3.0 points, while assessing the impact on policymaking at an average of 2.86 to 4.00 points.[28]
- *Review of discussion papers by outside experts.* Outside experts such as university professors in specialised areas are asked to evaluate the academic level of discussion papers on a scale of 1 to 5 (AA = 5, A = 4, B = 3, C = 2, D = 1). Respondents give an average rating of 3.57 to 4.07.[29]

Overall, RIETI takes the results of the evaluations of this particular medium–term plan period positively, stating that 'The products of research projects have contributed to planning at ministry departments and led to a stable evaluation of RIETI within the METI, which is a positive development' and that the 'Ratings on RIETI's various publications are consistently at high levels, and it can be said that the institute has played a significant role in proposing and spreading policies' (RIETI, 2012). While it is difficult to determine to what extent such a positive assessment reflects reality, it can reasonably be concluded that RIETI has a certain degree of involvement in policy formulation.[30] However, it should be noted that there is inherent tension between RIETI and METI. The more independent RIETI becomes as distinguished research institute, the less it is controlled by METI.

The degree of involvement in policy formulation by the three institutes varies, as the nature of operations at the respective ministries differs. The cases of these three institutes cannot be used to generalise about all 13 institutes, but it can be safely assumed that the position of research and studies in the process of policy formulation is not yet very high. This is not only the conclusion drawn from the analysis in this thesis, but also the actual feeling I have, having been involved in all three institutes in one way or another. The reasons can be summarised as follows. First, most institutes are not obliged to contribute directly to policymaking from the legal point of view. Second, the involvement of them in policymaking depends on the nature and characteristics of the business of their parent ministries. Some institutions such as ESRI can contribute as they are actually expected to. Third, there must be a trade-off between scientific analysis and policymaking.

It is right to understand that the objective of policy analysis lies in presenting a heuristic approach (based on learning from experience) in determining desirable policy options, and its foundation partially rests on administrative science and, in particular, on a more extensive analysis of the system (Miyakawa, 1995:57). Notwithstanding this, policies are always accompanied by political values and are often incompatible with science. Policies are not determined after a thorough analysis of all the related matters, or decisions made based on the results of such analysis; in reality, they are determined under various constraints, uncertainties or political influences. Meanwhile, academic neutrality and expertise are expected in research work; research that is performed to justify specific policies tends to lack reliability. On the other hand, studies that emphasise neutrality or are conducted from a medium- to long-term perspective tend to have less impact on policy formulation. This is where the fundamental trade-off exists between research and policy. The trade-off is an inherent problem of the policy research institutes that belong to ministries. In summary, it is necessary to strike the right balance between the two, and if an institute becomes too inclined towards one, it becomes necessary to re-emphasise the other.

Conclusion

In this chapter, I have analysed the functions of policy research institutes of ministries, focusing on the three institutes of ESRI, PRI and RIETI. While it is difficult to generalise the degree to which each institute becomes involved in policy formulation at their respective ministries, it can be said that there is a trade-off between policy formulation and research, and it is not easy for such institutes to become actively involved in policy planning. This point can be expanded into an overarching problem that concerns policy formulation at the central bureaucracy at Kasumigaseki. However, there have been signs of deterioration in such a policy process in recent years. Specific examples are policies under the administration of the Democratic Party of Japan beginning in 2009, such as child benefits and the relocation issue of the Futenma Air Base on Okinawa. Shiroyama et al (1999) point to limitations in the entire policy formulation process, as follows: (1) sectionalism between ministries; (2) limitations in transparency; (3) limitations from economic and societal structures; and (4) limitations at assistant manager level. These issues cannot solely be attributed to the leading political party, but Tanaka (2012) pointed out that the main factor in the deterioration of the quality of policymaking lies in the fact that the process of policy consideration is not 'contestable'.[31] Consultations with advisory panels may be taking place more frequently than in the past, but analysis and deliberation in the policy process is carried out exclusively by the bureaucracy, and, in fact, the basic data and the methods of compiling such data are not made public in a satisfactory way. Ultimately, policies should be determined by politicians based on the rule of democracy. Still, it is desirable to reduce the risk in the process of policy decisions by taking approaches such as analysing issues based on data and evidence, comparing and considering alternatives, consulting with outside experts, and hearing opinions from stakeholders, but the Kasumigaseki bureaucracy continues to be lacking in such areas.

One key issue in policy research by ministries is how to tackle such problems. Although people believe that governments need more research on and analysis of policy problems, they apparently intend that their elected officials somehow should call on the services of analysis and experts without abdicating political authority to them (Lindblom and Woodhouse, 1993: 6). This is not limited to the way policy research institutes are, but extends to the system of civil servants and the management of such personnel. In March 1999, the Advisory Council on the Public Service Personnel System issued a report (Advisory Council on the Public Service Personnel System, 1999), in which it pointed out the problem of limitations in the ability of policy formulation by the bureaucracy system and proposed further openness, diversification, flexibility and transparency, greater emphasis on individuals' ability and performance, and personal accountability. Also, Shiroyama and Hosono (2002: 369) state that while, in the past, policy was formed chiefly by generalists, to meet the needs of the new era, a good balance should be struck between generalists, specialists and professionals, and all such personnel should participate in policy formulation.

In order for policy research institutes to improve their policy analysis abilities and to play more active roles in policy formulation, it is particularly necessary to train personnel with expertise.[32] Such personnel may well detach themselves from the internal bureaus of ministries, which tend to be confined to short-term views, and may well engage in research and studies at policy research institutes and refine their specialist knowledge. Working at policy research institutes may also help such individuals to network with outside experts and scholars. In policy planning and deliberation, a wide variety of players are involved, including not only government organisations, but also political parties, think tanks, business lobbies, citizen groups, NPOs, journalists, policy researchers and universities. Policy research institutes can be positioned as the hub of all these players. At any rate, the necessity of policy research institutes, which are uniquely Japanese institutions, must be studied further in the context of the trade-off between policy formulation and research.

Notes

[1] In some countries, ministries or government agencies have their own policy research institutes. For instance, the Federal Institute for Vocational Education and Research in Germany was funded in 1970 on the basis of the Vocational Training Act as a federal government institution for policy, research and practice in the field of vocational education and training. The National Institute of Economic Research in Sweden is a government agency operating under the Ministry of Finance and performs analyses and forecasts of the Swedish and international economy and conducts related research.

[2] A think tank can be defined differently. McGann and Weaver (2000: 2–6) define think tanks as 'third sector'/'civil societal' organisations, which are not-for-profit in their legal statute, relatively independent/autonomous from the government/state, and dedicated to impacting public policymaking by playing a number of critical roles. Pautz (2010: 276) defines think tanks as non-governmental institutions that are independent from government, political parties or organised interests. Boucher (2004) suggests nine criteria for think tanks, one of them being that they 'are not responsible for government operations'.

[3] Lindblom and Woodhouse (1993: 63) point out that policy formulation by the bureaucracy can become problematic when:

> administrators focus on protection of their own budgets, power, or policy turf; fall into preoccupation with process instead of results; and become captured to an indefensible extent by one narrow set of interests, and fail to attend to consideration necessary for sensible action within their realm of responsibility.

[4] Normally, 'policy' refers to public policy, which is defined differently. Dye (2008: 1) describes public policy as 'whatever governments choose to do or not to do'. Peters (2004: 4) defines public policy is the sum of government activities, whether pursued directly or through agents, as those activities have an influence on the lives of citizens. Jenkins

(1978: 15) defines comprehensively that set of interrelated decisions taken by a political actor or group of actors concerning the selection of goals and the means of achieving them within a specified situation where these decisions should, in principle, be within the power of these actors to achieve.

[5] Lasswell (1956) defined the policy process as including intelligence, recommendation, prescription, invocation, application, appraisal and termination. Lasswell's approach formed the basis for other models. For instance, Howlett et al (2009: 12) define five stages in a policy cycle: agenda-setting, policy formulation, decision-making, policy implementation and policy evaluation.

[6] Policy analysis can be defined differently from policy research. According to Weimer and Vining (2005), the objective of policy research is to predict the impacts of changes in variables that can be altered by public policy, while that of policy analysis is systematic comparison and evaluation of the alternatives available to public actors for solving social problems. However, this chapter does not distinguish between them.

[7] NIRA was a special public corporation founded in 1974 based on the National Institute for Research Advancement Act. This law was abolished in 2007, when NIRA changed its organisation to an incorporated foundation. In 2011, it changed to a public interest incorporated foundation. JIIA was first authorised as an incorporated foundation in 1960 under the Ministry of Foreign Affairs and was reorganised as a public interest incorporated foundation in 2012.

[8] The description of ESRI's main function is quoted from its website. Article 43 of the Order for the Organisation of the Minister's Secretariat of the Cabinet Office stipulates that the function of ESRI is as follows: (1) to conduct studies (excluding those carried out by universities or jointly with universities) based on economic theories or other theories of a similar nature regarding economic and social activities; (2) to maintain and improve the national economic accounting system; (3) to perform national economic accounting; and (4) to conduct training concerning tasks that fall under the charge of the Minister's Secretariat.

[9] Quotes from ESRI's website, www.esri.go.jp/en/esri/menu-e.html

[10] Specifically, I participated in the 2007 international joint study 'Sustainable Growth and Fiscal Reconstruction Against the Backdrop of an Ageing Population', and in the 2009 international joint study 'A New Method of Macroeconomic Analysis – Labor and Social Security Policies'.

[11] It is said that the idea of setting up a research institute within the Ministry of Finance was first proposed at a 1973 seminar concerning the organisation and structure of the ministry. As the first step, the Fiscal and Monetary Research Office was set up within the Survey and Planning Division in July 1979.

[12] Specifically, the following five points were proposed: (1) topics should be set not only from a medium- to long-term perspective, but also from a practical point of view closely related to policy formulation; (2) the institute should consider inviting world-class

economists to take over key positions, such as president of the institution; (3) the institute should consider inviting able researchers both from Japan and abroad to create an environment conducive to freedom of publication with credit to the individual researcher; (4) the institute should make sure that visiting scholars and private-sector experts are able to play an important role in formulating policies through frequent exchanges of opinion with the ministry's departments and ensure that the research works are widely put to use; and (5) a group of advisors, consisting of scholars, private-sector experts and other qualified individuals, should be established with a view to enabling exchanges of opinion regarding overall economic policy.

[13] The function of PRI is stipulated in Article 67 of the Order for the Organization of the Ministry of Finance, and is as follows: (1) to conduct basic or overall research and studies regarding policies under the charge of the Ministry of Finance and other matters regarding domestic and world finance and economy and to collect, store, compile and provide documents, information and publications; (2) to compile basic or overall statistics about domestic and world finance and economy; (3) to compile statistics about the real situation of corporate accounting; (4) to handle matters related to the Ministry of Finance Library, a branch of the National Diet Library; (5) to conduct necessary training for employees at the Ministry of Finance to engage in tasks at the ministry as well as at Local Finance Bureaus; and (6) to cooperate on an international level with tasks falling under the charge of the Ministry of Finance.

[14] The passages that follow are based on my own experience between 2001 and 2003 when I was working at PRI and on interviews involving people related to PRI.

[15] Quoted from RIETI's website, www.rieti.go.jp/en/about/index.html

[16] Article 3 of the Research Institute of Economy, Trade and Industry Act stipulates as follows:

> the Incorporated Administrative Agency Research Institute of Economy, Trade and Industry aims to conduct basic research and studies about circumstances of the economy and industry both at home and abroad and about economic and industrial policies in an efficient and effective manner, to contribute to the planning of Japan's economic and industrial policies through the use of research results, to work to promote public knowledge and understanding about the economy and industry, and to thereby contribute to the development of the economy and industry and to secure mineral and energy resources in a stable and efficient manner.

[17] Article 12 of the REITI Act stipulates the following objectives of the institute: (1) to conduct basic research and studies about circumstances of the economy and industry both at home and abroad and about economic and industrial policies; (2) to work to disseminate the results from objective (1) and to propose policies; and (3) to collect, store, compile and provide publications and documents about the conditions of the economy and industry both at home and abroad and about economic and industrial policies.

[18] On the RIETI website (www.rieti.go.jp/en/about/index.htm), the institute is introduced as:

a policy think tank established in 2001. Its mission is to conduct theoretical and empirical research, maximize synergies with those engaged in policymaking, and to make policy proposals based on evidence derived from such research activities ... [working] to break the conventional administrative and policy framework and invigorate the policymaking capacity. Through such actions, Japan, as a member of the international community, will then be able to proactively implement more dynamic and innovative policies.

[19] Quoted from RIETI's website (www.rieti.go.jp/en/about/index.htm).

[20] Quoted from RIETI's website (www.rieti.go.jp/en/about/index.htm).

[21] On the policymaking process in Japan, see also Reed et al (2009) and Stockwin (2008).

[22] However, it was not that politicians of the Liberal Democratic Party gave complete freedom to bureaucrats; rather, they controlled and monitored them (Ramseyer and Rosenbluth, 1993).

[23] I cannot deny that this is a subjective assessment, but it is based on my first-hand experience working at PRI, as well as on interviews with several people with ties to the institute.

[24] There are only four presidents who have served for two years or more.

[25] I have also participated in research projects as a consulting fellow.

[26] For example, regarding the 'Study on an innovation system to maintain international competitiveness' as part of the performance evaluation for fiscal year 2007, the directors of the Industrial Technology Policy Division, the Technology Promotion Division and the R&D Division of the Industrial Science and Technology Policy and Environment Bureau were appointed as representatives for the major policy research domains.

[27] Specifically, when asked if the content of research reflected the needs of ministry departments, the following percentages of respondents gave an affirmative answer: 88% for fiscal year 2006; 100% for 2007; 87.5% for 2008; 87.5% for 2009; and 100% for 2010. As to whether research findings contribute to policy planning at the ministry departments, the following percentages of respondents replied 'yes': 100% for 2006; 100% for 2007; 75.0% for 2008; 75.05% for 2009; and 77.8% for 2010.

[28] In fiscal year 2006, average ratings by respondents regarding the degree to which specific research met policy needs were as follows: 3.00 points for the ageing society; 2.86 for innovation; and 3.00 for the world and Asia. Regarding the impact on policy formulation, the average ratings were: 3.75 points for the ageing society; 3.14 for innovation; and 4.00 for the world and Asia.

[29] Scores by fiscal year are as follows: 3.57 points for 2006; 4.07 for 2007; 4.01 for 2008; 3.93 for 2009; and 3.89 for 2010.

[30] Under this system, evaluations are not to be conducted internally, but by METI's Independent Administration Agencies Evaluation Committee.

[31] Conditions that are necessary for better policymaking are discussed in Lindquist et al (2011) and Sunningdale Institute (2009).

[32] For details on the issue of the specialties of civil servants, see Tanaka (2012).

References

Adachi, Y. (2009) *Kokyoseisaku-gaku to ha Nanika* [*What is the Study of Public Policy?*], Minerva-shobo.

Advisory Council on the Public Service Personnel System (1999) *Komuin-seido-kaikaku no kihonteki-houko ni kansuru toushin* [*Report Regarding the Basic Direction of Public Service Personnel System Reform*], download from the following www.cas.go.jp/jp/gaiyou/jimu/jinjikyoku/990518.htm

Boucher, S. (2004) *Europe and Its Think Tanks: A Promise to Be Fulfilled, an Analysis of Think Tanks Specialised in European Policy Issues in the Enlarged European Union*, Norte Europe.

Dye, T.R. (2008) *Understanding Public Policy* (12th edn), Pearson Education.

Hayakawa, Y., Utsumi, M., Tamaru, D. and Ohyama, R. (2004) *Seisaku Katei Ron* [*Discussion on Policy Process: Introduction to Policy Science*], Gakuyo-shobo.

Howlett, M., Ramesh, M. and Perl, A. (2009) *Studying Public Policy: Policy Cycles and Policy Subsystems* (3rd edn), Oxford University Press.

Jenkins, W.I. (1978) *Policy Analysis: A Political and Organizational Perspective*, London: Martin Robertson

Lasswell, H.D. (1956) *The Decision Process: Seven Categories of Functional Analysis*, University of Maryland Press.

Lindblom, C.E. and Woodhouse, E.J. (1993) *The Policy-Making Process* (3rd edn), Prentice Hall.

Lindquist, E.A., Vincent, S. and Wanna, J. (2011) *Delivering Policy Reform*, Australian National University, E-Press.

McGann, J.G. and Weaver, R.K. (2000) *Think Tanks and Civil Societies: Catalysts for Ideas and Action*, New Brunswick, NJ, and London: Transaction Publishers.

Miyakawa, K. (1995) *Seisaku-Kagaku Nyumon* [*Introduction to Policy Science*], Toyokeizai-sinposha.

Nakamura, M. (2010) 'Seisaku-keisei-jiku to Jinzai no Henka ni Yureru Think Tank' ['Think Tanks Affected by Change of Policy-Making and Human Resource'], in Y. Koike (ed) *Seisaku Keisei* [*Policy Making*], Minerva Shobo.

Nishio, T. (2012) *Gendai Gyosei-gaku* [*Modern Public Administration*], Open University of Japan Press.

Pautz, H. (2010) 'Think Tanks in the United Kingdom and Germany: Actors in the Modernisation of Social Democracy', *British Journal of Politics and International Relations*, vol 12, pp 274–94.

Peters, B.G. (2004) *American Public Policy: Promise and Performance* (6th edn), CQ Press.

Ramseyer, J.M. and Rosenbluth, F.M. (1993) *Japan's Political Marketplace*, Harvard University Press.

Reed, S., McElwain, K.M. and Shimizu, K. (2009) *Political Change in Japan: Electoral Behavior, Party Realignment, and the Koizumi Reforms*, Walter H. Shorenstein Asia-Pacific Research Center.

Research Institute of Economy, Trade and Industry (RIETI) (2012) *Chuki-mokuhyo-kikan Gyomu-jisseki-hyoka* [*Performance Evaluation Report for Medium-Term Target Period (fiscal year 2006 through 2010)*], download from the following www.meti.go.jp/committee/summary/0001630/report2011/rieti_eva.pdf

Shiroyama, H. and Hosono, S. (2002) *Chuo-shocho no Seisaku Keisei Katei: Sono Jizoku to Henyo* [*The Policy Process of the Central Government in Japan: Its Continuance and Transformation*], Chuo University Press.

Shiroyama, H., Suzuki, K. and Hosono, S. (1999) *Chuo-shocho no Seisaku Keisei Katei* [*The Policy Process of the Central Government in Japan*], Chuo University Press.

Stockwin, J.A.A. (2008) *Governing Japan: Divided Politics in a Resurgent Economy* (4th edn), Blackwell Publishing.

Sunningdale Institute (2009) *Engagement and Aspiration: Reconnecting Policy Making with Front Line Professionals*, National School of Government.

Suzuki, T. (2007) *Nihon no Minshushugi o Kigyo-suru* [*Encourage Japanese Democracy*], Daicihi-shorin.

Tanaka, H. (2012) 'Seisaku-katei to Seikan-kankei' ['Three Models of the Policy Process in Japan: Changing Roles of Politicians and Bureaucrats'], *The Annals of the Japanese Society for Public Administration*, vol 47, pp 21–45.

Tani, S. (1985) 'Tachi Ryuichiro ni Kiku', ['The Establishment of the Institute of Fiscal and Monetary Policy: Interview to the First President Ryuichiro Tachi'], *Finance* (monthly journal published by the Ministry of Finance Japan), May, pp 59–64.

Uchiyama, Y. (2007) *Koizumi Kaikaku* [*Structural Reforms by Prime Minister Koizumi*], Chuko-shinsho.

Weimer, D.L. and Vining, A.R. (2005) *Policy Analysis: Concepts and Practice* (4th edn), Pearson Prentice Hall.

EIGHT

A policy analysis of the Japanese Diet from the perspective of 'Legislative Supporting Agencies'

Jun Makita

Introduction

The Legislative Supporting Agencies (LSAs) are agencies supporting the legislation of the Diet and legislative activities by its members. In the Japanese Diet, the Research Bureau of the House of Representatives (RBHR), the Research Bureau of the House of Councillors (RBHC), the Legislative Bureau of the House of Representatives (LBHR), the Legislative Bureau of the House of Councillors (LBHC), the Research Bureau of the National Diet Library (RBNDL) and the Policy Secretary are all considered to be LSAs. Although playing a role through information provision and support for drafting a member's bill, they seldom attract attention because of their role in supporting legislative activities from the sidelines. However, because of their role, LSAs are deeply related to the Diet and its members' activities, and they and the other political institutions and political actors have a mutual effect on each other. In this respect, more attention could be paid to them when examining the function and state of the institutions and actors in the legislative process. Based on these issues, this chapter will focus on LSAs and, through comparison with other countries, clarify their constructions and functions, as well as how they participate in the policy analysis of the Diet.

In the second section, the definition and classification of LSAs will be given. Subsequently, in the third section, LSAs of the US, UK, Germany and Japan will be compared and their differences will be examined. In the fourth section, the role of LSAs in the Japanese legislative process will be assessed. Finally, in the fifth section, the specific function of each LSA will be examined from the perspective of policy analysis.

Definition and classification

Definition

First of all, it is necessary to clarify the meaning of the term 'Legislative Supporting Agency'. However, there is still no clear definition and the term is interpreted differently by different individuals.[1] Normally, a definition should be established through detailed examination of the elements that compose the words 'Legislative', 'Supporting' and 'Agency', and then determining the meaning of each word in the political context. Nonetheless, many pages would be required to document such a process and it exceeds the object of this chapter. Therefore, in this chapter, the following two conditions shall be adopted: (A) to have a duty directly contributing to the legislative acts of the Diet and the legislative activities of its members, such as research, analysis and making documents; and (B) to be an internal or attached institution of the Diet and to have staff who are civil servants. Institutions that meet these two requirements are referred to as 'Legislative Supporting Agencies'.

Classification

Based on the preceding two conditions, agencies that are included in the category of LSAs have been determined. Figure 8.1 shows a classification of LSAs. First of all, they are divided into the 'Diet-Attached Agency' and the 'Policy and Legislative Secretary', and the former is further classified into six agencies.

Figure 8.1: Classification of the LSAs

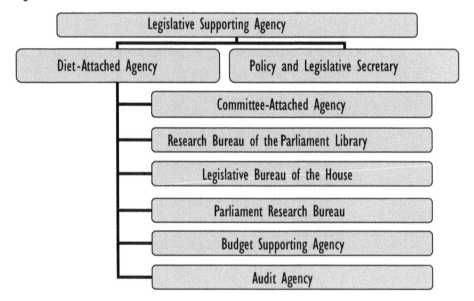

A simple explanation of each agency is as follows:

- Committee-Attached Agency – An agency that is attached to a committee and performs research and analysis about the related policy field of that committee.
- Research Bureau of the Parliament Library – A bureau established in the secretariat of the parliament library for legislative research.
- Legislative Bureau of the House – A bureau in the House Secretariat for the examination and drafting of rules and regulations, especially bills presented by members.
- Parliament Research Bureau – A bureau founded in the House Secretariat, but not attached to the committee, for research and analysis about policy matters.
- Budget Supporting Agency – A parliamentary agency for research and analysis, especially about the budget and finance matters.
- Audit Agency – An agency for auditing government expenditures.

• Policy and Legislative Secretary – A secretary that supports the policy planning and legislative activities of a member.

Comparison of different countries

This section will compare LSAs based on the classifications given earlier. The countries being compared are Japan, the US, the UK and Germany. This selection of countries, except Japan, is attributed to differences in the basic political systems, that is, the US adopts the president system, the UK employs the parliamentary cabinet system and assemblyism, and Germany uses the parliamentary cabinet system and committeeism.[2]

Tables 8.1 to 8.5 show the names, number of staff and duties of LSAs in each country according to the classification in the preceding section.[3] When examining these figures, the development of the US stands out. In terms of scale, the number of staff at almost all US LSAs overwhelms the other countries. Also, only the US has a Budget Supporting Agency and Audit Agency. In terms of duties, the US LSAs are engaged in a high level of work, for example, the committee staff participate in drafting bills and amendments, which makes the US LSAs mature compared to other countries.

Table 8.1: Committee-attached agencies of Japan, the US, the UK and Germany

Japan	US	UK	Germany
The Research Bureau of the House of Representatives and Councillors (560 staff members) Duties include: research about the committee's policy field; making a draft of bills' summary, etc.	Committee Staff of the Senate and the House of Representatives (2,752 staff members) Duties include: agenda setting; research and analysis about bills; drafting bills and amendments; making committee reports, etc.	Special Committee Staff of the House of Commons and Lords (237 staff members) Duties include: making committee reports; research about the committee's policy field, etc.	Committee Staff of the Bundestag and Bundesrat (213 staff members) Duties include: clerical work for the committee management, etc.

Table 8.2: Research Bureau of the Parliament Library of Japan, the US, the UK and Germany

Japan	US	UK	Germany
The Research Bureau of the National Diet Library (194 staff members) Duties include: research and reference service based on members' request; voluntary research, etc.	The Congressional Research Service (705 staff members) Duties include: legislative proposal, analysis, assessment and evaluation about the government's advice; research and reference service to Senators and members, etc.	The Research Bureau of the Library of the House of Commons and Lords (90 staff members) Duties include: research and reference service to members; voluntary research; writing reports, etc.	—

Table 8.3: Legislative Bureau of the Houses of Japan, the US, the UK and Germany

Japan	US	UK	Germany
The Legislative Bureau of the House of Representatives and Councillors (157 staff members) Duties include: drafting members' bills and amendments, etc.	The Legislative Counsel of the Senate and the House of Representatives (104 staff members) Duties include: drafting Senators' and members' bills and amendments; checking bills in terms of the legislative technique, etc.	The Public Bill Office of the House of Commons and Lords (17 staff members) Duties include: advising members on drafting members' bills, etc.	–

Table 8.4: Parliament Research Bureau, Budget Supporting Agency and Audit Agency of Japan, the US, the UK and Germany

	Japan	US	UK	Germany
Parliament Research Bureau	–	–	–	The Research Service of the Department for Research and External Relations, Bundestag (about 100 staff members) Duties include: research and reference service to members; voluntary research; writing reports, etc.
Budget Supporting Agency	–	The Congressional Budget Office (235 staff members) Duties include: support for making budget resolutions based on research about economy and finance, etc.	–	–
Audit Agency	–	The Government Accountability Office (about 3,300 staff members) Duties include: inspection of the government's work and financial affairs; assessment of policy and programme, etc.	–	–

Among the three countries other than the US, Japan's relative development attracts attention. The Policy and Legislative Secretary exists in Japan, not in the UK and Germany, and the Committee-Attached Agency, Research Bureau of the Parliamentary Library and Legislative Bureau of Japan are also highly developed in terms of the number of staff and contents of duties. Conversely, the LSAs of the UK and Germany are small-scale, and their duties are limited. In addition, there are few agencies in the UK and Germany that correspond to LSAs. Such conditions are symbolised by the member's secretary in the two countries. A member's secretary does not correspond to an LSA in this chapter because they lack the status of a civil servant (this is the reason that descriptions about the secretary in Table 8.5 are parenthesised).

Table 8.5: Secretary to members in Japan, the US, the UK and Germany

	Japan	US	UK	Germany
Policy and Legislative Secretary	Policy Secretary (one per member)	Senators and members employ their staff within the allowance paid by the Senate and the House (Senate: average of 35 per Senator; House of Representatives: average of 15 per member) (There is a special allowance for the Legislative Staff)	Members employ their staff within the allowance paid by the House of Commons (average of two per MP – House of Commons only) Note: staff members are not civil servants, but private citizens	Members employ their staff within the allowance paid by the Bundestag (average of six per member, but with many part-time workers among them – Bundestag only) Note: staff members are not civil servants, but private citizens
Other Public Secretary	First and Second Public Secretary (two per member)			

Considering the circumstances mentioned earlier, the following can be stated about LSAs in each country. First of all, US LSAs overpower the others in terms of their scale and role, and are most developed among the four countries. Japan's LSAs are relatively developed among the remaining three countries. On the other hand, LSAs in the UK and Germany show a low level of development.

This chapter does not analyse in detail the cause of differences in terms of the degree of LSA development because such a matter is beyond our objective. However, their overwhelming development in the US is deeply related to the presidential system in which Congress exclusively possesses the legislative right. Japan's relative development is connected with committeeism, a characteristic of the 'transformative legislature' (the UK adopts an 'arena legislature', which leads to assembly-centred debate), and a Diet environment in which there are no institutional guarantees for the activities of actors possessing the legislative supporting function (eg government bureaucrats and party staff) other than the LSAs. (In Germany, a parliamentary institution in which both the government party and opposition can utilise the bureaucrats and denomination staffs for legislative activities exists.)

Role of Legislative Supporting Agencies in Japan's legislative process

Involvement of Legislative Supporting Agencies in the legislative process

In the preceding section, the fact that Japan's LSAs are relatively developed among the countries adopting the parliamentary cabinet system has been clarified. However, this is entirely about an institutional form. Within the actual legislative process, there is no guarantee that LSAs are fulfilling a function that is equivalent to this institutional development. Thus, the following sections will investigate the role of Japanese LSAs in the legislative process, which will lead to understanding the actual state of policy analysis in the Japanese Diet.

In Figure 8.2, the Japanese legislative process is divided into six categories and the LSAs' role in each stage is shown. The LSAs' involvement in each stage is signified by an arrow from each LSA to the stage, and the arrow is thick when the LSA plays a central role in the stage.

Figure 8.2: The roles of Legislative Supporting Agencies in the Japanese legislative process

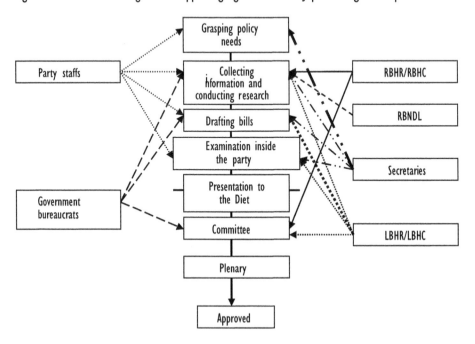

Looking at the figure, it is obvious that the Japanese LSAs mainly participate in the pre-Diet stages. The member's secretaries centrally take part in the 'Grasping policy needs' stage, and the LBHR and the LBHC play a central role in the 'Drafting bills' stage. Also, many agencies, including the RBHR, the RBHC and the RBNDL, participate in the 'Collecting information and conducting research' stage. However, after the presentation of bills to the Diet, LSAs are not involved in the actual legislative work except for the participation of the LBHR/LBHC in the presentation of amendments to the committee. Party staff and bureaucrats are the agencies that possess the legislative supporting function other than LSAs. The former takes part in the pre-Diet stages, and the latter is involved in broader stages, including the inter-Diet process.

Function of the Diet and role of Legislative Supporting Agencies

The involvement of LSAs in the legislative process is deeply related to the practical roles of the Diet. While judging the Diet function of Japan with respect to Polsby's (1975) classifications of 'Transformative Legislature' and 'Arena Legislature' is quite difficult because of the adoption of both the parliamentary cabinet system and committeeism, when considering the actual state of Diet operation, it has a clear tendency towards the 'Arena Legislature'. This refers to an open committee with question-based deliberation in the committee instead of holding discussion article by article, with few amendments,[4] a difference in approval ratio between government bills and members' bills,[5] and so on.

The tendency towards the 'Arena Legislature' means that the content of bills is almost entirely fixed when being presented to the Diet. Consequently, there are very few amendments in the Diet process. As shown in Figure 8.2, the participation of the LSAs in the legislative process is mostly limited to the pre-Diet stages. This is a characteristic of an 'Arena Legislature' in which the opportunities of legislative work are inherently limited in the Diet process.

Role of other actors having a legislative supporting function

The role of LSAs is also significantly influenced by the existence of other actors having a legislative supporting function, as well as by how such actors take part in the legislative process. Among these actors, particular attention should be given to government bureaucrats. Bureaucrats generally have an advanced legislative ability in countries adopting a parliamentary cabinet system in which the government can present bills to the parliament. Therefore, the type of involvement of such bureaucrats in the legislative process has a great effect on the legislative activities of the party and members.

For example, in Germany, the participation of bureaucrats in the legislative process is institutionalised as attendance at the committee. In actuality, they support the members' legislative activities in several respects, including drafting bills and amendments. Moreover, while members of the ruling party can use the bureaucrats of the central government, members of the opposition can also utilise the bureaucrats of the state in which that party is in power. In short, both the ruling party and the opposition can be supported by the bureaucrats.

In Japan, members of the ruling party can receive support from bureaucrats, though that support is not institutionalised, like in Germany. Members of the opposition can also be assisted by bureaucrats, at least in simple work like information provision. Actually, it is common for bureaucrats to attend the party's policy meeting, to provide information and to explain several policy matters. Furthermore, when drafting a member's bill, a hearing from the bureaucrats involved about the present environment of the policies and the related laws is a precondition of entering into concrete legislative work. Considering that, in Japan, the party and members in both the ruling party and the opposition party are in a political circumstance in which they can use the bureaucrats for legislative activities, such conditions obviously tend to decrease the degree of use of LSAs by the party and members. When coupled with the tendency of the 'Arena Legislature' operation discussed earlier, this reduces demand for legislative support from LSAs.

Difference of institution and function

The facts outlined in this section and the last show that there is a difference between the institution and the function of the Japanese LSAs. Namely, while being relatively developed in the institutional side, in terms of function, they do not play a role that corresponds to their institutional development. Based on this difference, the following sections will examine the duties performed by each LSA and how each LSA is positioned in the policy analysis of the Japanese Diet.

Duties of each Legislative Supporting Agency

Research Bureau of the House of Representatives, Research Bureau of the House of Councillors and Research Bureau of the National Diet Library

Information provision function

The RBHR, RBHC and RBNDL all handle duties that can be classified as legislative work in terms of related laws and regulations. Regarding the RBHR, Article 1 of the 'Basic Principles for the Committees' Research Duties Conducted by Research Bureau Staff', and regarding the RBHC, Article 5 of the 'Rules for the Standing Committee Research Bureau', respectively, provide that drafting a bill's summary is a duty of each bureau. In addition, regarding the RBNDL, Article 15-3 of the National Diet Library Law prescribes the provision of bill-drafting services as one of its duties. However, actual opportunities to be engaged in this legislative work are quite few. Almost all of this legislative work is performed by the legislative bureaus of the two houses.

It can be said that, through the research about basic facts and the collection/provision of some dates and materials, the three research bureaus play a role of information provision to the parties and their members, rather than a legislative role. Core duties of the RBHR and the RBHC include: the analysis of bills presented to the related committee; the making of several research materials based on that analysis; research based on the members' requests; and original research. Also, those of the RBNDL include research based on the members' requests and prediction research. In terms of information, these works support the policy activities of members, including committee deliberation.

Policy analysis

Although this information provision and material collection supports the policy activities of the parties and members, such activities are nothing more than the furnishing of materials about facts. Arguably, there is little policy analysis that goes deeper than providing information about facts.

The RBNDL classifies research requests from members into four types: 'Literature Introduction' (introduction and provision of literatures), 'Drafting' (drafting and planning of members' bills), 'Research' (collecting information on details and facts for policy matters) and 'Analysis' (adding a researcher's original interpretation, verification and proposal to the 'Research').

Figure 8.3 shows the ratio for each type of request among total requests after 1965. Looking at this graph, it can be seen that the majority of requests are 'Research'. For other types of requests, 'Drafting' and 'Analysis' remain at a low level throughout the period, while 'Literature Introduction' increases a little. Accordingly, 'Research' accounts for the majority of requests to the RBNDL and there is very little more advanced policy-related support. This indicates that research about facts is a core duty of the RBNDL.

Figure 8.3: Ratio of each type of request to the Research Bureau of the National Diet Library

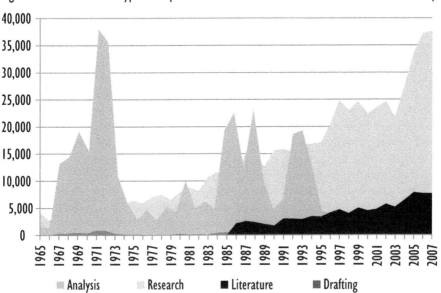

While such statistics are not available for the RBHR and RBHC, the same trend is obvious when looking specifically at the materials made by these bureaus. For instance, when a bill is presented to the Diet, the bureaus make a report about it to contribute to the deliberation of the committee. However, most of the report's content is facts, including the bill's summary and the history and background of the policy concerned. Although the original views of the bureaus are sometimes shown in the form of the 'Point at Issue of the Bill', the quantity of such material is quite small when viewed from the entirety. More detailed analysis is also very rare.

As a specific example, let us consider the Renewable Energy Bill. In the report made by the Research Office on Economy, Trade and Industry, an office of the RBHR, the first items explained are the points and main contents of the bill. Next to be stated is the 'background and history of the presentation of the bill to the Diet', which describes the Japanese energy environment, the circumstances of each energy use, trends in renewable energy and so on. The subsequent section is the 'Point at Issue', which points out the unclearness of the people's benefit realised by this bill and the vagueness of the management plan of the bill. Finally, the reference materials are introduced.

The object of this bill is the spread of renewable energy, and thus, at the committee deliberation, an important point is how the system should be designed and managed to spread each form of energy. Accordingly, a simulation analysis is needed to show how much electricity generated by renewable energies, including solar power, wind velocity, geothermal power, hydraulic power and so on, is bought to secure a profit for suppliers, and, as a result, how many suppliers enter into the electric market and how wide a spread of energy is forecasted. However, such a detailed analysis does not exist in the report. While analysis is performed as a matter of course by the Ministry of Economy, Trade and Industry (METI), the presenter of the bill, an original analysis of the Diet is not performed by the research office in charge.

Legislative Bureau of the House of Representatives and Legislative Bureau of the House of Councillors

Flow of bill drafting

Because the roles of the three research bureaus discussed in the previous section are limited to material collection and information provision, almost all support for actual legislative activities as represented by drafting members' bills is provided by the legislative bureaus of the two houses. The LBHR/LBHC's bill drafting starts after receiving a request of a member, party or committee. The section receiving the request first examines the contents of the request and arranges the points at issue. Subsequently, the bureaus analyse existing legislative institutions related to the contents of the request, examine the consistency of the request with present legislation and review the novelty that is necessary for new legislation. As a result of this work, the basis of the institution and measure adopted in the bill are determined through cooperation with the requester. After the framework of the bill is decided, the bill's outline will be made.

After the outline is made, the next step is drafting the bill itself. Based on the contents of the outline, the bureaus edit the text of the bill and it becomes an original proposal of the section in charge. The proposal is inspected by the Commissioner of Legislation, the Deputy Commissioner General and the Commissioner General, and at each stage, it is reviewed from various angles. Finally, drafting is finished when approval is gained by the Commissioner General. The bill will be presented by the section in charge to the requester.

The requester to which the bill is presented holds discussions among the members or the parties/denominations, and makes a final determination about the contents and time for presentation to the Diet. The LBHR and the LBHC participate in this stage by providing materials about the bill and attending the member's or inter-party's meeting to provide an explanation.

After the bill is presented to the Diet, the person in charge of the bureau engages in deliberation for the bill by providing a memorandum for the requester's answers and answering questions in the Diet.

Conduct of Legislative Bureau of the House of Representatives and Legislative Bureau of the House of Councillors when drafting

The primary role of the legislative bureaus is reflecting the thinking of policy that the requester would like to realise in the text of bill, not researching and analysing the policy. From a view of policy analysis, the required role is definitely different from that of the RBHR, RBHC and RBNDL. The LBHR and the LBHC do not pass judgement regarding the policy contents of the request. Despite making a report to serve as material for judging the points at issue in the bill-drafting process, this work is nothing more than providing information on facts, which is the same work performed by the three research bureaus.

Due to the character of the LBHR/LBHC, no policy judgement is passed regarding requests. Still, the general duties of legislative bureaus include judging a bill's content from a legislative perspective, including the constitutionality of the policy and consistency with the existing legislative system (Asano, 1999: 16).[6] Thus, if the bureau does not recognise a policy's legislative validity, a part of the policy cannot be reflected in the text, and, in some cases, the bill itself cannot be formed. Many such cases have been pointed out. For example, Osamu Shibutani, an ex-member of the Diet who belonged to the Socialist Party, wrote a book that described his experience of opposing the bureau over the idea of public nature for land utilisation when making a proposed amendment to the City Planning Act. Shibutani discusses how his opposition almost caused a setback in the presentation to the Diet (see Shibutani, 1994: 91–3; see also Nishikawa, 2002: 271–2).

A core duty of the US Legislative Counsel is technical support for bill drafting, including the wording of the text. Although the Counsel points out constitutional issues and consistency with the existing legislative system, the final judgement is entrusted to the presenter (see Strokoff, no date; Shibutani, 1994: 55–62). Actually, there are many bills that contradict the provisions of existing law. There are also many bills that are inconsistent with existing interpretations and are presented to change the legislative construction of the court.[7] The drafting conduct of the legislative bureaus is related to the very basis of their duties. Accordingly, said conduct is a very significant matter that can sometimes influence the form of the member's bill. Actually, it has been pointed out that the Japanese LBHR/LBHC's insistence on consistency with existing legislative interpretations and the legislative system positions it as a 'barrier' to members' bills and reduces the total number of members' bills (see Nishikawa, 1998: 96–9). In the parliamentary cabinet system, it is thought that the Parliament/Diet tends to attach great importance to the existing legislative system, the majority of which are government laws, because of the close proximity between the Parliament/Diet and the government and because most approved bills are presented by the government. Arguably, the drafting conduct of the legislative bureaus may be a reflection of such trends. Such trends in the LBHR/LBHC's work are the result of influence by the parliament cabinet system, which is the basic government structure, as well as the RBHR, RBHC and RBNDL, whose main duty is information provision, including factual research, as mentioned earlier.

Policy Secretary

Frequency of Policy Secretary's duties

According to Article 132-2 of the Diet Law, the duties of the Policy Secretary are defined as 'mainly supporting the policy planning and legislative activity of the Diet member'. However, the type of work actually performed by the Policy Secretary differs from office to office. In order to ascertain the frequency of the Policy Secretary's duties and to grasp the real state of LSA utilisation by members, the author of this chapter conducted a questionnaire with the Diet members of Japan. Results of the questionnaire are shown in Figure 8.4.[8] The questionnaire asked members to rate the frequency of their Policy Secretary's duties by writing the applicable number from the following: '1. Very frequent', '2. Relatively frequent', '3. Relatively few' and '4. None'. Members responded with regards to the following nine duties: 'A. Supporting the drafting of members' bills'; 'B. Preparing questions for the Diet'; 'C. Collecting general information about policy matters'; 'D. Attending a meeting of the political party as a substitute for the member'; 'E. Accounting'; 'F. Making a member's magazine or pamphlet'; 'G. Collecting money'; 'H. Making clerical documents'; and 'I. Making the rounds of the member's supporters'.

Figure 8.4: Frequency of Policy Secretary's duties

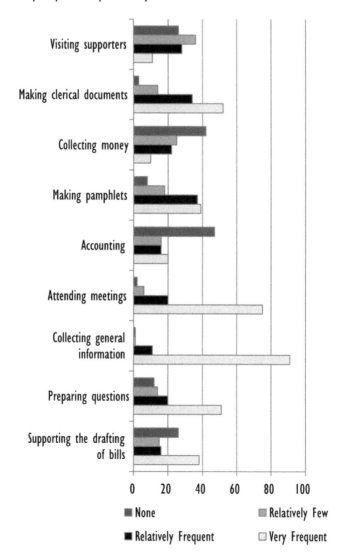

When looking at the figure, '1. Very frequent' was the most common answer for 'A. Supporting the drafting of members' bills'. On the other hand, a considerable number of members also selected '4. None'. The answer '1. Very frequent' stands out for 'B. Preparing questions for the Diet', 'C. Collecting general information about policy matters' and 'D. Attending a meeting of the political party as a substitute for the member'. This shows that these tasks are particularly common as daily work of Policy Secretaries. In addition, a relatively high number of members selected '1. Very frequent' and '2. Relatively frequent' for 'F. Making a member's magazine or pamphlet' and 'H. Making clerical documents'. Conversely, many members selected '3. Relatively few' and '4. None' for 'E. Accounting', 'G. Collecting money' and 'I. Making the rounds of the member's supporters'. Accordingly, Policy Secretaries are engaged in deskwork inside of the office rather than the jobs moving around outside, and in clerical work rather than the collection of votes and money.

Specific work of the Policy Secretary

In the previous section, the general frequency of duties was ascertained by referring to the questionnaire. In the following section, an interview with the Policy Secretaries serves as the basis for a more detailed examination of their work. Stated in the following are the three typical policy-related works, that is, supporting the drafting of members' bills, preparing questions for the Diet and attending a meeting of the political party as a substitute for the member.

- *Support for the drafting of members' bills.* There is little opportunity for the Policy Secretary to participate in drafting the contents of bills. In most cases, the Policy Secretary collects material by using the Diet Library and the research bureaus of the two houses, and facilitates communication and adjustment for the people concerned, including members, the legislative bureaus and bureaucrats.
- *Support for preparing questions.* Another principal work of Policy Secretaries is support for preparing questions that the member will ask at the Diet. The extent to which a Policy Secretary participates in this work differs according to the method for preparing questions. When the member prepares a manuscript before the question, the Policy Secretary is engaged in the drafting work. When preparing a question, the Policy Secretary often asks the three research bureaus of the Diet to collect information. In order to gather an even wider range of information, the Policy Secretary frequently issues requests to both the RBHR/RBHC and the RBNDL. Generally, the Policy Secretary arranges the materials collected, collates the necessary information, discusses with the member and makes a draft.
- *Attending policy meetings as a substitute.* In each party, various meetings on policy matters are held every day.[9] Types of meetings include policy meetings, research meetings, study meetings and a project team. It is not uncommon for some meetings to take place at the same time, especially when the Diet is in session.[10] Attendance at most of the meetings is optional and a member attends the meeting in which he/she is interested. When the member cannot attend, his/her Policy Secretary attends as a substitute. In most of meetings, the Policy Secretary does not have the right to speak. Therefore, the Policy Secretary's main duty is to take notes and relay the contents of the meeting to the member.

Policy analysis of the Policy Secretary

Based on the preceding, the opportunity for a Policy Secretary to be engaged in substantial policy planning and legislative activity in the real work is generally quite limited. Therefore, it can be said that the role of a Policy Secretary is collecting, arranging and summarising information and then correctly conveying that information to the member.

Summary of Japanese Legislative Supporting Agencies' activities

As examined earlier, Japanese LSAs mainly provide information for Diet members and political parties, and communicate and adjust with the person concerned. It is quite rare for Japanese LSAs to make a detailed policy analysis based on the information obtained. Also, except for the legislative bureaus, it is unusual for LSAs to be engaged in practical legislative affairs, even though legislative work is defined as a duty of LSAs in related laws and regulations.

Arguably, such a trend can be attributed to the institution surrounding the LSAs. In the parliamentary cabinet system, the Parliament/Diet functions less as a place enacting legislation and tends to serve increasingly as a place for the expression of intentions and discussion. Accordingly, in such a Parliament/Diet, the opportunity for LSAs to participate in practical legislative affairs is inherently limited. Furthermore, because of the close proximity to the government, the Parliament/Diet's awareness of observing the present administration tends to be weak. Such facts create a situation in which members of both the ruling party and the opposition party can utilise the bureaucrats for legislative activities. As a result, the main duty of LSAs is information provision, and there is very little detailed policy analysis conducted by them.

Conclusion

Despite a high level of institutional development when compared to other countries adopting the parliamentary cabinet system, the Japanese LSAs actually do not play a role that reflects this development. This leads to a gap between the institution and function. From a policy analysis point of view, this problem is obvious because it is highly unusual for Japanese LSAs to conduct detailed analysis and dissection, thus exceeding the normal work of collecting and arranging material and then providing that material to members and parties.

However, in no way does this imply that LSAs fail to satisfy an existing need. The Japanese Diet is a place not for legislation, but for an expression of intentions and discussion. Accordingly, the political environment does not require policy-related support other than the provision of information on facts.

Notes

[1] Among existing literature introducing LSAs, there is a difference in agencies referred to as 'LSAs'. For example, see Asano (2003), Oyama (1997), Harada (1997), Hirose (1999), Nakashima (2007), Sakakibara (2008), Hirata (1998), Ishimura (1997) and so on.

[2] The UK and Germany can be described as the 'Westminster Type' and the 'Continental Europe Type'. However, the latter, in particular, does not have an obvious definition and its meaning is not evident. For a contrast between the Continental Europe Type and the Westminster Type, see Oyama (2003); for a contrast between the Consensus Model, which is considered as a type of the Continental Europe Type, and the Westminster Type, see Lijphart (1984, 1999).

[3] Tables 8.1–8.5 were made with reference to Makita (2013: ch 2).

[4] The amendment rate in 2010 was 10.14%, with the average amendment rate from the first Diet being 20.39%.

[5] The approval rate of government bills in 2010 was 55.95%, while the approval rate of members' bills was 23.81%. Also, while the average approval rate of government bills from 1947 was 89.22%, that of members' bills was 30.98%.

[6] As a specific example, see Tani (2003: 329), who describes the legislative process of the NPO (Non-Profit Organization) Bill.

[7] An example is the case of the Metropolitan Washington Airport Act (see *Bond Buyer*, 1991; *Washington Post*, 1998).

[8] The number of valid response was 112. The response rate was 15.5% (112/721, the total number of Diet members).

[9] Each political party has several meetings corresponding to the respective policy fields in the policy research bureau. Discussion and approval in the meetings is a necessary process to determine the party's guidelines for each policy. For the Democratic Party of Japan, corresponding meetings are the Section Meetings set up in the Policy Research Department. For the Liberal Democratic Party, corresponding meetings are the Section Meetings formed in the Policy Research Department.

[10] Generally, during the Diet session, various party meetings are held from 8:00am. This time is set to enable attendance by members, as the Diet committees usually start from 9:00am.

References
Asano, I. (2003) *Kokkai-Nyumon* [*An Introduction to the Japanese Diet*], Shinzansya-Syuppan.

Asano, Y. (1999) 'Diet Members' Legislation and the Legislative Bureaus' (in Japanese), *Gikaiseijikenkyu*, no 50, pp 28–37.

Bond Buyer (1991) 18 June.

Harada, K. (1997) *Gikaiseido* [*The Diet System*], Shinzansya-Syuppan.

Hirata, Y. (1998) *Giin-Hisyo no Kenkyu* [*A Study of Secretary to the Diet Members*], Souseisya.

Hirose, J. (1999) 'A Policy Making Process of Diet and the Legislative Supporting Agencies' (in Japanese), in H. Shiroyama, K. Suzuki and S. Hosono (eds) *Chuousyouchou no Seisaku-Keisei-Katei* [*The Policy Making Process of Central Government Offices*], Chuoudaigaku-Syuppanbu, pp 275–309.

Ishimura, K. (1997) *Giinrippou – Jitsumu to keiken no nakakara* [*Diet Members' Legislation – from the Practice and Experience*], Shinzansya-Syuppan.

Lijphart, A. (1984) *Democracies: Patterns of Majoritarian and Consensus Government in Twenty-One Countries*, Yale University Press.

Lijphart, A. (1999) *Patterns of Democracy: Government Forms and Performance in Thirty-Six Countries*, Yale University Press.

Makita, J. (2013) *Rippouhosakikan no Seido to Kinou – Kakkoku Hikaku to Nihon no Zissyoubunseki* [*Institutions and Functions of the Legislative Supporting Agencies – a Comparison with the Countries and a Positive Analysis on Japan*], Kouyousyobou.

Nakashima, M. (2007) *Rippougaku* [*Science of Legislation*], Houritsubunkasya.

Nishikawa, S. (1998) 'The Legislative Bureau – an Examination on the Organization and Function' (in Japanese), *Seikeironsou*, vol 66, nos 5/6, pp 405–58.

Nishikawa, S. (2002) *Shirarezaru Kancho – Shin Naikaku Houseikyoku* [*An Unknown Government Office – the New Cabinet Legislation Bureau*], Satsuki-Syobou.

Oyama, R. (1997) *Kokkaigaku-Nyumon* [*An Introduction to the Science of Japanese Diet*], Sanseido.

Oyama, R. (2003) *Hikakugikaiseiji-Ron* [*A View of Comparative Parliamentary Politics*], Iwanami-syoten.

Polsby, N.W. (1975) 'Legislatures', in F.I. Greenstein and N.W. Polsby (eds) *Handbook of Political Science, Vol 5: Governmental Institutions and Process*, Massachusetts, MA: Addison-Wesley, pp 257–319.

Sakakibara, Y. (2008) 'A Trend and Problem on the Reform of Legislative Supporting Agencies' (in Japanese), *Hokudaihougakuronshu*, vol 59, no 2, pp 397–451.

Shibutani, O. (1994) *Gikai no Jidai* [*An Era of Diet*], Sanseido.

Strokoff, S. (no date) 'How Our Laws Are Made: A Ghost Writer's View', Office of the legislative Counsel (House). Available at: http://legcounsel.house.gov/HOLC/Before_Drafting/Ghost_Writer.html (accessed 14 January 2013).

Tani, K. (2003) 'Legislative Supporting Function – Legislative Supporting Activities of Policy Secretary' (in Japanese), in K. Tani (ed) *Giinrippou no Jissyoukenkyu* [*A Positive Study of Diet Members' Bill*], Shinzansya-Syuppan, pp 359–444.

Washington Post (1998) 17 November.

NINE

Councils, policy analysis and policy evaluation

Kiyoshi Yamaya

Introduction

As policy studies becomes more advanced in Japan, the role of governmental councils (*Shingi-kai*) in the policy process is attracting a degree of scrutiny. Some of these are formal councils established by ministries and agencies in line with law, others are set up informally. As of July 2012, there were 118 formal councils. Informal councils are impossible to count, and the nature of their work is also diverse. Here, the discussion will focus on how both formal and informal councils analyse and evaluate policy, with particular reference to experiences over the last 12 years since the system of policy evaluation was established in Japan.

Councils in Japan

The characteristics and realities of councils in Japanese central government will be explained with reference to three sources. The first is the National Government Organization Act 1948, which provides for the establishment of consultative bodies under the name of councils and investigation committees. Their prescribed mission is to fill gaps in government knowledge with expertise from the private sector, broadly reflect public opinion in the administration and ensure the fairness and gravity of government (Okabe, 1967: 168). The second is an explanation based on a guidebook used by government officials. This is the *Shingikai-souran* (*Council Handbook*), published every year by the Institute of Administrative Management. The Institute was set up in 1977 as a think-tank body for the Administrative Management Agency (now the Ministry of Internal Affairs and Communications). The fact that it is published by the think tank of a body responsible for the administrative management of Japanese central government means that any organisation listed in the *Handbook* will be recognised as a formal council.

The third source lies in explanations by Japanese political scientists. In their critical explanation of councils lies the reality of councils in Japan. Specifically, their criticism is that 'Council discussions usually follow a script set by administrative bodies, turning councils into a mere mouthpiece of the government' (Sato, 1985). It became a problem that ministers and bureaucrats selected council members and tried to control the meetings and policy discussions (without policy analysis).

A famous example of this negative image came during the tenure of Prime Minister Nakasone (1982–87). He was criticised for directly adopting reports, opinions and advice presented by his informal councils and private advisory committees, and using them when forming policy, thus bypassing the national Diet. Also, in the 1980s, pressure groups and lobbyists forged close links with the ruling Liberal Democratic Party (LDP), inviting criticism from Japanese political scientists that councils provided venues for this activity. Criticism of the role played by councils in the policymaking system, dubbed 'Japanese neo-corporatism', even moved public opinion. This was eventually reflected in a revision of councils, coinciding with the reform of central government bodies. Basically, the Japanese government decided to abolish the policymaking council and the policy-enforcement council (Article 30 of the Basic Act on Central Government Reform 1998).

This decision was reflected in the 'Basic Plan on Reorganisation and Rationalisation of Councils' (Cabinet Decision of 1999). Under this plan, the government reduced the number of councils from 212 in 2000 to 110 by 1 July 2006. Those targeted for reduction were dormant councils that had elected no new members for five years or more, councils that met exceptionally rarely and councils whose work was becoming increasingly irrelevant due to changes in social circumstances and the drive towards deregulation.

Despite these institutional reforms, however, the Japanese media still criticise councils for having an undue impact on policy – and they have a point. During the revision of medical fees in 2002, for example, management executives of the Japan Dental Federation bribed members of the Central Social Insurance Medical Council (CSIMC) to issue statements in favour of dentists. As a result, the executives and members of the Japan Dental Federation, LDP Diet members, local assembly councillors (legislators) and others were indicted on corruption charges, and all were found guilty. However, another problem was still to come. That was the Fukushima nuclear power accident following the Great East Japan Earthquake disaster on 11 March 2011. Now, the public lost trust in the councils and specialist committees of the Cabinet Office, the Ministry of Economy, Trade and Industry, and the Ministry of Education, Culture, Sports, Science and Technology, as they had prioritised the revenues of power companies and had done nothing to anticipate an 'unexpected' disaster. This loss of trust was equally directed at the system of councils itself.

But what exactly are these 'councils' anyway? Article 8 of the aforementioned National Government Organisation Act defines a formal council as 'an organ having a council system for taking charge of the study and deliberation of important matters, administrative appeals or other affairs that are considered appropriate to be processed through consultation among persons with the relevant knowledge and experience'. However, within the category of 'councils', this author would also include informal councils – that is, committees, specialist committees, round-table meetings, research groups and 'private study groups' of directors-general, directors and other bodies with no legal basis. This is because their roles are actually quite similar. Like formal councils, informal councils not only 'guarantee the objectivity and neutrality of the administration' and 'reflect representative views of various social interests', but are also involved in policies in a variety of forms. A way of organising this diversity of councils is to look at the basis for their establishment. This can be found in 'Guidelines on the Establishment of Councils, etc.', an attachment to the aforementioned 'Basic Plan on Reorganisation and Rationalisation of Councils' (1999). When categorised on this basis, councils fall into the six patterns outlined in Table 9.1.

These councils and other groups play a large number of roles. They include the roles of deliberating on and judging specific themes, consultation and advice on

Table 9.1: Categories of the councils

Types	Examples	Main functions
1. Councils established under the Act for Establishment of the Cabinet Office	The Food Safety Commission; the Public Records and Archives Management Commission; the Central Council for the Promotion of Measures for Disabled Persons; the Local Government System Research Council; the Election System Deliberation Council; the Council for Relocation of the Diet and Other Organisations; the Statistics Commission; the Information Disclosure and Personal Information Protection Review Board; the Public Interest Corporation Commission; the Reemployment Surveillance Commission; and the Consumer Commission	Deliberating on and judging a specific theme fairly and equally
	The Commission on Policy Evaluation and Evaluation of Incorporated Administrative Agencies (IAAs) of the Ministry of Internal Affairs and Communication	Sometimes scrutinises IAA activities like audit and inspection
2. Bodies established by various ministries and agencies based on Article 8 of the National Government Organisation Act	Leading examples are the Legislative Council of the Ministry of Justice; the Medical Ethics Council; the Central Council for Education; and the Labour Policy Council	Deliberating on and judging a specific theme
3. Specialist committees and advisory councils created ad hoc when drawing up or amending 'Program' or 'Basic Plans'	The Committee for Policy Planning on Disaster Management (an expert review committee of the Central Disaster Management Council); specialist committees set up when revising the Framework for Nuclear Energy Policy; the National Defence Program Guidelines; the Official Development Assistance (ODA) Charter, etc	'Home tutors' for directors-general and divisional directors charged with deciding policy directions
4. Groups set up by the cabinet and government agencies based on specific laws	Central Social Insurance Medical Council; The Council for Gender Equality based on the Basic Act for Gender Equal Society; the Central Environment Council based on the Basic Encouragement Law; the Council for the Promotion of Policies for Crime Victims based on the Basic Act on Crime Victims, etc	Consultation and advice on the policy
5. Evaluation committees for IAAs	IAAs set up by 12 ministries and one agency based on the Act on General Rules for IAAs. Each ministry has a committee that monitors and checks IAA activities and performances (the total number of IAAs in 2014 is 98)	Measuring and monitoring the performance of IAAs
6. Specialist committees on policy evaluation created on a private, round-table discussion basis by ministries, agencies and others	21 ministries and agencies[a] have specialist committees based on their internal rules	Evaluation of ministerial evaluation policy, meta-evaluation of policy evaluation and confirming the authenticity and credibility of data gathered and surveyed

Note:[a] 1. Cabinet Office; 2. Imperial Household Agency; 3. National Public Safety Commission; 4. Ministry of Defence; 5. Ministry of Internal Affairs and Communications; 6. Ministry of Justice; 7. Ministry of Foreign Affairs; 8. Ministry of Finance; 9. Ministry of Education, Culture, Sports, Science and Technology; 10. Ministry of Health, Labour and Welfare; 11. Ministry of Agriculture, Forestry and Fisheries; 12. Ministry of Economy, Trade and Industry; 13. Ministry of Land, Infrastructure and Transport; 14. Ministry of the Environment; 15. Nuclear Regulation Authority; 16. Environment Dispute Coordination Commission; 17. Financial Services Agency; 18. Reconstruction Agency; 19. Specific Personal Information Protection Commission; 20. Japan Fair Trade Commission; and 21. Consumer Affairs Agency.

the policy, 'home tutors' for directors–general and divisional directors charged with deciding policy directions, the work of gathering and analysing data when evaluating or reviewing policy and organisations, and confirming the authenticity and credibility of data gathered and surveyed. What must not be forgotten, however, is that the aforementioned Basic Plan on Reorganisation and Rationalisation of Councils sets out the principle of 'basically abolishing the functions of deliberating policy and creating standards'. In spite of that, councils and committees are still involved in deliberating or discussing policy. Even if there were a 'basic principle of non-involvement' between deliberating policy and creating standards, would it really be possible to achieve? To answer that question, we will need to look at the realities of policy analysis and policy evaluation in Japan.

Policy analysis and policy evaluation by councils in Japan
Policy analysis

It was in the early 1970s that many Japanese students and researchers of governmental activities first knew of the existence of policy sciences. At the same time, systems analysis, cost–benefit analysis, operations research (OR), social engineering, system engineering and analysis using economic models were imported as methods of analysing policy. As such, the actual content of policy sciences in Japan was policy analysis, sometimes used synonymously with 'systems analysis' (Miyakawa, 1973). This was due to the influence of the Planning Programming Budgeting System (PPBS), which was popular with the Japanese government from the late 1960s to the beginning of the 1970s; systems analysis was seen as 'preliminary analysis' for policymaking in Japan. Thus, policy analysis became synonymous with systems analysis, and also came to be recognised as a 'rational' (read: quantifiable) technique for improving governmental decision-making and policymaking. In the 1970s and 1980s, Japanese students and government officials regarded policy sciences as the academic field wherein to research this science.

In Japan, policy analysis posts were set up in some administrative bodies, but, in most cases, the analysis was commissioned to a think-tank organisation in the private sector. At the time, there were no institutions in Japan offering systematic education in policy sciences or policy analysis, and no institutes of higher education awarding degrees in policy sciences. Instead, the general method was either that Japanese bureaucrats would study for a degree (master's and doctoral) in the US and then take charge of educating their peers in the workplace on their return, or that economists and professors of engineering would teach at the training facilities of administrative institutions. The problem here, however, was that it limited the spread of policy sciences and policy analysis because this kind of knowledge had not originally been required of civil servants when they were hired.

In that case, do Japan's councils often carry out policy analysis? The answer is 'no' because council members are not selected for their knowledge of policy sciences and policy analysis. Many council members are university professors with expertise in economics, statistics or social engineering, university professors of politics or public administration, renowned economists, think-tank leaders and economists, lawyers, certified public accountants, and former bureaucrats; very few have any experience of policy analysis. Therefore, the work of councils involves giving advice on the content or substance of policy (eg education, diplomacy, welfare, environment), presenting the results of policy analysis undertaken by administrative bodies and hearing the views of individual members. This means that as long as there is no particular opposition, the council accepts the results of policy analysis.

Actually, the essential content of policy sciences in Japan has changed greatly over the last 20 years or so. Now, importance is placed not only on positivistic quantitative analysis in the form of policy analysis, but also on qualitative analysis. The values held by policy analysts have also come under scrutiny. In Japan, these changes are seen as movements towards 'policy studies'. The trigger for this came when Japanese political scientists and public administration scholars focused their attention on the movement of political scientists in the US, the Policy Studies Organization (PSO), in the 1980s. The 'plan–do–see' cycle was frequently cited in discussions by the PSO, and when the 'see' part of this cycle attracted attention as policy evaluation, the same interest expanded into actual practice.

Policy evaluation

Policy evaluation developed as a research field when evaluation research influenced research on the policy process and implementation in politics and public administration studies. It is also a feature of administrative practice. Attention was drawn to the 'see' part of the cycle because in Japan, as in the US, there were researchers and government officials who knew, from their experience of PPBS, that pre-analysis would be extraordinarily difficult. Then, some government officials and academic members in Japan had the idea of starting from retrospective ex post research, or a summative review in which the results of policy are scrutinised, so-called 'from analysis to evaluation' (Shick, 1971).

Let us take a closer look at methods of policy analysis and policy evaluation, with a view to distinguishing between them. In typical forms of policy analysis, quantitative data are quantitatively analysed, using various techniques devised within the specific methods of economic analysis and cost–benefit analysis. Examples include benefit incidence table analysis, the travel cost method, the hedonic approach, the contingent valuation method, input–output analysis, econometric model analysis and the linkage model. On the other hand, qualitative analysis of qualitative data is commonly seen in evaluation research, the prototype of policy evaluation. For this, the techniques used include participant observation, monographs, fieldwork, ethnography, social surveys and interviews. Although it is extremely difficult to subject qualitative data to qualitative analysis and predict effects in advance, ex post surveys are comparatively easy. Conducting evaluation research on policy tools and the programmes that serve as their operational manuals is known as 'programme evaluation' in Japan. This programme evaluation is the essence of policy evaluation. Methods of programme evaluation are diverse, but principal methods such as the following have been devised (Rossi et al, 2004):

- assessing the need for a programme;
- expressing and assessing programme theory;
- assessing and monitoring programme process;
- measuring and monitoring programme outcomes;

- assessing programme impact – randomised field experiments;assessing programme impact – alternative designs;detecting, interpreting and analysing programme effects; andmeasuring efficiency.

If council members were involved in policy evaluation, they would need to have some understanding of these methods of programme evaluation. However, there are not many examples of this. Again, if councils were to carry out policy evaluation, a very important point would be whether the members could understand methods of gathering and analysing data. Often, however, in Japan, councils merely look at data gathered and analysed by policy analysts in the think tank, or data prepared within the ministry. It may sound ironic, but even members who know nothing of specialist analytical tools and techniques can work in a council.

The relationship between policy analysis and policy evaluation in councils

The functions of analysis and evaluation are often divided according to the various stages of the policy process (plan–do–see), not only in practical policy analysis and evaluation, but also in the practical work of evaluating Official Development Assistance (ODA) and others. That is, they are divided into the processes of: policy analysis and formative evaluation before the event; monitoring and formative evaluation during the event; and summative evaluation, evaluation review and programme evaluation after the event. If a council were involved at each of these stages, it would first have to reach a consensus on 'evaluation policy', including the objects of analysis and evaluation, the schedule, the selection of techniques, the timing of reports, and so on. Then, it would have to verify the validity of the analysis and evaluation techniques. Of course, policy analysis and policy evaluation are difficult work that requires specialist knowledge and expertise; they also incur a large working cost. Members of councils, most administrators, ministers, senior vice-ministers and parliamentary secretaries of ministries do not know the difference between analysis and evaluation, and they are not interested in how to use quantitative analysis and qualitative evaluation. This is why they sometimes commission analysis and evaluations from think tanks and consultants in the private sector.

The reality of councils

In Japan, there were critiques of councils that they were used to ratify and justify government preferences. However, there are two new styles in which councils can be involved in policy.

The first is meta-evaluation of policy evaluation. Examples of meta-evaluation by councils include: (i) reviews of how policy evaluation (self-evaluation) should be done; (ii) using a third-party eye to monitor self-evaluation by government agencies; (iii) seeing the results of completed evaluations and stating opinions; and (iv) advice on how the evaluation results should be reflected in policymaking and the budgeting process.

The second new style is advice and proposals on the practical content of policy. Here, when analysing and evaluating major single-policy issues, like nuclear power, suicide prevention and ODA, members with specialist knowledge are involved.

Meta-evaluation

In around 2002, there were various discussions in government agencies on the activity of specialist committees for policy evaluation. Now, a decade later, the activity of specialist committees has converged on the following key points:

- deciding the objects of policy evaluation (ex post evaluation, regulation and deregulation, tax system, etc);
- deciding on the system for implementing evaluation;
- checking a government agency's basic plan for policy evaluation as the framework for policy evaluation;
- checking the agency's plan for implementing policy evaluation;
- deciding on the annual schedule;
- scrutinising ideal evaluation forms and formats;
- organising solutions to issues in implementation (reflecting evaluation results in budgeting and policymaking, setting performance targets, selecting performance indicators, etc)
- responding to problems in policy evaluation practice identified by the Ministry of Internal Affairs and Communications, and advising on principles for responding to instructions and request from the ruling political parties.

As will be clear from this, the work of each ministry's specialist committee on policy evaluation is completely different from the images that students of the Japanese policy evaluation system have; it is a question of being involved in formal aspects of evaluation (how to carry out evaluation). In some situations, it is difficult for this to be turned into analysis and evaluation of policy. This means that it is possible, even without knowing too much about the content and substance of policy (eg diplomacy, welfare or environment), to evaluate diplomatic policy, welfare policy or environmental policy. The reasons for this is that since the system of policy evaluation is shared by all ministries and agencies (Government Policy Evaluations Act 2001), a cross-agency format needs to be developed, and interest is concentrated in the development of this format for the evaluation system.

Substantial involvement in policy

The Final Report of the Administrative Reform Council (December 1997) instructed that 'When councils need to be created, they should be general bodies not beholden to the framework of ministries and agencies, and their matters for deliberation should be specifically limited'. Certain councils have a mission based on this instruction, and are involved in policy as inter-agency bodies. Specifically, these are the working groups and committees established within the Council for Gender Equality. They provide a good illustration of policy analysis and policy evaluation in practice.

The Council for Gender Equality was established in the Cabinet Office in January 2001, based on the Basic Act for Gender-Equal Society. To promote its specific mission, several specialist study groups have been set up as committees within the Council for Gender Equality.

Research Group on Gender Equality Impact (created December 1999)

Measures planned, proposed and implemented by the Japanese government can have differing impacts on men and women. This research group was created to discuss ways of surveying and evaluating these impacts. The outcome was the 'Research Group on Gender Equality Impact Report – Reconstructing the Policy Process from the Viewpoint of Gender Equality' (December 2000). The report outlines approaches and methods of '*programme impact evaluation*', of which there are few examples in Japan.

Specialist Committee on Monitoring and Handling Complaints (created April 2001

This specialist committee surveyed whether the various ministries and agencies were steadily implementing the Basic Plan for Gender Equality. It published its findings in the 'Discussion Paper on the Handling of Complaints Relating to Measures for Gender Equality and Relief for Victims of Human Rights Infringement' (April 2002), 'Monitoring of the Implementation of Measures to Promote the Formation of a Gender Equal Society' (July 2002), 'Comment on Enhancing and Strengthening Systems on the Handling of Complaints Relating to Measures for Gender Equality and Relief for Victims of Human Rights Infringement' (October 2002), 'Survey on Gathering, Organization and Provision of Information on Gender Equality' (July 2003), 'Promoting ODA from the Viewpoint of Gender Equality' (April 2004), and 'Proposals for Promoting the Adoption and Dissemination of the Convention on the Elimination of All Forms of Discrimination against Women, ILO Conventions and other Conventions as well as International Norms and Standards into Japan' (July 2004).

Specialist Committee on Monitoring and Impact Surveys (created October 2004)

This surveyed government measures aimed at forming a gender-equal society. The outcome took the form of the 'Report on Results of Research and Examination on Assignment of Advisory Council Members in Prefectures and Government-Designated Big Cities Based on Government ordinance' (October 2006), 'Report on Monitoring and Impact Assessment on Policies for Capacity-building and Lifelong Learning to Facilitate Diversity of Choice' (March 2007), 'Report on Monitoring and Impact Assessment on Support for the Independent Life of the Elderly' (June 2008), and 'Report on Monitoring and Impact Assessment on Men and Women Facing Living Difficulties Amid New Socio-Economic Trends' (November 2009).

Specialist Committee on Monitoring (created April 2011)

This was created under Article 22 paragraph 4 of the Basic Act for Gender-Equal Society. The outcome of its deliberations has been as follows:

- 'On the Monitoring of the Final Opinion Follow-up of the Committee on the Elimination of Discrimination against Women (Amendment to the Civil Code, Temporary Special Measures)'

- 'On the Monitoring of the Performance Targets and Reference Indices Incorporated in the Third Basic Plan for Gender Equality'
- 'On the Monitoring of the State of Progress of Concrete Measures Specified in the Third Basic Plan for Gender Equality'
- 'On the Assessment of the Content of Complaints Concerning Measures to Promote the Formation of Gender Equality, etc., and the System of Relief for Victims of Human Rights Infringements Related to Gender Equality'

There are four ways in which these committees have been involved in policies. The first is by monitoring the observance or non-observance of international agreements. The question here is whether Japanese laws and policies are compatible with the Convention on the Elimination of All Forms of Discrimination against Women, ILO conventions, and other global standards. The second is by monitoring the setting of policy targets and progress towards them, and if progress is slow, surveying the reason (programme evaluation). The concept of 'Measure and Evaluation' (performance *measurement* and programme *evaluation*) found in Western countries can be seen here. The third is by surveying what kind of impact various government programmes have. Finally, the fourth is by examining methods of feedback and verifying the implementation of feedback to see how the knowledge thus gained is incorporated in 'plans'.

The research groups and specialist committees of the Council for Gender Equality are classic examples of councils being substantially involved in policy analysis and policy evaluation in Japan. The members assembled in these research groups and specialist committees are experts in evaluation, experts in administrative practice, gender researchers, heads of local governments (mayors), international law scholars, lawyers and researchers in social welfare and welfare economics, among others. The groups and committees are endowed with human resources on a par with Western research task forces, and stand as unusual examples in which substantial deliberation on policy has been possible. However, rather than encouraging policy change through their evaluation and analysis, their role has focused more on supporting policy with 'research'.

Conclusion

Members of councils involved in policy analysis and policy evaluation are expected to be 'analysis and evaluation literate'. For policy analysis, the main form of literacy is expertise in cost–benefit analysis and cost–effect analysis, or systems analysis. The mandatory pre-evaluation (analysis) of regulations imposed on ministries and agencies from 2007 has expanded opportunities for activity by these literates in this kind of analysis. Again, pre-analysis and ex post evaluation were carried out in the policy evaluation of special taxation measures (in 2010). Literacy in analysis and evaluation was also strongly required here. For policy evaluation, similarly, there have been growing demands for the results of policy evaluation to be reflected in the budgeting process in Japan since 2003, under the initiative of the Council on Economic and Fiscal Policy. In 2011, however, a decision was made to promote a shift to 'target-management-style policy evaluation' (Management by Objectives-style performance measurement), centred mainly on the 'performance measurement' type of performance evaluation as one method of policy evaluation, and this was adopted by various ministries and agencies. As members of the Diet and most bureaucrats in Japan are not policy analysts and evaluators, this shift was welcomed.

As council members were not conversant with policy analysis and evaluation, it was quite difficult for them to understand the significance of these shifts. Then, the only role that they could actually play would be to check and confirm the data and performance indicators presented by government officials. It would be impossible for them to check the validity, reliability, accuracy and usefulness of the social science tools used in policy analysis and evaluation, or to confirm the validity of analysis results, that is, the real mission expected of policy analysis and policy evaluation. Thus, the role of a council lacking literacy in analysis and evaluation would be merely to ratify and justify the results of policy analysis and policy evaluation carried out by think tanks commissioned by government officials in the ministries. In this case, the major premise of the cabinet decision, that is, that councils should not be involved in the policy process, would be upheld.

In Japan, like the nuclear-electric power stations in Fukushima, policymaking, policy decisions, implementation and evaluation of policy have been politically controlled. Here, I would like to distinguish the concepts of analysis and evaluation of policy, the clarity of these concepts and their objectively appropriate use can withdraw 'ill-designed' policy advocacies and their political influences over the councils, the media and the Diet. However, these distinctions are not universally accepted. Policy analysis as a universal design will be necessary for policy studies in Japan.

References

Miyakawa, T. (ed) (1973) *Shisutemu Bunseki Gairon – Seisaku Kettei no Shuho to Oyo* [*Overview of Systems Analysis – Techniques of Policy Decision and their Application*], Yuuhikaku.

Okabe, S. (1967) *Gyosei Kanri* [*Administrative Management*], Yuuhikaku.

Rossi, P., Lipsey, M.W. and Freeman, H.E. (2004) *Evaluation: A Systematic Approach* (7th edn), Sage.

Sato, A. (1985) 'Gyousei to Shimin [Public Administration and Citizen]' in I. Kato, Y. Kato, A. Sato, and W. Yasuo, *Gyouseigaku Nyuumon* [*Introduction to Public Administration*], Yuuhikaku, pp 219–20.

Schick, A. (1971) 'From Analysis to Evaluation', *The ANNALS of the American Academy of Political and Social Science*, March, pp 57–71.

TEN

Local governments and policy analysis in Japan after the Second World War

Toshiyuki Kanai

What is policy analysis?

Policy analysis is, in a sense, the investigation of policy in order to guide future decision-making while considering the ground reality. The five-stage model of the policy process includes: (1) agenda-setting; (2) policy formulation; (3) decision-making; (4) policy implementation; and (5) policy evaluation. Policy analysis occurs in the policy formulation stage and is regarded as being situated at the 'P' (plan) stage of the PDCA (Plan-Do-Check-Action) cycle.

In other words, policy analysis is the intellectual investigation by policymakers working at the stage of policy formulation. It is not limited to scientific or academic analysis. Coordination among stakeholders, the most unscientific and political activity at first glance, is based on the analysis of political situations. Coordination without analysis of politics will result in failure. Policy analysis involves information activities such as human intelligence (HUMINT).

Policy analysis by local governments in Japan after the Second World War

The centralised intergovernmental system and local governments without policy analysis

Local policy analysis is significantly influenced by the local government policy process. It occurs at the policy formulation stage, leading to the decision-making stage. Under the centralised intergovernmental system, local governments are generally not in charge of decision-making. Therefore, they need not conduct policy analysis.

In centralised post-war Japan, the national government is responsible for decision-making. The local governments are primarily responsible for policy implementation. Agenda-setting and policy formulation, which occur prior to decision-making, are carried out largely by officials of the ministries and agencies of the national government. These ministries and agencies of the national government often refer to themselves as 'policy offices'. They research, plan and formulate policies. Policy study is important for the officials in 'policy offices' because it is a distinctive activity of national policy bureaucrats. Agenda-setting is naturally affected by outside influences and is subject to inputs, including demands from politicians and interest groups, the tone of mass media and public opinion, policy trends in other countries, and discourses in research and academia.

While decision-making is primarily prepared by officials, the final decisions go through an approval process by government parties, the cabinet and the Diet, implicitly or explicitly. According to the principle of collegiality of the cabinet, ministers must reach consensus for the decision to be approved. To gain the proper approval and agreement of the ministries, national officials spend the majority of their time coordinating, rather than researching and planning. These officials are known as 'realistic officials' (Satake, 1998), 'political officials' (Muramatsu, 1981) or 'coordinating officials' (Mabuchi, 2009). While they are devoted to policy formulation and decision-making, they become bureaucrats without policy professional skills. Experts who advise the bureaucrats also lack expertise. Study groups and research committees consisting of outside experts have also been referred to as 'study groups without study' and 'research committees without research'.

Under the centralised intergovernmental system, a division of roles and functions has developed. Local governments are responsible for policy implementation. As they are not engaged in policy formulation and decision-making, they do not conduct policy analysis. Instead, they lobby the national government, similar to other interest groups. These efforts contribute to agenda-setting, or policy formulation, by national government officials, but do not directly lead to policy formulation by local governments. It is important for local officials to analyse political situations and understand local issues. Local investigation ultimately constitutes part of the policy analysis by the national government.

A chronological change

Under the centralised intergovernmental system, local governments are generally not engaged in policy analysis (Kitami, 2010: 85). However, if one local government wishes to conduct its own policymaking, it must also conduct its own policy analysis. It is possible to generally characterise the chronology of policy analysis of local governments as follows (Isozaki et al, 2014: 30–2).

The first period of local government policy analysis occurred in the 1950s among pro-development local governments. In the aftermath of the Second World War, there was confusion over the food supply, restoration and reconstruction following war damage, and frequent disasters that occurred both during and immediately following the war. In attempts to develop their localities, some local governments launched aggressive policies to promote economic recovery and economic growth. These policies were in line with similar initiatives by the national government. In addition to cooperating with the national government on policies, they began attempting to industrialise and modernise their communities. As a result, local government planning divisions formulated development projects. Influenced by national economic plans, local development plans were established, with policy studies and analyses conducted by local officials.

Following the economic growth of the 1950s, the second period of local government in the 1960s–70s was known as 'progressive'. The progressive local governments demanded action on environment regulations and welfare services. They had to balance many policy goals from economy to welfare or ecology. Therefore, they asked for management systems based on comprehensive plans with both medium- and long-term perspectives. In order to take action against pollution or to create welfare measures on their own, they had to make plans without waiting for national policies to guide them. They also developed skills to make comprehensive general plans, involving public and local officials, and monitoring (Tsujinaka and Ito, 2010: 99–103). Similar to the pro-development governments of the 1950s, the progressive local governments' planning divisions were engaged in policy study, analysis, planning and coordination.

The third period of local governments in the 1980s promoted 'the municipal policy research movement'. The oil shocks that increased fiscal deficits, the environmental and welfare policies incorporated by the national conservative government, and the increase in the number of conservative-centrist mayors and prefectural governors all contributed to the loss of the uniqueness of progressive local governments. This did not, however, lead the conservative-centrist local governments to apply national policies irresponsibly. Local governments continued to pursue their own policies. This trend was referred to as the 'age of localities'. As a result: local officials improved their policymaking abilities; voluntary policy research groups by local officials increased; the Japan Association of Autonomous Government Studies was established in 1985; and the 'policy-oriented legal-affairs movement' of local officials also developed (Kaneko, 2012: 80–1). This period is characterised by disclosure of the government information system (freedom of information), public participation and the refinement of local land-use ordinances.

Local governments in the fourth period were known as 'reformists' in the 1990s. In the 1980s, local governments backed by (nearly) all political parties increased. Party coalitions were slow to reform, and they had adopted development and welfare policies that were ineffective in revitalising their communities. Following the long-term depression, local governments began reviewing existing policies in the name of 'reform'. They attempted to streamline local governance through administrative reform and evaluation. They conducted policy assessment, a technique to review existing policies, as part of their administrative evaluation, while also pursuing techniques to promote affordable policies. These actions by local governments led to the decentralisation reform and the nursing-care insurance system in 2000.

In the fifth period in the 2000s, local governments were characterised by their paralysis. Local policy formulation was stagnant (Omori, 2008: 77–145). Following the decentralisation reform in 2000, local governments have been occupied with responding to the annexation initiative promoted by the national government (Kawamura, 2010: 29). They were also tackling long-term depression and local financial crisis. Their abilities to develop policy were decreasing. Recognising their limitations, they have proposed reforming the metropolitan system (Kitamura, 2013: 207–45) and the regionalisation ('*Do-Shu*') system (Morita and Kanai, 2012: ch 3).

Four elements of local policy analysis

Even though local governments are under the centralised intergovernmental system, they have also conducted policy formulation and decision-making according to local needs based on local/field knowledge (Omori, 2008: 66–7). Policy analysis by them can be roughly classified into the following four elements.

The first element is expert/professional policy analysis. It investigates the social environment, analyses residents' needs and public opinion, studies international and national policy trends, introduces expertise in each policy area, and assists local governments in policy formulation. Expert policy analysis is not value-neutral, but includes the logic of appropriateness (March and Olsen, 1995: 30–1), that is, the appropriateness of a policy. Accordingly, the policy orientation of experts plays a crucial role. Local governments are affected by the paradigm inherent in the professional community. If desired, they can also selectively choose experts or expertise closer to their own policy preferences. Although the policy preferences of local governments are naturally influenced by partisan ideologies embraced by politicians, they are also highly sensitive to public opinion, residents' needs or objective environments (Muramastu and Inatsugu, 2009: 24–6). The study and analysis by the local government of such needs becomes important.

The second element is also expert policy analysis in its strictest sense. Assuming a given policy goal, the expert analyst examines the technical feasibility of achieving the goal by deciding and implementing certain measures. It is relatively value-neutral. It does not address whether a policy can, in fact, be decided or implemented. Rather, it examines whether the goal can be achieved if a policy is decided and implemented according to the policy design. The logic of appropriateness, associated with policy goals or policy evaluation, is unnecessary here. It is then possible to conduct professional, neutral and independent policy analysis.

The third element is the analysis of politics. The goal of policy formulation is to create a policy that can be decided upon. It is not about drawing on a blank piece of paper. Achieving political consensus among influential stakeholders becomes the key for decision-making. It is essential for officials to predict how stakeholders will respond to a proposed policy's effects on their interests. Needless to say, public officials do not always strive for wide consensus, but when faced with opposition, they periodically have to make judgements about whether they can overcome the potential conflicts. This analysis is not expert policy analysis, but analysis of a political situation. Local officials need to have an understanding of the political climates facing their local governments (Iio, 2008: 33).

The fourth element of policy analysis is implementation-oriented. Policy formulation attempts to formulate a policy that can be implemented. Infeasible policy cannot be implemented, even if consensus among influential stakeholders is achieved. Public officials have to analyse factors enabling policy execution. A typical issue analysed is the possibility of obtaining administrative resources. Public officials assess whether they can ensure the budget and personnel, whether they can obtain necessary information, or whether they are entitled to implement the policy. When examining the possibility of whether a policy can be implemented, public officials analyse people who might oppose, be indifferent, ignore or escape. These activities often involve consensus-building and working out agreements with those with administrative resources or the clients of a policy. These activities are not always performed at the stage of decision-making, so public officials need to begin the de facto policy implementation stage during the policy formulation stage.

Actual policy formulation by local governments is conducted through policy analysis, combining all or some of the four elements listed. The following sections will discuss three types of policy analysis by local governments in a centralised intergovernmental system. The three types are categorised by initiative taker.

The voluntary type: in local initiative

The voluntary type of decentralised local governments

The voluntary type is a local initiative one. If local governments have strong internal desires to achieve policy goals, they conduct policy analysis according to their own judgement as regards the policy goal (Omori, 2011: 280).

Local governments are usually faced with two kinds of environment and begin their policy analysis by studying these environments (Soga, 1995). The first environment is the local one. It is important to discover local risks and opportunities and understand residents' needs. In the process of creating programmes to solve local questions, local governments also have to find local resources. In addition, they analyse the possibility of building consensus according to the local power structure in order to further decision-making.

The second environment is the national one. It is mainly the national government, but it includes other local governments nationwide. A local government in a locality within the sovereign nation state cannot act without considering the national environment. In particular, local governments in Japan after the Second World War found it essential to examine whether their policies were in conflict with national laws. They tried to avoid the political or legal 'anger' of the ministries and agencies of the national government and courts. National government subsidies can result in a net increase in revenue. It is favourable for them to get subsidies, and subsidies can also result in political support from the national government's ministries and agencies. In addition, it is important that local governments achieve a reputation, support, fame and a following within the nationwide local government community.

These two types of environment can sometimes form a trade-off relationship. Local governments need to analyse the best solution in both environments. For example, if they put too much emphasis on the national environment while trying to obtain subsidies, they could neglect the policy analysis of the local environment and make policies useless to local needs. Subsidies are generally understood as a centralised tool because they divert local government policy analysis from the local environment. However, if local governments conduct well-founded policy analysis in accordance with the local environment, they would achieve their policy goals more easily with the financial support of the national government. The effectiveness of the subsidies ultimately depends upon the quality of the voluntary type of policy analysis by local governments.

The original style and demand style

In general, the planning division of a local government conducts the voluntary type of policy analysis. As long as the analysis is voluntary, others cannot compel it. In addition, if local officials responsible for policymaking take the initiative, they can further policy analysis by establishing think tanks within their local governments, contracting private think tanks, involving the knowledge of experts or businesspeople at will, or recruiting officials temporarily assigned from the national government.

Whether local policy analysis is conducted at will or not is extremely sensitive. For example, in the voluntary type of policy analysis, if local governments have access to national government officials who are familiar with subsidies or national laws and policies, and who also have connections within the ministries and agencies of the national government, they should obtain the support of the officials. If the national officials attempt to transplant policy goals of the national government to local government, however, they undermine the local voluntary initiative. They might strengthen the centralised system. To understand their actual effects, it is necessary to examine precisely how they are working. Voluntary-type policy analysis has to assess how national officials would work.

Local governments conducting voluntary-type policy analysis and achieving policy formulation, decision-making and implementation on their own have adopted the original style. The voluntary type of policy analysis is generally associated with the original style, which is localised and autonomous.

However, in some cases, even though local governments employ the voluntary type of policy analysis, they then file petitions or proposals to the national government in attempts at influencing policies. The demand style is extremely centralised in the decision-making stage, where local governments petition the national government and depend on national governmental decision-making. The implementation of national policies enacted in response to the local demands is often delegated by the national government to local governments.

Although the enactment of policies based on petitions and proposals assumes decision-making by the national government, policy analysis itself is not necessarily centralised. It is essential for local governments to conduct policy analysis of local needs, and judge the appropriateness of policy goals and their feasibility, prior to demanding the national government to enact special programmes or subsidies. In addition, national government officials are limited in their abilities to analyse policy in the real world. The policy analysis conducted by local governments benefits and informs both the national and local governments. Policy analysis by local governments can lead to the improvement of the national government's policies. Local governments want improved quality in policymaking by the national government, given the centralised intergovernmental system. However, policy analysis by local governments sometimes falls short of the national standard by only expressing local demands without national public interest.

The consideration type: from local initiative to national or other local thinking

The consideration type of adaptive-style local governments

The consideration type is the policy analysis conducted by a local or national government, while considering policy formulation, decision-making and implementation by other local governments. The consideration type consists of the diffusion style and the absorption style.

A local government adopting the diffusion style uses policy analysis conducted by other local governments for its policy formulation (Iio, 2013: 40–1). In response to early policy innovation by local governments, policies spread horizontally among local governments. Some policies are copied precisely, but other policies are adopted by imitation, causing adjustment in many cases. The latter is regarded as a consideration type. Local governments adopting the diffusion style do not necessarily copy policies literally.

The absorption style of policy analysis is conducted by the national government. When the national government carries out policy formulation while considering precedents established by local governments, they absorb or 'import' local government policies. In some cases, after the national government formulates and decides upon policies, it vertically directs local governments to implement them. This is very suitable to the centralised intergovernmental system. The leading local governments serve as materials for policy formulation by the national government, though their policies are not always fully adopted.

The consideration type of policy formulation does not always constitute expert policy analysis. It must judge between what should and should not be introduced from existing policies. With the consideration type, governments do not have to formulate initial policies, but they can imitate or modify existing policies and, as a result, keep political and/or administrative costs and risks low. If they attempt to make new policies, they could fail prior to formulating them. In this sense, expert policy analysis is necessary for new policy formulation, but the consideration type asks for only a small proportion of expert support. When considering the logic of appropriateness, governments can justify policies by the trend of the times, stressing that other local governments found them appropriate.

In the diffusion or absorption style, 'leading' local governments provide political or moral support for policy practices to 'following' local governments or the national government. Political and/or administrative costs are low. The consideration type, including both the diffusion style and absorption style, is also supportive in facilitating the emergence of leading local governments. The followers justify the innovators. Leading and following local governments are in a reciprocal relationship: leaders need followers and vice versa.

Policy practices by leading local governments serve as demonstrations of the policies for following local governments and the national government. The practices reduce burdens related to the policy analysis of politics and implementation-oriented policy analysis. They demonstrate that policies can be introduced politically and implemented in actuality.

Of course, a policy that is possible for a local government might not necessarily be possible for other governments. Therefore, policy practices by leading local governments do not reduce the necessity for policy analysis of politics or implementation-oriented policy analysis by followers. Rather, the practices by leaders constitute an important element of those analyses by followers. In addition, it is possible to conduct expert policy analysis of existing policies, including policy evaluation, but it is difficult for the consideration type because it can delay the decision-making.

Positioning among local governments

In the consideration type, a local government analyses its own position among all governments. This is known as positioning-in-population analysis and is an important element in the policy analysis of politics.

For local governments adopting the diffusion style, positioning analysis will determine whether they follow the same track paved by the leaders or go down their own, different track. Generally speaking, those who easily use terms such as 'advanced/leading' and 'following' assume the same track. Because one track is chosen, a competition among governments is organised. In the single-track model, as seen in the theory of modernisation, local governments embrace the value judgement that being 'advanced' is desirable (Rostow, 1960). However, the 'advanced' is not necessarily desirable to each local government.

Given the same track, local governments are divided into: the first-rider and top-runner; the leading and advanced group; the second group; the majority in the middle; the rear; the backward; and the delayed group. It is extremely important for local governments to conduct policy analysis to reveal how the diffusion race is progressing as a whole, where they are now positioned and where they are trying to position themselves. This diffusion race is not only about the chronological relationship concerning when policies are considered, but also about the level of quality of policies. The highest level is referred to as the best way (Taylor, 1911). Policy analysis based on it is called the benchmark or best practice.

Local governments may position themselves in the different quality level of policies and do not consider their policies as copying another's. That is, even if they consider policies, their policies are not the same. As long as they position different policies along the same track, their policy analysis involves analysis of the single-track model. However, differentiations in various degrees emerge in the process of consideration. The following local governments conduct expert policy analysis and policy analysis of politics. This leads to differentiation on the same track. They inject uniqueness by using the advantages of followers. Different tracks may also emerge, with the slogan 'the only one rather than number one' sometimes being heard (Kim, 2009: 21–2).

Some local governments develop their own track or niche rather than following the same track. They do not strive for the 'first-rider' position on the same track. 'The only one' is always the case during stages of originality or leadership. Whether a local government adopting the original style becomes 'the number one' or 'the only one' depends on whether they are followed by other governments or not. Sometimes, positioning analysis is also important, however, in order to formulate policies that are difficult to follow. In other cases, positioning analysis is important for local government to justify based on policy trends not on expert policy analysis.

Power struggles between governments

The policies of advanced foreign countries are considered by the national government through policy analysis by national government officials and research by experts and researchers (Iio, 2013: 339). The national government sometimes considers policies of local governments, too. It collects successful cases of local governments and analyses them, making value judgements regarding the cases as successful or failed, in accordance with the national political preference or professional logic of appropriateness of it. Policies chosen by local governments according to their own policy preference are judged by the national government according to their policy preferences. This judgement creates power struggles between levels of governments.

Local governments are incentivised to advertise their success stories. If the national government certifies these cases, intergovernmental power struggles do not occur. If it does not certify the successful experiences of local governments, the struggles happen. As these are power struggles, it is favourable for local governments to form a policy advocacy coalition (Sabatier and Jenkins-Smith, 1993). In this respect, the diffusions have a political meaning, too. The national government cannot but admit when policies are spread among a majority of local governments. Local governments who want to avoid such diffusions or absorption and keep their unique track can still experience power struggles between governments. In this way, policy analysis of politics between governments sometimes becomes more important than expert analysis of policies.

The adjustment type: central initiative with local reaction

The adjustment type of centripetal local governments

The adjustment type concerns various small policy analyses to implement policies within the policy framework of the national government. This type assumes the division of roles under the centralised and interfused intergovernmental system. The national government formulates and decides policies and local governments implement the policies. The core element of the adjustment type of policy analysis is implementation-oriented policy analysis.

In its strictest sense, expert policy analysis technically reveals the results of proposed policy goals and tools. Practices of implementation by local governments are fields that enable local officials to conduct implementation-oriented policy analysis as routine work. Some local officials may make full use of these opportunities, but, in other cases, they just carry out daily business without policy analysis. The superiority of local officials over experts and researchers outside government or national officials lies in their great accessibility to the real implementation information sources enabling those analyses.

In attempts to collect information, officials of the national government often make demands that local officials submit materials for their policy study. Experts and researchers sometimes invite frowns from local officials by adding to their workload with questionnaires or interviews. Even under the centralised system, local governments can increase their bargaining power by using the national government's dependence on them for implementation (Rhodes, 1988). They can also strategically use their superiority in information resources (Muramatsu, 1988).

A small adjustment within the national policy framework may be a big issue for residents of local communities. Local officials attach importance to policy analysis. Whether policy by the national government proceeds smoothly depends upon the skill and ingenuity voluntarily involved in the implementation stage by local governments. Imperfect policy made by the national government can be re-made to function through adjustment at the local implementation level. The local adjustments make the centralised intergovernmental system work. Without adjustment by local governments, they would be criticised by the people who suffer. To avoid this, they become devoted to the adjustment type of policy analysis. They help national officials whose quality of policy analysis is low. However, in doing this, they deprive national bureaucrats of opportunities to realise the low levels of their policy analysis and to learn analytical skills. This means that in the centralised intergovernmental system, the national government's abilities for policy analysis cannot progress – the stupid central master is supported by smart local butlers.

Policy analysis by centripetal local governments

When the national government formulates and enacts a policy, local officials conduct policy analysis to understand and assimilate the policy. To accomplish this, they need to have policy literacy, high levels of ability to recognise and comprehend circulars, laws or policy manuals issued by the national government, and ability to understand what is spoken at explanatory meetings called by the national government.

However, improving these abilities also has a harmful effect on a locality. Local officials who are too familiar with the national policy automatically implement it without adjustment. They are identified with the policy trends of the national government, but do not pay sufficient attention to policy analysis that is responsive to the needs of local communities; moreover, they can prevent original local policy analysis.

The centripetal local governments have four options after policy analysis. First, those who adjust conduct ex ante and ex post analyses of problems in implementing national policies and ask the national government for improvements. This implementation analysis involves expert policy analysis, implementation–oriented policy analysis and policy analysis of politics. It also leads to the demand style of the voluntary type. Local governments responsible for implementation avoid the policy mess caused by the insufficient policy analysis of the national government. They implicitly support the national government. There are, however, few national officials or experts and researchers who appreciate this local support. They have little ability to recognise their own analytical impotence.

Second, in some cases, local officials do not express their complaints and dissatisfaction even if they analyse problems in implementing national policies. They do not understand why the national government is pursuing such a senseless policy, but they follow it because it was decided by the national government. As a result, dissatisfaction or confusion emerges within local governments or in local communities. However, it is enough to apologise to local residents, saying that it was what the national government decided. In making such an apology or avoiding responsibility, they have to clearly analyse what the national government decided. To justify themselves to residents, some local officials say that the decisions are made not by them, but by the national government. Behind such an attitude is the policy analysis of politics, the analysis of whether an issue can be politically settled more easily by shifting responsibility to the national government.

Third, local officials conduct policy analysis for discretionary policy implementation in accordance with local situations and within the national policy framework. The policy framework is already decided by the national government, but it is rare that local governments have no discretionary competence. Therefore, within their discretionary power, local governments conduct policy analysis in the same style as the original style and demand style. In some cases, the existing national policy framework is not practical. Therefore, local governments deviate from it. However, if local governments deviate openly, the national government could become aware of de facto local policymaking, which could potentially develop into power struggles between governments. Policy analysis by centripetal local governments examines the possibility for covert discretion.

Centripetal local governments implement policies discretionally without being noticed by the national government. Policy analysis is important, and analysis of politics plays an especially major role. There are so many local governments that national bureaucrats cannot supervise them closely. 'The majority of local governments rule' is an important element of the diffusion style (Kaneko, 1997: 252). However, the adjustment type is based on the principle of 'it's all right if not found out'. Local governments cannot publicise their successes or progressiveness, so they concentrate on optimising policies through adjustment without being noticed nationally.

Fourth, if policies presented by the national government sometimes allow local governments to select menus or measures, such as schemes, projects and subsidies, local officials compare them and analyse which ones should be selected. The superiority of local governments over the national government lies in their local multifunctional generality (Kanai, 2007: 12). In negotiations between governments, they choose policies formulated and decided upon by national and sectional ministries and agencies, which compete with each other. In reality, however, it is rare that those national policies constitute 'a shopping list' from which local governments can select policies. Rather, local governments are usually forced to accept sectional and inefficient policies, and face difficulties in implementing them. The adjustment type needs to analyse the problems caused by too many sectional policies and to improve them, and also to address those problems comprehensively in implementation.

Conclusion

Policy analysis of politics and implementation-oriented policy analysis account for a large proportion of policy analysis conducted by local governments. Conversely, expert policy analysis does not play a significant role in the centralised intergovernmental system. This is inevitable. There was an era when local governments were praised because they developed new policies, but this was the product of the centralised regime. New or independent policies do not always mean that they are necessary for local people. Local governments are required to carry out policy formulation and decision-making based on expert policy analysis.

This chapter has revealed that various kinds of policy analysis must be conducted across local governments, not only by the planning division, but also by the sector division. However, local officials who can conduct policy analysis, particularly expert policy analysis, are few in number. Many officials confine themselves to implementation-oriented policy analysis and policy analysis of politics, analysing the application of the laws or schemes made by the national government to enable new policies with the approval of the national government and without incurring its anger.

Faced with a gap between supply and demand, a new policy analysis called a 'corporate type' is emerging (Ueyama, 2010: 199). It industrialises policy analysis, considering the mechanism of the original and demand styles, and the diffusion and absorption styles adopted by local governments. It is an attempt to outsource policy analysis. A policy business would 'sell' policy analysis to local governments. Building on successful results for a local government, it advertises the results and tries to 'sell' its policy to other local governments or the national government. Policy entrepreneurs, not local officials, conduct policy analysis for local governments. Local governments purchase policy analysis. In this case, local governments do not internalise policy analysis. If the corporate type, with its abilities for expert policy analysis, increases, the quality of policy analysis for (not by) local governments might improve to a certain extent.

Profits for policy entrepreneurs include fulfilling political and career ambitions and economic returns (Mabuchi and Kitayama, 2008: 315–16). A policy analysis business can be opened by professional politicians, public officials, consultant firms and think tanks. Even researchers at universities, critics and experts can become policy entrepreneurs. As it involves policy market competition, not everyone can succeed. Local officers who commission policy entrepreneurs might be lacking in literacy of policy analysis by business, being customers lacking in abilities to discriminate between good and bad policy and/or policy analysis. Consequently, policy entrepreneurs need to be understood by politicians. Although they pretend to conduct expert policy analysis, they have to conduct policy analysis of politics for their marketing.

Reference

Iio, J. (2008) *Seikyoku kara Seisaku he* [*From Political Climate to Policy*], NTT Shuppan.

Iio, J. (2013) *Gendai Nihon no Seisaku Taikei* (*Policy System in Contemporary Japan*), Chikuma Shobo.

Isozaki, H., Kanai, T. and Ito, M. (2014) *Horn Book Chihou-Jichi* [*Local Government*] (3rd edn), Hokuju Shuppan.

Kanai, T. (2007) *Jichi Seido* [*Self Government System*], Tokyo University Press.

Kaneko, M. (1997) *Gyousei Hougaku* [*Administrative Law*], Iwanami Shoten.

Kaneko, M. (2012) *Henkakuki no Chihou Jichi Hou* [*Local Government Act in Changing Age*], Iwanami Shoten.

Kawamura, K. (2010) *Shichouson Gappei womeguru Seiji Ishiki to Chihou Senkyo* [*Political Attitudes, Local Elections and Municipal Mergers in Japan*], Bokutakusha.

Kim, J.O. (2009) *Chihou Bunken Jidai no Jichitai Kanryou* [*Policy Performance and Organizational Behaviors of Bureaucrat in Local Government*], Bokutakusha.

Kitami, T. (2010) *Chihou Jichi Gosou Sendan* [*Local Governments as Slow Vessels*], Jigakusha Shuppan.

Kitamura, W. (2013) *Seirei Shitei Toshi* [*Metropolis by Decree*], Chuuou Kouron.

Mabuchi, M. (2009) *Gyousei Gaku* [*Public Administration*], Yuuhikaku.

Mabuchi, M. and Kitayama, T. (eds) (2008) *Seikai Saihenji no Seisaku Katei* [*Policy Process during Political Realignment*], Jigakusha Shuppan.

March, J.G. and Olsen, J.P. (1995) *Democratic Governance*, New York, NY: Free Press.

Morita, A. and Kanai, T. (eds) (2012) *Seisaku Hen'you to Seido Sekkei* [*Policy Change and Institutional Design*], Minerva Shobou.

Muramatsu, M. (1981) *Sengo Nihon no Kanryousei* [*Bureaucracy in Postwar Japan*], Touyou Keizai Shinpousha.

Muramatsu, M. (1988) *Chihou Jichi* [*Local Self-Government*], Tokyo University Press.

Muramatsu, M. and Inatsugu, H. (eds) (2009) *Bunken Kaikaku ha Toshi Gyousei Kikou wo Kaetaka* [*Were Municipal Government Organizations Changed by Decentralization Reform?*], Daiichi Houki.

Omori, W. (2008) *Henka ni Chousen suru Jichitai* [*The Prospects of the Changing Local Government*], Daiichi Houki.

Omori, W. (2011) *Seiken Koutai to Jichi no Chouryuu* [*The Changing Local Government with the Alternation in State Power*], Daiichi Houki.

Rhodes, R.A.W. (1988) *Beyond Westminster and Whitehall*, Routledge.

Rostow, W.W. (1960) *The Stages of Economic Growth: A Non-Communist Manifesto*, Cambridge University Press.

Sabatier, P.A. and Jenkins–Smith, H.C. (eds) (1993) *Policy Change and Learning: An Advocacy Coalition Approach*, Boulder, CO: Westview Press.

Satake, G. (1998) *Taikenteki Kanryou Ron* [*Experienced Bureaucratic Theory*], Yuuhikaku.

Soga, K. (1995) 'Ninon no Aaban Gabanansu' ['Japanese Urban Governance (1)'], *Kokka Gakkai Zasshi*, No. 7/8, pp 1-75.

Taylor, F. (1911) *The Principles of Scientific Management*, New York, NY: Harper & Brothers.

Tsujinaka, Y. and Ito, S. (eds) (2010) *Roukaru Gabanansu* [*Local Governance*], Bokutakusha.

Ueyama, S. (2010) *Osaka Ishin* [*Restoration of Osaka*], Kadokawa.

PART THREE
PARTIES, INTEREST GROUPS AND ADVOCACY-BASED POLICY ANALYSIS

ELEVEN

Policy analysis and policymaking by Japanese political parties

Takahiro Suzuki

Background to the bureaucracy-centred policymaking system in Japan

The bureaucracy has been the primary vehicle for policy analysis and the policymaking process of Japan since the Meiji Restoration. While there have been numerous changes in Japan's domestic political landscape since the Second World War, the end of the 1955 system and other events, there has not been a major change to this policymaking process. While there have been some attempts in the past to alter this bureaucracy-centred mechanism, changes thus far have been very incremental and nothing dramatic.

The following is a list of major characteristics associated with the policymaking process in Japan:

- policy is initiated by the central government/administration;
- the ruling party (or coalition) that forms the cabinet is heavily dependent on the administration;
- the legislative body remains weak as it functions merely as a place to pass bills; and
- public opinion is collected mainly by the bureaucracy, which has not functioned properly in recent times.

With these characteristics in mind, it is important to understand what kind of role political parties play in Japan's policymaking process.

Political parties' limited role in Japan's policymaking process

It is often said that Japan's policymaking process has long been bureaucratised, that is, the bureaucracy has penetrated Japan's policymaking process and consequently led to the decline in the role of the Diet as an independent legislative organ in post-war Japanese politics. Simply put, the bureaucracy mainly collects information on policy, analyses it and makes policy ideas and bills. The ruling party then discusses policy drafts and bills based on the aforementioned policy ideas, often referring to voices and opinions from various people/organisations, such as party members, supporters, voters, supporting groups/organisations and other concerned parties. It then makes bills within the party with strong support from the bureaucracy, based on discussion and adjusting them with the other parties forming the cabinet before submission to the Diet.

As demonstrated by the aforementioned process, the bureaucracy remains a dominant force in Japan's policymaking process as it is the main vehicle for conducting preliminary policy analysis and then creating policy drafts thereafter. This is not to say that the bureaucracy alone makes policies; the bureaucracy does work with a number of other actors, such as politicians, party staff members and other policy experts, but it is clear that the bureaucracy takes a clear lead and plays a dominant role in drafting bills from start to finish.

On some rare occasions, some Diet members themselves create policy drafts and bills by initiating discussions in their respective party policy committees and task forces. They then conduct their analysis and research by gathering information from specialists in the concerned fields, business circles and other concerned entities, with these analyses being fed into further internal party discussions, ultimately leading to party-generated policy drafts and bills. Non-ruling parties often receive little or no support from the bureaucracy, so if Diet members from the non-ruling party want to go out of their way to draft a bill, then this is often the way for them to do so.

Generally speaking, there are two major ways to make a law in Japan. One is legislation introduced by the government. The other is legislation introduced by Diet members. The former is conducted through coordination between the bureaucracy and ruling parties, and accounts for the majority of legislation in post-war Japan. The latter method of politician-led legislation does not happen very often as the current policymaking system does not incentivise politicians to take a lead and independently draft bills.

As a result, the following could be said about the bureaucratisation of Japan's policymaking process:

- The bureaucracy is the dominant vehicle in conducting policy analysis and then drafting bills/policies.
- Political parties play a very small role in Japan's policymaking process (the Japan Communist Party [JCP] is a major exception to this norm but will not be discussed in depth because the JCP is not a mainstream political party and has never been part of the ruling coalition to date).
- On those rare occasions that political parties (of the ruling coalition) take a lead in drafting bills, it has only been to make some minor modifications to existing policies/bills, not necessarily to draft bills from scratch.
- The bulk of the information/specialists necessary for policy analysis/policymaking exists within the bureaucracy, further reducing incentives for Diet members to self-initiate the policymaking process on their own.

With this background in mind, I would like to zoom in on the real roles that political parties play in Japan's policymaking process, with case studies of bills drafted by the Liberal Democratic Party (LDP) and the Democratic Party of Japan (DPJ). As the following cases will illustrate, the LDP has long executed a policymaking process that has relied extensively on the bureaucracy, a model they later attempted to tweak with some minor adjustments along the way. The DPJ, after defeating the LDP, attempted to reform this bureaucratised policymaking process but their attempts failed and did not culminate in a more independent law-making process.

The Liberal Democratic Party: extensive reliance on the bureaucracy with incremental changes

The LDP has been known to rely extensively on the bureaucracy-led policymaking process since the establishment of the 1955 system. This bureaucratised policy-drafting process has continued to function effectively at least throughout the 1955 system, but the shortcomings of the system incrementally led to malfunctions and fatigue in the process, thereby leading to some minor efforts to revise the system incrementally (but did not lead to a fundamental overhaul of the system).

The Liberal Democratic Party as the ruling party

The policymaking process within the LDP before the change of government in 2009 is shown in Figure 11.1. The current process after the LDP regained its ruling party status in 2012 is almost identical to that in Figure 11.1.

Figure 11.1: Flow in policymaking/bill-making

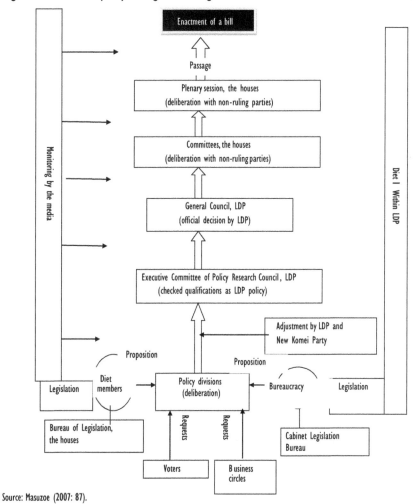

Source: Masuzoe (2007: 87).

The general flow of how bills are drafted by the LDP is outlined as follows.

Legislation introduced by the government

The process consists of the following three steps: (1) discussions within the Policy Division (PD) of the Policy Research Council (PRC) of the LDP; (2) further discussions with ruling coalition partners to make any modifications to the proposed policy drafts; and (3) a final decision in the LDP General Council (which is a complicated and lengthy process on its own).

The discussions in the PD are held as follows. When bureaucrats intend to make a new bill or modify a law, they solicit opinions from senior members in a PD related to the bill. If they receive positive feedback without any major issues, they then proceed to draft a preliminary version of the bill, which then gets reviewed by the Cabinet Legislation Bureau. They then put the draft bill to discussion within the PD, where Diet members with relevant political appointments (eg a minister in the relevant field) are required to attend a meeting in which they will be asked to give all the necessary input and feedback until it is ready for approval. In these discussions at the PD, the bureaucrats often provide the bulk of the policy information as they 'explain' to the involved Diet members everything there is to the policy draft.

As this shows, bureaucrats play a dominant role in facilitating policy-related discussions and drafting bills within the LDP, especially when it is the ruling party. As a result, the PRC and its PD function as 'a portal site of government ministries'.[1] On some occasions, the PD may attempt to conduct its own policy discussions, but it rarely conducts its own data collection or policy analysis without any help from the bureaucracy.

After obtaining the necessary approval from the executive committee consisting of the top members of the PRC, the draft bill must then obtain final approval from the General Council, an entity within the LDP that has the ultimate say in overall LDP management, before it is submitted as an LDP bill in the Diet. Once the bill is submitted to the Diet, LDP members are technically obligated to vote for the bill according to the official stance of the LDP (eg LDP Diet members are not technically allowed to vote against an LDP bill that the LDP officially endorses).

This process has a set of problems, which has been criticised extensively by the DPJ and other opposition parties in the past. First, there is the issue of advanced screening by the LDP before Diet deliberations. Second is the problem of a dual policymaking system, that is, as the ruling party and as the government/cabinet, which has caused a number of issues and confusion in the past. It is fair to say that the bureaucracy has manipulated some of these flaws in the policymaking process so as to maintain its dominance and power in controlling the policy-drafting process.

Independent legislation

This legislation is applied to bills that cannot be dealt with by bureaucrats or initiatives that should be undertaken by politicians in bill formulation. In this legislation, Diet members must conduct their research and examination by themselves and/or obtain ideas and cooperation from specialists and so on with the help of their staff members and party staff members.

However, as the ruling party receives support from bureaucrats, the party tends to depend on legislation introduced by the government. Even legislation introduced by Diet members is often conducted and/or assisted by bureaucrats as bill draft writers, supporters and so on.

The Liberal Democratic Party's past experience as a non-ruling party and the present

In 2009, the LDP underwent the worst defeat for a ruling party in contemporary Japanese history and thereby became a non-ruling party, consequently affecting the bureaucracy-led policymaking process and the role of the PRC in drafting bills. This meant that the bureaucracy no longer supported the LDP in drafting policies and bills, with a few exceptions, and the bureaucrats were now only legally obligated to 'explain' policies and bills in a PD. That is to say, the LDP and its Diet members then had to collect policy information, conduct research and draft bills virtually on their own and by soliciting outside help networks outside of the bureaucracy. In these cases, expenditures included only lecturer compensation and transportation expenses, limited budgets for making new data and policy information collection, and funds for the frequently conducted public opinion polls for elections.[2]

Let us examine this policymaking process here with a focus on a case that I was directly involved in, 'The Growth Strategy (Japan Phoenix Strategy) ... The Three Years of Decision and Execution to Materialize the Strategy' (Interim Report, 14 May 2010, in Japanese). This report was the result of the activities of the Special Policy Division for Growth Strategy of the PRC from January to May 2010, which was led by the head of the PD, his personal staff and party staff members, with cooperation from external staff members, in order to collect information independently, organise 40 interviews with external specialists and draft a comprehensive report thereafter.

The PD leader simultaneously collected policy recommendations from the main members of the division, and adjusted the draft with those recommendations accordingly. He further adjusted the draft by soliciting views from chairs of relevant policy divisions and obtaining their consent in finalising the draft. In that process, he also gathered more comments from bureaucrats, journalists and specialists in his own individual network to improve the draft.

Unfortunately, supporting staff members could only focus on general information collection efforts and could not conduct their own surveys or other modes of original data collection due to limited time and funding. The LDP was able to manage the financing of the hiring of the aforementioned external staff members, but this was actually an exceptional, rare case.

As this case illustrates, in the past, the LDP heavily depended on the bureaucracy for policy analysis and policymaking when it was the ruling party, and conducted its own policy analysis and policy research only on a very limited scale when it was a non-ruling party. Other than public polling surveys for elections and party public relations (PR), the LDP rarely conducts any of its own policy information collection activities or large-scale policy research. Additionally, non-ruling parties and their affiliates often resort to working with the Research Bureau of the House of Representatives, the Investigation Section of the House of Councillors and the Research and Legislative Reference Bureau of the National Diet Library because the bureaucracy is not legally obligated to serve anyone besides the ruling party and its affiliates.

The LDP regained control of the government as the result of the election in December 2012. This meant that the LDP could once again return to the old-fashioned means of depending on the bureaucracy in policy analysis and policymaking. However, the LDP began experimenting with new means of policymaking (as illustrated in more detail later), though the traditional means of the bureaucracy-dependent policymaking process continued as the mainstream.

Such experimentation was especially prominent in the May 2013 recommendation report, 'LDP's Economic Revitalisation for Japan' (Interim Report, 10 May 2013, in Japanese), which was undertaken by the Headquarters for Japan's Economic Revitalisation.

Let us trace the concrete process of making the report. There were two main points in the process, as follows:

1. Discussion and adjustment within the LDP and with the government.
   - Discussion in the headquarters.
   - Discussion and recommendations by Working Groups of Diet members, which were established to work on the interim report:
     - The Working Groups mainly consisted of young Diet members who were elected once or twice. These groups held their own discussions and submitted their own recommendations.
     - Eight Working Groups such as Macro Economy, Fiscal and Monetary Policies, and Regional Economic Revitalization were established.
   - Collecting opinions and increasing participation from local municipalities:
     - Making special recommendations for the revitalisation of the local economy, which Prime Minister Abe instructed the headquarters to make.
     - Launch Headquarters of Local Economic Revitalization, the chiefs of which are the chairs of the PRC of each federation of prefecture/metropolitan LDP branch.
     - Each headquarters made recommendations on economic revitalisation for each related area.
2. Utilisation of external staff members.
   - Twenty-seven interviews with outside specialists.
   - Academics were involved in supporting Diet members in drafting the report and policy recommendations.

This example shows that the LDP is now experimenting in its policymaking process by utilising outside personnel and collecting information/views from local municipalities.

Japan has long depended heavily on the bureaucracy for policy analysis and policymaking, which has resulted in long-term deadlock. In order to break free from such a deadlock, Japan is in dire need of new policymaking means, as illustrated earlier. The LDP's new experimentation with policymaking certainly deserves further consideration and scrutiny so that it can be expanded into a more systematic, regularised commitment in the future (eg regularised use of outside experts and personnel).

Liberal Democratic Party staff members

Additionally, the importance of party staff members has been heightened as the role of Diet members and political parties has also increased in policy analysis and policymaking in recent years. The LDP has about 30 policy staff members in the PRC and the PB in the House of Councilors, regardless of whether or not it is the ruling party.

Their main tasks are organising meetings of policy divisions and making contacts for the meetings. They draft meeting agendas, conduct previous arrangements for interviews and arrange for bill screenings with bureaucrats. During electoral cycles, they draft party platforms as well as make adjustments with concerned party divisions and ministries. The staff members of the PB support Diet members by drafting their speeches and questions for Diet sessions.

When the LDP is the ruling party, party staff members are able to maintain very close relations with the bureaucracy. However, they, too, need their own network for policy analysis and policymaking because they cannot depend on the bureaucracy when they are a non-ruling party. Personnel administrative rotation takes place once every few years among party staff members. Senior staff members may from time to time be able to influence the policymaking process due to their expertise and strong ties with influential Diet members.

Democratic Party of Japan: the rise and fall of their attempts to change the bureaucracy-centred system

This part explains some attempts by the DPJ to change the traditional policymaking process that has long been utilised by the LDP in the post-Second Word War era. The bureaucracy-centred policymaking process has failed to take into account many changes in domestic politics, as well as international relations, consequently leading to malfunctions and policy fatigue in recent times. As such, the DPJ tried to change the policymaking process when it was able to become the ruling party. However, the DPJ was unable to make fundamental changes to the traditional policymaking process, though it was able to make some minor changes and adjustments along the way.

Democratic Party of Japan as a non-ruling party

When the DPJ was a non-ruling party before September 2009, its Diet members, especially Diet members such as ex-bureaucrats who have experience in policymaking, generally made policy ideas and bills with party staff members and outside specialists. These specialists included not only people who helped the LDP make policy ideas, but also affiliates from the non-profit sector and labour unions.

Since its establishment, the DPJ has always held a keen sense of awareness regarding political reforms, but also on issues related to governance. These reforms included: making manifestos since the general elections in 2003; collecting opinions from non-profit organisations (NPOs)/non-governmental organisations (NGOs), other relevant organisations, local assemblymen and labour unions; and conducting their own research and discussions on how to manage the cabinet. This meant that the DPJ sought different approaches from the LDP in managing the cabinet and policymaking.

The DPJ tried to realise its reform ideas by introducing the state strategy office, the Government Revitalization Unit and the Big Three of each ministry: the ministry minister, the ministry vice minister and the parliamentary secretary.[3]

During the period as the ruling party and afterward

The DPJ had long advocated for a 'break from bureaucratic control' and for 'politician-led decision-making' and severely criticised the LDP's duality in policymaking between the ruling party and its cabinet before gaining political power in 2009. The DPJ tried to change this situation by abolishing its PRC so that the cabinet alone could initiate policy ideas and bills.

The office of the Secretary-General collected petitions and requests from people, local municipalities and various groups through Diet members and Federations of Prefecture/Metropolitan Party Branches, sorted and prioritised them, and made requests of the DPJ to be conveyed to the cabinet. These measures meant that the DPJ was attempting to depart from the old means of policy analysis, policy discussion and policymaking that traditionally relied on the bureaucracy.

On the other hand, Diet members who could not join the cabinet lost a place where they could discuss policy ideas within the DPJ. Instead, bills and policies examined by the government were explained to them in Policy Councils, the host of which was a vice minister of each ministry. The Policy Councils were places where the government only explained things to Diet members. They could ask questions, exchange opinions and make demands and recommendations there, though only the government could judge or decide whether they would be accepted. A policy research meeting for each policy division was held every week. The results of the meetings were conveyed to the Big Three through its director.

These changes made it difficult for policy discussion to easily result in party policy, unlike in the past, when the DPJ was very active in their own policy discussions. Diet members who could not join the government became highly frustrated and eventually called for the revival of the PRC. The PRC was revived in June 2010, but did not return to being an active and substantial venue for policy discussion, as before. Instead, there were various activities from various project teams within the DPJ. However, the PRC failed to function in making its party policies based on the unity of opinions and discussions.

Ironically, the DPJ fell into the situation where it had no system and personnel to conduct policy analysis and discussion within the party after regime change. It 'forced them out' to the government. Consequently, policy analysis, policy discussion and policymaking were only conducted by the government.

From the preceding meaning, we should consider the various attempts of the DPJ government as those of 'forcing them out' when we think about policy analysis and policymaking by the DPJ. The DPJ made the following attempts after gaining political power:

• To unify the duality in decision-making between the cabinet and the ruling party, the Big Three formed government policy, adjusting policy among concerned ministries through their executive meeting. Other attempts included closing down the PRC, holding Policy Councils, unifying the collection of requests through the office of the Secretary-General of the DPJ, and the abolishing prior screening bills.

- Abolishing the Conference of Administrative Vice-Ministers and initiating cabinet committees. The cabinet committees could not be a place for concerned ministers to have real discussions and were only a place for the final decision because the ministers were all, and always, busy. Policy adjustments were made over ministry-crossing issues in meetings of vice-ministers, which were not open to the public. As each vice minister bore interests in his own ministry, the function of policy adjustments was not conducted successfully there.
- The elimination of division into ministries and the establishment of the State Strategy Office[4] in order to realise the strong leadership of the prime minister and his staff members in the prime minister's office.
- The establishment of the Government Revitalisation Unit, which implemented a review programme to eliminate wasteful spending in ministries and agencies and to re-evaluate the national budget. The programme sought to maintain the transparency of government agencies, investigate public spending and sources of revenue, determine whether certain agencies or ministries were still necessary, and expose future issues concerning domestic policy, administrative systems, governmental organisations and so on.

Almost all of these attempts were introduced as new systems. They did not function as well as expected and regressed later on. Some of the attempts were successfully executed, while others failed and returned to the old ways. Some simply did not function as expected.

Some new attempts as case studies

After gaining political power, the DPJ undertook new attempts in policy analysis and policymaking that were different from the traditional methods employed by the LDP. Let me explain some of them here as concrete cases.

The New Public

The DPJ tried to realise the concept of the 'New Public' in policymaking, as noted in the following:

> The administration undertook important roles in the socioeconomic system in the twentieth century. However, as the economy and society matured, values among individuals became increasingly diversified, and as a result, their needs or social needs were not met by public activities of the administration, of which decision-making was done, based on unified and centralized judgment.... We have to change the public activities monopolized by the administration into those cooperatively conducted by citizens, businesses and the administration. This is the idea of 'New Public'.
>
> Present systems such as laws and the budget system have been made within the existing old framework. People who undertake roles in 'New Public' couldn't undertake important and active roles in those old ones. We, the DPJ will discuss how to make new systems and policies with those people in order to make rules to create 'New Public' and rules on the roles of such people.[5]

The Roundtable Committee on the 'New Public' and the 'New Public' Promotion Committee were established to materialise the concept. To strengthen the civic sector, the Roundtable Committee meetings were held:

> in order to consider concrete directions on citizens' public benefit tax systems such as donation tax systems and 'a system of nonprofit organizations operated by investments from citizens' as future issues and to sort through the merits and future issues related with those items. (Policy Research Council of Citizens, 2009: 8)

The Promotion Committee was held to make policy recommendations, such as the introduction of tax credits, a review of the public support test on authorising NPOs and a call for the introduction of a provisional authorisation system for NPOs, and to discuss various issues to strengthen the sector. Some of them were materialised.

These committees consisted of cabinet members such as the prime minister, deputy prime minster, chief secretary-general, the minister on 'New Public', executive members of the PRC of the DPJ and civic committee members. The Promotion Committee includes 'more committee members from NPOs/NGOs, NPO banks and consumer cooperatives than the Roundtable Committee' (Policy Research Council of Citizens, 2009: 9).

We can see a start of the idea of the 'New Public' and its activities in the making of the manifestos of the DPJ before gaining political power. For example:

> In 2003, the DPJ collected policy demands from its local assemblymen and local organizations, from intellectuals and NPOs, and from economic organizations and labor unions, and exchanged opinions with them. The DPJ made its manifesto based on their demands and opinions. The DPJ thought in its strategy that it would commission a research company and an advertising agency to inform people of the manifesto. (Yakushiji, 2012: 185)

Changes of policy for persons with disabilities

The enactment of the Act for Supporting the Independence of Persons with Disabilities had increased the burden of their use of vocational facilities and extinguished many chances or places for them to act or make a life. Against this situation, 'the new legal system was made in order to include socially persons with disabilities and create places for them to act' (Yamaguchi, 2012: 121).

The Headquarters for the Promotion of Reform on the System for Persons with Disabilities (chaired by the prime minister) was the centre to discuss the policy. The Subcommittee on General Welfare was established under the Headquarters. Many activists from various organisations for persons with physical and/or mental disabilities took part in the Subcommittee under the basic principles of the sovereignty of the persons concerned and sent new ideas to the public, considered new bills and discussed related policies and their revision or reform.

Deliberative poll

The DPJ and its government introduced a new method of deliberative poll (DP) to draft a basic policy on nuclear power plants and energy in the summer of 2012. DP is a public opinion poll method to investigate changes in opinions through discussions on politically divisive issues, and the DPJ changed its nuclear power plant policy based on its results. The introduction of DP illustrated the DPJ's willingness to engage in an alternative policy-analysis process by paying more heed to public opinion, which has always been a significant component of the DPJ's founding principles.

On the other hand, there were many policies that the DPJ failed to execute. These include issues related to environmental taxes, global warming, pension systems, US military bases in Okinawa, the cancellation of dam constructions and the DPJ manifesto.

When we compare these issues and activities, we can reach the following conclusions. The DPJ could, to some degree, succeed in dealing with issues for which concerned parties were limited and on policies that it had previous experience when it was a non-ruling party. Furthermore, the DPJ was eager to involve new actors, such as NPOs/NGOs, labour unions and persons with disabilities, who were traditionally not mainstream actors in LDP-dominated policy discourse, and, to some limited degree, they were successful in producing new policies.

However, when the DPJ was forced to confront politically divisive issues with complicated interests or when it faced powerful resistance from major political establishments, it had no mechanism in effectively responding to such situations and consequently could not make any effective counter-strategy. This meant that, in some cases, the DPJ succeeded in changing the framework and ways of policy analysis and policymaking, but it failed as a whole to manage the government as it had not had enough preparation and experience to realise its plans and ideas given the reality of politics and policymaking. The party returned to being the opposition in December 2012. It is still unclear at the present moment as to what kind of policymaking system the party will have from now on.

Policy staff members in the Democratic Party of Japan

The DPJ had about 20 staff members in its PRC when it was a non-ruling party. These staff members were people with various backgrounds, such as working in the private sector and other political parties, and also with policy expertise. As, in the past, the DPJ could not depend on the bureaucracy for policy analysis and policymaking, it made alternative policies and bills by: making use of these staff members; collecting ideas and information from outside intellectuals; criticising government bills; and presenting its opinions to the public.

These staff members organised daily meetings of the PRC, and their main function was to conduct interviews with bureaucrats on the proposed policies of the government or bills that were submitted to the Diet in order to present doubts and questions to the cabinet. However, after the DPJ became the ruling party, the PRC was abolished (though it was eventually revived). Its staff members then joined the government. After returning to being the opposition party again, it seems that DPJ policy staffs also returned to their former roles.

Comparison between the Liberal Democratic Party and the Democratic Party of Japan in policy analysis and policymaking: different points

Table 11.1 summarises the aforementioned points about the LDP and the DPJ as the ruling party.

Table 11.1: Comparison between the LDP and the DPJ

Party items	LDP	DPJ
Dependence on bureaucracy	Heavy	Try to make less heavy
Main actors	Bureaucrats, specialists, important people in the business world, etc	Bureaucrats, specialists, important people in the business world, NPOs NGOs, labour unions, persons concerned, etc
Systems	Bureaucracy-centred DM Duality in DM between party and cabinet	Politician-led DM Unifying in DM, the Big Three, abolishing the PRC and conference of vice-ministers, State Strategic Office, Government Revitalization Unit, etc
Notes	Even the LDP understands the present situation with trials for some changes in policymaking, though it does not seem to have an intention to make big changes	The DPJ had an intention and made some attempts to make big changes in policymaking. However, it could not make a new policymaking system to take over from the bureaucracy-led policymaking system

Note: DM = decision-making.

Some other countries: more activities and systems in policy analysis and policymaking

Here, I would like to note some examples from other countries in order to compare and contrast with policymaking processes in Japan. In the US, political parties are only an association of state-level party organisations that select a party presidential candidate, and they have weak capabilities in conducting policy research/analysis.

On the other hand, there are many systems, organisations and staff members with varying capacity to conduct policy research/analysis in/around the Federal Congress, the Executive Office of the President and in the non-profit/private sectors. This means that there is pluralistic and multi-tiered policy research/analysis in society as a whole, and its significance permeates various layers of society. It is also very popular for political parties, congressmen and candidates to use political marketing in political activities.

In the UK, party manifestos are formed in a lengthy and time-consuming process, such as internal party discussions with supporting organisations, and the process is dominated by political parties: 'Major politicians of a party and theorists with a relationship with the party take part in the process, and will have and feel responsibilities through the process' (Yamaguchi, 2012: 140). The parties make use of the results in policymaking by understanding the will of the people/voters through political marketing and other measures: 'From about 110 to 120 Parliament members such as floor leaders control the bureaucracy by holding cabinet positions, although it loyally serves the cabinet and achieves the realization of the policies of the ruling party' (NDL et al, 2002: 1).

There are sometimes differences in opinion between the cabinet and rank-and-file members of the ruling party in implementing policies that are not in the manifesto, or in how and when to start executing new policies. The floor leaders and parliamentary private secretaries who undertake a liaison role to communicate with rank-and-file members then persuade members to oppose the bill. The role of floor leaders and so on as coordinators is very important in monitoring activities and discussions in plenary sessions, parliamentary committees and various meetings within the ruling party, and in trying to understand the public will and conveying the demands/requests of rank-and-file members to the cabinet and executives of the ruling party (NDL et al, 2002: 1).

In Germany, policies of political parties are often presented to the public as a basic platform, an election programme or a manifesto. The parties establish a platform committee to draft the platform. Many experts in various fields from inside and outside the party are gathered to join in the process of making the draft. There are various examinations and considerations at each level of the party as the party engages in varying policy discourse.

Political parties are organised similarly in Japan and South Korea. Let me describe the drafting of the 2008 manifesto of the Grand National Party in order to understand the policy analysis and policymaking of political parties in South Korea.

The process started after the primary election to select the presidential candidate of the party, which ended on 20 August 2008. First, it put out the main public promises of each policy field that the candidate addressed during the primary election period, which was then drafted into a more concrete shape as the manifesto of the party in mid-September 2008.

The official headquarters for the presidential election campaign was set up, together with the Committee on Visions as a First-class Nation within it. The Committee drafted the manifesto, holding 15 subcommittees on public promises for each policy area, with 15 subcommittee chairs and 400 experts.

After that, Lee Myung-bak (the candidate) and the Policy Board of the party joined the Committee in adjusting and modifying the manifesto draft. The modified draft was announced to the public and was further modified and adjusted based on opinions from the public. On 7 December, the official manifesto was announced and was released to the public. After Lee was elected president, his government took over the manifesto with some modifications and proceeded to the implementation process.

As the preceding shows, it is clear that some other countries have more activities and formalised systems in policy analysis and policymaking within/around political parties than in the Japanese case.

Think tanks affiliated with political parties: some attempts in Japan and cases from other countries

General background

Among movements to change the bureaucracy-centred policymaking process, there were also past attempts to establish think tanks affiliated with political parties that could conduct their own policy research/analysis and collect policy information independent from the bureaucracy. This resulted in Public Policy Platform (Platon), established in 2005 by the DPJ, and Think Tank 2005, Japan (TT2005), established in 2006 by the LDP, which I was directly involved in as regards their establishment and management.

Both parties had various types of internal or external policy-related organisations or divisions. For example, the LDP has its Forward Policy Study Unit as a party organisation, of which its main functions are educating people loaned from private companies and allowing them to collect policy information (the unit continues to exist to this day).

There were some research institutions related to the DPJ, such as the Policy Research Council of Citizens (*Shimin-ga-tsukuru-seisakuchosakai*)[6] and Think Net 21, which the DPJ subsidised through grants for research activities, but their research was not always utilised by the party. The Japan Communist Party has the Social Science Institute (*Shakaikagaku-kenkyujo*) as a subsidiary think tank, but the products of the Institute's research, such as lectures and papers made by its in-house researchers, remain unclear to outsiders. A policy group of the Socialist Party of Japan (currently called the Social Democratic Party) also held its own think tank, called the Contemporary Research Group (*Genzai Sogo Kenkyu Shudan*), which specialised in issues related to structural reform.

Case studies

Let me examine TT2005 and Platon as recent examples of political party think tanks in Japan.

Think Tank 2005, Japan

Established in 2006 under the supervision of the LDP, TT2005 was eventually dissolved in February 2011 as the organisation was fraught with numerous problems from the start. Having said that, many people saw the necessity for alternative sources of policy information for the LDP and TT2005 was certainly able to make some concrete achievements, as outlined in the following.

Support for the 'Rising-tide Policy'

The research project 'Economic Policy toward 3% Growth in the Japanese Economy' of TT2005 contributed to the policy analysis and policymaking of the LDP by providing the policy information that was the base of the 'Rising-tide Policy' in 2006, which was the major policy of the party and the government, and counteracting resistance from the bureaucracy towards the policy. As a result, TT2005 helped the LDP realise politician-led policymaking.

In Japan, policy information has almost always been monopolised by the bureaucracy, and there has been a limited amount of accurate information on economic policy from non-bureaucratic sources. However, in this case, the bureaucracy could not protest and the LDP and politicians could persuade them because information from the project proved to be accurate.

There is no precedent in the policymaking history of Japan like this case, in which a political party made its own policy by independently conducting data analysis or policy analysis through the use of simulation modelling.

Efforts of policy marketing

The electoral system known as the single-seat constituency electoral system has become increasingly important in politics and in changes of a political party in power. On the other hand, the importance of politics and politicians has increased in policymaking. As a result, bureaucracy-centred information collection from business circles and understanding public will and opinions through Diet members selected by a medium electoral district system have not functioned well in making policies and conveying policies to people.

For these reasons, politicians and political parties have come to require the development of a new method to understand the will and opinions of the people/voters. Recently, some political parties have often conducted public opinion polls, though this is insufficient. Methods and systems such as political/policy marketing are required to carefully understand the people's will in each constituency, to continue to collect/analyse information on the people's will and to make policies and election plans based on them. Given this understanding, TT2005 conducted some policy-marketing projects, such as 'Project Hashikawa Family' and 'Election Navigation 100 for Victory', to analyse policies in electoral districts not from the perspectives of politicians, but from those of the voters/people. These results were not fully made use of by many Diet members and the LDP because the results were new and unique, though interesting and useful, but were used by some Diet members for election campaigns.

Although TT2005 conducted new attempts using new methods and obtained some results, after the LDP lost control of the government and had financial difficulties, TT2005 was dissolved in February 2011.

Public Policy Platform

The main activities of Platon were as fololows. Brown Bag Lunch (BBL) types of discussion sessions were held a few times each month, and research projects and support in making the manifestos of the DPJ and local area manifestos were conducted under the concept of community-based-solutions. Platon aimed at: being a place of assemblage for bold and ambitious people, such as academics, private people and bureaucrats as individuals; brushing up the political ideas and philosophy of the DPJ; strengthening the foundation for making policies; and gathering policies of good quality. Platon also tried to: make policy recommendations flexibly under a local area/field-centred model to counter the centralised policymaking system led by the bureaucracy; accumulate intellectual knowledge; and have first-rated people participate in network-type research projects for full-scale, total reform.

Its operating policy is to conduct policy research projects and policy recommendations in policy areas using the project-based method. Academics specialised in policy fields, opinion leaders and practitioner experts tried to make basic policies for the DPJ with its Diet members.

However, after the executives of the DPJ changed and the preparations for the election in which the party expected to gain political power became increasingly important, Platon lapsed into a dormant state, and it was not fully made use of even after the party came to power.

Problems and issues

There were some new attempts and approaches in conducting policy research/ analysis/discussion and building human networking for political parties in TT2005 and Platon. However, both institutes did not function as well as expected. The problems and issues are explained as follows:

- The relationship between a political party and its think tank is unstable because its executives often change after short periods.
- A political party tends to put more priority on the next election than policy research. This means that more financial weight is focused on coming elections, with other expenses being controlled.
- The previous point means that budgets for policy research projects are limited.
- The very limited budget covers very few human resources and activities.
- There were big gaps between the ideal and reality of other policy resources to be materialised against the bureaucracy.
- There were large gaps between research projects, which need some time to obtain results, and the political situation, which changes rapidly and dramatically.
- Diet members and political parties tend to value short-sighted results and effects.
- Diet members and political parties lack or do not have literacy on research in order to use policy research results for policymaking.
- There are some difficulties in using specialists as staff members for Diet members and political parties.
- There are some difficulties and conflicts in the division of labour among Diet members, their staff members, party staff members and so on.
- There are various opinions among Diet members even in the same political party.
- There are many limitations on the schedules and time of Diet members.

Some other countries

In the US, there are various types of think tanks, some of which, such as the Heritage Foundation, are closely related to political parties, though there are no formal think tanks within US political parties. These institutions contribute a great deal to policy analysis in the US.

In the UK, influential parliamentarians often have systems like political think tanks that help them in policy research/analysis and provide them with policy staff members.

In Germany, political foundations contribute to the manifesto-drafting process of political parties, often in the form of providing results from their policy research projects. Political foundations are unique to Germany and are organisations that conduct policy research and political activities based on the political ideals of a party close to each foundation. They are supported through tax subsidies.

In South Korea, political parties have their own think tanks that influence internal policymaking within parties. The revision of the Political Party Law and the Political Fund Law in 2004 imposed legal obligations for political parties to use 30% of government subsidies for the establishment, operation and project expenses of their think tanks.

Although these think tanks conduct research projects that are mainly short-term in nature, many of their 50–60 researchers hold advanced degrees such as a master's or PhD and are engaged in numerous policy-related activities that facilitate political parties to conduct their own policy analyses.

There are many policy research institutes and think tanks in the government, business and private sectors, some of which are large and proactive. As a result, they have significant policy influence over such institutions as ministries and presidential executive offices.

As these examples illustrate, in many countries, there are far more systematic institutions and staff members who are tasked with conducting their own policy analyses as a way to support the policymaking process of politicians and political parties than in Japan.

Conclusion and recommendations: need for systematic changes in Japan's policymaking processes

As this chapter shows, Diet members and political parties (especially the ruling party) in Japan have historically depended on the bureaucracy under the bureaucracy-centred policymaking system in the post-Second World War era. On the other hand, such a policymaking system, with an orientation on sectionalism and heavy reliance on precedent, has made it difficult for Japan to cope with drastic changes in both domestic and international contexts, exacerbating many of the underlying problems and complicating fundamental issues even further. Under such a context, some Diet members and political parties have tried to reform the bureaucratised policymaking process as a way to rectify the situation. Unfortunately, their attempts were limited in scope and did not materialise in fundamental reforms.

Alongside changes being made to the legislative and administrative branches, I therefore argue that political parties, not just the policymaking process, also need to be reformed. My recommendations for reforming Japanese political parties are outlined in the following.

Functions of marketing and communication

Japanese political parties have traditionally obtained their party members and voters and built their business networks by relying on the individual efforts of Diet members, rather than through a systematic effort by the party as a whole. As such, voter opinions and business preferences were often relayed to the political parties through individual

Diet members, which meant that political parties were unable to collect their own policy-relevant information or communicate effectively with their constituents on a systematic basis. Such an approach may have been useful at the time of the medium electoral district system, which was a system before the present single-seat constituency electoral system had been introduced, and in eras of relatively slow social change, but they have proved ineffective during times of rapid social change and single electoral systems. Additionally, the traditional means of the bureaucratised policymaking process that rely heavily on the bureaucracy–business alliance simply cannot cope effectively with rapidly changing public and social needs.

It has been increasingly difficult to understand the present situation as we are now witnessing highly individualised viewpoints as Japanese society becomes more pluralised, with varying opinions and trends becoming far more diverse than ever before depending on the sector, business or the region. In such a context, political parties must develop more systematic means to communicate with their constituents and promote their policies. Such new policy marketing and communication strategies will also help political parties to gather their own policy information as a means to counter the bureaucracy.

Functions of policy research/analysis

Ruling parties in Japan have historically produced policies by heavily relying on the bureaucracy. However, political parties must conduct their own policy research and/or policy analysis if they are to produce their own, independent policies in times of rapid social change and changing public needs. The time has come for political parties to have their own organisational units and personnel to conduct policy analyses that are independent of the bureaucracy. In order for such modifications to take place, Japan must make significant institutional and legal changes (and other incentives) so that political parties will be able to establish new organisations that can effectively utilise alternative information resources and policy intellectuals that come from outside the traditional bureaucratic policy networks. Independent policy research/analysis will prove to be a strong tool for Diet members and political parties to effectively counteract the highly bureaucratised policymaking process.

Functions of sharing and accumulating information within the party

Additionally, political parties will also need to have better internal functions of sharing, collecting and accumulating information within the organisation so as to maintain effective and independent policymaking mechanisms. At present, in political parties where Diet members occupy all of the important roles, information is often used to strengthen the influence of Diet members, rather than for general organisational purposes. As such, political parties must invent new functions/systems of sharing and accumulating information internally so that Diet members cannot hoard information on their own for personal gain, and so that their information can be shared for the greater good of the party as a whole. Such a system would make political parties more powerful in their policymaking function since it can contribute to strengthening the capabilities of their policy analysis and policy research in the long run.

It has become painfully clear in recent years that the current policymaking system that has been dominated by the bureaucracy is not sustainable and requires fundamental change. As such, there is now a stronger need for new political parties with new functions and institutions if Japanese politicians are to materialise their long-held goal of a politician–centred policymaking system and depart from traditional bureaucratised policy analyses. It is becoming more important to create a new political party based on new ways and functions, such as outlined earlier; otherwise, there will be no new development in Japanese politics that can materialise a politician–centred policymaking system.

Notes

[1] As stated by a senior staff member of the PRC of the LDP.

[2] These public polls are only for electoral or political reasons, such as understanding the public support ratio of a government, not for policymaking.

[3] Some ministries had a policy office under the Big Three to provide support in policy analysis, planning policy drafts and so on (Yakushiji, 2012: 51).

[4] The State Strategy Office was supposed to expand into the State Strategy Agency, but this was not realised because of political calculations and considerations.

[5] From 'New Public' by the DPJ. Available at: http://public.dpj.or.jp/about/ (accessed 8 February 2013).

[6] This organisation still exists. Its website is available at: http://www.c-poli.org/main/category/14

References

Masuzoe, Y. (2007) *Nagatacho-vs.-Kasumigaseki---Saikokenryoku-wo-dattsshusuru-nohadareka* [*Nagatacho Versus Kasumigaseki:Who Gains the Supreme Authority*], Kodansha.

NDL (National Diet Library), Politics and Parliamentary Affairs Division, and Research and Legislative Reference Bureau (2002) 'Policy-Decision and Parliamentary Political Party Organizations in the Labour Party and the Conservative Party in the U.K.' (in Japanese), 24 May NDL.

Policy Research Council of Citizens (*Shimin-ga-tsukuru-seisakuchosakai*) (2009) 'The Planning a New Government to Be Strengthened/the First Proposal. About Participation and Involvement of NPOS/NGOS in Policymaking … Toward Managing the Cabinet in Terms of a Bottom-Up Approach to Management in Where Citizens and Dwellers Are the Main Players', 17 August, www.c-poli.org/main/article/c/52

Yakushiji, K. (2012) *Shogen … Minshutoseiken* (*The Testimonies – The Government of the Democratic Party of Japan*), Kodansha.

Yamaguchi, J. (2012) *Seikenkotai-towa-nandattsutaka* [*What Was the Change of Government*], Iwanamishoten.

TWELVE

Business associations and labour unions

Takao Akiyoshi

Political system and interest groups in Japan

Conventional systems of interest group politics

In Japan, a close relationship between business associations and regulatory agencies is maintained through a framework known as 'the whole responsibility system', under which regulatory agencies with jurisdiction over industry are held responsible for everything that occurs in that industry (Iio, 1998). Hence, to better fulfil this responsibility, these regulatory agencies are strongly committed to all phases of the regulatory process: policy planning, policymaking, policy implementation and compliance inspection.

Although there are different views on the degree of control of regulatory agencies over industry in Japan,[1] it is commonly said that the relationship between them is generally not hostile, but close and cooperative, built through daily contact with each other.[2] Regulatory policy has been developed by a limited number of actors within divided and closed political arenas (Akiyoshi, 2007). In that context, policy alternatives are formed by the regulatory agencies and then adopted through a process of debate by related actors, such as members of the Policy Research Subcommittee of the Liberal Democratic Party of Japan (LDP) and particular committees of Congress with jurisdiction over regulated industry. Therefore, the strategy of being in contact with such related actors has been more for the politically expediency of business associations than to appeal to the general public.

In contrast, the relationship between labour unions and regulatory agencies has been weaker than the latter has with business associations. Labour unions had a close relationship with the Japan Socialist Party (JSP) during the time that the LDP held the reins of government. After the dissolution of the JSP, labour unions formed the same relationship with the Democratic Party of Japan (DPJ) and the Social Democratic Party of Japan (SDP), which collectively represent the successor of the JSP.

Changes in the political environment of interest groups

'The 1940s' regime' (Noguchi, 1995), the political-economic system that included these interest groups, was formed to cope with preparations for the Second World War in the 1940s. This system continued after the end of the Second World War, becoming the foundation of the political-economic system that supported the well-known 'Corporate Japan'.

This system has evolved since the mid-1990s, however, triggered by the promotion of deregulation by the central government. As the experience of deregulation in the

US was introduced to Japan, the problem of governmental regulation became the focus of the agenda at the Second Provisional Council on Promotion of Administrative Reform, which began in 1987. According to the report of that council, the Takeshita administration created 'the outline on the promotion of deregulation', which delineated the specific measures for deregulation. Building on this, the Hosokawa administration, which took power from the LDP in 1993 after 38 years' of absence from power, placed deregulation as one of its priorities for economic policy and established a private council on the reform of the economic system in Japan. According to the interim report of that council, 'economic regulation should be basically liberalized' (Council on Economic Reform, 1993, 1) and 'social regulation should be basically changed to the principle of self-responsibility' (Council on Economic Reform, 1993, 2). Consequently, public opinion in support of deregulation was shaped and encouraged.[3]

The following administration also set deregulation as an important policy agenda. Councils to promote deregulation were established, as directed by the prime minister, and several reforms were implemented. Additionally, the government used the opportunity of 'regulatory reform' since the late 1990s to change its orientation from abolishing regulations to making a more competitive system. These attempts to promote deregulation had an effect on the political environment of interest groups, and caused two changes with regard to regulatory policy.

First, the relationship between interest groups and regulatory agencies changed. A new regulatory system was introduced along with the deregulation, requiring clear rules on regulation in advance; this meant a decrease in the use of discretion among regulatory agencies, as well as a decline of their power (Kurita, 2005). Furthermore, the necessity of establishing independent regulatory agencies was brought up in debate, also having an effect on the relationship between regulatory agencies and interest groups (Kishii, 2002). Although the organisation of agencies themselves did not actually change, the issue of 'the whole responsibility system' was another issue of concern. In sum, the once-close relationship between interest groups and regulatory agencies was on the cusp of change.

Second, the arena of regulatory policymaking changed, especially with regard to institutional positioning. As mentioned earlier, the Hosokawa administration placed a high priority on deregulation as an important agenda item for economic policy. The debate on deregulation had been held not within the regulatory agencies, but in the councils where the prime minister had the initiative and direct control. As these councils were given the role of creating the master plans for government reform, it was difficult for regulatory agencies to put forth their intentions with regard to regulatory policy. The result was that interest groups could have no effect on policymaking by being in contact with regulatory agencies.

In addition to this change in the seat of decision-making power, the style of policymaking evolved, especially with regard to the manner of debate. As transparency of administrative procedures was required, the clarity of the debate process in the council, which was controlled directly by the prime minister, was also required. Accordingly, the Subcommittee on Deregulation of the Committee on Administrative Reform, which was established in April 1995, opened the issues of debate to the public as '*Ronten*' ('policy issues') written by members of the committee (Office of Committee on Administrative Reform, 1997). Similarly, the policy debate between related actors who were inclined to promote or prohibit competition was opened to the public as '*Koukai Touron*' ('open policy debate') (Office of Committee on Administrative Reform, 1997).

Interest groups and policy analysis

Interest groups and policy knowledge

Although there are multiple definitions of policy analysis, according to the policy sciences, policy analysis is defined as the activity of providing decision-makers with a range of information to improve policymaking. As well as the scale of organisation and finance, policy information and knowledge of particular industries are political resources of interest groups that have an effect on the decision-making of policymakers. Hence, policy analysis by interest groups is defined as the activity of collecting and analysing policy information and providing policy knowledge to the appropriate policy actors.

The kinds of knowledge used in each phase of policymaking can be divided into 'theoretical knowledge' and 'experimental knowledge'. Theoretical knowledge is the scientific knowledge to construct principles and instruments of public policy, as justified by specific systems of theory. Theoretical knowledge, called 'know-why' in knowledge management theory (Kusunoki, 2001: 54), is acquired by research and shows some causal relationship.

In contrast, experimental knowledge is the practical knowledge to implement public policy, as justified by experience and practice in the public policy process. Experimental knowledge is called 'know-how' in knowledge management theory (Kusunoki, 2001: 55), and is acquired by policymaking and policy implementation. The policy knowledge that interest groups provide is this experimental knowledge. Specific knowledge of an industry is be accumulated not by theory, but through the experience of practice or policy implementation in that industry.

Experimental knowledge has two functions in the policymaking process: justification of theoretical knowledge as policy knowledge; and justification of policy alternatives. With regard to the first function, theoretical knowledge is knowledge justified only by the specific system of theory. Also referred to as an 'impractical proposition', it is sometimes not usable in public policy, even if it is true in theory. Hence, it is necessary for experimental knowledge, which is acquired by the experience of policy implementation, to demonstrate that specific theoretical knowledge can be used in public policy formation.

Second, experimental knowledge functions to justify policy. Although theoretical knowledge justifies policy in theory, one cannot know from this that policy is suitable in an actual social situation. Hence, it is necessary for experimental knowledge, acquired by the experience of other countries, to demonstrate the policy's validity.

Formation of policy discourse

Policy analysis that is conducted by interest groups not only provides policy-oriented information, but also creates discourse about policy. In the dimension of ideals, discourse serves two functions (Schmidt, 2002: 213–14): cognitive and normative. The cognitive function is to reveal alternatives for policy problems. The normative function is to express the ideas and political goals of a programme in order to appeal to multiple values in society.

In another context – the political process of mutual interaction – discourse also has two functions (Schmidt, 2002: 218–19, 230–1): coordinative and communicative. The coordinative function is to coordinate and share policy ideas between policy actors by providing a language and framework for the political system. The communicative function is to obtain the support of the public by translating policy programmes into ideas.

Facing changes in their political environment, interest groups began to recognise policy discourse as an important factor. Under the conventional system of politics, it was important for interest groups to find a way to put pressure on politicians or bureaucrats to protect their rents. However, because their close relationship with agencies had come under scrutiny, and the organisation controlled directly by the prime minister now had a powerful effect on policymaking, it became inefficient for interest groups to depend on this strategy. Furthermore, as policy debate during the policymaking process had been opened to the public due to the establishment of the Subcommittee on Deregulation, it became important for interest groups to consider new ways of expressing and justifying their interests. Contributing to the formulation of policy discourse by using the knowledge provided by policy analysis appeared to be an important avenue for accomplishing this.

The developing policy discourse also had a critical effect on institutional change. The cognitive function and storyline of discourse give certain meanings to particular social-economic conditions as 'problem situations'. This led to the shared idea that the institutions presented a problematic situation (Hall, 1993; Oliver and Pemberton, 2004). A discourse coalition was formed by members who shared the storyline of discourse (Hajer, 1995: 65), and this coalition, while coping with the dominant collation that has power over existing policy, accelerated the development of a common perception of the defects of existing institutions. Furthermore, during the phase of the selection of ideas that form the basis of institutions, the cognitive function of discourse persuades the public by showing the legitimacy of certain ideas through the logic of 'necessity', while the normative function of discourse uses the logic of 'appropriateness' (Schmidt, 2002: 218–19, 230–1).

Policy analysis by nationwide organisations

Institutions of policy analysis

Nationwide organisations of business associations in Japan, called 'Zaikai', are important actors in the political system (Kikuchi, 2005). Nippon Keidanren (the Japan Business Federation) is the largest such organisation in Japan, composed of 1,282 major companies, 129 major industrial nationwide associations and 47 local economic associations (Yamakoshi, 2010). Nippon Keidanren was established by the merger of Keidanren (the Federation of Economic Organisations) and Nikkeiren (the Japan Management League) in 2002, both of which conducted policy analysis.

Keidanren established an internal committee system to conduct policy analysis.[4] Executives of member companies joined several kinds of committee to examine relevant policy issues and propose policy alternatives (Koga, 2000). Three types of committee existed for this purpose: Policy Committees; Regional and Bilateral Relations Committees; and Special Committees.

Policy Committees, such as the General Policy Committee, the Tax System Committee and the Administrative Committee, were organised based on policy agendas. Regional and Bilateral Relations Committees, such as the America Committee and the Europe Region Committee, were organised to discuss international relations. Special Committees, such as the National Defense and Production Committee, were organised to discuss special policy issues in relation to the future of society. The major committees also had subcommittees,[5] in which technical issues were addressed and policy alternatives were drafted for committees.

The Secretariat of Keidanren supported the activities of these committees,[6] providing adequate support for their operation. In addition, headquarter organisations at the Secretariat of Keidanren, economic headquarters, industrial headquarters and earth environment headquarters, negotiated with the bureaucrats of the central government to reflect their opinions in policy alternatives.

As with Keidanren, Nikkeiren also established several kinds of internal committees. After reorganisation of this committee system, there were 10 committees, including the Social Security Committee and the Labor Economic Committee. Important issues for management, ranging from labour problems to higher education needs, were analysed in these committees. Although, Nikkeiren conducted policy analysis as 'research activities' (Crump, 2006), the resulting analyses were intended to provide not alternatives for economic policy, but proposals for managers of member companies.

The nationwide organisation of labour unions in Japan is Rengo (Japanese Trade Union Confederation), which was established by the merger of four nationwide organisations in 1989. As of 2012, Rengo is composed of 53 industrial unions, which are organised per industry. Rengo has researched and analysed several policy issues related to labour problems in order to propose policy alternatives to the government.

In addition to its own policy analysis activity, Rengo has established the think tank Rengo-Soken (Research Institute for Advancement of Living Standards) as a group organisation.[7] Although Rengo-Soken conducts several kinds of activity, there have been three types of activity focused especially on policy research:[8] Major Survey and Study; Education and Public Affairs; and Exchange with Other Organizations. Major Survey and Study has been conducted by several Study Committees, such as the Economic Society Study Committee and the Survey Study Committee on Fixed-Point Observations about the Quality of Workers' Lives, to research and analyse labour problems. Education and Public Affairs has focused on holding symposiums[9] and publishing Study Reports and Monthly Reports. Exchange with Other Organizations has worked with other similar research institutes. Rengo-Soken formed cooperative relationships and shared results of policy analysis or views on policy at the exchange forum.

Effects on policy argumentation

The policy analysis conducted by these nationwide organisations has a certain effect on policymaking. First, policy analysis by these organisations has sometimes been opened to the public through the publishing of the research reports or being noticed by the mass media. In addition, these organisations have been actively and directly involved in the policymaking system, attempting to have an effect on the contents of policy. For example, with regard to the stabilisation of financial system in the late 1990s, the Financial Institution Committee of Keidanren published a research report that included several policy proposals, such as introducing a government guarantee of the borrowing of funds of the Deposit Insurance Corporation; these proposals were adopted for the Act concerning Emergency Measures for Early Strengthening of Financial Functions established in 1998 (Koga, 2000).

As noted earlier, Keidanren and Nikkeiren lobbied bureaucrats and politicians, and proposed the results of policy analysis, or policy alternatives, to them as 'policy requirements'.[10] In addition, they sent their members to several councils at regulatory agencies. In Japanese policymaking, specific policy issues are discussed in councils, which are established and controlled by the bureaucrats of these agencies. Senior members of Keidanren or Nikkeiren were able to join the councils as members, and in this capacity, could share their opinions on policy alternatives that were then formed by bureaucrats. This activity also had a bearing on the contents of policy.[11]

Second, Rengo published policy reports on the results of its policy analysis, such as 'Policy and Institution; Requirements and Proposals' and 'Important Policy of Rengo' (Kume, 1998). Rengo-Soken also published Study Reports, such as 'Report of the 11th Questionnaire Survey on the Work and Life of Workers' and 'Study Committee on Economic Development and Labor in East Asia', as well as Monthly Report 'DIOs' ('Data Information Opinions').[12]

As did Keidanren and Nikkeiren, Rengo also attempted to have connections to bureaucrats and politicians with responsibility for policy issues. Senior staff members of Rengo were also requested to become the members of councils by the government, to secure representativeness. At councils, they expressed their opinions on policy alternatives from the viewpoint of maintaining working conditions, also affecting policymaking.

Policy analysis by interest groups: re-regulation of taxi transportation

Outline of the case

In order to consider policy analysis conducted by each interest group and its effect on the policymaking process, this study examined the case of re-regulation of taxi transportation. The regulatory agency for taxi transportation in Japan has been the Ministry of Transportation (MOT), which regulates the industry strictly under the Road Transportation Act 1951 (Yamauchi, 1988). Regarding regulations for entry into the industry, a certification system was adopted, by which the minister of the MOT would certify each company for entry into the market under Article 5 of the Road Transportation Act. Here, the most important issue was the 'Demand and Supply Regulation', through which the business area and the number of cars in the relevant area was set by the MOT. With this authority, the MOT severely restricted not only the entry of new companies, but also any increase in the number of cars by existing companies.

Regarding price regulation, a permitting system was adopted for the minister of the MOT to permit each company to set or alter the price of their services under Article 8 of the Road Transportation Act. The most important issue in this regard was the principle of 'Same Price in Same Area', which was introduced by the administrative guidance of the Director of Automobiles in July 1955. Independently of the business area of entry regulation, the MOT set the pricing area (the 'Block of Pricing') and permitted only equal pricing within areas. Consequently, pricing competition among companies was prohibited in the taxi industry.

Deregulation of the taxi transportation industry had been considered a challenge because of the features of the industry and experiences of other countries (Akiyoshi, 2012). Regardless of this, problems in the regulation of the industry had been pointed out since the early 1990s, and deregulation had been discussed at several councils of the MOT and the central government. In 1993, the Subcommittee on Regional Transportation of the Committee of Transportation Policy of the MOT laid out a path for revising the principle of 'Same Price in Same Area'. The Subcommittee on Deregulation of the Committee on Administrative Reform also pointed out the problem of regulation of the taxi industry to the administration in a discussion on the reform of transportation policy (Office of Committee on Administrative Reform, 1997). According to this discussion, the MOT revealed a way to abolish the 'Demand and Supply Regulation' of all transportation industries, and established a council to discuss the introduction of a new rule of competition in each industry. The new rule of taxi industry competition and its supplementary policy was discussed at the Subcommittee on Automobile Transportation of the Committee of Transportation Policy of the MOT, and the Road Transportation Act was revised in May 2000 according to the resulting subcommittee report. With the introduction of this revised law, the deregulation of the taxi transportation industry began in February 2002.

As deregulation was implemented in other transportation industries, it seemed that the Ministry of Land, Infrastructure and Transport (MLIT) had the will to promote competitive policies in the taxi industry.[13] However, MLIT began to consider changing the competition policy of the taxi industry in October 2005, and showed that the programme did not permit the new entry or an increase in the number of cars in specific business areas in November 2007. Furthermore, a Special Act on justifying and activating ordinary car transportation business in specific areas, the Taxi Justifying and Activating Act, was established in June 2009, enabling control over the number of cars in the market, effectively reinstating regulation of the taxi industry.

Business associations and labour unions in the taxi industry

Although there are many business associations in the taxi industry, Zenjhoren (the Japan Federation of Taxicab Associations) has been the representative nationwide organisation of taxi companies.[14] Zenjhoren has conducted several kinds of activity, from research to presenting policy requirements to government, and has several committees on specific policy issues. On deregulation of the taxi industry, Zenjhoren has attempted to be in contact with members of Congress, especially with LDP members of the United Association of Taxis and Hires, and to exchange opinions with these members at opportunities such as the General Meeting of Zenjhoren. Zenjhoren also established a special committee on regulatory reform to research pertinent regulatory policy. Bureaucrats of MLIT, especially the director of the Automobile Transportation Bureau and the assistant manager of the Passengers Division, appeared at that committee to explain current policy issues, and Zenjhoren sought contact with them in particular.

As with business associations, there are also many labour unions in the taxi industry. Zenjikohren (the National Federation of Automobile Transportation Labor Unions) has been the representative nationwide organisation of labour unions. Zenjikohren is composed of several automobile transportation companies, including those with taxis, vehicles for hire, sightseeing buses and driving schools; members of Zenjikohren perform the activities of labour movements in each region. Zenjikohren also conducted political activities to present policy requirements to government, called 'Policy Activity'. With regard to deregulation, Zenjikohren researched regulatory policy and attempted to maintain contact with members of Congress, especially members of the LDP, and the bureaucrats of MLIT.

Policy analysis and re-regulation discourse

Deregulation of the taxi industry, which started in 2002, caused the new entry of companies and an increase in the number of cars of existing companies in the three major metropolitan areas of Tokyo, Osaka and Nagoya, and also in major cities like Sendai, Fukuoka and Sapporo. As competition within the taxi industry was accelerated by deregulation, new systems of pricing were introduced into the market, such as the 'One-coin (¥500) Hatunori fare' (minimum fare, which is the first amount of charge), 'Discount for long-distance travel', 'Flat-rate fare' and 'Commuter fare'. Similarly, new transportation services, such as 'Elder-care taxis' and 'Sightseeing taxis', were introduced, in proportion with the intensification of competition.

However, in spite of these positive effects of deregulation, some problems persisted, such as the decline of wages of taxi drivers and an increase in traffic accidents, and it was thought that competition was the cause of these problems. Labour unions and business associations researched these negative effects of deregulation and tried to form an advocacy coalition of anti-deregulation to require revision of the government's deregulation policy.

Yasuhiro Machidori, Chief Secretary of Zenjikourouren, published several papers on the decline of wages and the long hours of work of taxi drivers from the late-1990s (Machidori, 1997, 1998, 2001, 2003a, 2003b, 2005). Furthermore, Zenjikourouren dispatched Machidori to several councils as a member to represent the opinions of labour unions.

On the decline of wages of taxi drivers, Zenjikourouren emphasised that the average yearly income of taxi drivers had dropped each year since 1991. In 2004, it was about ¥3 million, or ¥2.4 million lower than that of all industries (Machidori, 2005).[15] This situation of taxi drivers was widely reported in sensational media publications, with titles such as 'Doraiba zankoku monogatari' ('The Cruel Story of Taxi Drivers').[16] On the long hours of work of taxi drivers, Zenjikourouren pointed out that even before the start of deregulation, the commission system that was the standard wage system for the taxi industry forced long hours for drivers. Zenjikourouren also emphasised that this situation was responsible for traffic accidents; the number of accidents involving taxis had increased about 60% since 1993 (Machidori, 2005). Furthermore, Zenjikourouren established a policy forum, 'Hire and Taxi Forum', with Kouturoren (the Federation of Labor Unions of Transportation) in January 2005 to present various policy requirements.

Zenjhoren, the representative organisation of business associations, tried to form an advocacy coalition for re-regulation and created the venue 'Forum on Taxi and

Hire Policy' in February 2005. Related business associations, such as Zenjikourouren and Zenkokyo (Japan Associations of Privately Owned Taxi), and related members of Congress became core members of this forum, and other interest groups, such as the All Japan Consumer Groups' Liaison Association and Harbor Modernization Promotion Council, also participated in this forum. Furthermore, it was a major achievement when Zenjhoren succeeded in inviting Hirotaka Yamauchi, a professor at Hitotsubashi University, who was known to be in favour of promoting deregulation (Akiyoshi, 2008).[17] Zenjoren also established a committee to propose policy alternatives involving re-regulation to MLIT in February 2008. They requested Kiyoshi Okada, a professor emeritus at Seijyo University, who supported the discourse of anti-competition, to become the chairman of this committee.

Policy argumentation

Due to responses to this report by the media and the political activity of interest groups, MLIT considered the problems in the taxi industry that were caused by deregulation. MLIT established the Subcommittee on the Future Vision of Taxi Service at a Sectional Meeting on Automobile, Sectional Committee on Surface Transportation of Transportation Policy Council, in October 2005. Yamauchi was appointed chairman of this subcommittee, and persons with relevant knowledge and experience, as well as representatives of the media, were appointed as members or temporary members of the subcommittee. Representatives of the taxi industry, Zenjohren and Zenjikourouren, were appointed as expert members of the subcommittee. The situation of the taxi industry after deregulation was considered, and members of this subcommittee recognised the problematic issues of the lower wages of taxi drivers and traffic accidents caused by deregulation. Furthermore, the future vision of the taxi industry was considered, and the orientation of policy, 'Important Public Transportation Which Maintains Regional Transportation System', was presented in this subcommittee.

According to this policy debate, MLIT began to strengthen the regulation of the taxi industry. In November 2007, MLIT set the 67 regions nationwide where there were signs of oversupply of taxis as 'Special Monitoring Areas'. Of these regions, MLIT designated six regions where the situation of oversupply of taxis was problematic as 'Particular Special Monitoring Areas', and then decided to implement measures for new entry and increases in taxis. Furthermore, in July 2008, according to the revision of the Circular Notice of Director of Automobiles, measures for controlling the supply of taxis were strengthened. 'Particular Special Monitoring Areas' were expanded from six to 109 regions, and 'Special Monitoring Areas' were also expanded from 67 to 537 regions nationwide.

As this gradual re-regulation was implemented, the Taxi Justifying and Activating Act was established in June 2009, and enforced in October 2009. According to this law, regions where oversupply of taxis is confirmed are designated as 'Particular Areas' by MLIT, and in those regions, permission by the minister of MLIT is required for new entries or increases in taxis.

Conclusions

As this chapter shows, policy analysis conducted by business associations and labour unions in Japan is not policy analysis in a narrow sense, such as cost–benefit analysis or cost-effectiveness analysis, but, rather, policy analysis in a broad sense: providing experimental knowledge based on the specific characteristics of the industry and experiences of policy implementation. The importance of this experimental knowledge is pointed out in policy studies showing that there are two effects of experimental knowledge on policymaking: justification of theoretical knowledge and justification of public policy.

In Japan, the political activities of business associations and labour unions were changed by the attempt to deregulate, beginning in the 1990s. Deregulation caused changes in the political environment, in the relationships between regulatory agencies and these groups, and in the transformation of the policymaking venue. Furthermore, these changes enhanced the importance of policy debate. Moreover, policy analysis not only provided policy-oriented information, but also formed the policy discourse. As the re-regulation process of the taxi industry demonstrates, it is important for business associations and labour unions to adopt the strategy of using specific discourses to revise existing policy.

Notes

[1] Richard Samuels pointed out that the 'jurisdiction' of regulatory agencies did not mean the control over industry by regulatory agencies, and described the notion of 'mutual consent' between them (Samuels, 1987).

[2] There were several channels between them. Formally, executives of major companies or business associations of industry visited bureaucrats of regulatory agencies to report on the economic situation of their industry. Informally, they met at venues such as meetings of industry representatives and exchanged views on the industry with each other.

[3] In that year, as the word 'Deregulation' was nominated for Japan's Keywords-of-the-Year contest, heightened attention was focused on the deregulation policy of the Hosokawa administration.

[4] The organisational structure of Nippon Keidanren is the same as Keidanren, and there is also a committee system in Nippon Keidanren (Yamakoshi, 2010).

[5] For instance, the Financial Institution Committee established multiple subcommittees, such as the Special Subcommittee of Financial Reform, the Special Subcommittee of Social Security Institution and the Working Group on National Burden Ratio (Koga, 2000: 132).

[6] The Secretariat was an organisation with a workforce of about 200 employees. Known as '*Minryo*' ('private bureaucrats'), they were selected from famous universities in Japan, such as Tokyo University, Waseda University and Keio University, and they had the policy knowledge to derive policy alternatives as well as bureaucrats could (Koga, 2000).

[7] Rengo-Soken has been established as a Public Interest Incorporated Foundation. It has been under the joint oversight of four government agencies.

[8] The Rengo-Soken homepage is available at: http://rengo-soken.or.jp/english/en-about/activities.html (accessed 4 August 2013).

[9] The most important symposium is the 'RENGO-SOKEN Forum', which is held annually. In this forum, the Annual Economic Situation Report is publicly announced.

[10] Keidanren also had several informal channels to bureaucrats and politicians. For instance, 'power breakfasts' were held every week, in which they exchanged views on economic policy with each other (Koga, 2000).

[11] On some important policy agendas, such as administrative reform or economic system reform, the chairman of Keidanren was requested to become the chairman of the council.

[12] The Rengo-Soken homepage is available at: http://rengo-soken.or.jp/english/en-about/activities.html (accessed 4 August 2013).

[13] According to the reorganisation of the central government ministries and agencies, the MOT, the Ministry of Construction, the National Land Agency and the Hokkaido Development Agency were unified, becoming MLIT on 6 January 2001.

[14] Zenjhoren changed its name to Zentakuren (the Japan Federation of Hire-Taxi Associations) in 2008. This chapter uses Zenjhoren consistently to avoid confusion.

[15] However, the decline in wages differed regionally. In particular, in several areas, such as Tokyo, Saitama, Aichi and Kyoto, the average income of taxi drivers was higher than that of 2001 (Yamazaki, 2009).

[16] Syuukan Toyo Keizai, no. 5996, pp 60-63. In addition to this, it was critical that the TV programme 'Taxi Drivers Cannot Sleep: Competition Caused by Deregulation' was broadcast by NHK (the Japan Broadcasting Corporation) on 17 September 2005. In this programme, problems of deregulation, such as the decline of wages and the long hours of work of taxi drivers, were mentioned; attention was focused on the deregulation of the taxi industry after the end of the broadcast of this programme.

[17] Zenjhoren also succeeded in inviting Seiji Abe, a professor at Osaka City University, who was known as a supporter of anti-competition policy of the taxi industry (Abe, 1993, 2005).

References

Abe, S. (1993) 'Taxi Industry and Public Regulation' (in Japanese), *Koueki Jigyou Kenkyuu*, vol 46, no 1, pp 133–47.

Abe, S. (2005) *Koukyou Koutuu ga Abunai: Kisei Kanwa to Kamitu Roudou (The Perilousness of Public Transportation: Deregulation and Long Working Hour)*, Iwanami Booklet.

Akiyoshi,T. (2007) *Koukyou Seisaku no Hennyo to Seisakukagaku : Nitibei Koukuu Yusou Sangyou ni okeru Hutatuno Kiseikaikaku* [*Policy Sciences of Policy Change:Two Regulatory Reforms in US–JAPAN Airline Industry*],Yuhikaku.

Akiyoshi,T. (2008) 'Knowledge and Policy Change:"Politics of Knowledge" in the Process of Second Regulatory Reform of Airline Industry' (in Japanese), *Koukyo Seisaku Kenkyuu*, vol 8, pp 87–98.

Akiyoshi, T. (2012) 'The Transformation of Interest Group Politics in an Age of Deregulation:The Politics of Discourse in Deregulation of Taxi Transportation' (in Japanese), *Nenpou Seijigaku*, vol 2, pp 110–33.

Council on Economic Reform (1993) *Kisei Kanwa ni Tuite: Tyuukan Houkoku* [*On Deregulation: Interim Report*], Council on Economic Reform.

Crump, J. (2006) *Nikkeiren: Mouhitotuno Sengoshi* [*Japan Management League: Another Postwar History*], Sakurai Shoten.

Hajer, M.A. (1995) *The Politics of Environmental Discourse: Ecological Modernization and the Policy Process*, Oxford University Press.

Hall, P.A. (1993) 'Policy Paradigms, Social Learning, and the State', *Comparative Politics*, vol 23, pp 275–96.

Iio, J. (1998) 'The Phase of Relationship between Bureaucrats and Industry' (in Japanese), *Nihon Koukyou Seisaku Gakkai Nenpou*, vol 1, pp 1–11.

Kikuchi, N. (2005) *Zaikai towa Nanika* [*What is Zaikai?*], Heibonsya.

Kishii, D. (2002) 'Regulatory Reform of Public Utilities and Antimonopoly Act:"A Particular Area Regulation", Antimonopoly Act, and the Fair Trade Commission' (in Japanese), *Nippon Keizaihou Gakkai Nenpo*, vol 23, pp 33–76.

Koga, J. (2000) *Keidanren: Nippon wo Ugokasu Zaikai Shinkutanku* [*The Federation of Economic Organizations: Think Tank of Zaikai That Had an Effect on the Economics of Japan*], Shincho Sensyo.

Kume, I. (1998) *Nihongata Roushikankei no Seikou: Sengowakai no Seijigaku* [*Success of Japanese Style of Management–Labor Relationship: Politics of Postwar Reconciliation*], Yuhikaku.

Kurita, M. (2005) 'Relationship between Regulatory Agency and Agency on Competition: In Comparison with the United States' (in Japanese), in D. Kishii and A. Torii (eds) *Koueki Jigyou no Kisei Kaikaku to Kyousou Seisaku* [*Regulatory Reform of Public Utilities and Competitive Policy*], Housei Daigaku Shuppankai, pp 85–123.

Kusunoki,T. (2001) 'The Differentiation of Values and Coexistence of Constraints: Creation of Concepts and the Organization Theory' (in Japanese), in Hitotsubashi University Institute of Innovation Research (ed) *Tisiki to Inovation* [*Knowledge and Innovation*],Toyo Keizai Shinpousya, pp 51–102.

Machidori,Y. (1997) 'Deregulation Policy without Considering the Features of Taxi Industry' (in Japanese), *Roudou Keizai Jyunpou*, vol 1584, pp 15–20.

Machidori, Y. (1998) 'Confusion and Pains in the Frontlines of Taxi Industry by Deregulation Policy' (in Japanese), *Gekkan Syakaiminshu*, vol 512, pp 21–5.

Machidori, Y. (2001) 'Securing the Safety and Trust of Taxi Transportation Service by the Proper Conditions of Employment and Working' (in Japanese), *Gekkan Syakaiminshu*, vol 548, pp 16–19.

Machidori, Y. (2003a) 'Lowering the Wages of Taxi Drivers under the Excessive Competition' (in Japanese), *Gekkan Roudou Kumiai*, vol 450, pp 30–3.

Machidori,Y. (2003b) 'An Approach to Strengthen the Social Regulation' (in Japanese), *Gekkan Roudou Kumiai*, vol 451, pp 58–61.

Machidori,Y. (2005) 'Lowering the Wages of Taxi Drivers and Threatening the Safety of Taxi Transportation: Putting a Brake on Running to Ruin of Taxi Industry by Taking Objection to Deregulation' (in Japanese), *Gekkan Roudou Kumiai*, vol 482, pp 20–2.

Noguchi,Y. (1995) *1940 Nenn Taisei: Saraba Senji Keizai [The 1940 Regime:The End of Wartime Economics]*,Toyo Keizai Shinpousya.

Office of Committee on Administrative Reform (1997) *Soui de Tsukuru Atarashii Nippon: Gyousei Kaikaku Iinkai Kisei Kanwa no Suishin ni Kansuru Iken Dainiji [Creating New Economic System of Japan: Secondary Proposals of Committee of Administrative Reform to Promote Deregulation]*, Gyousei Kanri Kennkyuu Senta.

Oliver, M.J. and Pemberton, H. (2004) 'Learning and Change in 20th-Century British Economic Policy', *Governance*, vol 17, pp 415–41.

Samuels, R. (1987) *The Business of the Japanese States: Energy Markets in Comparative and Historical Perspective*, Cornell University Press.

Schmidt,V.A. (2002) *The Futures of European Capitalism*, Oxford University Press.

Yamakoshi,A. (2010) 'Participation of Private Companies and Business Associations for Policy Making' (in Japanese), in H. Koike (ed) *Seisaku Keisei [Policy Formation]*, Minerva Shobou.

Yamauchi, H. (1988) *Taxi Sangyou Ni Okeru Kisei Seisaku [Regulatory Policy on Taxi Industry]*, Nikkouken Series, A-119-3-2, Nihon Koutsu Seisaku Kenkyuukai.

Yamazaki, O. (2009) 'Taxi Industry' (in Japanese), in National Diet Library (ed) *Keizai Bunnya Ni Okeru Kiseikaikaku no Eikyou to Taisaku [Influence of Regulatory Reform on Areas of Economy and Measures of Its Effects]*, National Diet Library.

THIRTEEN

Current state of non-profit organisations and the 'New Public Commons'

Takafumi Tanaka

Introduction

Lately, there are many books that discuss the non-profit sector or civil society in Japan.[1] They mainly focus on the civic movement after the 1995 Hanshin Awaji earthquake, and on the making of the new Law Concerning the Promotion of Specific Non-Profit Organisation Activities (NPO Law). However, this chapter deals with the revision of the Civil Code and the NPO Law after the Great East Japan Earthquake of 11 March 2011.

The administration of the Democratic Party of Japan (DPJ), which was in power from September 2009 to December 2012, expected non-profit organisations (NPOs) to play a public role, such as being the supplier of public services and disaster relief, as symbolised by its the 'New Public Commons' slogan. In particular, following the Great East Japan Earthquake, the DPJ stressed the role to be played by NPOs in disaster areas in terms of reconstruction, relief and rebuilding people's lives. Reflecting this, the administration appointed many people affiliated with NPOs to participate in government meetings, such as the Commission of Enquiry. Moreover, a number of policies appeared for NPOs, including those aimed at job creation. To develop a civil society for the future, the view was that NPOs, other civic groups and civic activities would constantly increase in importance. In this chapter, first we will consider the systemic revisions pertaining to NPOs that have been implemented since 2008. We will also study the current state of NPOs. We will then investigate the role of NPOs in terms of the 'New Public Commons'. Following this, we will consider the levels of awareness about NPOs among citizens, as the group of people that support NPOs, as well as the importance of education in order to increase that level of awareness. Finally, we will summarise issues that should be dealt with in the future.

Systemic revisions pertaining to, and the current state of, non-profit organisations

Revisions to the Civil Code and a shift to a new system

Three laws designed to reform the public interest corporations system were enacted on 1 December 2008: (1) the Law on General Incorporated Associations and General Incorporated Foundations; (2) the Law on Authorisation of Public Interest Incorporated Associations; and (3) Public Interest Incorporated Foundations, and the

Arrangement Law. In addition, sweeping reforms were made to the Civil Code that pertained to the public interest corporations system. Specifically, Article 34 of the former Civil Code (1896) provided that, 'Any association or foundation relating to any academic activities, art, charity, worship, religion, or other public interest which is not for profit may be established as a juridical person with the permission of the competent government agency'. The decisions of whether or not an NPO serves the public interest and/or whether or not the relevant organisation should be given a juridical personality were made by the government agency providing permission, on a discretionary basis. This prevented citizens from voluntarily forming an organisation that might obtain the benefits of the law but not serve the purpose that the law meant to support.

Given the principle-based approach adopted in General Incorporated Association and Foundation Law, NPOs (associations or foundations that do not have the distribution of surplus as an activity objective) are now able to acquire a juridical personality, regardless of the activities in which they engage. Pursuant to the Charitable Status Recognition Law, if an organisation satisfies the charitable status recognition standards and if it is approved by the Public Interest Corporation Commission, similar to the Charity Commission in England and Wales, or a council system body in 47 prefectures, it can become a public interest corporation. Under the standards, the principal objective of the business must be to operate for public interest purposes. The revenue pertaining to such businesses is *not* to exceed the amount representing the reasonable cost for its operation, and the ratio of the business for public interest purposes is expected to exceed 50%. The result is that in the new system, decisions regarding whether an organisation may have a juridical personality have been separated from those regarding whether the organisation serves the public interest. Consequently, a two-level structure has been created, with the Law on General Incorporated Associations and General Incorporated Foundations being the first level and the Law on Authorisation of Public Interest Incorporated Associations and Public Interest Incorporated constituting the second level.

Because of the 2008 fiscal year revisions to the tax system, those businesses that were recognised as being for public interest purposes became exempt from taxes even if, for example, their business corresponded to a profit-making business according to the Order for Enforcement of the Corporation Tax Act. In addition, they could be treated as having increased their deemed contribution ratio and as a special public interest promotion corporation among public interest corporations. Moreover, following the 2011 fiscal year revisions to the tax system, when an individual contributes to a public interest corporation that satisfies the Public Support Test (PST) requirements, they can choose to receive a tax deduction either in the form of a tax credit or a deduction from taxable income. However, if a public interest corporation has already been recognised by the Public Interest Corporation Commission as serving the public interest, it will be considered a special public interest promotion corporation under tax laws. As a result, the additional PST requirements that will be imposed on it are ultimately a superfluous measure that will only serve to place an additional burden on public interest corporations.

As of January 2013, 84% of the public interest corporations in the former system made applications to switch to the new system. Among these corporations are those with special exceptions in the Civil Code in the new public interest corporations system (Cabinet Office, 2013). Among the 24,443 corporations that are special exception corporations in the Civil Code, 20,808 corporations have indicated that they want to switch to the new public interest corporations system. This number includes those that intend to apply in the future. The remaining 3,635 corporations plan to dissolve, merge or take some other action. Among the 20,808 corporations that intend to switch to the new public interest corporations systems, 17,452 corporations had already filed their application as of the end of January 2013. Among the 4,066 corporations that filed an application with the Cabinet Office, 2,048 corporations had been approved as public interest corporations (50.4%), while 2,018 corporations (49.6%) had been approved to switch to become a general association or foundation. Elsewhere, of the 13,386 corporations that applied to prefectural governments, 6,222 (46.5%) were approved as public interest corporations, while 7,164 (53.5%) had been approved to switch to become a general association or foundation. Combining these two results, it appears that 8,270 corporations had been approved as public interest corporations, while 9,182 have been approved to switch to become a general association or foundation.

How is the new public interest corporations system perceived by the organisations and professionals that are governed by it? In 2012, the Japan Association of Charitable Organizations conducted a survey among its member organisations, to which 3,441 corporations responded. The most frequently identified reasons for choosing to become a general association or foundation, among multiple possible answers, was 'Management has comparative freedom in a general corporation'. This answer was chosen by 52.3% of those who responded. Other answers given were: (1) 'Viewed from our objectives and business, it is more appropriate for us to be a general corporation', which received 45.7% of the responses; and (2) 'The workload for the application for authorization as a public interest corporation, and also after the authorization, is excessive', which received 33.2% of the responses (Yamauchi et al, 2013). From the results of this survey, the extent to which the public interest corporation reforms are contributing to the development of public interest activities by citizens is not clear.

Revisions to the Law Concerning the Promotion of Specific Non-Profit Organisation Activities

The 'NPO Law' was created because of the demands and appeals of volunteers and citizen groups that participated in the reconstruction and relief efforts following the Great Hanshin Awaji Earthquake (1995) (law enforced in 1998). The purpose of this law is to promote the sound development of specified non-profit activities in the form of volunteer and other activities freely performed by citizens to benefit society, through such measures as the provision of corporate status to organisations that undertake specified non-profit activities, and thereby to contribute to advancement of public welfare (Article 1).

The NPO Law was revised in April 2012 and the revisions included the following: (1) a review of the certification system; (2) changes to the competent authorities; and (3) revisions to authorisation standards for approved specific non-profit corporations (hereinafter referred to as 'approved NPO corporations'). The review of the certification system entailed: the addition of three activity fields; the simplification of procedures; the cancellation of unregistered corporation certifications; the clarification of accounting procedures through the introduction of NPO accounting standards; and the registration of the range and limits of directors' rights to represent. The changes to the competent authorities affected corporations that have offices in several of Japan's prefectures, which were transferred from the Cabinet Office to the prefectural government in which the corporation's principal office is located. In the case of a corporation that has only one office in a district in a government-designated major city, the competent authority was transferred from the prefectural government to the relevant government-designated major city.

Finally, the revisions to certification standards, applicable to corporations that seek to become an approved NPO corporation, pertained to one of the certification requirements, the PST, in addition to the relative-value standards that had been used up to that time within this test. Standards designated by individual ordinances were also introduced. Moreover, a new temporary certification system that exempted some corporations from PST requirements was introduced. Through this system, corporations without a reason to be disqualified within five years of their establishment, and that applied for certification, were exempted from the PST requirements.

Further, through revisions to the tax system, the approval of NPO corporations that had previously been carried out by the National Tax Agency was instead carried out by local governments. Additionally, individuals who contributed ¥2,000 or more to a corporation that had received certification or temporary certification could receive a tax deduction by selecting either a tax credit or a deduction from taxable income. The amount of the deduction when it takes the form of a tax credit is 'contribution amount multiplied by 40%' and when in the form of a deduction from taxable income is 'contribution amount multiplied by the marginal tax rate'. When combined with a 10% reduction in resident tax, this tax credit can be as much as 50% of the contribution amount.

Table 13.1: Main non-profit organisations in Japan

Legal entities	Number	As of	Investigation agency
Public interest corporation (PIC)	8,621	Nov 2013	Cabinet Office
General non-profit corporation	33,029	April 2013	Cabinet Office
Specific non-profit activities corporation (SNC)	48,985	Mar 2014	Cabinet Office
Approved specific non-profit activities corporation (ASNC)	428	June 2014	Cabinet Office
Social welfare corporation	19,498	Mar 2012	Ministry of Health, Labor and Welfare
Medical corporation	47,825	Mar 2012	Ministry of Health, Labor and Welfare
School corporation	7,938	April 2012	Ministry of Education, Culture, Sports, Science and Technology
Rehabilitation aid corporation	165	Oct 2012	Ministry of Justice
Religious corporation	182,396	Dec 2010	Agency for Cultural Affairs
Neighbourhood associations (NHAs)	294,359	2008	Ministry of Internal Affairs and Communication
Approved neighbourhood associations (NHAs)	35,564	2007	Ministry of Internal Affairs and Communication

Source: Information from each investigation agency.

Current state of non-profit organisations

Table 13.1 shows Japan's main NPOs and the number of organisations. In the US, NPOs receiving a favourable tax treatment are lumped together regardless of active field under section 501c3 of the Internal Revenue Code. On the other hand, Japan has a plural system in which there are many laws regulating NPOs and several government offices related to them. Within Table 13.1, while neighbourhood associations (NHAs), do not have a juridical personality, they are recognised as a type of civic organisation unique to Japan (Pekkanen, 2006). Pekkanen (2006, pp 118–20) considered that while, on the one hand, NHAs are full of 'vitality' and are 'independent' civil society organisations, on the other hand, they are 'members without advocates' that do not 'have an influence on methodologies and policy decisions in the public domain'.

Next, we will discuss the current state of NPO corporations and the problems they face. We can see an uneven distribution and concentrations in the locations of specific non-profit activities corporations (SNCs) throughout the country. Approximately 20% of all NPO corporations (9,331 corporations) are located in Tokyo (as of 30 November 2012). Of those, the organisations are concentrated in urban areas such as Kanagawa Prefecture, Kyoto Prefecture and Osaka Prefecture. When we look at the number of NPO corporations per 1,000 people, we find that Tokyo has 0.7 corporations, which is the highest figure nationwide. As a result, there are regional differences in the distribution of NPO corporations; there are also major discrepancies in the roles being played by NPO corporations depending on the region that they are located in.

Figure 13.1: The top seven activities field of 48,985 specific non-profit activities corporations as of 31 March 2014

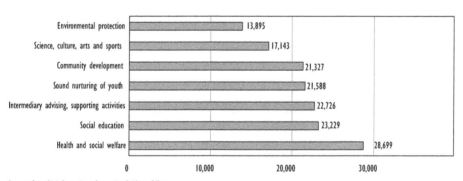

Source: Compiled from data from the Cabinet Office.

Figure 13.1 shows the number of organisations (multi-answer) in seven of the 20 activity fields from the corporations engaged in specific non-profit activities that were shown in Table 13.1 (as of 31 March 2014). From Figure 13.1, when we look at the activity fields of specific non-profit activities corporations (SNCs), we see that, overall, the largest fields are 'Health and social welfare', which constitutes 59.5% (28,699) of the total organisations. After these, the order is as follows: 'Social education' at 48.1% (23,229); 'Intermediary advising or supporting activities' at 47.1% (21,858); 'Sound nurturing of youth' at 44.7% (21,588); 'Community development' at 44.2% (21,327);

'Science, culture, arts and sports' at 35.5% (17,143); and 'Environmental protection' at 28.8% (13,895).

According to the Cabinet Office (2014), the average total revenue of SNCs in fiscal year 2012 was ¥36.91 million and the median total revenue was ¥6.89 million. Among approved or temporary approved SNCs, the average total revenue was ¥90.69 million and the median total revenue was ¥20.43 million. Looking at the distribution of total revenues for NPO corporations, the greatest number (29.1%) falls within the range of ¥10 million to ¥50 million, while 5.8% were in the range of ¥100 million or more. In addition, among approved or temporary approved SNCs, 14.9% were in the range of ¥100 million or more, from which it can be surmised that they are larger in scale than SNCs. Breaking down the revenues generated by SNCs, earned revenues constitute 55.3% of total revenues, contributions are 5.3% and subsidies and grants are 16.7%. For approved or temporary approved SNCs, contributions constitute 52.2% of total revenues, while subsidies and grants are 14.5%.

According to the Cabinet Office (2012), which compared responses from before and after the occurrence of an earthquake, 3.9% of people before the earthquake responded that they were 'Very interested or interested' in SNCs, but this rose to 10.7% after the earthquake. In other words, people's interest in SNCs increased due to the earthquake. The recent revisions to the NPO Law are considered a result of requests from the NPOs themselves, public comment and the lobby activities of a cross-party alliance of Diet members.

According to the data in Table 13.1, it appears that the number of approved specific non-profit activities corporations (ASNCs) does not reach 1% of all SNCs. In addition to the fact that the approval system is not very well known by the NPOs themselves, the trivial size of this percentage points to various other problems, including that many corporations find it difficult to satisfy the PST absolute-value standards and the complexity of the preparations required for an authorisation application. According to the Cabinet Office (2012), among all the people who contributed to an organisation that qualifies them for a contribution tax deduction, 37.8% did not declare this contribution even if they filed a final tax return. Looking at the reasons for this, the most common reason provided, by 26% of respondents was 'I did not know about the declaration system'. Therefore, it can be concluded that increasing the levels of awareness about the tax system for contributions will promote an increase in contributions to NPOs.

The role to be played by non-profit organisations in the New Public Commons

The Democratic Party of Japan administration's expectations for non-profit organisations

Each of the three prime ministers in the DPJ administration talked about the public role to be played by NPOs. In his keynote address given on 26 October 2009, Prime Minister Hatoyama stated that the New Public Commons is a signal that:

> we want a support role to be played not only by people working in government, but also through the participation of each person working in all regions in areas such as education and childcare, city planning, crime

prevention and disaster prevention, and medical and welfare services, as this will create a new sense of values of working to support society as a whole.

He described how the role of government would only be to eliminate those surplus regulations that impede the activities of NPOs.

In a policy speech given on 24 January 2011, Prime Minister Kan stated that:

> It is vital that we promote the New Public Commons that will undertake the realization of a 'society of minimized unhappiness.' As the residents of *Nagato-cho and Kasumigaseki* [ie the district where the government offices are located], we should change our attitude that has interpreted 'public' in a narrow range and actively support activities in this area. Therefore, in the new fiscal year, we will introduce a groundbreaking new system so that when a person contributes to an approved NPO corporation or other organization playing a role in the 'New Public Commons,' that contribution can become a tax credit. In conjunction with this, we will significantly relax the requirements required to be recognized as an approved NPO corporation.

As promised, his administration relaxed the requirements to become an approved NPO corporation and introduced a tax credit system.

In a policy speech given on 29 October 2012, Prime Minister Noda indicated that his government would provide support for NPOs for the purposes of post-earthquake recovery. He stated that:

> Going forward, the Reconstruction Agency will serve as a control tower and we will carry out the reforms that need to be made, while also providing various types of support, such as continuous human support, reconstruction special zones, and reconstruction grants. The Government will as one body support the efforts of citizens and local governments who are striving to clear away the debris and restore vitality to hometowns, while at the same time it will coordinate with companies, NPOs, and other relevant organizations.

As promised, his administration supported the efforts of NPOs for restoration from the earthquake disaster.

During the DPJ administration, in addition to the appointment of people affiliated to NPOs as special advisors to the Cabinet Office, many were also appointed to sit on the Commission of Enquiry and other committees. Those as special advisor to the Cabinet Office were Yasuyuki Shimizu, a representative of Lifelink, a support centre designed to prevent the termination of SNCs, and Yuasa Makoto, the Secretary General of MOYAI, an independent life support centre, and the Secretary General of the Anti-poverty Network. In addition to roundtable meetings on social responsibility and the 'New Public Commons', meetings to promote the New Public Commons, and working groups resulting from these meetings, 50 affiliates of NPOs were appointed to tens of committees and meetings. Further, several professionals affiliated to NPOs also became committee members of the Employment Strategic Dialogue.

The content of the New Public Commons

The New Public Commons is a philosophy relating to the provision of public goods and services by citizens, NPOs, companies and other organisations. It entails opening up areas previously monopolised by government bureaucrats to the 'public' so that those aspects of it that cannot be dealt with by bureaucrats alone can be managed through collaboration between the government and citizens (The New Public Commons Support Project, 10 March 2011). In the following, we will consider specific measures implemented for the New Public Commons. Additionally, a summary identifying new trends in NPOs and non-governmental organisations (NGOs) will be provided.

New Public Commons

Based on Prime Minister Hatoyama's keynote address, the New Public Commons philosophy and the expectations for it were widely disseminated to citizens, to companies and within the government administration itself. Then, in January 2010, the New Public Commons Roundtable was established, with the objective of holding discussions on the direction that Japanese society should take in the future and the systems and policies that should be created in order to achieve the society envisioned. The Roundtable produced The Declaration of New Public Commons (4 June 2010), which stated that the Government must:

> open up to the New Public Commons services and functions that it has long monopolized, and it can increase the number of options available to the people while implementing such measures as institutional reforms and reviews of operational procedures. For the New Public Commons to be truly effective, the government must take specific measures to build a society in which the people become part of the decision making process.

The Roundtable also proposed various measures, such as government-supplemented financing systems for NPOs and similar organisations, and actively introducing a system of payments for outsourced operations. Concerning these proposals, in its new growth strategy, the government stated that 'It is vital that a supply of capital be secured for start-ups and companies newly entering this area, for society-orientated companies, for NPOs, and for similar organizations', going on to say: 'in order to facilitate the smooth supply of capital to NPOs and similar organizations, we will progress reforms to regulations and systems and the tax system' (Cabinet meeting decision, 18 June 2010). Finally, it established the New Public Commons Support Project with a budget of ¥8.75 billion.

The ¥8.75 billion was divided between and distributed to each of Japan's prefectural governments as grants. The funds were used to support the services provided by the organisations responsible for the New Public Commons, such as NPOs, and for specific activities undertaken by NPOs and similar organisations, in collaboration with the government and related bodies. The organisations targeted for support were private sector non-profit organisations, including SNCs, volunteer groups, public interest corporations, social welfare corporations, school corporations, territorial organisations and cooperative associations (hereinafter referred to as 'NPOs, etc').

The project was made up of the following six elements: (a) support for the establishment and maintenance of infrastructure for the activities of NPOs; (b) support for the collection of contributions; (c) support to facilitate the use of financing; (d) interest subsidies for bridge financing; (e) a model business for the creation of venues for the New Public Commons; and (f) a model business to promote social innovation.

Support for job creation in disaster areas through reconstruction support (also known as Social Enterprise Support Fund)

Reconstruction support was provided in place of the original project entitled Support for Job Creation in Local Communities. Its goal was to create and promote business start-ups, as well as job creation, to contribute to the reconstruction effort after the Great East Japan Earthquake disaster. 'Social enterprise' start-ups were supported so that innovative businesses would solve regional difficulties in disaster areas, and so that the training of human resources to work in these enterprises would be provided. The total budget for the project is ¥3.2 billion (from the third supplementary budget in fiscal year 2011). The 12 business operators selected by the Cabinet Office Selection and Evaluation Committee are to carry out both or one of the types of business described as follows:

- Social start-up incubation businesses offer support for the start-up of social enterprises in disaster areas, or support for the start-up of social enterprises by victims of the disaster. Their aim is to provide support for 600 people to start up a business.
- Internships for the creation of human resources for social enterprises offer support for the training of human resources for social enterprises in disaster areas. Their aim is to provide support for the training of 2,000 people.

Within the 12 business operators, 10 were NPOs.[2] After a review of these projects by the government, it was decided at the end of fiscal year 2012 to abolish both the New Public Commons Support Project and support for job creation in disaster areas through reconstruction-type support. However, from the beginning, both projects were only scheduled to run until the end of fiscal year 2012. Given that both projects were short-term, going forward, it will still be necessary to verify what concrete benefits they produced and what impact they had.

Use of sleeping accounts

Sleeping accounts were a facility discussed at the meetings to promote the New Public Commons. Generally, a sleeping account refers to a deposit account in a financial institution (including banks, credit unions, the Japan Post Bank, agricultural cooperatives, fishery cooperatives and labour credit associations) that holds funds for a long period. During that time, the depositor does not withdraw funds or perform any other type of transaction, and the financial institution is unable to correspond with the depositor. In the Special Investigation Committee on the Best Methods for Public Contracts, between the Government and Citizen Sectors that was established through the meetings to promote the New Public Commons, the use of sleeping accounts was proposed by Hiroki Komazaki, who is the founder of the ASNC Florence.

Excluding accounts in the Japan Post Bank, it is said that 14 million sleeping accounts are generated each year and that about ¥50 billion is deposited within them, waiting to be withdrawn. Following deliberations, a government policy was concluded that allowed money deposited in sleeping accounts, from fiscal 2014, to be used to support venture companies, companies with cash-flow difficulties due to the earthquake and NPOs. Because of this resolution, a new organisation was established to group together and manage these funds. It was initially envisaged that the scale of the project would be around ¥50 billion, but the sleeping deposits will be carried over each year. Consequently, the money that can be used will increase. The specific design of this system, such as the financing conditions, the managing organisation and the methods of management, is expected to be completed within fiscal year 2013.

Use of support funds

As part of the reconstruction efforts following the Great East Japan Earthquake, a special mention should be made of the private sector, financing that was provided by citizens, companies and other organisations without any participation by national or local governments. Thanks to the activities of 'NPOs, etc' and citizen groups, significant sums were contributed to various support funds.

Private-sector funds meant for disaster relief flowed into two types of funds: relief money and support funds. In the case of relief money, citizens, companies and other organisations contributed funds to the Japanese Red Cross Society, the Central Community Chest of Japan and the fund-raising campaigns run by various TV stations and newspapers. In principle, the money is paid directly to the victims as relief money to support the reconstruction of their homes and lives. Based on decisions of the Japanese Red Cross Society committee, which allocates donations along with the allocation committees of the prefectures in the disaster areas, the money is distributed to the victims via their local authorities. As of 12 June 2013, the total amount donated to relief funds was ¥367.7 billion.

In contrast, while the support fund is also made up of contributions from citizens, companies and other organisations, it is used as the source of funds for citizen groups' rescue activities (distribution of goods, provision of medical services, distribution of boiled rice, etc) and reconstruction-support activities. For example, it is allocated to 'NPOs, etc' carrying out support activities meant to provide victims with support in disaster areas. In this respect, it differs from the relief money that is distributed directly to victims. In the case of support funds, contributions from citizens, companies and other organisations go through aid organisations and intermediary organisations, which are distributed to citizen groups, such as NPOs, NGOs, foundations and associations, and Japan Platform (JPF) organisations. However, the reality is that the various funds are intertwined in a complicated manner. In addition to aid organisations and intermediary organisations, support is also provided by industry organisations, support funds, fund-raising sites and overseas NGOs. From the materials published by these various organisations and information provided on their homepages, the total amount of support funds donated at the end of April 2013 was estimated to be approximately ¥71.1 billion.

Despite the size of donations, the standards and principles used to distribute funds collected by aid organisations and intermediary organisations to NPOs and other citizen groups is not clear. In addition, unlike relief money, when a support fund is distributed, it is assumed that necessary costs (direct and indirect costs) will be recorded, and so the question is: how much is required for these expenses? Going forward, it will be necessary to explore these issues and questions.

New trends in non-profit/non-governmental organisations

Finally, we will discuss new trends in NPOs and NGOs, which include the contribution made by NGOs to the post-earthquake reconstruction, and the anti-nuclear power movement driven by a number of citizen groups. After the Great East Japan Earthquake, memories of the contributions to emergency support and reconstruction support that were made by NGOs remain. Up until recently, these NGOs had mainly been active in the international cooperation field, but when assisting with the earthquake disaster, they were able to utilise the knowledge, experience, ideas and methods that they have acquired in providing urgent humanitarian aid in less-developed countries and trouble spots throughout the world. For instance, the JPF (which was formed in 2000 through a collaboration of three groups), NGOs, the economic world and the government provide humanitarian support overseas. After the earthquake, the JPF immediately rushed into action and contributed greatly to reconstruction support by raising a large sum through donations, among other things. Indeed, overlooking a crisis in Japan itself would have violated the principles set out for its establishment (Yamauchi et al, 2013).

Moreover, in August 2012, when the government carried out the first discussion-type public opinion poll, a large-scale anti-nuclear power movement was generated, and every Friday night, a large number of citizens gathered outside the Prime Minister's Office to hold the so-called 'Friday demo'. On 22 August, 10 members of the Metropolitan Coalition Against Nukes visited Prime Minister Noda at the Prime Minister's Office and directly told him of their organisation's opinions, which was considered to be an groundbreaking event. The Metropolitan Coalition Against Nukes, which does not have a juridical personality, is a network of several groups that are opposed to nuclear power and argue that Japan should reduce its reliance on nuclear power. Many of the organisations participating in the network are voluntary groups, and hardly any of these have a juridical personality (Yamauchi et al, 2013). It is thought that, going forward, there will be increasing opportunities for this sort of loose network to utilise Social Networking Service (SNS) and the Internet in order to function as a new form of advocacy.

Levels of awareness about non-profit organisations and the need for education about them

Levels of awareness about non-profit organisations

As was described earlier, due to revisions to the Civil Code, the NPO Law and the tax system, there has been a significant increase in the space available for the activities of private NPOs, including NPO corporations. Further, the presence of NPOs within the efforts to recover from the Great East Japan Earthquake and other natural disasters has steadily risen. However, has the public's awareness of NPOs also risen in conjunction with the increased significance of the presence of NPOs?

Figure 13.2: Organisations regarded as non-profit organisations

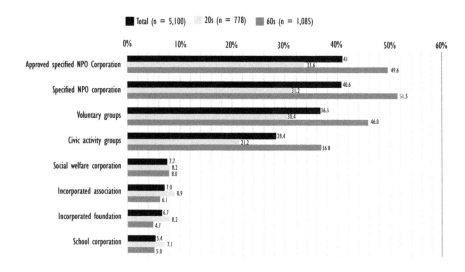

Note: N = 5,110.

Source: Intage Inc. (2011)

In December 2011, an Internet survey was conducted by Intage Inc (*N* = 5,110) asking respondents to select from among 15 NPOs and choose those organisations that 'You regard as NPOs'. Multiple answers were possible. The overall order of answers was as follows: (1) 'Approved NPO corporation' at 41.0%; (2) 'NPO corporation' at 40.6%; (3) 'Volunteer groups' at 36.6%; and (4) 'Civic activity groups' at 28.4% (see Figure 13.2). On the other hand, organisations that were regarded as NPOs by less than 10% of respondents were: (1) 'Social welfare corporation' at 7.7%; (2) 'Incorporated association' at 7.0%; (3) 'Incorporated foundation' at 6.7%; and (4) 'School corporation' at 5.4%. From this result, people comparatively know 'new-type NPOs' and it was apparent that levels of awareness about these 'traditional' organisations as NPOs was particularly low. In addition, the choice of 'I do not know/not any of them' was selected by as much as 39.7% of respondents.

Moreover, from the survey, it became apparent that the younger the respondent, the lower their level of awareness about NPOs tended to be. Among these respondents, those aged from 20 to 29 (*N* = 778) had the following respective levels of awareness: (1) 'Approved NPO corporation' at 33.6%; (2) 'NPO corporation' at 31.2%; (3) 'Volunteer groups' at 30.4%; and (4) 'Civic activity groups' at 21.2%. However, 'I do not know/not any of them' was selected by 48.6% of this age group, meaning about half of the members answered that they do not know anything about NPOs.

In contrast to this, among those in their 60s (*N* = 1,085): 49.6% were aware of an 'Approved NPO corporation'; 51.5% of an 'NPO corporation'; 46.0% of 'Volunteer groups'; and 36.8% of 'Civic activity groups'. From this, it was understood that the older the age of the respondent, the higher their level of awareness about NPOs. However, even among respondents in their 60s, the level of awareness about a 'Social welfare corporation' was lower than would be conventionally expected, at only 8.0%.

This sort of age gap in levels of awareness about NPOs probably has something to do with mass-communication reporting, as the media tends to focus on NPO corporations from among the different types of NPOs (Yamauchi et al, 2010).

The need for education about non-profit organisations

In order to increase levels of awareness about NPOs, it is vital to enhance education about NPOs. It is hoped that a role will be played by human resource training such that trainees understand the roles and functions of the NPO sector and consequently become able to utilise it. Additionally, in recent years, graduate schools have been established that are providing courses in public policy and public management, referred to as public policy graduate schools. In 2003, a system for professional graduate schools designed to train students to become specialists in their profession was introduced in Japan.

Through this system, the focus in graduate schools is to train students to be professional practitioners. In addition to training conventional researchers, the purpose of establishing many of these graduate schools was to train professionals who can play a positive role in public policy and public management at actual work locations. These graduate schools have been actively accepting mature students and have become a new place of learning for government personnel, as well as company employees who want to contribute to tackling social problems. In addition, joining NPOs and NGOs is a path being pursued by students after they graduate, and hopes are rising that these institutions will be able to increase the understanding that government personnel and company employees have about NPOs.

We conducted an investigation of the research courses being provided in the 48 master's programmes (first term of doctoral course) and professional courses being run by the 44 graduate schools that are considered to provide courses in the field of public policy and public management. Based on the 2011 fiscal year lecture outlines published on the homepages of each of the respective research courses, an investigation was carried out for the NPO/NGO-related subjects to ascertain 'Who will carry out the lectures?', 'What is the subject name?', 'What is the content?' and 'What text will be used?'. Table 13.2 shows the numbers of graduate schools investigated in terms of their forms of establishment.

By looking at the course outlines and syllabi of the research courses, we investigated whether there was an NPO/NGO-related subject (hereinafter referred to as 'NPO-related subject') on the outline. NPO -related subjects are those subjects that deal with the themes of NPOs and NGOs, social enterprises, community businesses, social capital, and the formation of civil society.

Looking at the number of subjects in the NPO field, it appears that a research course contains 2.7 NPO-related subjects on average; the median was zero (12 research courses had this value). Thirty-three research courses, which is equivalent to 70% of the total, contained less than the average of 2.7 subjects and it became apparent that many research courses provide very few subjects in the NPO field (see Figure 13.3).

Table 13.2: The number of public policy graduate schools (professional schools)

	Number
National	19(6)
Private	29(3)
Sum	48(9)

Source: Compiled from data on the homepages of each university.

Next, we classified the content of NPO-related subjects in terms of whether they were theory- or practice-focused. We will give some examples of subjects classified as theory-based. 'NPO Theory', provided in the policy major of the Graduate School for Creative Cities, Osaka City University, is an introductory course aimed at providing students with an overall understanding and acquisition of knowledge about NPOs. 'International Cooperation Research' on the governance research course of the Graduate School of Meiji University takes an interdisciplinary viewpoint on the various problems relating to development assistance carried out by government agencies and NGOs and the methods of ascertaining its effects.

Figure 13.3: Number of non-profit organisation-related subjects

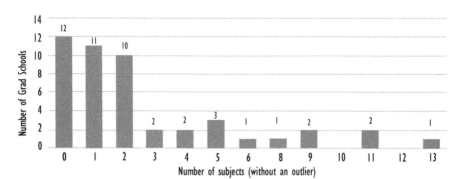

Source: Tanaka and Osawa (2012).

We will also give some examples of subjects classified as practical subjects. In the 'Special Course on Local Community Revitalization' in the regional policy research course of the Graduate School of the Takasaki City University of Economics, students research the activities of NPO corporations within Takasaki City, visit local communities in the Haruna and Kurabuchi districts, and study measures to revitalise local communities within Takasaki City. In 'Social Business Product Development and Promotion' at Keio University's graduate school, research courses on policy and media require students to analyse social changes at the social business frontier from the perspective of the development and promotion of products and services.

When we consider the 36 research courses that have established NPO-related subjects, we see that only 17 research courses, or 35.4% of all courses (17/48), offer a curriculum that provide students with both subjects on NPO theory and management practice. From this, it can be said that there are not many research courses in Japan that focus on both theory and practice.

In the US, the Nonprofit Academic Centers Council (NACC) sets a standardised curriculum for those NPO-related subjects that should be taught in graduate schools and by university faculties. The NACC (2007) guidelines are divided into two parts. The first part is on 'The role of the nonprofit and volunteer sectors in society', and describes the theories that the students should be familiar with by the time they complete the course. Items in the first part include 'Nonprofit organizations, volunteering, and philanthropy', 'Public policy and law' and 'Public services and citizen participation'. The second part is on 'Management and leadership in nonprofit organizations' and describes the applied knowledge and skills required to be a manager in an NPO. Items in the second part include 'Management and leadership in nonprofit organisation', 'Fund raising', 'Financial management', 'Nonprofit marketing' and 'Assessment methods for decision making'. What we must be aware of here is the scope of the term 'NPO'. For example, when the term 'NPO' is used in the US, it includes not only organisations that correspond to 'new-type' NPO corporations in Japan, but also a variety of other 'traditional' organisations, such as private schools, hospitals and welfare facilities, foundations, and so on.

From the results of this investigation, it has become apparent that, excluding some of the research courses, there are only a small number of NPO-related subjects in the research courses provided by Japan's public policy graduate schools, and that in terms of content, they are not achieving a balance between theory and practice. Moreover, among the lecturers teaching these subjects, it was found that nearly half of the research courses do not have full-time teachers or teachers holding additional posts. Further, practitioners are not teaching a sufficient number of these courses. As a result, it is clear that education regarding NPOs provided by Japan's public policy graduate schools is still very much a work in progress.

While there are graduate schools providing students with an education in the NPO field, more than a few of them are intended to train students to be researchers. Clarifying the reasons for this is one issue for future research, though one reason is thought to be that Japan's graduate schools are rooted in a conventional and traditional academic framework; moreover, it is likely that NPOs and NGOs do not have a fully established position within the existing academic framework. There is a need to investigate methods for teacher training and the participation of more practitioners. Finally, there is a need to establish common guidelines, similar to the NACC guidelines, in order to ensure both the quality and quantity of NPO educational programmes in the future.

Issues for the future

During the election of the House of Representatives in December 2012, practically no items relating to NPOs were included in the public policy commitments and manifestos of the 12 political parties competing at that time. It did not seem that this oversight was because of a lack of expectations for NPOs, but rather that a tentative infrastructure is already in place to support NPOs through the legal and tax systems, as had been requested by the NPOs themselves. In the future, NPOs are going to be asked to what extent they can play a role in compensating for the failures of government and the failures of the market, and they will be asked for the results. Of course, there are problems that need to be addressed. For example, there is a need to eliminate inequalities in the tax system between SNCs and social welfare corporations. There is also a need to construct a tax system that is consistent from top to bottom. Another problem is the management unclearness of general non-profit corporations. Because the information is not open, profit-oriented companies may be included in them. Finally, a debate will need to take place regarding unification of Japan's system of non-profit corporations, as a diverse range of such corporations exist within the country, which includes public-interest corporations, SNCs and social welfare corporations.

Notes

[1] For example, Nishide (2009), Osborne (2003), Schwartz and Pharr (2003), Vinken et al (2010) and Yamauchi (2003).

[2] These are: Ishinomaki Revival Support Network (NPO corporation); ETIC (Entrepreneurial Training for Innovative Communities) (NPO corporation); Groundwork Mishima (general association corporation); SAVE IWATE (general association corporation); Social Business Network (association corporation); Tohoku New Business Conference (NPO corporation); 20th Century Archive Sendai (public interest association corporation); JACEVO (The Japan Association of Chief Executives of Voluntary Organisations) (NPO corporation); Furusato Return Support Center (approved NPO corporation): and HIT (Hokkaido Intellect Tank) (general association corporation).

References

Cabinet Office (2012) *Fiscal 2011 Survey of Actual Conditions in Specific Nonprofit Activities Corporations and Usage Conditions of the System for the Approved Specific Nonprofit Activities Corporation.*

Cabinet Office (2013) *The Report from the Public Interest Corporation Commission*, 1 February.

Cabinet Office (2014) *Fiscal 2013 Survey of Actual Conditions in Specific Nonprofit Activities Corporations and Survey of Civic Social Responsibility.*

Intage Inc (2011) *The Survey of the Regard for NPOs* (in Japanese).

NACC (Nonprofit Academic Centers Council) (2007) *Curricular Guidelines for Graduate Study in Nonprofit Leadership, the Nonprofit Sector and Philanthropy*, Cleveland: Nonprofit Academic Centers Council.

Nishide, Y. (2009) *Social Capital and Civil Society in Japan*, Sendai: Tohoku University Press.

Osborne, S.P. (2003) *The Voluntary and Non-Profit Sector in Japan*, Routledge Curzon.

Pekkanen, R. (2006) *Japan's Dual Civil Society; Members Without Advocates*, Stanford University Press.

Schwartz, F.J. and Pharr, S.J. (2003) *The State of Civil Society in Japan*, Cambridge.

Tanaka, T. and Osawa, N. (2012) 'How Should We Teach the NPO/NGO-Related Subjects at Public Policy School for Building Civil Society? Japanese Case', paper presented at the Association for Research on Nonprofit Organizations and Voluntary Action, Indianapolis, 16 November.

Vinken, H., Nishimura, Y., White, B.L.J. and Deguchi, M. (2010) *Civic Engagement in Contemporary Japan*, Springer.

Yamauchi, N. (2003) *The Economics of the Japanese Nonprofit Sector*, Kyoto: Shoukadoh.

Yamauchi, N., Tanaka, T. and Okuyama, N. (2010) *NPO White Paper 2010* (in Japanese), OSSIP, Center for Nonprofit Research & Information.

Yamauchi, N., Tanaka, T. and Okuyama, N. (2013) *NPO White Paper 2013* (in Japanese), OSSIP, Center for Nonprofit Research & Information.

FOURTEEN

Think tanks and policy analysis: meeting the challenges of think tanks in Japan

Mika Shimizu

Introduction

What the late Robert S. McNamara described at a meeting of the 'Think Tanks to Japan'[1] project in 1991 reflects the challenges of 'think tanks' that Japan has faced for many years. He stated that:

> if I were the President of the United States, the first thing I would do is to pick up the phone and call to my friend to say dear friend, there are many things I would like to discuss with you, but the foremost thing I should tell you is to establish five think tanks tomorrow. Other things to discuss would follow that. (Cited in Ueno, 2009: 170)

What did he mean by that?

Existing studies indicate that many 'think tanks', generally defined as organisations that generate policy-oriented research, analysis and advice (McGann, 2012), do exist in Japan. According to the '2011 Global Go To Think Tank Rankings', Japan was ranked ninth in the world in terms of think-tank numbers (103) (McGann, 2012). The National Institute for Research Advancement (NIRA) in Japan has collected data on 'think tanks' (defined as 'organisations engaged in policy research') from 1982 through to the current year, and records 198 organisations in 1992, and 201 in 2012 (NIRA, 2011).

On the other hand, Japan has few think tanks if viewed in terms of strict definitions of 'think tanks' as characterised by specifically having: (1) 'relative autonomy'; (2) key functions based on policy analysis and evaluation; and (3) catalytic roles between governments and civil society (see the following section for details). This fact has not been understood well by the public or even by policy communities within Japan. Where does the gap come from, how is the gap related to the preceding comments by McNamara and how are the resulting relevant challenges interlinked to policy analysis, relevant social, economic or policy systems, and public policy in Japan?

In seeking answers to these questions, this chapter is designed to address the challenges of present Japanese think tanks, with a focus on policy analysis, through the following three areas of analysis. First, an overview of think tanks in Japan is provided by articulating relevant gaps with key ingredients of strictly defined think tanks. Second, an exploration of how think tanks have been incorporated into Japanese society is conducted by identifying the differences between think tanks in Japan and in the US, and articulating relevant policy and social systems interlinked to the state of think tanks. Third, a case study is presented of the 2011 Tohoku Disaster, which examines how the state of think tanks in Japan is relevant to specific public policy. Based on these three analyses, the final section concludes with a discussion of policy analysis and think tanks in Japan in the context of seeking alternative models.

Overview of 'think tanks' in Japan and gaps with key ingredients of think tanks

Overview of think tanks in Japan

According to 'Think Tank Information 2012' issued by the NIRA (2011), which provides data drawn from 201 think tanks in Japan as of 2011,[2] almost half of think tanks (99 organisations; 49.3%) are for-profit corporations. For others: 77 (38.3%) are foundations; 19 (9.5%) are *shadan* corporations (incorporated associations); three (1.5%) are *dokuritsu-gyosei* corporations (independent administrative corporations);[3] and two (1%) are non-profit corporations (NIRA, 2011).

Such think tanks in Japan have the following characteristics (see the details in Box 14.1 and the discussion in the preceding section):

- Economics and land development/utility account for almost 40% of expertise in think tanks.
- About 75% are funded by national or local governments and granted research is limited to 2.2%.
- More than half of think tanks do not provide outputs to the public (25.9%) or provide outputs in very limited ways (needs approval for 30.7%).

Box 14.1: Overview of existing 'think tanks' in Japan

Expertise: The major prioritised expertise of think tanks are: 1) economics (18%); 2) land development/utility (17.9%); and 3) industries. These are followed by different categories with minor percentages: transportation (6.0%); environmental issues (6.0%); politics and administration (5.5%); and so on.

Research Type/Funds: Of research projects (total numbers 3,078): 65% are contracted research; 32.8% are independent research; and granted research is limited to 2.2%. Among contracted research projects, about 75% are funded by national or local governments.

Publications: Of the 3,072 research projects that completed in fiscal year 2010: 25.9% do not make research outputs available to the public; 30.7% can refer their contents with the approval of commissioned/granted research organisations or research-conducted organisations; 31.7% provide reports to the public for free; and 11.6% provide reports available to the public for payment.

The origin of think tanks in Japan dates back to the 1970s. Around that time, the first major for-profit research organisations were established, such as the Nomura Research Institute (in 1965), the Japan Information Service (currently, the Japan

Research Institute) (in 1969) and the Mitsubishi Research Institute (in 1970). While the Japanese concept of a 'think tank' was modelled on US policy research institutions, such as the RAND Corporation and Brookings Institution (Ueno, 1998), which are major non-profit think tanks in the US, 'think tank' organisations established in Japan were for-profit institutions funded by Japanese giant enterprises.

Although it is not appropriate to consider for-profit institutions as not being think tanks just because they are for-profit, it is necessary to carefully examine how the functions of for-profit and non-profit institutions differ. In fact, this question is directly related to the reason why it is essential to examine think tanks from the perspective of the strictly defined criteria for think tanks (discussed in the following section). While the details of the differences between non-profit think tanks (originated in the US) and for-profit think tanks (rooted in Japan) are discussed in the following section, it has been pointed out by experts who studied Japanese think tanks that research conducted by Japanese think tanks is typically funded and designed to address a government agency's or private company's interests rather than the interests of the broader public (Telgarsky and Ueno, 1996).

In the decades following the first major wave, there were some changes in the environment of research institutes in Japan, which sometimes move forward but sometimes go backward. These include:

- The National Research Advancement Act was introduced in 1974 to institutionalise the implementation and provision of grants for research development for the public, which allowed the government and others to provide funds or assets for this purpose. This Act has led the government to set up the aforementioned NIRA. While the NIRA has played a role in promoting Japanese think tanks by providing research funds and coordinating policy research projects (Suzuki, 2011), the NIRA had to cut major functions after the Act was abolished in 2007.
- In the late 1980s, financial institutions and insurance companies rushed to establish their own affiliated for-profit research organisations, including the Sanwa Research Institute (later called Mitsubishi UFJ Research & Consulting), the Daiwa Bank Research Institute (later called the Resona Research Institute) and the Fuji Research Institute (later called the Mizuho Information Research Institute).
- At the beginning of the 1990s, many local governments funded the establishment of local think tanks, while some of them, including ones in Kochi and Kagoshima, had already been abolished .
- While political parties established the Public Policy Platform (Liberal Democratic Party in 2005) and 'Think Tank 2005 Japan' (Democratic Party of Japan in 2006), these were abolished in the midst of drastic changes in the political environment after the Democratic Party of Japan came to power in 2009.

Given the preceding, with some exceptions, the overall picture of think tanks in Japan, both in terms of scope and numbers, has not changed much for almost the past 20 years.

Key ingredients of 'think tanks' and existing gaps in think tanks in Japan

It is well-known that there are considerable difficulties in defining think tanks and, as a result, there is a range of definitions for 'think tanks'. Therefore, in examining the role that Japanese think tanks play in policy analysis, the perspective of a strictly defined think tank is required. The gaps between broadly defined and strictly defined think tanks are directly associated with the challenges of Japanese think tanks in policy analysis.

As a matter of fact, while there are different existing pieces of literature regarding think tanks, these tend to describe variations of think tanks regarding, for example, the size, financial sources and natures of the institutions. The key factors by which think tanks can be differentiated from other research organisations have not necessarily been synthesised in the existing literature.

In the following are listed three key ingredients of strictly defined think tanks drawn from the existing literature and from the author's experience in think tanks in Japan and the US. These ingredients tend to be lacking among Japanese institutions called 'think tanks'. Each ingredient is discussed in association with think tanks in Japan, as follows.

'Relative autonomy'

While think tanks are supposed to be independent of government, political parties, businesses and other interests in order to engage in independent policy research for the public, think tanks are 'relatively autonomous' organisations in that they are often in resource-dependent relationships with funding institutes (Stone and Garnett, 1998). On the other hand, although perfect independence or autonomy is not realistic given the resource dependency, think tanks are supposed to maintain research freedom and their research results should not be influenced by their funders, wherever the funds come from.

In terms of relative autonomy, for-profit think tanks (which are the majority of think tanks in Japan) need to rely on resources of specific interests since their ultimate goal is to gain profits for shareholders, who are their ultimate customers. Given that, it is apparent that for-profit think tanks have little relative autonomy (discussed in detail in the following section).

Key functions in the comprehensive policy process

Overall, think tanks are supposed to perform several key functions in the comprehensive policy process, especially in policy analysis, including: (1) identification of issues and policy problems; (2) policy analysis and evaluation; (3) policy recommendations; and (4) policy dissemination. While some think tanks in Japan engage in some of these functions, there are few think tanks for which it can be argued that they engage in the comprehensive scope of the key functions. For example, researchers in think tanks write reports on some policy issues, but the outputs are not necessarily based on policy analysis and policy evaluation, and they are not necessarily disseminated to policymakers or to the public.

Catalytic roles

Think tanks are supposed to play a catalytic role in policy communities among national and local governments, the Congress or Diet, businesses, the media, and universities, by providing critical information and knowledge, promoting policy discussions, and integrating interdisciplinary knowledge for problem-solving approaches to policy issues. More importantly, think tanks needs to play a catalytic role in bridging the gap between the public or civil society and government(s). For the public or civil society, think tanks are supposed to raise awareness of policy issues among the public, provide relevant information and knowledge in a timely manner, translate policy issues so that they become easy to understand for the public, and promote discussions among the public. On the one hand, think tanks are supposed to convey views from the public to policy communities based on experiences and knowledge, and provide policy options to the policy communities that account for the public's views. Given this role, think tanks are strongly related to open information and democracy, but very few think tanks in Japan engage in this role (see the detail in the following sections).

How have 'think tanks' been incorporated into Japanese society?

Given the overall picture of 'think tanks' in Japan and the existing gaps with key ingredients of strictly defined think tanks as identified previously, this section goes further to examine how 'think tanks' have been incorporated into Japanese society, with a focus on policy analysis. In examining think tanks from the aspect of policy analysis, it is not enough to just focus on one-time policy analysis in a report or in a project. A broader picture is necessary, which can be gleaned from the following three perspectives:

- The function of policy analysis in think tanks can work only when the function is incorporated into other key functions (this is related to 'Relative autonomy' and 'Key functions in the comprehensive policy process', previously outlined as key ingredients in strictly defined think tanks).
- Other than key functions at the organisational level of individual think tanks, those functions needs to be interlinked with other critical factors at market (industry) and social levels (these factors are relevant to the previously discussed key ingredient of 'Catalytic roles').
- The interlinkage of think tanks with the market and social levels are further interlinked with policy and social systems.

Given the preceding, the following examination addresses the question of how 'think tanks' have been incorporated into Japanese society from three dimensions at organisational, policy market (industry) and social levels, and policy and social systems, respectively.

Key functions of think tanks: non-profit versus for-profit (organisational level)

As specified in the preceding section, the majority of think tanks in Japan are for-profit, which means that they rely on the resources of specific interests and have little relative autonomy. This is not the only issue for autonomy itself, but the issue that impacts the key functions or operations of think tanks.

To articulate this, a typical type of for-profit think tank in Japan can be compared with a typical type of non-profit think tank in the US in terms of key functions or operations at an organisational level. Table 14.1 illustrates the comparative summary between a typical type of Japanese for-profit think tank and a typical type of US non-profit think tank, along with key factors, based on the author's more than 10 years of observations and her own research experiences in both non-profit US think tanks and Japan's for-profit think tanks.

Table 14.1: US non-profit think tanks versus Japanese for-profit think tanks

	Japanese for-profit think tanks	**US non-profit think tanks**
Relations between their major business and policy research	Research department is located alongside other business departments such as information technology system integration and business consulting departments Little policy research	Locate policy research as their central business Strong policy research
Financial resources	Research projects are commissioned by governments or businesses and the financial source of each project is usually one source	Foundations, governments, businesses and individual funding (multiple financial sources for a project)
Relations with different stakeholders	Governments and businesses that fund projects tends to be considered as 'clients' and major goals of the projects are to meet the requests from the clients	Play roles as a hub among different stakeholders, including governments, businesses and the public Overall, the funders do not get involved in policy research, but attempt to be involved in intellectual discussions
Human resources	Researchers do not necessarily have PhDs or policy-relevant careers and the researchers are rotated among other departments through business orders	In most cases, policy researchers have PhDs and have built up policy-relevant careers in think tanks, governments, universities, foundations or the media
Scope of policy research issues and terms	Scope of issues is influenced by clients/ customers, and most of the research is based on short-term requirements	Cover broad range of domestic/international issues on short-, mid- and long-term bases
Operations of policy research	Issue definitions and research approaches reflect client intentions or requests. Collaborative research projects beyond organisations are few In most cases, policy discussions are limited to meetings with customers or some specialists. Public forums and discussions during the process of projects are rare	Policy professionals are involved in policy research from issue identification and definition stages Many projects are conducted through collaboration with other organisations for multiple years and with a series of public forums and discussions
Outputs	Only a part of outputs from projects are accessible to the public In many cases, it is difficult for the researchers to track their reports and know how those outputs are used	Most outputs are accessible to the public through websites or publications Policy information, discussions and knowledge can be readily tracked

In summary, Japanese for-profit think tanks locate their research departments as a part of their businesses and policy research cannot be their major target in business operations, mainly because of the influence of financial resources and their clients. In turn, the state of their business is reflected in the human resources that are assigned to research, the limited scope of policy research issues and terms, the limited operations of policy research, and the limited access to outputs of policy research.

On the other hand, as for US non-profit think tanks, their core business focuses on policy research that is supported by different types of financial resources and within which they maintain their autonomy and play the role of a hub among different stakeholders. This operation is reflected in their professional human resources, their broad range of scope of policy research and terms, and their accessible outputs, which are easy to track.

The preceding analysis does not intend to rush into concluding that non-profit organisations are better than for for-profit organisations. However, at least in terms of the key functions of think tanks and policy analysis, non-profit think tanks in the US have better capacities and functions to play a role as 'think tanks' and commit to policy research and analysis. For-profit Japanese think tanks act as public consulting firms rather than think tanks.

Market and social levels

Policy market (market or industrial level)

In general, individual think tanks may be sustainable only if there is an economic and social platform, that is, a policy market (or industry) where different think tanks that engage in policy research and analysis can compete with each other and interact with other stakeholders in terms of functions, outputs and financial resources. Given this, to articulate the state of relevant markets related to think tanks in Japan, it is useful to compare the Japanese situation with that of the US. Figures 14.1 and 14.2 depict overall snapshots of think tanks and other stakeholders in Japan and the US at policy market levels, respectively. Based on these, the following things can be pointed out:

- (a) In Japan, most research projects related to public policy are funded by governments and are conducted mainly by for-profit think tanks and universities (and a small number of non-profit organisations). While foundations provide a few related grants, the numbers are small. (b) There are few interactions among stakeholders, and the rigid lines between governments and for-profit think tanks or governments and universities are major relationships among different stakeholders, though there are some exceptions. Given (a) and (b), the scope of the policy market is very limited in Japan.
- In comparison, the US has a large policy market where think tanks play major roles as catalysts through dynamic interactions with different stakeholders, including governments, businesses, the media, academic institutions and the public. A key factor that links different stakeholders is how to address 'public goods', that is, the public issues to be addressed.

Another major difference between policy markets in the US and Japan is that the US has major policy analysis and policy evaluation functions within governments, such as the Congress Research Service (CRS), Government Accountability Office (GAO) and Congressional Budget Office (CBO), which are lacking in Japan. Those institutions allow policy markets to thrive in that they promote policy discussions between think tanks and other institutions by providing information and knowledge, and, more importantly, seek different knowledge and information from outside think tanks. In essence, a solid policy market exists in the US where the functions of think tanks can work and policy analysis by think tanks can be utilised in public policies.

Figure 14.1: Overall snapshot of think tanks and other stakeholders in Japan at the policy-market level

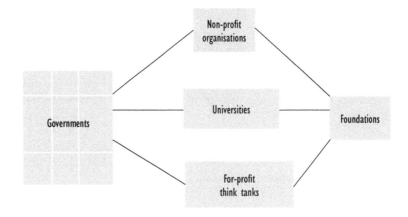

Figure 14.2: Overall snapshot of think tanks and other stakeholders in the US at the policy-market level

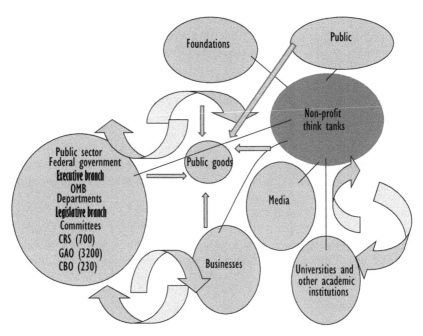

Notes: Numbers of staff in parentheses. CRS = Congress Research Service; GAO = Government Accountability Office; CBO = Congressional Budget Office; OMB = Office of Management and Budget.

One of factors that led to the current state of the policy market in Japan may be related to the involvement of civil society in public policy and democracy, as discussed in the following.

Civil society and democracy (social level)

Since the beginning of the 1990s, the initiators of the aforementioned 'Think Tanks to Japan' project (see the Introduction) have recognised the strengthening of civil society and democracy as a critical factor in establishing strictly defined (the project uses the term 'independent') think tanks in Japan, stating the following as a premise of their work:

> For democratic civil societies it is increasingly critical that citizens raise policy issues outside of government, and that they possess the capability of scrutinizing government policy decisions. Key to the public's ability to debate policies that affect them in an intelligent and informed manner is an accurate information base. Research institutions that operate separately from government or industry and that conduct objective, independent analysis of policy proposals can provide the foundation of knowledge upon which this 'informed debate' can be based. (Telgarsky and Ueno, 1996: 2)

The 'Think Tanks to Japan' project was conducted for five years (from 1991 through 1996) by its US and Japan initiators, who were eager to establish independent think tanks given their lack in Japan. This project was a so-called pioneering effort that contributed to raising awareness and discussion of think tanks in Japan. For example, the World Think Tank Forum, which was organised as part of a project in Tokyo in 1995, was attended by more than 530 Japanese Diet members, academics and researchers. Also, they published in-depth relevant books that examined what the challenges were in establishing independent think tanks, and what the options were given Japan's own social and economic systems, based on extensive research on more than 100 different types of think tank in 16 different countries.

However, in the midst of political and social dynamisms, the valuable research efforts did not lead to a plan to establish the independent think tanks that they envisioned.[4] After that, we have seen few developments in terms of strictly defined think tanks in Japan, apart from some exceptions (discussed in the following case study and Conclusion).

It may be possible to explain the status in different ways, but reflecting the original driver in promoting independent think tanks in Japan, the followings can be pointed out. First, it has not been well-understood by the majority of policy communities and the public how think tanks are interlinked with civil society and democracy. Second, Japanese societies have not had enough capacities of civil society and democracy to establish (strictly defined) think tanks. The capacities of civil society may be related to the involvement of civil organisations outside of governments in policy analysis and policy discussions; the capacities of democracy may include open information, which allows the public to be involved in the policy process, and a system of checks on the government from a third party (see the following section).

Policy and social systems

In terms of policy and social systems, past studies have pointed out different policy and social systems that hampered the emergence of (strictly defined) think tanks in Japan. They include legal barriers and tax laws for non-profit organisations and philanthropic funds, limited access to information, Japan's rigid education and employment system, and the lack of a policy evaluation system (see Suzuki, 1993; Ueno, 1998, 2004).

To overcome these obstacles, some policy changes have been made over the past 15 years and some new laws have been introduced (see major changes in Table 14.2). These changes provide a basic foundation for strengthening the previously discussed capacities of civil society and democracy.

Table 14.2: Major relevant policy changes

Policy Evaluation Law	The Government Policy Evaluation Act was introduced in 2001 to mandate government ministries and agencies to conduct policy evaluation within their institutions
Non-Profit Organisations Law	The Law to Promote Specified Non-Profit Activities was introduced in 1998 to recognise the significance of non-profit organisations and provides legal status for those institutions. Later, the Law was reformed in 2011, mainly for simpler procedures of setting up non-profit organisations. Along with this reform, the Charity Law was reformed, which includes measures such as easing the process of getting favourable tax status for non-profit organisations and easing regulations for tax exemptions for non-profit organisations from individuals and corporations
Access to Information Law	The Administrative Information Disclosure Law was introduced in 1999 to promote disclosures of administrative information to the public. Later, in the Public Records and Archives Management Act introduced in 2009, the role of public records was specified as an intellectual resource to be shared by the people in support of the basis of sound democracy and provides procedures for public records and archives management

However, it is important to note that the new laws in Table 14.2 have not necessarily been implemented or are not enough to promote the capacities of civil society and democracy, particularly from the point of view of think tanks and policy analysis, as shown in the following.

Policy evaluation based on policy analysis and think tanks

While the Government Policy Evaluation Act was introduced in 2001, the Act is basically designed to evaluate policies by parties in charge within government ministries and agencies. Although the Act refers to 'the acquisition and utilization of findings of persons with relevant knowledge and experience', evaluations by independent third parties, which are a critical part of policy evaluation, are not formally incorporated in this Act. Furthermore, the evaluation results reported by each ministry or agency based on the Act are not formally linked with other critical functions of governments, such as budget planning.

Going further in terms of the policy evaluation system, the National Diet does not have its own policy analysis and evaluation-focused institutions, such as the aforementioned CRS, CBO and GAO in the US. For example, the primary roles of the Board of Audit in Japan should not be understood in the context of the GAO in the US: while the primary roles of the GAO in the US are to conduct policy evaluation based on policy analysis for governments, and, as a matter of fact, the GAO publishes more than 900 policy evaluation reports annually, the Board of Audit's primary role is in accounting, and is basically not intended to conduct policy evaluation. Having said that, after the Reform in the Board of Audit Act in 1998, it was institutionalised that the Board can report to the Diet if the Diet requests the Board to do so. However, there are few cases of the Board reporting to the Diet; as of 2012, the Board has made reports to the Diet in nine cases, and for others, the numbers are limited to less than five cases a year. As such, policy analysis and evaluation are not formally systematised in governments, which provide less opportunities for think tanks to be involved in policy analysis and evaluations because of a lack of demand for policy analysis and policy evaluation in the policy market.

Non-profit organisations and think tanks

The Law to Promote Specified Non-Profit Activities introduced in 1998 was a cornerstone in recognising the significance of non-profit organisations after the Great Hanshin Earthquake in 1995, providing legal status for those institutions, and the reform in the Law in 2011 was a step forward in creating simpler procedures for setting up non-profit organisations. However, in fact, although the numbers of non-profit organisations that have the special tax status has slightly increased since the law was reformed, as of September 2013, the current numbers are still limited to 247 organisations.[5] At the current time, we need to see how the reformed law impacts the numbers of non-profit organisations. On the one hand, from a policy analysis and think tank perspective, it is important to note that few non-profit organisations engage in policy analysis and evaluation, as indicated by the fact that non-profit organisations account for a considerably small percentage (around 1%) of research organisations that engage in policy research, as specified earlier.

The Reform of Charity Act encourages non-profit organisations to have a stable financial environment. It is important to note that giving by corporations and individuals has historically been quite small, though the situation has gradually been changing. According to the Japan Fundraising Association, the total amount of annual individual giving was estimated to be ¥545.5 billion in 2009, which accounts for only 0.12% of the nation's nominal gross domestic product (GDP), and ¥518.2 billion (0.11% of the nation's nominal GDP) in 2011 (except for giving for the Tohoku Disaster). On the other hand, it is important to note that around ¥600 billion has been donated by individuals in 2011. Regarding the total amount of corporate giving, it was ¥494 billion in 2008, which only accounts for 1.4% of the total amount of corporate annual income, while it increased to ¥695.7 billion in 2010, which is equivalent to 2.1% of the total amount of corporate annual income.

Access to information and think tanks

Access to information is critical for think tanks to engage in policy analysis and policy evaluation. Access to information is ensured by the Administrative Information Disclosure Law 1999, which promotes disclosures of administrative information to the public, and the Public Records and Archives Management Act 2009, which specifies the role of public records as an intellectual resource to be shared by the people. However, different cases have been seen where these acts were not necessarily implemented. For example, immediately after the Great East Japan Earthquake in 2011, then-Vice Prime Minister Katuya Okada reported to a ministerial meeting that 10 out of 15 organisations that were newly established by the Prime Minister's Office, including the Emergency Disaster Response Headquarters, Special Response, the Headquarters to Support Victims, the Nuclear Disaster Response Headquarters and the Reconstruction Headquarters, did not make any notes or records and he stated that it is likely that members of the organisations were too busy to record them.

In summary, reflecting the problems pointed out by previous studies, while there are some positive signs for possible change, most of the problems are still valid and enduring challenges exist.

Case study of the Tohoku Disaster: needs and relevance to functions and roles of think tanks

The Great East Japan Earthquake in 2011 (the Tohoku Disaster), which killed approximately 16,000 people, tremendously shocked Japanese society in a range of ways. The Tohoku Disaster brought about physical, economic and social challenges and posed critical challenges to policy structure. The following provides an overview of the major structural policy challenges that the Tohoku Disaster poses and how they are relevant to the functions of strictly defined think tanks discussed in the previous sections.

Multidisciplinary and multi-sectoral approach to extreme, complex and synergetic disaster risks and impacts

Overall, the Tohoku Disaster, caused by a tripartite (earthquake, tsunami and nuclear) disaster, brought wide-ranging short- to long-term social and economic effects and has impacted at least six major policy domains: disaster management; environment (removal of tons of debris); energy; public health; local economy and industry (eg fisheries, agriculture); and international relations (eg radioactive contamination of sea and air). These different issues are intricately linked in extremely complex and uncertain ways since each problem is linked with different policy domains beyond individual sectors.

The policy structural challenge is not just unique to the Tohoku Disaster, but, rather, part of global changes in emerging synergetic and complex disaster risks at local, national and global levels. Many of those disaster risks are related to globalisation, urbanisation and climate vulnerability. These risks are synergistically interlinked and dramatically changing the scope, severity and impact of many modern-day disasters. For example, impacts of earthquakes, hurricanes and tsunamis are linked with disaggregated infrastructures and population densities, which are dramatically increasing in urban and coastal areas all over the world, especially in Asia. These risks are also related to water, food and energy security.

Basically, the kinds of synergised risk specifically have three major characteristics, that is: (1) they interlink with other risks in complex ways to produce cascading disaster risks; (2) they cause multidimensional (human, physical, social and economic) and multi-sectoral effects and impacts; and (3) they bring different uncertain factors, particularly in terms of what the disaster risks bring about and when and how disaster risks bring about disasters.

The challenge requires systematising multidisciplinary and multi-sectoral policy research on risks and complex effects of risks on a continuous basis. To enable the systematising of research requires different institutions that can be engaged in policy analysis and evaluation through a comprehensive policy process and that can link with other stakeholders independently on a long-term basis. These required functions are closely related to the aforementioned three key ingredients of strictly defined think tanks, namely, relative autonomy, engagement in a comprehensive policy process, and catalytic roles.

Knowledge co-production required for addressing uncertainties

Given the aforementioned characteristics in emerging disaster risks, particularly uncertainties, the co-knowledge production system that links experiences and knowledge based on policy analysis and policy evaluation is critical. The Tohoku Disaster has shown that even when critical information and problems were identified by someone or some organisation, many of them were addressed separately from the overall disaster management system and public policy (Shimizu, 2012). To address uncertain and complex issues effectively requires far more systemic knowledge production than is normally required for conventional disasters. The co-knowledge production process includes systemically accumulating, synthesising and integrating key information, experience, data and lessons learned, beyond conventional expertise, organisational or geographical boundaries, to produce actionable policies. Furthermore, the co-knowledge production system will be enabled by pluralising and systematising basic knowledge production systems beyond demarcations of expertise and interests. The knowledge production systems include systemic analysis and evaluation to produce operational information, and diverse dissemination mechanisms for conveying the knowledge to end users in the form of 'actionable policies' (see Figure 14.3). Co-knowledge production can be made possible through institutions that can engage in a long-term comprehensive policy process, which is very relevant to the key ingredients of strictly defined think tanks.

Figure 14.3: The knowledge production system

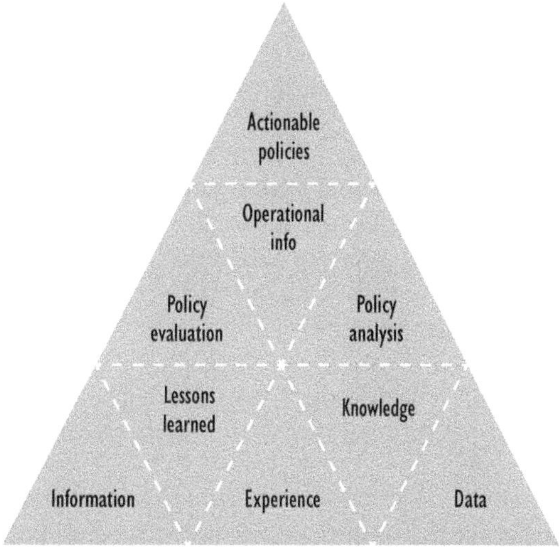

Source: Shimizu, 2012

Policy innovation based on policy analysis and evaluation required after disasters

After disasters, especially unprecedented large-scale disasters such as the Tohoku Disaster, policy evaluation-based policy analysis is required for policy renewal or innovation by identifying weaknesses of current policies through systematic and objective evaluation and by seeking what can be done to create better policies and how it can be done. In fact, after the Tohoku Disaster, different kinds of evaluations of the Tohoku Disaster have been conducted at different levels by different stakeholders (see Box 14.2).

Box 14.2: Overview of stakeholders engaged in evaluations of the Tohoku Disaster

- Government agencies and government committees
- Central Disaster Management Council
- Reconstruction Design Council (Advisory Panel of intellectual figures that was set up by the government of Japan in April 2011)
- Local governments
- Semi-public research institutions/academic groups
- The media
- Government Nuclear Power Accident Investigation Committee
- Japan Fukushima Nuclear Accident Independent Investigation Commission (NIIC; established by the national Diet)
- Rebuild Japan Initiative Foundation 'Fukushima Project'
- Tokyo Electronic Power Company (TEPCO) Fukushima Nuclear Power Plant Accident Committee

---

Overall, it is important to note that evaluations not only by parties of interest, such as different government agencies, but also third parties, such as independent commissions assigned by the Diet and the Rebuild Japan Initiative Foundation (which was founded as a non-profit foundation in March 2011), engaged to policy evaluations (mainly, the Fukushima nuclear power accidents). In particular, the NIIC, established by the national Diet on 8 December 2011, was the first independent investigative body in Japan's constitutional history to be established by the national Diet. According to the stipulations in the Law for the National Diet of Japan Fukushima Nuclear Accident Independent Investigation Commission, the chairman and commission members (nine) were appointed by the Speakers of the House of Councillors and House of Representatives and were selected from the private sector. Other important parts in the Act in terms of governance were that:

- The commission conducts its investigation of government based on investigative powers that insulate it from the influence of political parties and Diet members (Article 15).
- The Commission sets a goal of about six months from the date of appointment to submit to the Speakers of House of Councillors/House of Representatives a report listing the accident investigation results and proposals and to publish it (Article 16).[6]

However, in reviewing the evaluation processes and outputs of the aforementioned stakeholders, the following can be pointed out. First, overall, except for several cases pointed out earlier, most of the policy evaluations were limited to the ones by governments or related committees or organisations. Furthermore, even policy evaluation cases conducted by third or independent parties were limited to the challenge of the Fukushima Power Plant.

Second, while different governmental agencies, including the related governmental committees, conducted policy evaluations on individual issues, such as tsunamis, earthquakes, energy and telecommunication: (1) those policy evaluations tended to be made along stovepiped organisational lines; (2) few policy evaluation cases were based on objective data and policy analysis was limited; (3) few evaluations were open evaluation processes; and (4) most of the policy evaluations tended to be conducted on a one-time or ad hoc basis and it is hard to find linkages between policy evaluations and policy renewal or innovation.

Third, other than government-related organisations, policy evaluations have been conducted by third parties and independent committees, but those evaluations tended to be conducted on a one-time or ad hoc basis. It is important to note that even the NIIC, highlighted earlier, has been dissolved after publishing reports and conducting open forums based on the report. Furthermore, it turned out that the NIIC went through critical operational challenges, including: conducting research in such a short period; selecting capable research staff from outside that could engage in the review full-time for only a short period; and preparing the research infrastructure that underlay the investigation (see Suzuki, 2012).

As such, although different evaluations by different stakeholders tend to be made after disasters, the Tohoku case indicates that there is a lack of third-party or independent multilayered institutions that can engage in policy analysis continuously on a long-term basis in order to link with policy renewal or innovation. The lack of those institutions is relevant to the lack of strictly defined think thanks that have relative autonomy and can engage in a comprehensive policy process.

Conclusions and way forward for alternative think tank models

The analysis and discussion on think tanks and policy analysis in Japan has indicated three critical points. First, recognising 'think tanks' with a focus on the characteristics of (1) 'relative autonomy', (2) key functions based on policy analysis and evaluation, and (3) catalytic roles between governments and civil society is essential since those are interlinked with how think tanks can play roles with other stakeholders and what think tanks can provide through policy analysis. In particular, the key functions and roles include: i) identifying of issues and policy problems; ii) conducting policy analysis and evaluation; iii) making policy recommendations; iv) disseminating policy; v) raising awareness of policy issues among the public; vi) providing relevant information and knowledge in a timely manner; vii) translating policy issues so that they become easy to understand for the public; viii) promoting discussions among the public and conveying views from the public to policy communities based on experiences and knowledge; and viiii) providing policy options to policy communities. Very few think tanks in Japan have engaged in those functions or roles comprehensively.

Second, the state of Japanese think tanks is interlinked with the state of the policy market, democracy/civil society and policy and social systems. Japan lacks a solid policy market where different think tanks engage in policy research and analysis, compete with each other, and interact with other stakeholders in terms of functions, outputs and financial resources. The lack of a solid policy market is partly related to the lack of demand within governments for policy analysis and evaluation, since there are few relevant institutions within governments, and the lack of involvement of civil society in public policy, such as the involvement of civil organisations outside of governments in policy analysis and policy discussions.

Third, the case study of the 2011 Tohoku Disaster has demonstrated that the aforementioned three characteristics and nine functions or roles of think tanks are closely associated with the challenge arising from the Tohoku Disaster. That is: (1) extreme, complex and synergetic disaster risks and impacts require a multidisciplinary and multi-sectoral approach; (2) knowledge co-production is required to address uncertainties; and (3) policy innovation after disasters necessitates third-party or independent multilayered institutions that can engage in policy analysis continuously on a long-term basis. The very few existing think tanks in Japan contribute to this.

With this summary, readers may still wonder why Japanese think tanks have not engaged in (or have been prevented from engaging in) the aforementioned critical roles and functions of think tanks or why Japanese think tanks are so different from US think tanks. Different experts list a variety of related reasons, including historical, cultural and system-related aspects. For example, from historical and system perspectives, some say that since the concept of democracy was imported into Japan, the relationships among the government, private sector and civil society are still rigid and policymaking involving multi-stakeholders and relevant systems is immature. From cultural and system perspectives, some say that policy evaluation is culturally very difficult since 'evaluation' tends to be considered as a critique or as used to blame the actions of other people and relevant systems, which does not work well in Japan. Also from cultural and system perspectives, still others say that the employment system in Japan means that changing jobs between governments and the private sector is generally difficult, especially since the 'revolving-door' type of employment system in the US (former public servants going to work for think thanks, and congressmen and federal workers moving back and forth between government and the private sector) is not rooted in Japan, except for some exceptions, and that that kind of system may not fit with Japanese society from a cultural perspective.

For the aforementioned reasons, four things should be pointed out. First, looking at those reasons carefully, it can be recognised this is not just an issue of think tanks, but is more related to the whole society or broader picture of relationships among civil society, governments and private sector. Second, on the other hand, these reasons may not necessarily be true since there are emerging innovative groups of people who understand the importance of decision-making among multiple stakeholders, the evaluation of third parties and experiencing different jobs in different organisations, though this group of people are not the majority. Third, the preceding reasons should not be used as excuses for not facing the reality of the critical needs of the roles and functions of think tanks, as seen from the Tohoku Disaster. The underlying message here is not to say that Japan just needs US-type think tanks, but that critical roles and functions drawn from strictly defined think tanks are very necessary to fill in gaps, especially when facing complex policy challenges such as the Tohoku Disaster. Fourth, considering the second and third point, education may also be another important factor in changing the current state of think tanks in Japan. In this sense, although historical, cultural and systemic barriers exist, Japanese society should keep seeking to change the current state of think tanks through multiple channels, mainly through integrating education and system innovation (history and culture change will follow).

More specifically, given the challenges in the nexus of think tanks and policy analysis in Japan, how can the way forward be seen? Are there any alternative models for addressing the challenges? There are two different points of view on these questions.

First, it is critically important not only for governments and the policy community, but also for businesses, the media and the public, to understand the systemic challenges interlinked throughout the whole of society. Although the term 'think tanks' is broadly known in Japan, the term tends to be used as a buzzword or taken for granted, and the critical functions and roles of think tanks in association with public policy, society and civil society/democracy have hardly been discussed. As one of the ways of breaking through the current state, it is imperative to train innovative policy leaders, for example, mid-career government staff or researchers in the private sector or universities, who can understand the relevant challenges based on their knowledge and experiences and link those with their actions by disseminating the challenges and renewing their own activities and institutions for change.

Second, while the existing challenges are daunting, it may be a good idea to focus on some positive signs or practices and apply those to design or build innovative organisational models. Examples of positive signs/practices include:

- After the Tohoku Disaster, some private organisations, such as the Rebuild Japan Initiative Foundation (as stated in a previous section), and non-governmental organisation (NGO) networks, such as the Japan NGO Center for International Cooperation, have actively engaged in reviewing the Tohoku Disaster to provide policy recommendations and disseminate them to the public, and have expanded those activities into other critical issue areas.
- A number of social ventures that focus on solving social problems through businesses have been increasing over recent years. There are different types of organisations, small or large, for-profit or non-profit, or for-profit and non-profit, which engage in those social problem-solving efforts. In particular, the latter example suggests that discussions on think tanks should not be limited to non-profit versus for-profit; rather, a hybrid type of organisation, such as non-profit and for-profit (eg making profits through businesses and using part of the profits to fund the non-profit activities of think tanks), may be a possibility.

Finally, while this chapter focused on the Tohoku Disaster case to indicate the association of think tanks with the needs of public policy, there are emerging public policy issues that cannot be addressed only through traditional policy institutions and approaches, and require think tank roles and functions, especially in light of the multidisciplinary and multi-sectoral approach, knowledge co-production, and urgent policy innovation, including ageing/immigration, climate change, energy and food/water security issues. It is extremely urgent to face up to the challenges and to pave the way forward for think tanks and policy analysis in order to create a resilient and sustainable society.

Notes

[1] The project was initiated by the Urban Institute in the United States and the Sasakawa Peace Foundation in Japan in 1991.

[2] The data excludes 24 organisations that are university-affiliated and local government-affiliated organisations.

[3] National (government) research institutes changed status to become 'independent administrative corporations' after the administrative reforms of the 1990s.

[4] Interview with Dr Makiko Ueno, an initiator of the 'Think Tanks to Japan' project, 9 February 2013.

[5] See the Cabinet Office non-profit organisation page. Available at: https://www.npo-homepage.go.jp/ (accessed 13 September 2013).

[6] The final report was published in Japanese on 5 July 2012.

References

McGann, J.G. (2012) '2012 Global Go To Think Tanks Index Report'. Available at: http://repository.upenn.edu/think_tanks/7/ (accessed 1 February 2013).

NIRA (National Institute for Research Advancement) (2011) 'Think Tank Information 2012'. Available at: http://www.nira.or.jp/pdf/tt2012_gaiyo.pdf (accessed 1 February 2013).

Shimizu, M. (2012) 'December, Resilience in Disaster Management and Public Policy: A Case Study of the Tohoku Disaster', *Risk, Hazards and Crisis in Public Policy*, vol 3, no 4, pp 40–59.

Stone, D. and Garnett, M. (1998) 'Introduction: Think Tanks, Policy Advice and Governance', in D. Stone, A. Denham and M. Garnett (eds) *Think Tanks across Nations: A Comparative Approach*, Manchester: Manchester University Press, pp 1–20.

Suzuki, T. (1993) 'Policy Development and Think Tanks in Japan', in R.J. Struyk, M. Ueno and T. Suzuki (eds) *A Japanese Think Tank: Exploring Alternative Models*, The Urban Institute, Part 1.

Suzuki, T. (2011) 'Why have No "American-Style" Think Tanks been Developed in Japan?' (in Japanese), *Policy and Management Studies*, vol 2, pp 30–50.

Suzuki, T. (2012) 'Experiences in NIIC' (in Japanese), Workshop in Policy Analysis Network, 17 November.

Telgarsky, J.P. and Ueno, M. (1996) 'Introduction: Think Tanks and a Changing Japan', in J.P. Telgarsky and M. Ueno (eds) *Think Tanks in a Democratic Society: An Alternative Voice*, The Urban Institute, Chapter 1.

Ueno, M. (1998) 'Think Tanks in Japan: Towards a More Democratic Society', in D. Stone, A. Denham and M. Garnett (eds) *Think Tanks Across Nations: A Comparative Approach*, Manchester University Press, Chapter 9.

Ueno, M. (2004) 'Think Tanks in Japan: A New Alternative', in D. Stone and A. Denham (eds) *Think Tank Traditions: Policy Research and the Politics of Ideas*, Manchester University Press, Chapter 10.

Ueno, M. (2009) 'For the Students of Policy Studies; Remembering a Message by the Late Robert S. McNamara' (in Japanese), *Journal of Policy Studies*, no 32, pp 169–78.

FIFTEEN

Policy analysis in the mass media

Hirotsugu Koike

Introduction

The point of policy analysis is to help achieve better policies or enhance policies currently being implemented. For the latter, that may include proposing possible alternatives. For those involved, it is indispensable to accurately grasp policy tasks or issues and carefully analyse the effects of policies worked out by the government. Needless to say, such intellectual work requires talented individuals.

This requirement applies to all sectors of society, and the mass media is no exception. However, compared with other players in society, journalists often have easier access to the venues where government officials, politicians and others actually implement or influence policy. As such, the mass media bears an especially large responsibility for yielding fruitful results in digging up facts and inspecting the policies involved. Under such circumstances, the expectations placed on investigative reporting are growing larger, while journalism itself, in trying to meet these expectations, is working to enhance its methods and human resources for achieving this task.

More people in the Japanese media industry are recognising the necessity for and significance of policy analysis, one aspect of which is investigative reporting. One might say that in policy analysis, we can take advantage of the mass media's unique characteristics and bring people's attention to this uniqueness. Newspapers, in particular, need to enhance their capabilities in analysis and commentary because of the constraints on their news-delivery speed in the age of television and online news.

The mass media is also expected to have a critical viewpoint or stance towards the government in power. To understand the importance of this, one need only recall the investigative coverage by the *Washington Post* in the 1970s that uncovered a White House scandal and eventually forced the US president to step down.[1] Inspection and analysis from a critical viewpoint are precisely what is needed from the media in terms of policy analysis. The Japanese media has started to acknowledge this, though it still has room for improvement here.

As Japanese newspapers step up their investigative reporting, they are becoming more active in making policy proposals. This trend has become increasingly clear since the early 1990s, suggesting that the media is gradually playing a bigger role in policy analysis and formation. This is exactly the type of role that the media – with the large influence it wields relative to other players in society – should play.

Recognising the necessity of policy analysis, the Japanese media is working on ways to better serve this purpose. However, it has to be said that its efforts remain inadequate. Intensifying competition with online journalism is causing the business performances of traditional media organisations to deteriorate, and many expect this trend to continue. It is very possible that media organisations and the staff responsible for policy analysis – the media segment gaining the most importance – will gradually shrink. Such a development might weaken Japan's policy-analysis capabilities and even hinder the development of its democracy. It is therefore necessary for the established media to reinforce its analysis capabilities by establishing new business models and collaborating with academia and other players.

The thrust of this chapter is to give a broad overview of the functions of the Japanese media and how it relates to policy analysis, and to illustrate the media's efforts in policy analysis with specific examples. I will also explain and discuss the media's role in the policy-forming process. I would also like to refer to my own experiences as a journalist while explaining the functions of the media.[2] In doing so, I will present problems in policy analysis and clarify tasks that need to be accomplished before presenting a few policy proposals.

Whenever the word 'media' appears in this chapter, it refers to the mass media in principle, including newspapers and television broadcasters. I will take examples from nationwide daily newspapers, in particular, as they are more deeply involved in policy analysis. As for social networking services, I refer to them as 'online media' and distinguish them from 'media'. Finally, I would also like to stress that this chapter simply expresses my personal views and does not represent those of the institution to which I currently belong or the media company to which I used to belong.

Functions of the media and policy analysis

First, I will classify the functions of the media and then discuss their relationship with policy analysis. The functions may be classified into the following five types:

1. *Reporting and analysis/commentary as part of reporting.* As for public policies, media reports should be prompt, accurate and clear in conveying the news on moves towards forming and deciding policies, as well as the content of such policies. The ability to understand and analyse information and provide clear explanations is a must for any journalist.
2. *Evaluating policies.* The media provides information to readers to help them judge whether the policies hammered out by the government are valid, and also to help them find problems with the policies, if any. It is taken for granted today that the Japanese media compares the policy platforms, or manifestos, of each political party against each other. This is one of the media's roles in policy evaluation.
3. *Monitoring and checking.* The media keeps a close eye on whether politicians and/or bureaucrats are acting in accordance with the people's interests, whether they are engaging in illicit behaviour, and so forth. This function also includes examining and inspecting previous policies.
4. *Proposing policies.* In recent decades, newspapers have increasingly published their own proposals for constitutional amendments and/or revisions to the pension and medical care systems. The first such attempt among Japan's national dailies was the *Yomiuri Shimbun*'s suggestion for constitutional revision in 1994. In 1995, the *Asahi Shimbun* announced its proposal titled 'International Cooperation and the Constitution'. Since then, many newspapers have been publishing their own pension reform plans as if competing with each other.

5. *Hosting forums.* With increasing frequency, the media provides venues for policy debate so that they can report the content themselves. Most such events are held in the form of panel discussions or symposiums.

The first four functions have to do with policy analysis. The fifth one, hosting forums, can be taken as part of the media's own policy-analysis activity, as the debate covers policy analysis.

The emphasis placed on these functions differs among media organisations, and these companies can shift their emphasis over time. What is important is that many media companies came to be more aware of policy analysis in the 1990s and, based on that, started to work out their own policy proposals. Amid the impasse in the aftermath of the collapse of the economic bubble in the late 1980s, a growing sense of crisis among the media could have been one reason behind its shift in emphasis to policy analysis. Media companies started to get involved in policy analysis mostly as organisers of outside specialists, while sometimes taking the initiative in conducting research.

On the development of forms of media reporting, some observers say that recent years have seen the emergence of investigative journalism and 'proposal journalism', in addition to conventional objective reporting (Yomiuri Research Institute, 2002).

Efforts in policy analysis
Taking the initiative in analysis

I would now like to take a detailed look at policy analysis in the Japanese media, such as who heads such efforts and what their processes are. At Japanese newspapers, policy analysis is handled mainly by the editorial bureau and the editorial committee. These two groups always spearhead the efforts even if the research department at the newspaper or an outside research institute is involved in such a project.

The editorial bureau and the editorial committee are separate bodies within the company, and neither is accorded a higher status or allowed to interfere in the other's activities. The editorial committee is guaranteed independence from the editorial bureau. That said, both sides frequently swap personnel and regularly hold joint meetings. Since both are under the supervision of the president, it is possible that one side may exert influence over the other if it has a good relationship with the president.

The editorial bureau, with its many reporters, handles day-to-day reporting, while the editorial committee, to which editorial writers belong, is mainly in charge of the paper's editorials. An editorial writer rarely writes using a byline. The head of the editorial committee is primarily responsible for editorials, while the president holds the ultimate responsibility.

The organisational structures at newspaper companies in major countries are generally alike when it comes to such bodies as the editorial bureau and the editorial committee. However, I would say that the Japanese media has a greater number of reporters and editorial writers, and a relatively large number of Japanese reporters make it their career goals to one day become editorial writers. In contrast, many in the West seem to aspire to become columnists, who depend on bylines for recognition.

When starting a career as a reporter at a Japanese newspaper company, new hires (usually people fresh out of college) in the editorial bureau typically undergo training for a certain period and are then assigned either to a local bureau, a press club of a government office or a private organisation, or the company headquarters. It is generally thought to take about 10 years to build up full experience in news-gathering and reporting, though it differs from person to person. After that, the reporter usually works for about five years as a team leader (called a 'cap' in Japanese media organisations). At this point, a reporter has two choices of career path if he or she is to remain in the editorial bureau. One is to write bylined stories using the title of senior staff writer or special correspondent. The other is to take a post of assistant manager, or 'desk' in the Japanese media industry (because the job requires them to remain stuck at a desk), whose job is to edit stories submitted by staff writers and engage in administrative work, such as assigning people to posts. This position combines the duties of editor and manager. As for the position of editorial writer, it is usually given to a senior staff writer recognised as a specialist in a certain field. At the *Nihon Keizai Shimbun*, where I used to work, many senior staff writers double as editorial writers, and some editorial writers double as senior staff writers. From the management side, this can be considered an effective use of human resources. However, from a reporter's perspective, it means more work because it requires having to wear two hats.

As I mentioned earlier, policy analysis at newspaper companies is handled by front-line reporters, senior staff writers and editorial writers. At the *Nihon Keizai Shimbun*, there are 25 editorial writers, and this group may spend more time on policy analysis than the others. This number includes the chairman of the editorial committee and five vice chairmen, each of whom heads his or her own section. Of the 25, 10 are based in the editorial committee, while the rest call the editorial bureau home and concurrently serve as editorial writers. The *Mainichi Shimbun*, a national daily that provides general news, has a total of 20 editorial writers (including the chairman), all of whom are based in the editorial committee. Two of them hold the vice chairmanship, while five also serve as specialised senior staff writers.

Front-line reporters are usually required to cover a wide area. When one is assigned to the Ministry of Finance, his or her coverage ranges from fiscal policy to taxation to the international financial system. In the case of a reserve reporter in the city news section, that person must follow virtually everything. As the topics they are assigned are always changing, the reporters do not have enough time to delve deeply into one particular area. In rare cases, a reporter may be allowed to follow a particular topic from early on in his career, but front-line reporters do not usually have the physical or mental energy left to specialise as well.

In the Japanese media, reporters have no leeway to explore a specific, single issue. That may partly be because they even have to handle regular announcements of official data, the kind of releases that US newspapers pick up from news agencies. Another reason may be that most of their energy goes into getting a scoop. Later, I will discuss in more detail what is expected of Japanese reporters.

As for policy analysis, reporters can do this effectively to some extent, but never on the same level as specialists or researchers. Therefore, they rely on outside specialists in commentary and analysis. Some reporters can work on high-level policy analysis, but, in many cases, reporters' activities are limited to a mediating role: they find out information from specialists, write a commentary based on that information and introduce the views of the specialists to readers.

Compared with front-line reporters, senior staff writers and editorial writers have more time for policy analysis because they are exempted from following day-to-day news items. Senior staff writers are not assigned a particular place to cover, but they need to write a bylined commentary when big news comes out. Editorial writers, who, in principle, are responsible only for writing editorials, usually have more time available than senior staff writers. Senior staff writers place more emphasis on commentary, while editorial writers generally stress their own views and proposals. The time available for policy analysis increases as one moves from front-line reporter to senior staff writer to editorial writer.

Also requiring mention regarding policy analysis by the media is the importance of collaborating with outside specialists and pundits. As I said earlier, a front-line reporter incorporates the views of specialists and pundits when writing a commentary. However, the collaboration goes beyond that when it comes to policy formation. Newspaper companies often invite specialists and researchers to open symposiums or in-house seminars, from which it may take cues for its future reporting and in forming an opinion. It may also publish the content of a debate in the form of proposals and sound out the public's reaction.

Day-to-day flow

How does the media actually deal with policy analysis? The following provides an example from Japanese newspapers and, in particular, the *Nihon Keizai Shimbun*. As mentioned earlier, the editorial bureau and the editorial committee engage in policy analysis. I will show the workflow for both sides.

First, let us take the editorial bureau. Japan is rare in that the same newspaper issues both morning and evening editions. Here, I will focus on the process of making a morning edition. On weekdays, each of the editorial bureau's sections – political, economic and so on – comes up with a 'menu' of news items to be released in the morning edition the next day. They will write brief explanations about each item and enter the information into the editing system. Based on the list of all the news items, a final decision on the basic thrust of the paper is reached through discussions at three different stages – first by the bureau's deputy directors, then by the section managers and finally by the assistant mangers (or 'desk' editors). The desk editors then communicate the decision to front-line reporters.

Flexibility is required in this regard because news is always shifting and developing, and something new can happen at any time. After holding a meeting in the evening, the desk editors meet again at least once before the final deadline to discuss further details. The editorial bureau has several deputy directors, each of whom takes charge of the day's edition by rotation.

In making the day's edition, the deputy director in charge has the primary responsibility and serves as the 'control tower'. Also, each section has several assistant managers (desk editors) taking turns each day at being responsible for the section. In terms of newspaper editing, therefore, the primary responsibility goes to the day's deputy director (for the editorial bureau as a whole) and the day's 'desk' (for each section of the editorial bureau).

For policy analysis, reporters and bureau sections work on an individual basis. However, what is important for newspaper companies is the meeting process, which starts with deputy directors, then section managers and finally desk editors, as mentioned earlier. The meetings are more for forming a consensus than for exchanging opinions. However, in the event of major news, the debate can often get quite heated.

Regarding a specific policy hammered out by the government, quick decisions must be made at the meetings on the gist of the policy, who will provide commentary and how they will provide it. It is generally the case that news about a government policy rarely just suddenly pops up; usually, it steadily and continuously develops. Even when the editors have to deal with time constraints, we can expect quality output because the analysis on a certain government policy has already been under way to a considerable extent in collaboration with in-house and outside specialists.

As for specific policy issues, front-line reporters and senior staff writers handle the first-stage analysis. The findings are then expanded upon at the meetings of each section or the entire editorial bureau. Further analysis may soon become difficult because the company as a whole is swamped by daily news articles. The possibility of continued and deeper analysis depends on the competence of each senior staff writer or editorial writer, rather than on the newspaper company as a whole.

Also, I would like to briefly mention the workflow in the editorial committee. Although the details may differ somewhat at each company, generally, the committee decides on two main things: (1) the topics of the editorials for the next day's morning edition (usually two pieces a day); and (2) who will write the pieces and in what manner/tone.

The head of the editorial committee is busy with management and administrative tasks, as well as with coordinating roles in and outside the company. The committee's editing work and other daily routines are done by deputy chief editorial writers (also called 'desks' in Japan), who take weekly shifts. Each company has slightly different approaches. At the *Mainichi Shimbun*, all the editorial writers attend the daily meetings around noon from Monday through Friday, while the *Nihon Keizai Shimbun* has editorial writers meet in the early afternoon on Monday for one hour to set up the week's editorial schedule. In either case, the companies can anticipate when the news on government policies will come out. As such, they can discuss the issues and appoint the editorial writers beforehand in many cases. Such an advance schedule needs to be modified in accordance with changes in the situation. Also, the committee sometimes sets a date for big discussions on policy topics besides having occasional ad hoc talks.

At an individual level, editorial writers are always required to work on their specific areas of focus and produce satisfactory output whenever requested. With their 'preparedness', they should demonstrate not only an accurate understanding of government policies, but also a grasp of the problem in question. Moreover, they are required to always pay attention to what tone their company should take in developing their argument.

Editorial writers must also make it a rule to exchange views with colleagues and chief editors to avoid discrepancies in the company's articles. In this sense, each editorial writer's analysis capabilities are extremely important because they could greatly influence society's view of the company. At the same time, it is also important for the editorial committee to provide an atmosphere where members can hold discussions freely and liberally. The committee needs to be independent from other parts of the company, and discuss and speak out freely on their own. Accordingly, the media company's competence in policy analysis depends not only on individual editorial writers, but also on how the committee functions and performs.

Medium- to long-term efforts

Now, I would like to take a look at the medium- and long-term efforts made by newspaper companies in policy analysis. As described earlier, the editorial bureau and the editorial committee are the two main players in policy analysis at a newspaper company. Both have senior staff writers and editorial writers well-versed in their relevant policy fields. In the case of a big policy issue, a newspaper company not only makes reports, but also is requested to publish its own evaluations and views, which, in turn, may help further the discussion among people at all levels of society. In many cases, the editorial bureau and/or the editorial committee organise a research team or study group with members from across the company to focus on a specific subject for one year or longer. A typical example can be seen with the issue of pension reform. Most newspaper companies have such a research group to compare and examine the proposals set forth by the government, each political party, private-sector institutes and academia. Based on the research, the research group drafts its own proposal, which is then published in the newspaper. Moreover, the company is sometimes asked to explain its own proposal at a Diet meeting or in other public forums.

Newspaper companies are always asked to express their own views, and they are expected to do so with greater speed and coherence than other players in society. The government does not necessarily wait for newspapers' analyses before making policy decisions. A newspaper company therefore needs to present its own proposal at an early stage to influence policymaking. Even if views differ within the company, it must find common ground in order to express a 'unified view'. One newspaper cannot simultaneously hold multiple 'company opinions' in a single issue. Some may say that it is not impossible for a senior staff writer or editorial writer to voice views different from those of the company, but this would be highly unlikely because of the pressure that the writer would face from his peers in such a case.

In the case of the media, those involved in policy analysis tend to emphasise promptly reaching a unified opinion. This may be natural given the characteristics of the media, but it also runs the risk of eroding the quality of policy analysis, and the resulting opinion may end up being bland or noncommittal.

In recent years, many media companies, nationwide dailies in particular, have been establishing research institutes within the company or as an affiliate to focus on medium- to long-term policy issues. Behind such moves may be growing demands for high-level policy analysis in the face of increasingly complex policy issues.

For example, the *Yomiuri Shimbun*, the first in the Japanese media to launch activities for policy proposals, set up the Yomiuri Research Institute (YRI) in 1982 for this purpose. Many of the research fellows are *Yomiuri* news reporters who have been transferred to the institute and tasked with conducting surveys and research for a certain period of time.

The *Nihon Keizai Shimbun*, as an economics-oriented media organisation, has so far focused the efforts of its think tank, the Japan Center for Economic Research (JCER), on the field of economics. JCER has corporate and individual members and accepts research fellows from Nikkei group companies as well. The survey and research staff are therefore a mixture of former Nikkei reporters and those dispatched from group companies. Besides conducting their own surveys and research, both YRI and JCER engage in activities involving specialists and researchers outside the media. In this way, the media can also be positioned as organisers of policy-analysis projects.

I should also mention the Japan National Press Club (JNPC), an organisation of Japanese media companies. The members – newspapers and television broadcasters – cooperate with each other on a diverse range of levels. While its main activities are to plan and hold press conferences in an organised manner, the members continue to engage in a variety of activities involving study groups. Many such groups publish the results of research online or via other means.

Attention should be paid to 'Media Watch 100', a site set up in 2011 by the Media Evaluation Research Group. It mainly consists of former staff writers of national dailies who check and evaluate the content of newspaper reports. Broadly speaking, it can be said that one of their functions is to monitor how the media conducts policy analysis.

Case study on policy analysis

Policy analysis in the media often follows two basic patterns: (1) the editorial bureau and the editorial committee form a joint study group and repeatedly hold discussions to ensure timely output; and (2) a company organises a broad-based research team by gathering not only in-house staff, but also specialists from outside the company. Before even the latter happens, front-line reporters often form a cross-sectional team inside the company to gather information and conduct surveys.

Let us look at a remarkable example of policy analysis in action. The *Asahi Shimbun* set up a team of reporters after the Great East Japan Earthquake of 11 March 2011, and the Fukushima nuclear accident that immediately followed. Reporters were selected from various sections in order to better uncover the truth of the power plant disaster. The team's work was published in serial form under the title 'The Trap of Prometheus', starting in October 2011, attracting considerable public attention.

After the initial reporting was finished, the newspaper added some new information and published the series as a book. In expressing the team's determination to tackle the issue, Takaaki Yorimitsu, head of the special reporting section and leader of the team, said, 'We must thoroughly study and inspect this human-caused absurdity' (Asahi Shimbun Special Reporting Section, 2012, 266).

As I have mentioned, the media has easier access than most to places and people when gathering information. The media can therefore take full advantage of its strength in gathering information and conducting surveys, the preliminary stage of policy analysis. The more this function is utilised, the more powerful and significant the media's policy analysis. In other words, if the preliminary stage of collecting data and doing surveys is performed inadequately, the quality of policy analysis as a whole suffers. In the worst-case scenario, a policy proposal is made based on insufficient and inaccurate primary data – a house of cards.

The reason the *Asahi* team was praised so highly by the public is that each reporter and editor on the team was extremely competent and capable. Much of the credit should also go to the company leaders who decided to form such a specially dedicated team and let it work on the issue for a comparatively long time. Having so many staffers focused on the same project must have added to the burden of other reporters. Furthermore, it is also important to note that the company as a whole was successful in providing a collaborative system for the project.

The importance of policy analysis was also driven home by the investigative reporting of the Japan Broadcasting Corporation (NHK), which pointed out waste in the budget allocated for rescues and restoration in the regions stricken by the

11 March quake. Although the problem had been raised during Diet deliberations and by some weekly publications, NHK examined each and every official budget-related document and analysed them with the cooperation of experts. The findings were organised into a television programme, broadcast on 9 September 2012, which pointed out many areas of waste contained in the budget. The report prompted the government and lawmakers at the time to review the issue, which eventually led to an inspection of the overall budget.

As for an example of policy analysis by a media company in cooperation with an outside research institute, in 2011, the *Nihon Keizai Shimbun* created the 'Virtual Think-Tank' jointly with the Center for Strategic and International Studies (CSIS) of the US. Organising experts from outside the media, it has conducted research and published proposals on security issues.

I would also like to mention a research group founded by a former reporter who came to recognise the necessity of policy analysis. Yoichi Funabashi, former chief editor of the *Asahi Shimbun*, drew attention to his Rebuild Japan Initiative Foundation and its independent, private-sector Independent Investigation Commission on the Fukushima Daiichi Nuclear Accident. This commission released an investigative report ahead of any other commission, including public ones, and clearly indicated the problems with Japan's so-called 'nuclear power village' – the web of connections between the nuclear industry and government officials. In the report, Mr Funabashi emphasised the importance of examinations and inspections, saying:

> Japan has failed to form a national consensus on never letting this country repeat the same failure. If the government makes a policy gaffe or a big mistake in disaster rescue operations, the government and the Diet must always try to find out the entire truth, learn lessons from it and present the results to the public.

Similar cases may arise in the future when people who once worked for the media decide to take advantage of their connections and influence to engage in policy-analysis activities. Such moves can be called an 'extensive development' of the media's policy analysis.

Comparison with the Western media

There are no significant differences between Japanese and Western media companies regarding their organisational structures and day-to-day approaches to policy analysis. However, it should be noted that major Japanese newspaper companies publish both morning and evening editions, whereas Western newspapers publish only morning or evening editions. This difference means that journalists at Western newspapers tend to have more time for policy analysis than their Japanese counterparts. That said, at Western media organisations – especially the *Financial Times* (*FT*), which has been pushing forward with the integration of its print and online editions – journalists are often required to write articles for both print and online editions, as well as take photographs, which cuts into their time for engaging in policy analysis.

Japanese newspapers generally have more editorial writers than Western papers. These writers devote more time to policy analysis than other writers and reporters within the organisation. According to my research, the *FT* had five people on its editorial board in 2008 – a chief plus four others who were responsible for writing most of the editorials. It would seem, then, that Japanese editorial writers have more time per article than their Western counterparts. It is worth noting that Japanese editorial writers are often involved in research committees and study groups related to policy analysis within and outside the news organisation. What the public especially expects to see in policy analysis by the media is investigative reporting. In this respect, Japanese media organisations have a lot to learn from their Western counterparts.

It is important to understand the background behind why the policy-analysis capabilities of the Japanese media have improved. As I mentioned earlier, since around 1990 – and especially after the collapse of the Japanese economic bubble – Japanese people, faced with a declining economy and a changing security environment brought about by the end of the Cold War, have been looking for policy alternatives designed to help the country cope with the new era. In the West, especially in the US, there are many independent and non-profit think tanks that research policy alternatives and make policy recommendations. In Japan, the relative dearth of think tanks means that media organisations – particularly newspapers – have assumed the role of US-style think tanks. That is why Japanese newspapers have established internal research arms, either within the company itself or the group, and make their own policy recommendations on important issues. We seldom see Western newspapers making their own policy recommendations like that. In this sense, Japanese media organisations, especially newspapers, are becoming institutions that play a combined role as a news organisation and think tank.

Problems with policy analysis
Weakness in analysis and lack of relevant skills

While the Japanese media is beginning to recognise the importance of policy analysis and is taking steps to provide a necessary structure for it, it still falls short in some key areas. First, I will touch upon how employees are nurtured. In most cases, Japanese newspaper companies employ new college graduates as reporters. They can hardly be said to have specialised in policy analysis at the undergraduate level. Their initial training does not cover policy analysis in particular, but is more about the 'dos and don'ts' of reporting and other basics, such as the protection of personal information and the ethics of news-gathering.

When such newcomers start their careers, they basically learn through on-the-job training, which means that their ability to become proficient at policy analysis mostly depends on their own efforts. Front-line writers are required to handle a variety of topics, and the diversification in the types of media – from newspapers to online news – is adding to each reporter's workload. It is a simple fact that reporters lack both the time and mental elbowroom to hone their skills for analysis. Overseas study programmes are often provided, but they are available to only a limited number of employees, and policy analysis is not necessarily the purpose of such programmes. In recent years, the *Nihon Keizai Shimbun* has increasingly been employing people who have obtained a master's degree. However, the number of those majoring in policy analysis is small.

When front-line reporters become senior staff writers or editorial writers, they can afford to spend more time on their own; some may have closer ties with academia, teach at universities or take part in research activities. However, front-line reporters hardly have the time or opportunity to attain policy-analysis skills. Reporters are the ones who actually gather news on policies on-site, and if their relevant skills remain weak, it is impossible to improve the quality of policy analysis in the Japanese media as a whole.

Difficulties in management

With the coming of the Internet era, the mass media has seen changes in its own industrial structure, just like many other industrial sectors. Online media enables vast amounts of information to be transmitted speedily and at low cost, traits that put it in a position to replace other established media. Most newspaper companies in advanced countries are seeing a decline in their revenues from sales and advertising. This trend also applies to Japanese newspapers, and although their revenue decline is not as steep as those in the West, some analysts call the newspaper industry 'a structurally depressed sector'. Japanese newspapers are placing increasing emphasis on online news distribution, but they are having a hard time making a profit from such efforts due to stiff competition. As newspaper companies are relative newcomers to the Internet market, their online services have not grown to the extent of replacing the long-established newspaper business.

It also must be pointed out that Japanese newspaper organisations have been slow in the area of globalisation. Newspapers are calling for the need to globalise, which means that they will have to compete under global standards. This also means that the Japanese media must be competitive in releasing and distributing news in English. Unfortunately, Japanese companies mostly provide news services in Japanese and are far from attaining global competitiveness when it comes to English-language news. We have to admit that the Japanese media is a major laggard in the two important areas – Internet services and globalisation.

If the management of a news organisation grows unstable due to insufficient revenues, it will naturally affect the quality of mainstream reporting operations. The fear is that such a situation might lead to a reduction in employees and funds allocated for policy analysis.

In the case of investigative reporting, the impact of financial instability is not hard to predict. If a company forms a team with reporters competent in various fields and tasks it with concentrating on a specific theme, the result will likely help improve the company's reputation in the long run but could cut the reporters' overall output in the short run. The management and chief editors have to decide whether the company should launch costly investigative reporting at the expense of short-term profits. Once in a while, they sacrifice immediate gains in favour of investigative reporting. However, generally speaking, when business performance weakens, newspaper companies can no longer afford staff for investigative reporting, reducing the time and personnel allotted for policy analysis.

Structural problems

As mentioned earlier, what is expected from the media in terms of policy analysis is: (1) abundant information on policy issues thanks to reporters' comparatively easy access to the people and places involved; and (2) insightful analysis with a critical view towards those in power. Here, I would like to take up the latter point.

Those in power, or top government officials, hold a massive volume of information on policies and distribute it to the public from time to time. The government has enhanced its public relations system in recent years, and because of such efforts, the sender of the information – that is, the government – is prone to possibly controlling who can access such information. In such cases, it might become difficult for the recipients to scrutinise the content and judge it correctly.

To improve the quality of policy analysis, it is by all means necessary to maintain a critical stance when checking the information given by the government. Without a critical attitude, it is difficult to maintain objectivity because there is always the possibility that the news organisation is basing its analysis on information that the government has fed it for reasons of convenience. This is why the media is expected to maintain a critical attitude. Unfortunately, the Japanese media does not fully possess this spirit.

Concerning this point, people often bring up the existence of Japan's 'press club' system. Although it has been criticised for a variety of reasons, the system has improved to some extent. Even so, many say that it remains 'closed'. Having a press club at each government ministry or agency is seen by some as a symbol of the media's collusive relationship with those in power. In some cases, journalists who cover politics are seen as being insiders, even fixers, in the political arena, and, as such, critics doubt if such journalists are able to view politicians with a critical eye. Makino (2012) says that Japan's bureaucratic system and mass media have actually formed an alliance. Of course, some Japanese media organisations and journalists see their roles as serving as a check on power, as in US-style watchdog journalism. However, as a whole, the relationship between the media and those in power in Japan appears less tense than in the US, and it undeniably affects the quality of the media's policy analysis.

Future tasks

Improving expertise: reviewing staff selection and training

What, then, will be required if we are to upgrade the media's skills and expertise in policy analysis in the midst of the media's 'winter'? First, I would like to touch on staff selection and training aimed at improving expertise. It is, to some extent, possible to give on-the-job training to new recruits who have very little experience with policy analysis. However, to have reporters who can rival experts in policy evaluation, specialised training is necessary. The media should employ people who have acquired policy-analysis skills at graduate school or who otherwise have strong experience with policy-related work.

Even after an employee is recruited, in-house training alone is not enough. Ideally, media organisations will establish programmes under which reporters are sent to graduate schools in Japan or abroad to concentrate on policy analysis-related research.

Establishing a new business model

Deteriorating business results at media companies can weaken their often-costly efforts in policy analysis. Such a situation could even threaten the basis of journalism.

Tsubota (2009) expressed his sense of crisis about this, saying: 'We have to avoid losing journalism by all means. If journalism were to disappear, democracy would be choked to death. In this sense, I would like to think about a new form of digital journalism'.

The business model used by the media thus far has focused on hiring new graduates and generating revenue from subscriptions and advertising, but we should recognise that this model is nearing the end of the road. We are entering an era when, without an alternative business model, it will be difficult to maintain journalism and secure expertise for policy analysis.

One new model now being used for journalism involves non-profit organisations (NPOs). This type of news service is widespread and developing in the US through the use of advanced media, and similar moves are certainly being sought out in Japan as well. However, unlike in the US, the practice of donating money has not yet taken root here, and the funding situation for NPOs generally remains weak. It is therefore not clear how far *NPO-type journalism will develop in Japan.*

Another way can be found in the form of citizen journalism. South Korea's *OhmyNews,*[3] which once wielded significant political influence, featured articles written by citizen reporters. Taking cues from that approach, it is possible to envision journalists from a major Japanese newspaper cooperating with citizens in reporting while engaging in policy analysis as part of such efforts.

It will also become increasingly important to have close ties with academia. The specialised knowledge that exists at universities is not necessarily fully utilised by society. Newspaper companies are equipped with the skills and tools needed to transmit useful information to the public and are also capable of organising human resources in various fields. They should leverage these characteristics to collaborate more closely with the academic world in promoting policy analysis. With business conditions growing more severe for the media, newspaper companies will find it even more important to have access to the specialised knowledge of outside institutes and help organise that know-how.

Conclusion

It was only about two decades ago that the Japanese media started acknowledging the significance of policy analysis and policy proposals. Before that, the media had, of course, engaged in policy analysis to a certain degree, though it was not referred to by that name.

What ultimately alerted the media to the importance of policy analysis and spurred it to create a framework for it was the increased uncertainty in the global situation in the aftermath of the collapse of the Cold War. It also had something to do with the lack of policy direction in Japan amid its economic downturn. Besides conventional reporting, the media was now also required to contribute more to improving public policies.

With the protracted economic slowdown, the Japanese media, printed newspapers in particular, appear to be weakening in line with the industry's structural problems. This is unfortunate because their business base is deteriorating at a time when the media is expected to play a greater role in policy analysis and improve its expertise in the field. The industry continues to search for a new business model to replace the current one. To upgrade the quality of policy analysis in Japan, sound and wholesome journalism is without a doubt necessary. It is also imperative to establish a new business model for the media.

Notes

[1] Known as the Watergate scandal, which ultimately forced President Nixon to step down in 1974. The series of *Washington Post* reporting is seen as a model of investigative journalism in Japan as well.

[2] The author worked for the *Nihon Keizai Shimbun* from 1974 to 2009 as an economic reporter, overseas correspondent, senior staff writer and editorial writer. From 2000 to 2006, the author served as director at the National Institute for Research Advancement (NIRA), an industry–government–academia think tank.

[3] South Korea's online news service launched in 2000 with ordinary citizens contributing reports. It once influenced the presidential election but later lost momentum and ran into the red.

References

Asahi Shimbun Special Reporting Section (2012) *Purometeusu no wana* [*The Trap of Prometheus*], Gakken Publishing.

Makino, Y. (2012) *Kanpo Fukugotai* [*Government–Media Complex*], Kodansha.

Tsubota, T. (2009) 'Rebirth of Media', *Contemporary Business*, 30 September (online edition).

Yomiuri Research Institute (ed) (2002) *Teiguen Hodo* [*Proposal Journalism*], Chuokoron-Shinsha.

PART FOUR

FUTURE DIRECTIONS OF POLICY ANALYSIS IN JAPAN

Policy education in Japan: a study of professional graduate public policy schools

Koichiro Agata

Development of public policy education

Policy affairs have largely been researched, discussed and taught in Japan at faculties and schools of law, political science and economics within several universities, where they are analysed from the perspective of each discipline. The first such undergraduate school, which is clearly oriented to policy study and whose name is associated with the notion of policy, was established in 1990 as a Faculty of Policy Management. This came about approximately 100 years after the first official university in Japan was organised.

The existence of the first undergraduate school of policy education had both a horizontal and a vertical influence on the constellation of Japanese universities. In particular, more policy education schools are being established at the undergraduate level, while the Faculty of Policy Management has added on a graduate school that has induced similar actions at other policy education undergraduate schools. Hence, there are now roughly 100 policy education undergraduate and graduate schools in Japan.

Due to these trends in policy education at both the undergraduate and graduate levels, the Ministry of Education, Culture, Sports, Science, and Technology (MEXT) has issued a guideline on graduate education, which will be described in the second section. If the existing system of graduate education could be referred to as containing 'academic' graduate schools, then we can assert that a new system of 'professional' graduate schools has been established, in which more emphasis is laid on the practical and vocational aspects of graduate education. In the framework of these professional graduate schools, a new type of graduate school for policy education – a professional graduate public policy school – has been established. Thus, in Japan, there are two different streams of policy education: the academic type at both the undergraduate and graduate levels; and the professional type at the graduate level.

The next section will discuss the development and perspectives of professional graduate public policy schools in the context of the coexistence of the two different types. It will also examine the institutional aspects of the professional school system. The third section will present a concrete example of these schools, while the fourth will introduce a special system for the quality management of professional graduate schools, particularly accreditation. Finally, the last section will review some characteristics and perspectives of these professional graduate public policy schools.

Building a system for professional graduate public policy schools

Ideas for professional graduate schools in Japan

Professional graduate schools have been established in Japan since 2003 as graduate courses that specialise in fostering advanced professionals. They were created in order that societal needs for people who play active roles in a globalised society and in an economy with highly advanced technology can be fulfilled. Three main characteristics can be attributed to professional graduate schools: 1) they foster talented persons with highly professionalised vocational abilities; 2) they provide highly practical graduate education that bridges the gap between theory and practice; and 3) they provide graduate education taught not only by research professors, but also by practitioner professors equipped with highly practical experiences and capabilities (MEXT, 2014). In order to achieve such purposes, three major considerations have been undertaken within the system: 1) flexible and practical graduate education; 2) development of practitioner graduate students; and 3) a wide scope of specialisations for professional graduate schools.

First, fostering talented persons with highly professionalised vocational abilities requires flexible and practical education in the specified vocational field. Therefore, educational methods in these schools are oriented towards seminars, case studies, fieldwork, workshops, simulation and role-playing, in which practitioner professors can generalise their own practical experiences and teach them to the students.

Second, professional graduate schools provide practitioner students with sites for external vocational training, where they can achieve higher specialisation and obtain new knowledge and technology. It is therefore important to accommodate these students with specific development strategies, such as admission processes specialised for them, evening graduate courses, satellite campuses or a system of one-year courses towards the master's degree. In the year 2012, there were about 20,000 professional graduate students in Japan, among whom slightly less than 40% were practitioner students.

Third, the specialisation scope of professional graduate schools is so wide that there are eight fields in which such schools now specialise: Business/MOT (Management of Technology), Accounting, Public Policy, Public Health, Intellectual Property, Clinical Psychology, Law and Teacher Education. In 2012, there were a total of 185 professional graduate schools in Japan; law schools comprise the largest number, at 74.

Concepts for professional graduate public policy schools

In the above-mentioned general constellation of professional graduate schools, professional public policy graduate schools are expected to educate persons who demonstrate a comprehensive ability in public policy affairs (problem finding, analysis, policymaking, evaluation, etc) so that they can work as policy analysts and policymakers in local, national and international organisations (MEXT, 2012). The concept of the professional public policy graduate school has been developed using the following background and logic (Agata, 2005).

In 2002, Japan's Central Education Council (CEC) issued an interim report entitled 'Fostering High-Level Professionals and Technicians at Graduate Schools' in order to suggest the necessity for creating professional graduate schools (CEC, 2002). Based on that report, the MEXT added to the existing academic master's and doctorate courses a third graduate course that specialised in the training of highly qualified professionals. It defined the graduate schools that gave these professional degree courses as 'professional graduate schools' (MEXT, 2003a).

In the year 2000, before the movement to conceptualise and institutionalise professional graduate schools, the National Commission on Educational Reform (NCER) asserted that there should be professional schools that train specialists in the field of public policy and that a master's degree should be postulated for careers in the national civil service and teaching (NCER, 2000). In this context, the National Personnel Authority (NPA) reported that it should place emphasis on the significance of graduate school education for fundamental knowledge of civil services, expect a conceptualisation of effective graduate school education and closely observe the development of such actions (NPA, 2000).

In addition, the Cabinet Secretariat (CAS), as the headquarters for the modernisation of civil services, proclaimed that it should review its examination system in order to recruit promising candidates with the competency and motivation to overcome complicated and diverse problems of public administration (CAS, 2001). The cabinet had already decided to strive to modernise the civil service system in many respects.

Based on this conceptual background, the MEXT considered the necessity for professional graduate public policy schools as one form of professional graduate schools and organised the Study Group for Professional Graduate Public Policy Schools (SGPP) to investigate curricula for professional education at the graduate level and to publish the 'Guideline for Curricula of Professional Graduate Public Policy Schools' (SGPP, 2003). An overview of that conceptual development is described in Figure 17.1.

Figure 17.1: Ideas and concepts

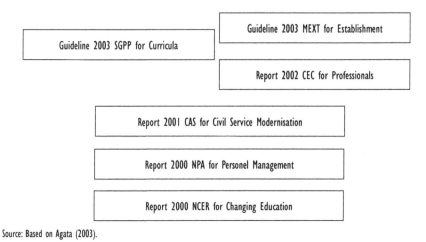

Source: Based on Agata (2003).

Permission for the establishment of graduate schools as a form of ex ante control

When universities in Japan are to be newly established, they must be permitted by the MEXT through a judgement of the Council for University Establishment and School Corporation (Section 3 of the School Education Law). This provision has also been applied to professional graduate schools since 2003, the year in which they were first institutionalised. There is a separate standard for such judgements for each of the three different kinds of higher education – undergraduate schools, academic graduate schools and professional graduate schools. Therefore, new professional graduate schools are permitted based on such a judgement by the Council in reference to the Professional Graduate Schools Establishment Standards (MEXT, 2003b). Founders of new professional graduate schools must submit an application before June each year, which is then judged by the Council. Such applications are examined on the basis of six elements: (1) purpose of the new establishment; (2) organisation and quality of teaching professors; (3) degree to be given and curricula of education; (4) admission system for new students; (5) financial situation of the school; and (6) facilities for education and research at the school. Distinctive features of professional graduate schools can be found in the constellation of professors: it is required that about 30% of the professors be practitioners with at least five years of practical experience outside of universities, and that the ratio of professors to students must be one to 15. This permission can be characterised as a form of control that is exercised in advance in order to secure the quality of professional graduate education.

The Council for University Establishment and School Corporations has two subcommittees: one for university establishment and one for school corporations. The latter committee is in charge of the financial and facilities aspects, while the former is in charge of everything else. The university establishment committee is organised further into the Working Group for Professional Graduate Schools, which examines

Figure 17.2: Permission to establish graduate school

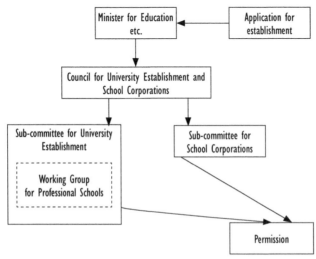

Source: Based on MEXT (2003a) and modified by the author.

the educational quality of the application. The final judgement as to establishment is delivered in December each year, so that a new professional graduate school can begin functioning in April. The above process is outlined in Figure 17.2.

Institution and practice of professional graduate public policy schools

Schools and students at a glance

Figure 17.3 shows us the progression of the number of professional graduate public policy schools and their professors since 2003. The first school was established in 2003, three more were added in 2004, one more each in 2005 and 2006, and the last one in 2007. Thus, by 2011, there were eight such schools: four in the Tokyo area, two in western Japan and two in north-east and northern Japan.

Figure 17.3: Numbers of schools and professors

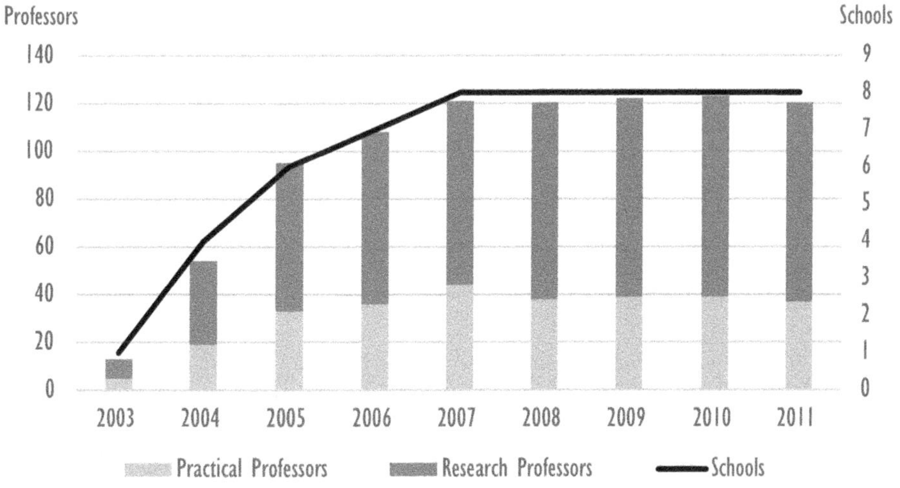

Source: Calculated and drawn by the author.

In the year 2011, a total of 120 professors were teaching at the eight public policy schools. About 30% of them were practitioner professors. This shows that the general standard for the ratio of practitioner professors to professional graduate schools was met.

Figure 17.4 shows the changes in the number of students in theory and practice over the last nine years. This development is coordinated with that of the total number of schools. In the year 2011, there were about 350 numerus clausus in place for professional higher education in the field of public policy. The number has remained almost unchanged since 2007, when the last public policy school was established. That development is depicted by the solid line. The number of graduate students who have entered these schools is depicted by the large-dotted line. Since 2005, slightly more students than the numerus clausus allows have entered these schools. In the peak year (2008), about 60 students more than the numerus clausus were admitted. This trend can indicate that the significance of professional graduate education through public policy schools has been acknowledged positively in Japan in the last few years, though a slight declining tendency is visible in 2011.

Figure 17.4: Numbers of students

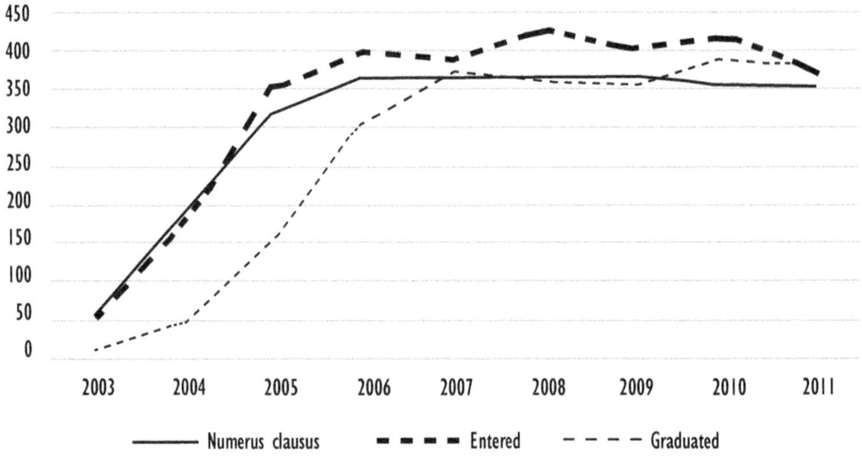

Source: Calculated and drawn by the author.

The small-dotted line shows us the development of the students who have graduated from the schools during these nine years. Institutionally speaking, that development should follow that of the students who entered two years later because most students graduate from these schools two years after their entrance. The line connotes the satisfactory results of professional public policy education in Japan, especially since 2010, during which time slightly more students than the numerous clausus graduated.

Curricula

The system of public policy schools in Japan is composed of two different courses: education for newcomers and advanced training for practitioners. 'Newcomers' are students without vocational experience who have recently completed their undergraduate degrees and who study a two-year course. 'Practitioners' have some years of job experience and can be trained in an intensive course for one year.

The purpose of the public policy school system in Japan lies in helping students to develop comprehensive competence in public policymaking, noble vocational morality and international competency. Upon completion of either a two-year or one-year master's course, the student earns the degree of Master of Public Policy (MPP) or Master of Public Management (MPM), and in such comparable fields as Public Law Policy, Public Economy and so on.

The system's curriculum is structured with a complex of subjects principally based on the three main disciplines of Law, Political Science and Economics. In principle, there are four categories of subjects: Basic Subjects, such as fundamental theories and necessary knowledge; Advanced Subjects, which involve higher and broader content in related specialised fields; Practical Subjects, such as fundamental methodologies for policy practice; and Case Studies, which involve applying knowledge using concrete policy cases. In the realm of public policy schools, because policy fields and the knowledge that supports them are very various, a certain variety in curricula among the public policy schools is allowed.

In the curricula of public policy schools, it is very important to cultivate policymaking abilities through quasi-practical experiences provided through simulation, role-playing and case studies (Ikuta, 2005). Students become eligible for graduation by taking more than 40 credit points towards their degree in either a one- or two-year programme. They can relatively freely combine subjects within the four different categories in order to fulfil the requirements for the degree. Concretely speaking, the main abilities that students develop at public policy schools are to appropriately apprehend the complex problems facing society, to design and execute measures for the resolution of those problems, and to evaluate the outcome (Tanabe, 2006). In the sense of bridging the gap between theory and practice, policy orientation through the logical reflection of goals and means should be balanced by political orientation through compromise or coordination (Adachi, 2009).

Case study[1]

General characteristics

This section contains a case study of Waseda University, which established the first professional graduate public policy school in Japan in 2003: the Graduate School of Public Management (GSPM), which awards an MPM. There are two different courses, a one- and a two-year programme, in which students can receive an MPM by earning more than 40 credits, including a master's thesis as an obligatory subject.

The GSPM sets three main principles for education: the definition of 'public management', the balance between equity and efficiency, and policy proposals through master's theses (Waseda University, 2003). Public management is defined as the division of functions and cooperation between the governmental, private and civic sectors, which share and solve societal problems that could not have been resolved without such trilateral cooperation. This allows for the development of sustainable practices at the national level and for a stable international society. There are at least three requirements, from a public management perspective, for the identification of issues for trilateral collaboration: first, some societal problems need to be common to or shared by the three sectors; second, these problems need to be solved only by collaboration among the three sectors; and, third, there must be preparedness for self-sacrifice among all sectors (Agata, 2013: 222).

The second principle – balance between equity and efficiency – can be traced back to a reflection of the New Public Management (NPM) movement that began in the 1980s. The NPM approach aims to introduce business management methods, especially performance evaluation, into public administration in order to make it as efficient as possible. However, in some cases this requirement is emphasised so much that equity cannot be secured when it must be unconditionally guaranteed. Public administration exists in order to supplement those things that market principles cannot alone resolve. Therefore, the GSPM has adopted the balance between equity and efficiency as it motto.

A special meaning can be ascribed to the system of the master's thesis as an obligatory subject. It is very important for students in general to set a research question, gather the necessary qualitative and quantitative data for problem solving, process that data logically, and compose a thesis based on the research question. Moreover, at a professional graduate public policy school, it would actually be very significant if the master's thesis could contribute to resolving societal problems in reality. Therefore, during the admission examinations for Waseda University, candidates must submit a precise research plan for a possible thesis. After their admission, the students design their study plan to include subjects that are as directly concerned with the research question as possible, both theoretically and practically. As about half of the registered students are practitioners, the outcome of a master's thesis can be a concrete solution to a problem if the concerned student has a clearly target-oriented problem consciousness and writes a well-structured master's thesis.

Curriculum

The curriculum of the GSPM is so structured that the idea and logic of the above-mentioned notion of public management can be fostered and the students can apply academic and practical tools to solving concrete societal problems in the context of public management. The core disciplines for structuring the curriculum are Political Science connected with Law and Economics; this is the case because the GSPM was established in close relation to the School of Political Science and Economics at Waseda University. The basic structure of the curriculum at the moment of foundation is based on the SGPP guideline: Stage I covers basic subjects and Stage II covers advanced, practical and case study subjects, as well as a Graduate Seminar for theses as case studies. Stage II, in particular, is composed of subcategories that reflect the basic concept of curriculum building. As will be explained, these subcategories have changed.

The GSPM has experienced two curriculum modernisations, though the main characteristics have not changed. The fundamental structure of the curriculum discussed in the third section has been retained. These curriculum modernisations are concerned with three things: whether obligatory subjects should exist; how many credit points one-year students should need to earn for graduation; and how subcategories should be structured. The modernisations were implemented in 2006, three years after the school's foundation, and in 2012.

Whether or not all students must study a certain number of obligatory subjects depends on the variety of their academic backgrounds. GSPM students have graduated from universities not only in the fields of human and social sciences, but also in the natural sciences. Therefore, we cannot easily expect them to share areas of knowledge that are basic to public policy education. In this sense, obligatory subjects can play the role of a provider of minimum standards for policy study. On the other hand, this system can also create the problem that those who have graduated from social science programmes are not motivated to repeat the minimum level of knowledge. At first, the GSPM introduced four obligatory and six elective obligatory subjects. However, this system was abolished in 2006 and reactivated in 2012 in a reduced form. The significance of obligatory subjects must be continually discussed.

At the time of the foundation of the GSPM, a MPM could be awarded to students who had achieved at least 40 credit points, including passing a master's thesis. The question was whether or not the burden of 40 credit points, including thesis writing, was too heavy for students in the one-year course. Before permission was given, the proposal provided that one-year-course students could receive a degree by earning 36 credits. However, in the process of gaining permission, it was claimed that a particular master's degree always deserves a particular number of credits. Therefore, the GSPM began with a unitary system of 40 credits. In actuality, it was not easy for one-year-course students to meet the requirement. Therefore, from 2006 on, such students were required to earn only 36 credits in order to graduate.

As already mentioned, the structure of the subcategories reflects a basic strategy for education. At the time that the GSPM was founded, three foci were stated as subcategories: Public Administration as a system; Public Policy as an output; and Public Economy as an outcome. This statement stemmed from the following way of thinking: public administration as a system implements public policy by supplying sets of outputs that influence the public economy as an expected outcome. Therefore, the focus of the Public Administration subcategory was structured around both theoretical and practical subjects regarding institutional, organisational and personnel aspects, while the focus of the Public Policy subcategory is concrete analyses of policy affairs in various sectors and on different governmental levels. The focus of the Public Economy subcategory includes theoretical and practical subjects for the purpose of analysing and evaluating actual societal and economic situations.

The further modernisation performed in 2012 reshuffled the subcategories into three other fields: Local Government and Administration; Political Science and International Affairs; and Public Policy. The basic concept behind this reshuffling lies in the idea that the subjects to be offered should be categorised in accordance with traditional disciplines. The structure of the curriculum can be seen in Table 17.1, which includes concrete examples of subjects and the number of subjects in each category. The SGPP column indicates which curriculum category correlates with the SGPP guideline.

Professors and Students

The number of professors registered at the GSPM is 13, based on the permission of the MEXT. Figure 17.5 shows the progression of the total number of GSPM professors, as classified into research and practitioner categories. As already mentioned, it is legally required that more than 30% of the professors at a Japanese professional graduate school be practitioner teachers. As shown in Figure 17.5, the GSPM has fulfilled this requirement. The practitioner professors at the GSPM mainly have public sector backgrounds. Some examples of subjects taught by practitioner professors include Policy Evaluation, Fiscal and Monetary Systems, Local Decentralisation, Local Autonomy, Case Study (Programming Management), Field Study (Local Revitalisation), Local Decentralisation, Local Autonomy and Internship (Local Administration).

Table 17.1: Structure of the curriculum

SGPP	Category	Subcategories	Examples	Subjects
Basic	Basic Subjects	Obligatory Subjects	Elementary Quantitative Methods	3
		Knowledge/Communication Literacy	Academic Writing in English	3
	Core Subjects	Local Government and Administration	Public Administration	7
		Political Science/International Relations	Issues of International Politics	4
		Public Policy Fields	Public Economics	10
Advanced	Advanced Subjects	Local Government and Administration	Policy Evaluation	19
		Political Science/International Relations	International Organisations and Administration	8
		Public Policy Fields	Environmental Economics	22
Practical/Case Studies	Practicum Subjects		Introduction to Public Management	36
			Field Study (Local Revitalisation)	
			Case Study (Top Seminar)	
Basic	Analytical Tools		Research Methods/Case Study Research	8
			Risk Management	
Practical/Case Studies	Seminars		Developmental Administration (Seminar)	35
			Quantitative Methods (Seminar)	
			Policy Evaluation System (Seminar)	
			Decentralisation Reform (Seminar)	

Figure 17.5: Research and practitioner professors

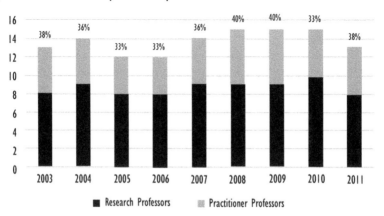

Source: Calculated and drawn by the author.

Figure 17.6: Students and graduates

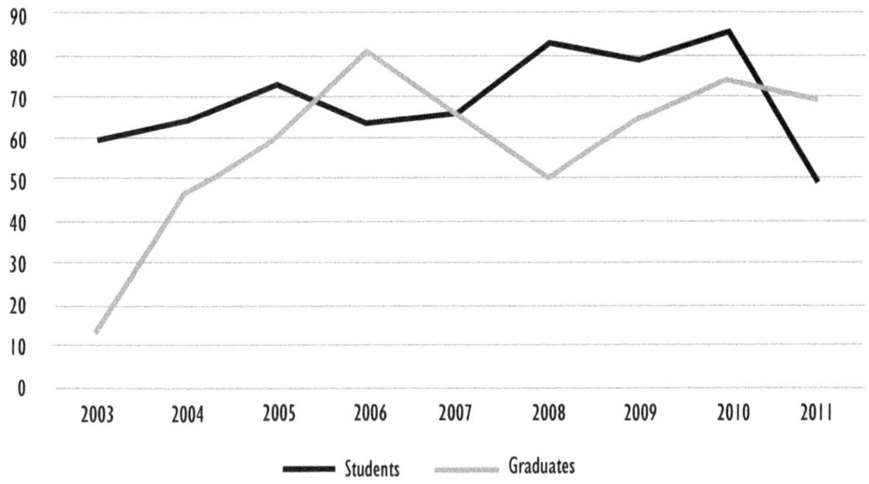

Source: Calculated and drawn by the author.

The chronological development of the number of students who have entered and graduated from the GSPM since 2003 is shown in Figure 17.6. The number of graduates in 2003 was much smaller than the number of entrants because, in that year, only the students in the one-year course graduated. We observe a pair of peaks among the graduates in 2006 and 2010. This seems to have occurred because there were a certain number of students who did not successfully graduate in the previous year. The dip in graduates in 2008 is supporting evidence for this. Judging from the basic fact that the numerus clausus of the GSPM accounts for 50 students, the results on the admission side can be positively evaluated. In the period between 2003 and 2011, about 650 students entered the MPM course, while about 520 received a degree. About half of these students were practitioner students.

The scholarship system at the GSPM is well-equipped. At Waseda University, there are two general sources of support: the university itself and the Japanese Student Service Organization, a government funding source. Adding to both sources, the GSPM has a third scholarship that is financed directly by private persons and corporations that support the university through patronage activities. In the year 2012, about 70% of the students who applied to the GSPM received scholarship funds from these three sources. A survey on the subject has shown that 59.9% of all master's students in Japan receive scholarship funds (JASSO, 2010). Thus, in comparison to this overall statistic, it can be said that the scholarship system at the GSPM can be positively evaluated.

Figure 17.7 demonstrates that there are not very many graduates of the GSPM who have assumed positions in the public sector, as the name 'professional graduate public policy school' implies. The number in each column represents the ratio of students who were recruited into or returned to the public sector. Their positions are located at the national, prefectural and local levels of government, with more than half working for a prefecture or municipality. Some of them have become elected politicians since their graduation or are working as policy staff for politicians.

Figure 17.7: Employment after graduation

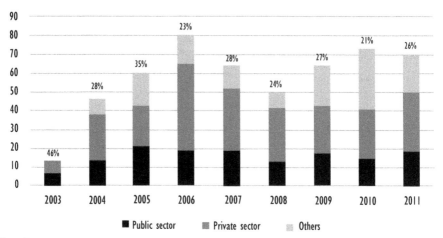

Source: Calculated and drawn by the author.

As Figure 17.8 shows, almost half of the graduates achieved occupations in the private sector. This trend was very clear in 2006. The three main types of private companies that hire GSPM alumni are think tanks, the mass media and non-profit organisations (NPOs). In the private and civic sectors, GSPM alumni can deploy the policymaking abilities that they have developed through the acquisition of systematic analytical skills and practical experience in their master's study.

Figure 17.8: Employment after graduation (% of total)

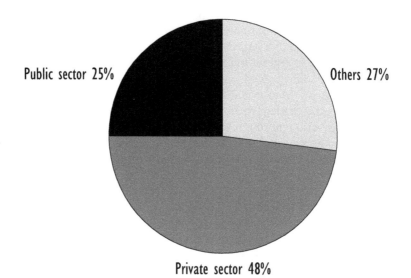

Source: Calculated and drawn by the author.

How can the outcome of graduate education at the GSPM be evaluated? It is very difficult to measure this aspect quantitatively, but on the qualitative side, there are two main outcomes. In 2009, an official GSPM Alumni Organisation was established;

it arranges an annual conference at which related communication and practical experience is exchanged in meetings and on the Internet. Directly after the catastrophe in 2011, the Alumni Organisation reacted by gathering donations for the affected areas. Moreover, in 2011, a group of alumni who work in the public sector organised three study groups in order to solve actual problems in reality. The study group is planning to publish interim reports on their own research. Such networks of alumni can have various effects in the coming years.

Accreditation of professional graduate public policy schools

Accreditation as ex post facto control

All of the universities in Japan must be evaluated for accreditation every seven years, while all of the professional graduate schools in Japan are evaluated every five years (Section 109 of the School Education Law and its associated ministerial ordinance). Such accreditation is conducted through organisations certified by the MEXT based on the Standards for Certification of Accreditation Organisations. Professional graduate public policy schools in Japan must be accredited by the Japan University Accreditation Association (JUAA), which has ordained a standard for the accreditation of public policy schools in Japan (JUAA, 2010). That accreditation can be regarded as ex post facto control for public policy schools because it requires them to be accredited based on viewpoints that examine the standards for establishment of the schools, as will be discussed in the next section.

The accreditation process begins with a self-evaluation by a given university or graduate school according to the accreditation standards. Universities or graduate schools must submit a self-report on their performance to JUAA every seven years, while JUAA must form a committee for accreditation – composed as a peer and third-party review organisation – every five years. The accreditation committee should examine the submitted self-report to judge the accreditation value of the concerned school. The process of the certification of an organisation for accreditation, and of accreditation itself, is reflected in Figure 17.9.

Standards and organisations for accreditation

The accreditation standards for the public policy schools in Japan can be traced back to a guideline determined by the National Institution for Academic Degrees and University Evaluation (NIAD-UE, 2006), which was drafted through a special committee comprised of professors and practitioners. Based on this guideline, JUAA published the 'JUAA Standards for Professional Graduate Public Policy Schools', which was drawn up by specialised professors and practitioners (JUAA, 2010). The standards include seven aspects for accreditation: (1) purpose of the school; (2) contents, methods and outcome of education; (3) teaching organisation; (4) admission; (5) facilities for education and research; (6) management; and (7) accountability. Accreditation is based on these standards, which are intended to verify the development of professional education at a given public policy school based on whether or not it has realised its intention at the time of the granting of permission for its establishment. Therefore, the accreditation system can be considered to be a form of ex post facto control.

Figure 17.9: Accreditation

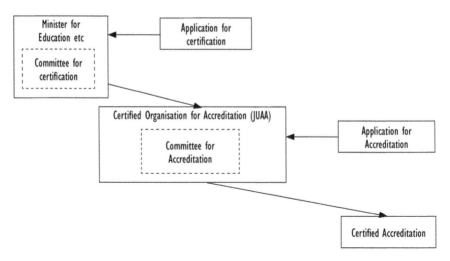

Source: Drawn by the author based on data from MEXT. Available at: http://www.mext.go.jp/b_menu/shingi/chukyo/chukyo4/013/index.htm

The qualifications for accreditation have been divided into 55 evaluation items. After accumulating the evaluated items, the performance of the school is evaluated in terms of each of the seven aspects as 'Advantages', 'Problems' or 'Recommendations'. The strictest evaluation for the school is the last one because it means that the school must improve the noted aspect in the coming five years before the next accreditation process. An evaluation of 'Problems' implies a suggestion for further development, while an evaluation of 'Advantages' points out value-added aspects of the school in the field of public policy education. In the worst possible case, an evaluation of 'Unaccredited' can be given, but the system implies that through this feedback, the quality of policy education can be amended, enhanced and secured in coming years.

Accreditation practice

As mentioned earlier, the accreditation process for public policy schools in Japan was introduced in 2010, but the professional graduate school system had already established an accreditation process in 2003. Therefore, until 2010, an external evaluation of public policy schools was conducted by a third party. The major difference between an accreditation and an external evaluation lies in the fact that the first must rest on accreditation standards as common and stable criteria, while optional and one-time benchmarks have been provided for the external evaluation of each public policy school. Such external evaluations were carried out a total of four times by newly organised committees, and the experiences of the external evaluations influenced the establishment of the common standards of JUAA. After the standard came into effect in 2010, two different public policy schools were accredited (Kanemoto, 2011; Mabuchi, 2012). Currently, in 2013, two more schools are being scrutinised. We should now monitor with caution whether or not the feedback provided by the accreditation process proves effective for the improvement of education and research at Japanese public policy schools.

Characteristics and perspectives of the system

Permission and accreditation as controls to secure education quality

The deregulation trend in global society suggests the importance of ex post facto control. The permission and accreditation system in Japan should be evaluated from this perspective. The deregulation of permission for universities in general in Japan was carried out in 1991 (MEXT, 1991). The establishment of a new undergraduate or graduate school must be permitted, but reorganisations of existing undergraduate or graduate schools may require coordination with the appropriate ministry and its committees regarding the curricula and the school's organisation management in order for the new school to be registered. Regarding evaluation, in 1991, a system of self-evaluation for such schools was introduced in order to scrutinise the quality of their education. The evaluation system has since been refined by the introduction of a third party in 1998 and the institutionalisation of accreditation in 2004 (NIAD-UE, 2008).

If we look at the situation of professional graduate schools in general with this background, they are clearly subject to both permission and accreditation –both ex ante and ex post facto control. The CEC suggested a necessary balance between both types of control for securing better-quality higher education in Japan, and emphasised the importance of both aspects in order to guarantee a level of graduate education that meets international standards (CEC, 2005a, 2005b). In the case of the law school evaluation system in Japan, it is said that accreditation contributes to a general understanding of the education system and its problems, as well as promoting its improvement. However, some negative aspects of the accreditation system have been pointed out (Noda et al, 2011). Therefore, we must examine how the regulation system for professional graduate schools should proceed in the future, especially in terms of the costs and benefits of the ex ante and ex post facto regulations.

Revision of accreditation standards

Before accreditation began, the need to scrutinise and modify the system had already been suggested because it was not easy to evaluate the various public policy schools comprehensively (Morita, 2007). For this reason, in 2012, JUAA initiated a revision of its accreditation standards for public policy schools by considering a balance with those of other professional graduate schools. Therefore, a commission to revise the accreditation standards for public policy schools was organised in the autumn of 2012; the new standards were ratified in summer 2013 (JUAA, 2013) and should take effect in 2015.

The revised standards include eight aspects, 22 sub-aspects and 104 items for evaluation. One of the important points of the revision is that an evaluation must be conducted according to the sub-aspects in order to sum up the accreditation in terms of the eight new aspects as an overall evaluation. The evaluation categories of 'Advantages', 'Problems' and 'Recommendations' remain unchanged. The revised standards place emphasis not only on the basic aspects of organisation and curricula, as before, but also on the vital aspects of facilities, education services and the evaluation system of the concerned graduate school itself. Furthermore, a post-evaluation feedback mechanism must be set up so that an evaluated public policy school is able to follow up on the recommendations for modernisation. Certainly, the implementation of the results of the evaluation is the most important aspect of the evaluation system (JANU, 2009). Therefore, the effect and significance of the new standards will be observed in future years. Furthermore, a system of workshops to be held after accreditation will be introduced to discuss the advantages of the accredited schools.

Vocational perspectives of graduates

A major difference between the law school and public policy school systems is that the education of the former is closely connected with the National Bar Examination, while that of the latter has no direct relation to the National and Local Civil Services Examination (Morita, 2004). Therefore, the vocational perspectives of students after graduation must be discussed. In 2004, Tokyo Prefecture introduced a recruiting system for master's degree-holders in the social sciences that places them on a specialised track for career building. On the national level, there were two such measures. First, two new examination subjects – Public Policy A and B – were added to the subjects list in 2006 so that alumni and students of public policy schools can better use their specially cultivated knowledge, way of thinking and skills (NPA, 2005). Second, in 2012, another modernisation was made to a specialised track only for graduates in the career category (NPA, 2011). These measures do not mean that alumni of public policy schools will have an advantage in the examination process, but they will be examined separately from candidates without master's degrees.

Based on the latest statistics, the proportion of all examinees and successful candidates in the specialised track of the whole career category is about 15% and 27%, respectively (NPA, 2014a). These statistics suggest that successful candidates in that track did, in fact, have better access to governmental offices in comparison with candidates in other tracks. In this respect, it can be said that graduate school education in general and official recruitment into the governmental sector have been more tightly combined than before. Therefore, the effect of such measures should continue to be monitored in the coming years, especially in the context of professional graduate public policy schools.

Cooperation between schools and vocational sectors for education and recruitment

Not only in the sense of the above-mentioned vocational perspective, but also for the improvement of the quality of professional education at Japan's public policy schools, further cooperation should be attempted between the schools on the supply side of the workforce and the vocational sectors on the demand side. The CEC recommended the necessity of collaboration between professional schools and vocational sectors for modernising not only the curricula, but also the evaluation system and vocational recruitment, by analysing the situation of the overall recruitment system in professional education (CEC, 2010).

At some of the public policy schools in Japan, a kind of advisory board has been organised in which the public, private and civic sectors are represented. Such meetings do not happen often, but they provide very good opportunities for the exchange of opinion between the schools educating students and the vocational sectors recruiting them. For example, a report and a self-evaluation of educational output are executed from the school side, while an evaluation of future needs is executed from the sector side. Such direct dialogues can promote the quality of education if the schools analyse actual problems and strive to modify them in order to meet the needs of the vocational sectors.

A system of internship can contribute to enhancing cooperation between professional graduate public policy schools and vocational sectors in terms of gathering relevant information and improving perception on both sides. For example, for every year since around 2007, the NPA has provided opportunities for around 40 internships in almost all the central ministries (NPA, 2014b). This internship system has also been implemented in other vocational sectors.

One of the important objectives of professional graduate schools in Japan is to develop people with highly professional vocational skills and to recruit or engage them in the concerned vocational sectors. Therefore, in the near future, the contribution of Japanese professional graduate public policy schools to this objective should continue to be examined.

Note
[1] The case study in this section is based on Agata (2003, 2004), as well as three pamphlets from the Graduate School of Public Management (GSPM) (Waseda University, 2003, 2009, 2012). The GSPM was established in 2003 under the name Okuma School of Public Management and reorganised and renamed in 2012.

References

Adachi, Y. (2009) *What is Public Policy Science?* (in Japanese), Tokyo.

Agata, K. (2003) 'Professional Schools and Human Resources Development' (in Japanese), *Toshimondai*, vol 55, no 6, pp 29–40.

Agata, K. (2004) 'Results in the First Year and Perspectives at the First Professional Graduate Public Policy School – At the Okuma School of Public Management of Waseda University' (in Japanese) (interviewed by J. Tokuyama), *Jinji Shiken Kenkyu*, no 192, pp 9–12.

Agata, K. (2005) 'Legal and Political Education in the Latter Higher Education – Possibility of Professional Graduate Public Policy Schools' (in Japanese), *Nomos*, no 16, pp 69–83.

Agata, K. (2013) 'Conclusion: Possibilities of Public Management', in T. Sakurai, I. Macdonald, T. Yoshida and K. Agata (eds) *Financing Public Services – Taxes, User Pay or Other Forms of Service Delivery?*, Tokyo: Waseda University Press, pp 221–6.

CAS (Cabinet Secretariat) (2001) 'Guideline for Civil Service Modernization' (in Japanese). Available at: http://www.gyoukaku.go.jp/jimukyoku/koumuin/taikou/honbun.pdf

CEC (Central Education Council) (2002) 'Fostering High-level Professionals and Technicians at Graduate Schools' (in Japanese). Available at: http://www.kantei.go.jp/jp/kyouiku/houkoku/1222report.html

CEC (2005a) 'Prospects of Higher Education in Japan'. Available at: http://www.mext.go.jp/b_menu/shingi/chukyo/chukyo0/toushin/05013101.htm

CEC (2005b) 'Graduate Educations in a New Era – To Build an Internationally Attractive Graduate Education'. Available at: http://www.mext.go.jp/b_menu/shingi/chukyo/chukyo0/toushin/05090501.htm

CEC (2010) 'Problems and Perspectives of Professional Graduate Schools', Working Group for Professional Graduate Schools. Available at: http://www.mext.go.jp/b_menu/shingi/chukyo/chukyo4/011/attach/1292189.htm

Ikuta, O. (2005) 'Aiming at Developing Highly Practical Competence through Simulation Experience of Policy Formulation' (in Japanese) (interviewed by J. Tokuyama), *Jinji Shiken Kenkyu*, no 194, pp 16–19.

JANU (Japan Association of National Universities) (2009) 'Handbook of Planning and Evaluation at National Universities'. Available at: http://www.janu.jp/active/txt6-2/hyo1910_01.pdf

JASSO (Japanese Students Services Organization) (2010) 'Students' Life Survey 2010' (in Japanese). Available at: http://www.jasso.go.jp/statistics/gakusei_chosa/documents/data10_all.pdf

JUAA (Japan University Accreditation Association) (2010) 'The JUAA Standards for Professional Graduate Public Policy Schools' (in Japanese). Available at: http://juaa.or.jp/images/accreditation/pdf/handbook/public_policy/2010/shiryou_01.pdf

JUAA (2013) 'The (Renewed) JUAA Standards for Professional Graduate Public Policy Schools' (in Japanese). Available at: http://www.juaa.or.jp/news/pdf/20130918_732681_1.pdf

Kanemoto, Y. (2011) 'The First Round of the Accreditation of Professional Graduate Public Policy Schools is Ended – Representing the Commission for the Accreditation of Professional Graduate Public Policy Schools' (in Japanese), *JUAA*, no 46, p 4. Available at: http://www.juaa.or.jp/images/publication/pdf/juaa46.pdf

Mabuchi, M. (2012) 'The Accreditation of Professional Graduate Public Policy Schools in 2012 is Ended' (in Japanese), *JUAA*, no 50, p 3. Available at: http://www.juaa.or.jp/images/publication/pdf/juaa50.pdf

MEXT (Ministry of Education, Culture, Sports, Science and Technology) (1991) 'Education and Culture Policy in Japan' (in Japanese). Available at: http://www.mext.go.jp/b_menu/hakusho/html/hpad199101

MEXT (2003a) 'Guideline of Standards for Establishment of Professional Schools' (in Japanese). Available at: http://www.mext.go.jp/b_menu/shingi/chukyo/chukyo4/gijiroku/021201g.pdf (accessed 31 March 2013).

MEXT (2003b) 'Professional Graduate Schools Establishment Standards' (in Japanese). Available at: http://law.e-gov.go.jp/htmldata/H15/H15F20001000016.html

MEXT (2014) 'Outline of Professional Graduate Schools' (in Japanese). Available at: http://www.mext.go.jp/a_menu/koutou/senmonshoku/__icsFiles/afieldfile/2014/09/02/1236743_01.pdf (accessed 31 March 2013).

Morita, A. (2004) 'Professional Graduate School of Public Policy' (in Japanese), *Gakujutsu no Doko*, no 96, pp 19–22.

Morita, A. (2007) 'Evaluation of Graduate School of Public Policy' (in Japanese), *Daigaku Hyoka Kenkyu*, no 6, pp 44–50.

NCER (National Commission on Educational Reform) (2000) '17 Proposals for Changing Education' (in Japanese). Available at: http://www.kantei.go.jp/jp/kyouiku/houkoku/1222report.html

NIAD-UE (National Institution for Academic Degrees and University Evaluation) (2006) '"Standards" Model for Certified Evaluation of Professional Schools' (in Japanese). Available at: http://www.niad.ac.jp/n_hyouka/jouhou/no6_12_senmon_kizyunmoderu.pdf (accessed 31 March 2013).

NIAD-UE (2008) 'Evaluation of Higher Education in Japan' (in Japanese). Available at: http://portal.niad.ac.jp/library/1179902_1415.html

Noda, A., Hayashi, T., Shibui, S., Tanaka, Y. and Nozawa, T. (2011) 'Current Situation and Issues of the Certified Evaluation and Accreditation of Law Schools Through the Review of the Evaluation System' (in Japanese). Available at: http://www.niad.ac.jp/n_shuppan/gakujutsushi/mgzn12/no9_16_noda_no12_04.pdf

NPA (National Personnel Authority) (2000) 'Report on Modernization of Personnel Management in the Civil Service' (in Japanese). Available at: http://www.jinji.go.jp/kankoku/h17/pdf/bessidai3.pdf

NPA (2005) 'On "Public Policy" as a new subject for the Examination Category I from 2006' (in Japanese), Available at http://www.jinji.go.jp/saiyo/public_policy.htm

NPA (2011) 'National Civil Service Examinations Will Be Modified in 2012!!' (in Japanese). Available at: http://www.jinji.go.jp/saiyo/pamphlet.pdf

NPA (2014a) 'Actual Situations on National Civil Service Examinations' (in Japanese). Available at: http://www.jinji.go.jp/saiyo/saiyo03.htm#24

NPA (2014b) 'Internships in Central Ministries for Students at Professional Public Policy Schools' (in Japanese). Available at: http://www.jinji.go.jp/saiyo/internship-koukyou.htm

SGPP (Study Group for Professional Graduate Public Policy Schools) (2003) 'Guideline for Curricula of Professional Graduate Public Policy Schools (Provisionally)' (in Japanese), internal material.

Tanabe, K. (2006) 'Aiming at Further Development at GraSPP after the First Graduation' (in Japanese) (interviewed by K. Yamada), *Jinji Shiken Kenkyu*, no 198, pp 14–17.

Waseda University (2003) 'The Okuma School of Public Management', pamphlet.

Waseda University (2009) 'The Okuma School of Public Management – Admission and Faculty', pamphlet.

Waseda University (2012) 'Graduate School of Public Management', pamphlet.

Appendix 1: List of official websites (all of the following websites without special remarks were last accessed on 31 May 2015)

Graduate School of Governance Studies, Meiji University. Available at: http://www.meiji.ac.jp/cip/english/graduate/governance/index.html

Graduate School of Policy and Management, Tokushima Bunri University. Available at: http://wwwt.bunri-u.ac.jp/sousei/daigakuin/top.html (in Japanese).

Graduate School of Public Management, Waseda University. Available at: http://www.waseda-pse.jp/gspm/jp/ (in Japanese).

Graduate School of Public Policy, University of Tokyo (GraSPP). Available at: http://www.pp.u-tokyo.ac.jp/en/

Hokkaido University Public Policy School (HOPS). Available at: http://www.hops.hokudai.ac.jp/home-e/entop.html

School of Government, Kyoto University. Available at: http://www.sg.kyoto-u.ac.jp/en/

School of International and Public Policy (IPP), Hitotsubashi University. Available at: http://www.ipp.hit-u.ac.jp/english/

School of Public Policy, Tohoku University. Available at: http://www.publicpolicy.law.tohoku.ac.jp/ (in Japanese).

SEVENTEEN

Job market for public policy programme graduates in Japan

Satoshi P. Watanabe

Introduction

Formation of public policy in today's multifaceted society is persistently challenged by numerous ongoing agendas, as well as newly emerging social issues, often inextricably interrelated at local, national and global levels, with potential beneficiaries on one side and typical defrayers that inevitably exist on the other. Guiding public policy towards optimised points of social equilibria, particularly with individuals and groups claiming mutually conflicting interests and rights for their own sake, is deemed an extremely arduous task for any intermediating agents as it involves strenuous efforts through lengthy political and administrative processes of governments, as well as laborious negotiation with individual actors and interest groups.

It seems fairly natural that the increasingly demanding administrative and technical environment surrounding the platforms of today's policymakers and analysts calls for fully fledged 'policy professionals' who are equipped with a wide spectrum of cutting-edge analytical skills and knowledge, as well as ethical minds, in order to effectively serve the broad public interest. To this end, the Ministry of Education, Culture, Sports, Science and Technology of Japan (referred to as MEXT) inaugurated a new scheme of graduate-level professional schools in 2003 in order to 'provide new graduate programs (professional degrees) that specialize in fostering high-level professionals to take leadership roles in all fields of social economy as well as active international roles' (MEXT, 2007). Directly following the preceding model of public policy schools in the US, universities in Japan then began to establish their own version of higher learning, with specific missions of nurturing policy professionals and citizens who would make beneficial contributions to their social health and well-being. As a result of this government-led effort, a modest number of graduate-level professional schools of public policy, administration and management (henceforth referred to as PPAM) were launched in a short period between the years of 2003 and 2007. As discussed in the following section, however, a non-negligible number of universities and colleges had already provided undergraduate and graduate programmes in the field of public administration and policy analysis, often as a branch subject within other social science departments, such as political science and economics. The newly established professional graduate schools are clearly differentiated from the former academic programmes in nature, as they stand alone as 'professional schools' specialising in preparing students for careers in public service and the non-profit sector, rather than educating students together with other social science majors for more generic placements in a broader range of occupational categories.[1]

Despite the logical validity and legitimacy of the rising supply and demand motives for the need of such professional higher-learning opportunities, there have been arguments that the employment capacity for the graduates of these professional schools has not yet fully developed in the domestic job market so as to provide them with sufficient career possibilities that suitably match their formal training and educational investment. It is also claimed that some indigenous factors and human resources practices uniquely institutionalised in Japanese organisations have also been imposing restrictions on the career formation of PPAM graduates. This chapter focuses on this very issue of the limited potential career opportunities presently faced by the public policy programme graduates in Japan, with supporting evidence obtained from various sectors of relevant labour markets. Further consideration is given to a search for possible remedies for mending the shortage of career opportunities for Japanese policy professionals, which would move towards the more effective deployment of well-trained social service manpower through cultivating new job market potential and laying out clear career paths.

Historical overview

Prior to the recent development of the professional graduate schools scheme, which was undertaken with the leadership of the MEXT, the primary mission of Japan's graduate university education had been widely recognised as the provision of highly advanced academic training to a handful of young traditional students, which typically prepared them for careers as faculty of universities and colleges, as well as specialists in scientific research in both public and private industries. Therefore, 'academic elitism', owing to the relatively small population in a meritocratic society, has provided a niche labour market to the completers of the conventional discipline-based graduate schools, which laid out straightforward career paths set forth within a narrowly defined realm of highly specialised occupations. Even during the post-war expansionary period of the country, such advanced graduate training was more or less exclusively provided through a research-based, hands-on apprenticeship style of instruction, through which students completed a degree thesis or dissertation under a mentoring advisor's guidance, rather than following an array of systematically designed coursework taught in large classrooms.

Around the turn of the 21st century, however, a nationwide call for the necessity of graduate-level professional training arose and was finally realised by the MEXT in 2003 with the inauguration of the new professional graduate schools scheme. It is perhaps no accident that the timing coincides with the upsurge of administrative reform initiatives led by the former Prime Minister Junichirō Koizumi and his cabinet (2001–06), who enthusiastically pursued various structural reforms of the country's public sector in order to mend the long-criticised inefficiencies, corroding ethics of public servants and lack of accountable and cost-effective systems of public service provision. A series of the cabinet's reform efforts over this period eventually resulted in, for instance: privatisation of the public postal services, which led to the founding of the new Japan Post in 2003; corporatisation (a 'big bang' for the ivory towers) of the national universities in 2004, which primarily aimed at retrenching the hefty government spending on the nation's public higher education system through drastically downsizing full-time employment in national universities;[2] and enactment of the Act for Promotion of Justice System Reform, which later brought about the launch of new graduate-level professional law schools in 2004,[3] along with the so-called *saiban'in* system, the Japanese version of a jury system, in 2009. Moreover, a chain of mismanaged and lost pension records of individuals detected in the Social Insurance Agency in the early 2000s eventually led to the dissolving of the Agency in 2009. The Social Insurance Agency was then replaced by the Japan Pension Service in 2010, for which employees no longer hold public servant status today.

The drastic structural transformation of these public agencies implemented by the cabinet no doubt gained its momentum with the tailwind of the New Public Management (NPM) paradigm, which spread throughout the world from the 1980s and had reached Japan's shores by this period. However, it is noteworthy that there existed another important factor behind the favourable reception and rapid diffusion of the graduate-level professional schools scheme in Japan. The expansion of graduate programmes, particularly those aimed at producing graduates for careers in professional occupations, was hailed by the community of higher education as many domestic universities and colleges had been struggling to recruit undergraduate students due to a continuously shrinking 18-year-old bracket population.[4] The graduate-level professional schools scheme would certainly provide an opportunity to rebuild financial strength for many of these institutions, permitting them to reinforce contracting undergraduate revenues with new matriculation of non-traditional students from a much larger population of the active workforce. As a result, in response to the government-led university reform initiative, many graduate schools opened their doors for the first time to a wider population of non-traditional, non-research-oriented applicants. Watanabe (2012) argues that regaining financial health was, therefore, the true incentive for many universities to jump on the new scheme offered by the MEXT in a timely manner.

Preceding the inauguration of the graduate professional schools scheme by the MEXT in 2003, Japanese universities and colleges had, in fact, already offered undergraduate and graduate programmes that led to conferment of academic degrees in the PPAM field. In terms of providing advanced training for workers of local public agencies, the Law for Establishment of the Local Autonomy College (*Jichi Daigakkō*) was enacted, which eventually set up the College in 1953 as Japan's only central training institution for the employees of local public agencies (Ministry of Internal Affairs and Communications, 2011).[5]

Figure 18.1 presents the student enrolment in the PPAM field by degree level in Japan for the selected departments and schools having 'public' ('*kōkyō*') and/or 'policy' ('*seisaku*') in their department or school name. The figure clearly shows that PPAM departments and schools in Japanese universities and colleges have particularly been concentrated in undergraduate degree programmes, which grew from 15,039 students in 2000 to 29,852 students in 2012, representing a staggering increase of 98.5% in 12 years. A similarly substantial increase (an increase of 85.9%; from 410 in 2000 to 762 in 2012) was also observed in doctoral enrolment during the same period. As the time-series trend in the figure demonstrates, however, the new launching fever seems to have been much weaker at the master's degree level (an increase of 33.7%; from 1,717 in 2000 to 2,296 in 2012), though the magnitude of the increase is undoubtedly non-negligible.

Historically, the formation of higher education policies in Japan has been led by political forces operating between councils set up as the prime minister's advisory panels and numerous committees formed within various ministries. For example,

Figure 18.1: Student enrolment at undergraduate, master's and doctoral 'public' and 'policy' programmes

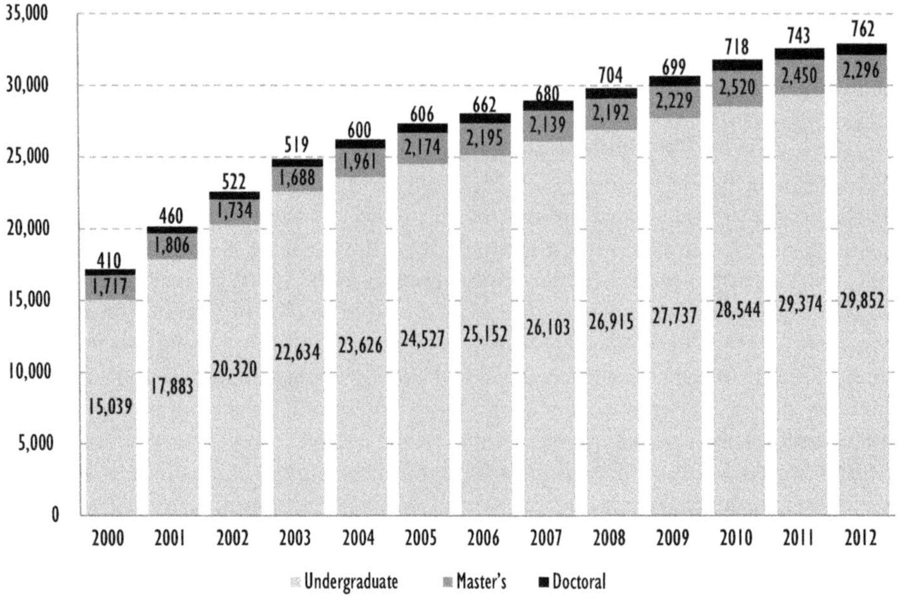

Source: Author's calculation based on the School Basic Survey released by the MEXT.

in agreement with Prime Minister Koizumi's firm belief in small government and minimised public interventions, the Structural Reform Policy for Universities, the so-called 'Tōyama Plan', was submitted to the Council on Economic and Fiscal Policy in 2001. The Plan, which was proposed by (then) Education Minister Atsuko Tōyama, emphasised increased efficiency and effectiveness of public higher education through the laissez-faire principle, while proposing mergers of national universities and the necessity of third-party evaluations, as well as accreditation systems, to assure the quality of all domestic universities and colleges. This movement towards market fundamentalism allegedly followed from an ideology that developed in the 1980s by the Second Provisional Commission for Administrative Reform, the ultimate aim of which was to conduct drastic administrative and financial reforms (Inoue, 2006).

As for the establishment of the graduate-level professional schools scheme, the Council for Higher Education in the Ministry of Education proposed the expansion of graduate schools in 1998 in order to produce highly trained professionals to meet the future needs of the globalising economy and knowledge society. However, as Fukuda (2011) points out, the only supporting ground provided by the Council for the pressing need of such graduate schools was the mere fact that the number of graduate students in Japan was 1.3 persons per 1,000 population in 1996, whereas those numbers in the US, the UK and France were 7.7, 4.9 and 3.5 persons, respectively. Fukuda (2011) further explains that the argument base found in a report by the Justice System Reform Council (2001) for establishing the law schools scheme was again simple Japan–foreign comparisons of the headcounts of lawyers, from which the Council concluded the urgent need for the launching of graduate law schools.

These discussions suggest that the recent expansion of Japanese graduate schools was perhaps not based on well-scrutinised planning by the central government. In conjunction with the pursuit of misguided self-interest by individual universities as a compelling driving force, a less than desirable outcome of the professional graduate schools scheme may be manifesting itself as a specific case of Japanese higher education policy falling short of its intended impacts.

Status quo at a glance

Shortage of demand for 'professionals'

For many Japanese universities and colleges that have historically relied on the traditional student population as opposed to non-traditional students, the rapidly shrinking 18-year-old bracket population has been posing enormous challenges in terms of acquiring sufficient student enrolment and maintaining robust institutional operations. Recently established professional graduate schools are not immune to this harsh reality of a chronic shortage of applicants. A report by the Central Council for Education (2010), which surveyed all the domestic professional graduate degree programmes in fields other than law and teacher education, shows that nearly one half (49.3%) of the professional graduate programmes were operating below the required enrolment quota in 2009.[6] In the same year, four out of eight existing graduate professional policy schools were found unable to fill the enrolment quota required by the MEXT.

Watanabe (2012) argues that the unpopularity of the new professional schools may be attributed to the unattractive career prospects provided for graduates. Employment prospects are particularly dismal for the graduates of the new law schools, most of which began admitting students in 2004 and are already flooding the domestic job market of the legal professions with newly trained Juris Doctors (JDs).[7] With only approximately a quarter of the bar examinees nationwide successfully passing each year (MEXT, 2012) and less than half successfully passing the bar within four years after graduation (Ministry of Justice, 2013), not only the unemployment (or underemployment) issue of new graduates, but also the poor design and planning of the professional law schools scheme itself, have drawn public attention and become the target of condemnation (*The Yomiuri Shimbun*, 2009). Many law schools today are on the verge of closing their doors as they continue to struggle with student recruitment and placement while trying to maintain healthy institutional operations.[8]

Presumably, a non-trivial proportion of PPAM graduates in Japan also experience difficulties in successfully landing a first job that suitably matches their educational training and investment. Although the statistics released by the MEXT (2010) boast an 85.3% overall placement rate for the recently launched professional policy schools in the country, the figure includes working individuals with full-time employment who returned to their employers upon graduation. Without counting the incumbent professionals at matriculation (37.2% in 2009) and those who continued on to doctoral programmes (3.3%), it is calculated that approximately one out of four (23.7%) professional policy school graduates were found to be unemployed after graduation. Clearly, Japanese professional graduate schools face a demand shortage both from their prospective applicants at the entrance market and from the potential employers at the exit market for their graduates.

Severe competition for public service jobs

In response to the high popularity among current and prospective students of landing public service jobs, many Japanese PPAM schools have customised their academic programmes and curricula towards preparing students for careers in public services at the central and local levels. However, public servant positions in Japan require the successful passing by applicants of a highly competitive public service recruitment examination, unless the position is a political appointment. Any individual with a university degree meets the eligibility requirement for sitting the advanced section of the National Public Service Recruitment Examination, which is perhaps regarded as the most selective examination administered for the country's public service positions.[9] The examinations are offered by the National Personnel Authority and taken by the applicants according to their undergraduate or graduate majors, such as political science, international relations, law, economics, human science and so on. These examinations are not available through the professional PPAM schools, and while the curricula may be designed to help students prepare for the required examination, there is not a strong direct link between attendance in a PPAM programme and successful completion of the qualifying examinations.

Table 18.1 shows the number of applicants for the National Public Service Recruitment Examination, as well as the proportion of those who successfully passed the examination in 2012. The table demonstrates how selective the examination is, with less than 1% of the undergraduate applicants in the political science/international affairs subsection passing with successful marks in 2012, and thereby able to take elite public servant careers in central government agencies. Overall, only 4.9% of the applicants with a bachelor's degree successfully passed the examination. For applicants with an advanced graduate degree, landing a public service job is less competitive, though the overall successful passing rate for the examination remains low, at only 10.4%.

A public service career may also be sought at the local government level after successfully passing similarly highly selective examinations. Figure 18.2 shows that the successful passing rate for the advanced section of the local public service recruitment examinations was generally around 10% over the period 2005–11. As Agata (2007) points out, because of the severely competitive nature of public service recruitment examinations for both national and local government agencies, Japanese PPAM schools tend to enrol full-time employed professionals and practitioners as part-time students, for whom the schools have less concern in finding new placements, while also contributing to a high placement rate, at least on the surface, for the graduates.

Non-profit organisations

Typically, the graduates of the PPAM programmes may well seek their career opportunities in the non-profit sector. Representative of the public voice in the US, numerous non-profit organisations (NPOs), non-governmental organisations (NGOs) and charitable and research organisations play critical and influential roles in enhancing social well-being and welfare in the domestic and international communities. While the career markets in such sectors are fairly mature in the US, the non-profit sector in Japan, for which an associated NPO Law was not enacted until 1999, provides much more limited job prospects for recent graduates of PPAM schools. The limited

Table 18.1: Numbers of applicants and successful applicants for the National Public Service Recruitment Examinations in 2012

	(1) Applicants (%)	(2) Successfully passed (%)	(2)/(1)
Applicants with an undergraduate degree:			
Agricultural engineering	186 (0.9)	20 (1.9)	10.8
Agricultural science, fisheries	491 (2.3)	33 (3.1)	6.7
Chemistry, biology, pharmaceuticals	839 (3.9)	37 (3.5)	4.4
Economics	2,789 (13.1)	219 (20.5)	7.9
Engineering	1,919 (9.0)	186 (17.4)	9.7
Forestry, natural environment	384 (1.8)	17 (1.6)	4.4
Human science	653 (3.1)	33 (3.1)	5.1
Law	9,532 (44.6)	418 (39.2)	4.4
Liberal arts	1,134 (5.3)	52 (4.9)	4.6
Mathematical science, physics, earth sciences	438 (2.1)	25 (2.3)	5.7
Political science, international relations	2,993 (14.0)	26 (2.4)	0.9
Total	21,358 (100.0)	1,066 (100.0)	4.9
Applicants with a graduate degree:			
Administration	1,222 (32.6)	130 (33.2)	10.6
Agricultural engineering	48 (1.3)	7 (1.8)	14.6
Agricultural science, fisheries	321 (8.6)	22 (5.6)	6.9
Chemistry, biology, pharmaceuticals	565 (15.1)	33 (8.4)	5.8
Engineering	789 (21.0)	91 (23.3)	11.5
Forestry, natural environment	196 (5.2)	18 (4.6)	9.2
Human science	178 (4.7)	27 (6.9)	15.2
Law	95 (2.5)	35 (9.0)	36.8
Mathematical science, physics, earth sciences	338 (9.0)	28 (7.2)	8.2
Total	3,752 (100.0)	391 (100.0)	10.4

Source: Data from the official website of the National Personnel Authority. Available at: http://www.jinji.go.jp/saiyo/saiyo03.htm

capacity and roles played by the non-profit sector as a potential pool of employers may be grasped by taking a look at the Global Civil Society Index (GCSI), which evaluates Japan's civil society sector with one of the lowest scores among developed countries (see Figure 18.3).[10]

The GCSI measures three critical dimensions of a country's civil society sector: (i) 'capacity', capturing the size of the sector, as well as the effort or activity it mobilises; (ii) 'sustainability', measuring the ability of the civil society sector to sustain itself over time – legally, financially and socially; and (3) 'impact', measuring the contribution that the civil society sector makes to social, economic and political life. According to the overall assessment of the health of the civil society sector based on the composite

Figure 18.2: Numbers of applicants and successful applicants of the advanced section of the local public service recruitment examination

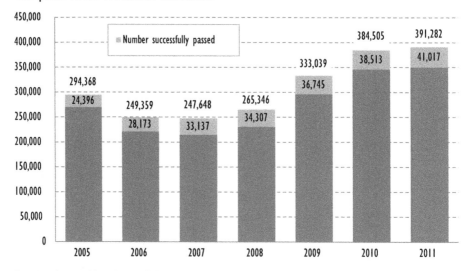

Source: Data from the Ministry of Internal Affairs and Communications of Japan. Available at: http://www.soumu.go.jp/menu_news/s-news/01gyosei11_02000030.html

Figure 18.3: Global Civil Society Index for 34 countries

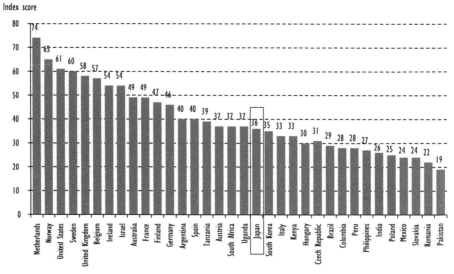

Source: Salamon and Sokolowski (2004).

index, Japan, with an index score of 36, was placed after Tanzania (GCSI = 39), Austria, South Africa and Uganda (all three countries assessed with GCSI = 37). This clearly highlights the immature nature of the health and vitality of Japan's civil society sector, particularly in comparison to the cohort of other developed countries.

The capacity of the civil society sector as a potential employer may also be measured rather directly by the scale of the workforce in the sector as a share of the economically active population. Despite the dramatic increase in the number of NPOs demonstrated over the last decade (see, eg, Watanabe 2012), the non-profit sector in Japan is not nearly as large as in the US, where almost 10% of the workforce is employed in the non-profit sector, accounting for 10% of the US economy (Killian, 2011). The size of its industrial scale alone, however, does not fully portray the entire picture of its limited employment capacity. A survey conducted in 2005 by the Research Institute of Economy, Trade and Industry (RIETI), which is charged with deliberating policy research that falls under the jurisdiction of the Ministry of Economy, Trade and Industry,[11] reveals not only that the proportion of paid workers in the non-profit sector was remarkably small, with only 50.5%, but also that their average annual salary was shown to be much lower, at only ¥1,300,000 (≈ USD9,931) than the average salaries earned in other sectors – ¥6,280,000 (≈ USD47,975) for public servants in the central government agencies (National Personnel Authority, 2005) and ¥4,370,000 (≈USD33,384) for employees in private industries (National Tax Agency, 2005).[12] As a result, substantive non-profit activities in Japan are often perceived widely as volunteer work, characterising the sector with a large proportion of unpaid staff being involved as the central actors. Therefore, the non-profit sector in the country may well be recognised as an unattractive industry for permanent career development by recent policy professionals with an advanced graduate degree, which typically incurs non-trivial burdens of direct financial, as well as opportunity, costs.

On this point, Salamon and Sokolowski (2004) also demonstrate, by level of development across 36 countries from 1995 through 2000, that among the developed countries, 4.7% of the non-profit sector workforce were paid staff, whereas 2.7% were volunteers, constituting 7.4% as a share of the economically active population. In comparison, although Japan, with 4.2% (3.2% paid staff and 1.0% volunteers) of the active population engaging in non-profit work, stands above the developing and transitional countries, which average 1.9% (1.2% paid staff and 0.7% volunteers), it is placed approximately on a par with the 36-country average of 4.3% (2.7% paid staff and 1.6% volunteers).

Think tanks and research organisations

Another important mission proclaimed by many PPAM programmes in Japanese universities is to produce fully fledged professionals who are capable of performing policy analysis and evaluation in private research organisations or think tanks. However, placing their graduates in such organisations entails other challenges. First and foremost, there are only a limited number of think tanks in Japan. According to research by McGann (2008), which covers some 5,550 think tanks worldwide in nearly 170 countries, there exist 105 think tanks in Japan, constituting only 1.9% of the entire think tank market in the world (see Table 18.2). The US particularly stands out in this figure, with 1,777 think tanks, constituting 32.5% of the industry worldwide. It is clear, therefore, that the employment potential provided by Japanese think tanks is substantially smaller and limited when compared to the US, upon which the curricula and missions of the Japanese PPAM programmes are modelled.

Second, most private think tanks in Japan are for-profit subsidiaries of financial, manufacturing or trade companies, rather than being non-profit and non-partisan entities. As Ueno (2005) points out, non-partisan independent think tanks capable of representing public opinion and evaluating public policies without financial restraint or commercial influence of a parent company are still rare in Japan. Suzuki (2011), in his self-inquiring article entitled 'Why Have No "American-Style" Think Tanks Been Developed in Japan?', attributes the underdeveloped state of the think-tank market of the country to the lack of the idea that (US) think tanks are 'tools and mechanisms for democracy'.[13] In fact, the foremost activities of these research organisations in Japan involve business consulting and the provision of information technology (IT) solution services to other private corporations and government agencies. Accordingly, Japanese think tanks have historically employed individuals with an advanced degree in engineering and physical sciences to meet the organisational emphasis on expanding IT services and system-integrating projects (Watanabe, 2012). As documented in Yamada and Tsukahara (1986: 142–3), this employment trend in the think-tank market has persisted since the 1970s. As a result, placing graduates in private think tanks continues to pose a serious challenge for Japanese PPAM schools.

International organisations

There has been a steady demand for professional staff in various arenas of international organisations. The versatile roles played by such multilateral entities further propel their significance and growth, with diversely complex issues emerging in rapidly

Table 18.2: Top 15 countries with the largest number of think tanks

	Country	Number of think tanks	%
1	US	1,777	32.52
2	UK	283	5.18
3	Germany	186	3.40
4	France	165	3.02
5	Argentina	122	2.23
6	India	121	2.21
7	Russia	107	1.96
8	**Japan**	**105**	**1.92**
9	Canada	94	1.72
10	Italy	87	1.59
11	South Africa	78	1.43
12	China	74	1.35
13	Switzerland	72	1.32
14	Sweden	68	1.24
15	Netherlands	55	1.01
Total		5,465	100.0

Source: McGann (2008).

globalising environments, for which member states are postulated to work through collaborative and interdependent processes. Figure 18.4 illustrates that the Japanese staff members employed at the professional (P1) level or above at the United Nations (UN) Secretariat has steadily increased from 404 in 1995 to 708 in 2009, representing a 75% increase in this period. The number of Japanese staff appointed at the level of director positions or above also reveals a steadfast increase of 63%, from 40 in 1995 to 65 in 2009.

Figure 18.4: Change in the number of Japanese staff employed at the United Nations Secretariat: professional

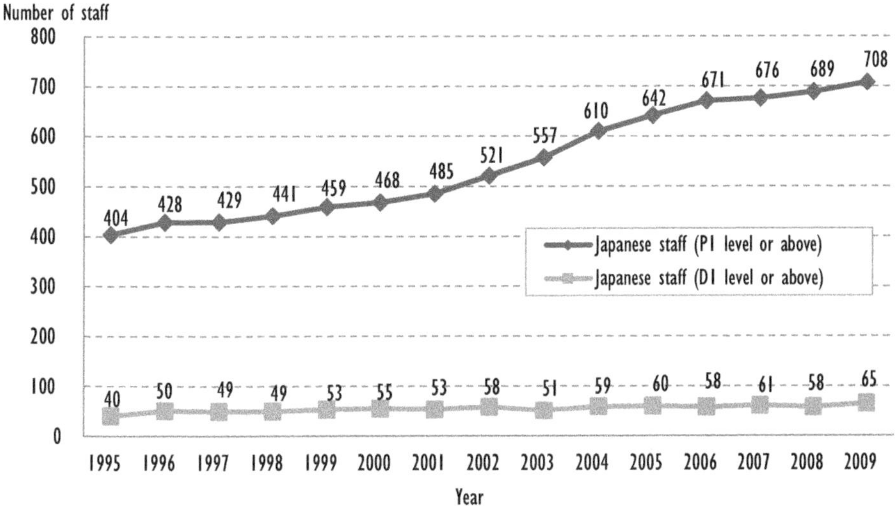

Source: Ministry of Foreign Affairs, cited by Nakauchi (2010).

However, despite the robust increase in Japanese representatives employed at the UN Secretariat, the further demand for such experts is predicted to grow, particularly for Japanese nationals. Typically, the desirable numbers of staff employees in multilateral international organisations are proportionately determined according to the financial contributions made by each member state. Table 18.3 shows a list of the top 20 countries in terms of the scale of staff members in decreasing order of the numbers of staff working at the UN Secretariat, along with the desirable range of staff employment, current share at the Secretariat against its overall demographic staff composition and the financial contribution in proportion made by each of the member country.

Among the top five member states, the UN Secretariat employs the nationals of Germany and France within the appropriate targeted range, while employment of Italian citizens slightly exceeds the desirable range. The US, with the largest share of financial contribution, is represented by staff members employed at slightly below the desirable range. In contrast, the UN Secretariat is falling seriously short of Japanese citizens as the country represents, in terms of the demographic composition of the Secretariat, less than one half of the lower end of the desirable range. Even with the second-largest financial contribution (16.6%) made to the organisation, Japan's share of staff members at the UN Secretariat remains modest, with only less than 4%. It is perhaps worth pointing out, however, that nearly 60% of the Japanese staff members at the UN Secretariat are female employees, representing the second-highest member state in terms of the female staff ratio, next to the Philippines (75.0%) and above the US (55.9%).

Towards further promotion of public policy, administration and management professions

It is often claimed that professional graduate school training in the PPAM field delivers fewer benefits and incentives than do other professional schools in Japan. For instance, successful completion of advanced legal training provided by professional law schools is specifically listed as an eligibility requirement for sitting the national bar examination, though an alternative option is offered through an equivalent examination in place of the JD degree. Completing the curriculum of professional accounting schools also permits partial exemption from the certified public accountant (CPA) examination.

Table 18.3: Number of staff at the United Nations Secretariat by country (as of 30 June 2009)

	Country	Staff numbers (female)	Desirable range (median)	Share (%)	Financial contribution (%)
1	US	333 (186)	352–(414)–476	11.85	22.000
2	Germany	170 (80)	140–(165)–189	6.05	8.577
3	France	132 (63)	104–(123)–141	4.70	6.301
4	Italy	117 (60)	85–(101)–116	4.17	5.079
5	Japan	111 (66)	265–(312)–359	3.95	16.624
6	UK	99 (39)	110–(129)–148	3.52	6.642
7	China	85 (46)	75–(88)–101	3.03	2.667
8	Russia	75 (11)	27–(32)–37	2.64	1.200
9	Canada	74 (30)	52–(62)–71	2.63	2.977
10	Australia	55 (29)	34–(37)–46	1.96	1.787
11	Spain	50 (22)	53–(62)–71	1.78	2.968
12	India	46 (17)	37–(44)–51	1.64	0.450
13	Netherlands	43 (14)	35–(41)–47	1.53	1.873
14	Mexico	40 (16)	43–(50)–58	1.42	2.257
15	Philippines	40 (30)	6–(10)–15	1.42	0.078
16	Argentina	39 (19)	9–(14)–19	1.39	0.325
17	Brazil	37 (15)	23–(28)–32	1.32	0.876
18	Korea	35 (12)	40–(48)–55	1.25	2.173
19	Switzerland	32 (14)	24–(29)–34	1.14	1.216
20	Austria	30 (15)	18–(23)–28	1.07	0.887
	Other	1,166 (466)			
	Total	2,809 (1,260)		100.0	

Source: Ministry of Foreign Affairs, cited by Nakauchi (2010). The original source is the UN (A/64/352).

The graduates of PPAM schools, in contrast, receive no such exemption merits or privileges in terms of taking the public service recruitment examination. In order to increase the demand for the country's PPAM programmes, therefore, a system of incentives needs to be created to stimulate committed individuals to obtain their academic training through the professional PPAM schools. This could be achieved simply by setting the PPAM degree as an eligibility requirement for certain public service jobs.

It is also worth noting that the majority of successful applicants for the advanced section of the public service recruitment examinations held only a bachelor's degree, typically earned from high-prestige elite institutions, and no significant distinctions were made in terms of expected responsibilities, remuneration, rank and career path based on the degree type held by the applicants. Therefore, an individual with a graduate-level professional PPAM degree, once employed by the central government, carries no value added even relative to those with only undergraduate training. In an attempt to rectify this condition, the National Personnel Authority established a new examination policy in 2011 to accommodate these issues by introducing separate career tracks and examinations for applicants with undergraduate diplomas and those with professional graduate degrees. The implementation of the new examination policy, which began in April 2012, is expected to enlarge the roles of and demand for the professional PPAM schools in Japan.

In the growing salience of today's globalisation and a knowledge-based society, in which producing highly skilled manpower is becoming a vital ingredient for building an opulent society, the nation is still challenged by the future agendas of further expanding the sector of NPOs/NGOs and think-tank markets. In this regard, readers are referred to Tanaka (Chapter Thirteen) on the development of NPOs in Japan and Shimizu (Chapter Fourteen) on Japanese think tanks and the policy market of the private sector included in Part Three of this volume, where the authors provide the historical background, current issues and future agendas. In particular, Tanaka (Chapter Seven, this volume), in his well-articulated discussion on an 'in-house policy research institute' found within each ministry of the central government, claims that 'analysis and deliberation in the policy process is carried out exclusively by the bureaucracy', and provides a valuable clue to the employment issue of PPAM graduates by pointing out that in order for these government-affiliated policy research institutes 'to improve their policy analysis abilities and to play more active roles in policy formation, it is particularly necessary to train personnel with expertise'.

It is pointed out that only a limited number of PPAM schools currently offer degree programmes with some international contexts of public affairs and policies. The English track international programmes are primarily designed for educating young non-Japanese professionals gathering from other parts of the Asia-Pacific region. In order to heed responsibly the voice from the global community, however, further efforts need to be made in recruiting Japanese students committed to crossing the border beyond domestic public services. Multidimensional challenges deriving from the globalisation of public policy schools, as well as public policy analysis and affairs in multilateral contexts, are discussed in Fritzen (2008). Designing an indigenous programme that is 'fit for purpose' across different countries is also a critical agenda of curriculum development (Geva-May et al, 2008). From the perspective of developing the international PPAM track in Japan, an Asia-Pacific-focused programme, rather than the generic 'international' emphasis, may be worth considering, as have some

European universities devoted efforts in developing university programmes specifically tailored to the needs of the European Union system. Rapidly expanding intra-regional activities within the Asia-Pacific region bring forth new complex agendas that require multilateral negotiations and professional leaders representing each nation.

Conclusions

In this chapter, we highlighted some critical issues currently faced by PPAM degree programmes in Japan, particularly from the perspectives of the job placement and career development of graduates. Evidence is provided that the government-initiated, supply-driven establishment of graduate-level professional schools scheme has generated an excess supply of professionals in the domestic job markets. The graduates of Japan's professional PPAM schools face both quantitative and qualitative mismatches at initial job entry, as well as over the course of their prospective careers, often being unable to fully maximise their professional knowledge and participate in the public service and policy arena to which they aspired when choosing to pursue their field of study. The topic covered in this chapter, therefore, may well serve as a case study portraying how and why this specific higher education policy initiated by the MEXT ended up falling short of its potential outcomes. Thus, it stresses the urgent need for government agencies, NPOs/NGOs and think tanks to create systems of employment where the professional knowledge and skills gained by these graduates is valued and maximised on the job.

Japanese PPAM schools are still in the early stages of development, with active mergers, closures, restructuring and redesigning of curricula. In the fluid nature of today's public debates, a thriving future of the PPAM schools and their graduates likely requires further modifications of the current systems in multiple respects, and critically hinges on their ability to effectively lead and heed the ongoing public debates at the local, national and global levels.

Notes

[1] In this regard, readers are referred to Chapter Seventeen by Agata in Part Four of this volume, where the author discusses various perspectives and issues faced by Japanese PPAM schools in terms of curricula, instruction, accreditation, faculty development and so on, with an interesting case study drawn from Waseda University's Graduate School of Public Management.

[2] There existed 100 national universities in 2003 prior to the corporatisation, which was cut down to 87 by 2004 through mergers of relatively small national universities in order to bring in the economy of scale, or a scale merit of expanded organisations, into these institutions. As of 20 December 2013, there exist 86 national university corporations.

[3] It is worth mentioning that even before the establishment of the graduate-level professional law schools, Japanese universities had long offered law degrees at an undergraduate level that qualified the graduates to sit the national bar examination. However, neither university education nor majoring in law was a requirement under the former examination system. Under the ongoing system, applicants for the bar examination

must have either graduated from a professional graduate law school or have successfully passed the equivalent examination in place of a graduate law degree.

[4] For example, the 18-year-old bracket population in Japan decreased from 2.03 million in 1990 to 1.51 million in 2000, and reduced further to 1.22 million in 2010, representing a 40% decline in two decades.

[5] For more detailed discussions on the emergence of progressive local authorities in the 1960s through 1970s and the provision of advanced training opportunities for local public officers, please refer to Chapter Three in Part One of this volume by Tsuchiyama.

[6] The enrolment capacity or quota must be approved for each degree programme in Japan by the MEXT, which then oversees the student enrolment status each year. A violation of this conduct, for example, enrolling a larger number of students beyond the approved capacity or being unable to fulfil the quota, is subject to pressure by the MEXT of reduced government subsidies.

[7] The number of lawyers has nearly doubled between 2000 and 2013, from 17,126 to 33,624, and has tripled since 1980, from 11,441 (Japan Federation of Bar Associations, 2013).

[8] Five law schools had already ceased admitting students by April 2013, and three more law schools have announced plans to do so by April 2015.

[9] Because of its high selectivity, the examination has often been referred to (more or less cynically) as the Japanese version of *Kējǔ*, which is a highly selective civil service examination system introduced as early as the Sui Dynasty (581–618 AD) in China.

[10] The GCSI, which provides 'a tested and reliable tool for assessing the health of the civil society sector in countries throughout the world', has been developed by the Center for Civil Society Studies at the Johns Hopkins Institute for Policy Studies. Detailed information on the Center and the GCSI may be obtained from their official website. Available at: http://ccss.jhu.edu/

[11] In Chapter Seven in Part Two of this volume, Tanaka provides a detailed discussion on the 'in-house think tanks' or research bodies that implement policy research within each ministry of the central government.

[12] The calculations are based on the currency exchange rate averaged for the year of 2005 at USD1.00 = ¥130.9.

[13] In Chapter Fourteen in Part Three of this volume, Shimizu also shares a similar view, making her point on the 'catalytic roles' played by think tanks as one of their critical ingredients, but seeing these as lacking for Japanese think tanks, which cannot, therefore, truly be called 'think tanks'.

References

Agata, K. (2007) 'Kōkyō Seisaku Daigakuin no Genjō to Tenbō', *IDE Gendai no Kōtō Kyōiku*, vol 493 (August–September), pp 23–30.

Central Council for Education (2010) 'Senmonshoku Daigakuin no Jittai Chōsa (Shiryō)'. Available at: http://www.mext.go.jp/b_menu/shingi/chukyo/chukyo4/011/gijiroku/__icsFiles/afieldfile/2010/02/08/1289889_2.pdf

Fritzen, S.A. (2008) 'Public Policy Education Goes Global: A Multi-Dimensional Challenge', *Journal of Policy Analysis and Management*, vol 27, no 1, pp 205–14.

Fukuda, M. (2011) 'Kyōiku to Keizai Shakai wo Kangaeru: Kyōiku ni Okeru Juyō to Kyōkyū no Misumacchi'. Available at: http://www7.ocn.ne.jp/~mfukuda/edec06.pdf

Geva-May, I., Nasi, G., Turrini, A. and Scott, C. (2008) 'MPP Programs Emerging Around the World', *Journal of Policy Analysis and Management*, vol 27, no 1, pp 187–204.

Inoue, S. (2006) 'Changing Japanese Society and Higher Education Reform: The Current Status and Continuing Problems from the Perspective of Comprehensive Policy Studies', *Shimane Journal of Policy Studies*, vol 11, pp 85–107.

Japan Federation of Bar Associations (2013) 'Bengoshisū no Suii (1950nen–2013nen)'. Available at: http://www.nichibenren.or.jp/library/ja/publication/books/data/2013/whitepaper_suii_2013.pdf

Justice System Reform Council (2001) 'Shihō Seido Kaikaku Shingikai Ikensho: 21-seiki no Nihon wo Sasaeru Shihō Seido'. Available at: http://www.kantei.go.jp/jp/sihouseido/report/ikensyo/pdf-dex.html

Killian, S. (2011) *Professionalizing the Field of Nonprofit Management: Is a Master of Public Administration Degree, Concentration in Nonprofit Management Effective for Today's Aspiring Nonprofit Management?*, Saabrücken, Germany: LAP Lambert Academic Publishing.

McGann, J.G. (2008) *The Global 'Go-To Think Tanks': The Leading Public Policy Research Organizations in the World*, The Think Tanks and Civil Societies Program, International Relations Program, University of Pennsylvania.

MEXT (Ministry of Education, Culture, Sports, Science and Technology) (2007) 'Ministry of Education, Culture, Sports, Science and Technology 2007'. Available at: www.mext.go.jp/list_001/list_016/__icsFiles/afieldfile/2009/03/19/mext_2007_e.pdf

MEXT (2010) 'Senmonshoku Diagakuin no Jittai Chōsa no Kekka Gaiyō'. Available at: http://www.mext.go.jp/b_menu/shingi/chukyo/chukyo4/011/gijiroku/__icsFiles/afieldfile/2010/02/08/1289889_1.pdf

MEXT (2012) 'Hōkadaigakuin Kyōiku no Saranaru Jūjitsu ni Muketa Kaizen Hōsaku ni Tsuite no Gaiyō'. Available at: http://www.mext.go.jp/b_menu/shingi/chukyo/chukyo0/gijiroku/__icsFiles/afieldfile/2012/07/24/1323733_15.pdf

Ministry of Internal Affairs and Communications (2011) 'Local Autonomy College English Pamphlet'. Available at: http://www.soumu.go.jp/jitidai/english.htm

Ministry of Justice (2013) 'Hōkadaigakuin-betsu Jukenshasū, Gōkakushasū Shirabe (Heisei 20nendo Shūryōsha)'. Available at: http://www.moj.go.jp/content/000115436.pdf

Nakauchi, Y. (2010) 'Kokuren ni Okeru Nipponjin Shokuin Zōkyō Mondai', *Rippō to Chōsa*, vol 305, pp 34–42.

National Personnel Authority (2005) Kokka Kōmuin Kyūyotō Jittai Chōsa. Available at: http://ssl.jinji.go.jp/hakusho/index.html

National Tax Agency (2005) Minkan Kyūyo Jittai Tōkei Chōsa. Available at: http://www.nta.go.jp/kohyo/tokei/kokuzeicho/minkan2005/menu/pdf/0405.pdf

Salamon, L.M. and Sokolowski, S.W. (eds) (2004) *Global Civil Society: Dimensions of the Nonprofit Sector* (vol 2), Bloomfield, CT: Kumarian Press.

Suzuki, T. (2005) 'Nippon ni Atarashii Seisaku Keisei System wo Tsukurō', *Ronza*, vol 120, pp 46–57.

Suzuki, T. (2011) 'Why Have No "American-Style" Think Tanks Been Developed in Japan?', *Kikan Seisaku Keiei Kenkyū*, vol 2, pp 30–50.

The Yomiuri Shimbun (2009) 'Kyoiku Renessance: (9) Shūryōsha Fue Shūshoku Kibishiku', 25 February.

Ueno, M. (2005) 'Seisaku ga Sangyō to Natta Beikoku', *Ronza*, vol 120, pp 82–7.

UN (A/64/352) 'Composition of the Secretariat, Report of the Secretary-General'. Available at: http://daccess-dds-ny.un.org/doc/UNDOC/GEN/N09/515/01/PDF/N0951501.pdf?OpenElement

Watanabe, S.P. (2012) 'Where Do They Belong in the Job Markets? Emerging Career Issues of Public Policy Program Graduates in Japan', *Journal of Comparative Policy Analysis: Research and Practice*, vol 14, no 5, pp 410–30.

Yamada, K. and Tsukahara, S. (1986) *Kagaku Kenkyū no Life Cycle*, Tokyo: University of Tokyo Press.

EIGHTEEN

Conclusion: future directions of the theory and practice of public policy analysis in Japan

Yukio Adachi

Introduction

The primary purpose of this final chapter is to enumerate and unravel the challenges of public policy analysis as an intellectual and practical activity in Japan. This is achieved by drawing on the numerous examples explored in previous chapters, and bringing together the analysis made to outline future directions for public policy analysis in Japan.

As was discussed in previous chapters, especially in Part Two, Japanese governments, both at the central and local levels, have never been indifferent to enhancing their employees' skills in relation to policy analysis. Every year, they have dispatched a number of promising young bureaucrats to top-level universities mainly in the US and European Union (EU), allowing them to participate in one- or two-year advanced policy-related programmes. They have established as many as 12 ministry-affiliated research institutions, while governmental organisations set up to support legislatures' policymaking activities are comparable with similar institutions in other advanced democracies. A few internal policy advisory councils have opened the door to outside policy analysts, though a great majority of them remain a tightly knit, closed community. Much effort has been made in developing more and more public policy programmes to foster and upgrade students' practical analytical skills. The urgent need to activate a policy market, where competing policy alternatives are advocated by major policy actors, such as political parties, business associations, labour unions, non-profit organisations (NPOs) and non-governmental organisations (NGOs), social movements, the media, and policy analysts working for universities or think tanks, is now widely acknowledged.

The existence of such positive trends should neither be ignored nor underestimated. Still, judging the more or less 'pessimistic' tone evident in almost all of the previous chapters regarding the state of policy analysis in Japan, there is much room for further improvement. To begin with, policy analysis has not yet been established as a fully fledged profession in Japan, and its application has consequently been quite limited. Moreover, it has rarely been successful in fulfilling its original mission of monitoring and correcting the 'democratic myopia'[1] by means of introducing systemic thinking into the policymaking process. Its limited application and poor performance might be mainly due to the insufficient understanding, on the part of the governmental, market and civic sectors, of the potential contributions that policy analysis can make for improved policymaking and policy implementation. Only a few members in each sector realise the vital need of consulting policy analysts when selecting and adopting a general stance on public issues. Politicians are no exception. Some responsibility for the unfortunate state of policy analysis in Japan, however, must be borne by the alleged policy analysts themselves. Policy analysts are urged to drastically upgrade the quality of their products if they ever hope to be listened to more attentively and have their products adopted into the policy process.

Therefore, enhancing the social and political prestige of policy analysis as a profession and promoting its application require a double reform. First, we need to reflect on what is missing or insufficient as part of the policy-analytical activities practised in Japan. Part of this enhancement should see the fostering of quality policy analysts who can serve as the clients' trusted advisors, not mere informants.[2] Second, a series of drastic system reforms need to be undertaken that require the government and non-governmental policy sectors to incorporate policy analysis before making a critical decision. This chapter focuses on the first issue – exploring the potential future directions of policy analysis in Japan – while only briefly touching upon widespread system reforms.

The need for more informed and realistic cost-effectiveness analyses

Accurately predicting the costs and benefits of a policy is extremely difficult even for the most accomplished analysts with the latest information and analytical tools. Prediction, therefore, needs to be made with maximum caution as a means to minimise errors, especially if there is a high probability of a policy causing serious and long-lasting impacts on people's lives. Fatal prediction errors must be avoided at all costs. It is, at times, necessary to anticipate the worst-case scenario, in which the benefits (positive effects) remain minimal and the costs (policy expenses plus negative effects) reach the maximum of what were predicted. In Japan, many policies have been formulated, adopted and implemented based on an optimistic prediction that estimates benefits higher, and costs lower, resulting in enormous social damage. Why have such fatal prediction errors repeatedly been made?

It has been common practice in Japan for governmental bureaus responsible for the promotion and implementation of policies to also analyse and formulate policies, despite the fact that most staff members in these bureaus are not adequately trained in the theories, skills and ethics of policy analysis. Bureaucrats have substantially led discussions in ad hoc commissions through the secretariat function they provide. They have also lobbied influential people, such as top lawmakers in the ruling and opposing parties, along with leaders of relevant organisations, and created reports and other materials on issues that they may not have been able to fully analyse for the Diet (national assembly). They have been known to even answer lawmakers' questions on behalf of ministers (on matters besides technical issues relating to pure administrative operations). To do all these things, they have exploited information collected and analysed by government agencies, or quasi-government organisations, including government-affiliated institutes and think tanks.

It is no easy task for government bureaucrats officially in charge of policy formulation and implementation to objectively and critically examine the validity of their own analyses and predictions. This is also the case with analysts working for government-affiliated institutes and think tanks; unless they are institutionally guaranteed a high level of independence from the government, objectivity is difficult to achieve. This underscores the importance of entrusting policy analysis to outside professional organisations, which have highly trained and experienced staff members, and are independent and specialised enough to work with the 'central mind of the government' on an equal footing (Dror, 2001). These organisations should be able to provide objective and expert advice on the projected costs and benefits of policies. However, both central and local governments have seldom sought their advice. When analysis has been commissioned to external organisations, there has been a tendency to selectively adopt only the information advantageous to the promotion of their favourite (often predetermined) policies. It has generally been of little interest to them to impartially compare and rank alternative policy options, in which the critical mission of policy analysis lies.

The following example supports this point by highlighting how a prediction error led to an overestimate of the demand for airport construction in Japan. In March 2010, the Ministry of Land, Infrastructure, Transport and Tourism (MLIT) announced the forecasted demand and the actual demand in 2008 for every airport in Japan, with the exception of 25 (the 24 airports that had been built before any demand forecasts were required, such as the Yamagata airport, and the Shizuoka airport, which had been open for less than a year). According to the announcement, the actual number of users was far below the forecasted demand at about 90% of all the investigated airports; some of these airports had an actual demand that was slightly over 10% of the forecasted demand. For instance, the Kitakyushu airport, which opened in March 2006, had only 1.11 million customers in 2007, which was about 40% of the demand forecast announced in 2004 by the Institution for Transport Policy Studies, whose leading members are retired high-ranking officials from the MLIT. The number of users has continued to decline at this airport, with no sign of increasing. In March 2011, this situation compelled the MLIT Kyushu Regional Development Bureau to modify their demand forecast for Kitakyushu airport for 2032 from 3.925 million to 0.985 million customers, a quarter of the original forecast. This case is a striking example of the widespread analysis that was frequently practised based on the unrealistic assumption that the population around the airport would continue to increase and the economy would continue to grow by several percentage points every year.[3]

Ability to adapt to changes in the policy environment and newly discovered facts

If the policy environment has changed significantly since the formulation and adoption of an existing policy, or if new facts have been found or scientific discoveries made, prompt and appropriate actions should be taken accordingly. Up until the beginning of the 1990s, when the Liberal Democratic Party's (LDP's) one-party dominance ended, policies were developed through the coordination of ideas among cabinet members, the ruling party's executive office and bureaucrats. One major problem that stood out during this period was the huge information gap between government bureaucrats and other actors involved in the policy process. Consequently, important matters that needed to be considered in policy formulation, such as the costs and benefits of alternative policies, were steered by government bureaucrats rather than specialised policy analysts. This gap gave bureaucrats considerable leverage in the policy-formulation process. During the LDP's tenure in office, agreement was often reached through bureaucrat-led policy networks composed of bureaucrats, *zoku-giin* – policy tribes that are made up of politicians with specialised knowledge, or at least intense interest, in a particular set of policy issues (Curtis, 2002: 6) – and relevant interest groups. These agreements were normally adopted as the cabinet's official policy proposal with only minor additions or modifications. This was the case for economic policy during this period, best identified through the slogan, 'Catch up with the West, get ahead of the West', which drove the country to achieve a full post-war recovery and economic growth, underpinned by a widely shared vision among political actors of building a Japanese-style welfare state. In effect, government ministries and agencies functioned as exclusive think tanks for the cabinet and the LDP's executive office. Counter-proposals occasionally suggested by independent think tanks, academic organisations and researchers in relevant fields were mostly ignored and seldom made it on to the agenda.

However, we should note that even during the period when the vision of establishing a Japanese-style welfare state through economic growth was developed, serious political confrontations still took place. Japan has a history of vigorous social movements, including anti-pollution movements, anti-nuclear testing movements, anti-US military base movements, pro-Constitution movements, labour movements and agrarian movements. The activists in these movements have used various means of approaching the ruling and opposing parties and journalists, including campaigning on the streets, in order to promote their interests, and have had a substantial impact on policymaking processes. Moreover, politicians, whose priority is to defend the interests of their constituencies, have advocated for job creation and regional development mainly through the implementation of large-scale public works in the name of equity or minimising regional gaps. Bureaucrats skilfully dealt with both sets of activists' interests and demands by somehow coining policies more or less acceptable to every stakeholder. The 'policy analysis' performed by bureaucrats was, in this sense, essentially interest coordination among conflicting parties. Bureaucrats sought to develop feasible and executable policies that would pass the political test. The Japanese bureaucrats were very capable in this respect, though it is also important to point out that this process was undoubtedly reinforced by the fast-growing economy, which provided the financial room for this kind of interest coordination and taming of staunch opponents to take place.

Thus, most policies during this period were: developed in bureaucrat-led policy networks; reconciled and compromised at times to satisfy influential political actors, including social activists; submitted to the Diet as government-sponsored bills; and finally adopted and implemented. Nevertheless, given the way that it protects the decision-making class from the periodic evaluation of voters, there are advantages to maintaining this style of policymaking, enabling them to think about long-term political changes that focus on developing society as a whole, rather than short-term objectives that focus on keeping active voters happy. In fact, this approach did make significant contributions to Japan's post-war recovery and economic growth.

At the same time, bureaucrat-led policymaking does cause undesirable effects. Most bureaucrats are naturally resistant to reviewing, let alone discontinuing, the policies that they have been involved in formulating and played a role in their implementation. Such policies often take on a life of their own in the name of commitment to legal continuity or consistency. In such cases, ministers' requests for a mid-course adjustment or cancelation of policies can often be sabotaged by bureaucrats (Curtis, 2002: 3–5).[4] Moreover, more often than not, regulatory bureaus fail to adequately fulfil their original functions because they become 'captured' by the very organisations that they are supposed to be regulating (Stigler, 1971). In such cases, legislatures, who are institutionally expected to supervise and monitor both the executive branch and bureaucrats, should take the initiative of reviewing policies. However, they tend to be rather reluctant to do so, perhaps because of an overarching hesitation to 'ditch' sunk costs, which should clearly not be a factor in deciding whether a project should be continued or discontinued. Psychological resistance to publicly admitting their original mistake of having approved the policy remains a guiding force.[5]

The Nakaumi reclamation project is a good example. The project plan was announced by the Shimane Prefecture in June 1954 and put into effect as a government-sponsored project in April 1963. The purpose of the project was to desalinate Nakaumi, which was originally a brackish lake, by reclaiming 2,230 hectares of paddy fields, which would ensure an agricultural water supply from the fields and the surrounding farms, covering 7,300 hectares in total. However, by 1968, when the major construction began, the rice surplus phenomenon had already grown evident and become a social problem. As solutions, the Ministry of Agriculture, Forestry and Fisheries of Japan (MAFF) launched a policy of reducing rice acreage in 1971. While carrying out reclamation projects, the government coerced farmers not to produce rice, which completely contradicted the reasoning behind this intervention. If the government had re-evaluated this reclamation project at this point, they would not have wasted 25 years and ¥72 billion. The MAFF then gave up on the original plan of creating rice paddies in 1984, but persisted with the project, now focusing on creating dry fields. With the intensification of anti-desalination movements led by those who were concerned about water pollution and environmental destruction (eg those engaged in fisheries), the Shimane and neighbouring Tottori Prefectures changed course, requesting the MAFF to postpone the execution of desalination (May 1985). Consequently, the MAFF was forced to officially announce the discontinuation of the project in 2002 after having drained just over 20% of what was originally planned.

The lack of prompt and appropriate responses from regulatory agencies to changes in the policy environment and newly discovered facts is partly responsible for the tragic reactor core meltdown accident at the Fukushima Daiichi Nuclear Power Plant in March 2011. This plant was built over 40 years ago when seismological knowledge was still in development. Advancements in this field repeatedly pointed to the possibility of a tsunami much larger than was projected at the time the power plant was constructed. The plant's vulnerability to reactor core damage in case of such an event had been made clear.[6] Despite this prediction, the Tokyo Electric Power Company (TEPCO) underestimated the risk and only undertook inadequate measures, with no margin of safety. The regulatory ministries and agencies were also aware of the vulnerability of the Fukushima Power Plant, and yet overlooked TEPCO's slow response. If all the responsible parties had taken the latest findings in seismology and newly revealed facts more seriously and prepared appropriate measures, this worst-case scenario could have been prevented.

Reluctance to imagine and prepare for a worst-case scenario

In order to avoid a worst-case scenario, whose chance of occurrence is extremely small but that will cause intolerable damage once it happens, what kinds of preventive measures need to be taken?[7] If a worst-case scenario should happen, how should relevant parties, including operators, the national government, local governments, the Self-Defense Force, the police, NPO/NGOs and local community associations, act to minimise the damage? Frankly, the study and practice of risk management, which focuses on such issues, is still at a primitive stage of development in Japan. Even when analysts did predict the occurrence of a worst-case scenario, their warnings were largely ignored by the industries concerned or regulatory agencies. We have been made fully aware of this dreadful fact through the Fukushima disaster.

It will suffice to list the following preventive measures that should and could have been taken to mitigate this worst-case scenario:

- the introduction of a method of injecting water into reactors and containment vessels using fire pumps;
- the installation of a pressure-resistant vent system;
- protecting against the risk of a total loss of electricity at neighbouring plants and in all the emergency diesel generators and power distribution buses;
- the appropriate provision of chief reactor engineers and ensuring that the operator shift structure is managed to effectively deal with simultaneous accidents at multiple plants; and
- special training of the chief reactor engineers in case of emergencies.

The most exacerbating negligence in relation to Fukushima was the fact that even TEPCO's extremely insufficient and inadequate measures to protect against severe accidents were overlooked by the regulatory agency, the Nuclear and Industrial Safety Agency (NISA).

Policy analysis backed by systemic policy thinking

A public policy, designed and implemented in order to deal with a specific public issue, is closely and intricately linked to other policies in the same or different fields through policy linkage. Thus, dealing with any policy, regardless of its subject matter, requires advanced and systemic analytical skills.[8] No analyst lacking such skills should be expected to design a truly appropriate policy. However, how is it possible to develop such a policy? Also, what exactly is systemic policy analysis?

The first phase of systemic policy analysis is to pay maximum attention to opportunity costs. There are few things in this world that can be obtained for free. If one is to gain possession of something important, he/she needs to be ready to sacrifice other things that are no less important to him/her, be it money, time or whatever else it may be. Policy is no exception. We gain a great number of things from implementing a policy, but a great number of things are also lost in return. The resources required for a specific policy are not easily transferable to another policy issue. The government generally operates under severe resource constraints, and often has to compete with the private sector over resources. Excessive resource consumption by the former can interfere with the business activities of the latter, causing negative impacts upon the economy in the long run. In addition, the government should allocate the limited resources available in relation to the private sector in the most efficient way to policies in various fields competing with each other for government resources. This is why analysts are always expected to search for and formulate the most cost-effective policy, which produces the desired effects at a minimum cost, regardless of the type of issues they are dealing with.[9]

Therefore, if analysts are to develop a new policy, they need to present a realistic case for securing enough funds for its implementation. This requires asking questions, such as, 'Which existing policies can be downsized or cancelled?', and 'Which competing policy proposals can be postponed?' This is even more important now given that high economic growth and related increases in tax revenues cannot be expected. Deliberating on the source of revenue for policies is more easily said than done, especially for politicians who tend to advocate popular (but costly) policy choices. This is best embodied in the 'manifesto' (an election promise with defined revenue sources) of the Democratic Party of Japan (DPJ), which beat the LDP-led coalition to power and achieved a historic change of government following the lower house election in August 2009.

In this election campaign, the DPJ presented a number of bold policy options in its manifesto that required a budget increase of ¥16.8 trillion (until the end of 2013), despite the economic crisis that the country was experiencing, which saw the balance of government bonds being twice as big as the country's gross domestic product (GDP). The breakdown of the budget is as follows:

- ¥5.5 trillion for the provision of child allowance and childbirth benefits (¥312,000 per annum for all children until they finish junior high school);
- ¥0.5 trillion for free public high school education, with equivalent subsidies to private high school students;
- ¥1.6 trillion for the renewal of medical and long-term care systems;
- ¥1 trillion for individual (household) income support for agriculture;
- ¥2.5 trillion for the abolition of provisional tax rates on gasoline, and so on;
- ¥1.3 trillion for the elimination of highway tolls;
- ¥0.8 trillion for employment measures;
- ¥3.6 trillion for other measures not listed earlier (eg the abolition of the Health Insurance Scheme for People Aged 75 and Over, the expansion of university scholarships, raising minimum wage levels, and assistance to small- and medium-sized enterprises).

The DPJ also promised in the manifesto that they would generate funding for these attractive policies through the elimination of wasteful government spending, such as public works (¥9.1 trillion), the effective use of reserves in special accounts or 'buried treasure' (¥5 trillion), and a review of taxation measures (¥2.7 trillion).

As groundbreaking and meaningful as these policies themselves may have been, the three years and four months of DPJ administration was a complete disappointment to the electorate, which had high hopes for the regime change. This poor performance cannot be justified even through the unprecedented disaster of the Great East Japan Earthquake or the so-called 'twisted Diet', which saw the House of Councilors, dominated by the opposing coalition, continuing to reject the DPJ's bills that were necessary in implementing their policies. While failing to either curtail wasteful government spending or find the 'buried treasure' that would have been required to deliver against their manifesto promises, Japan's dependency on government bonds continued to increase even more than during the LDP-led coalition government. Consequently, the DPJ was unable to put into action almost any of the major policies listed in the manifesto. As a natural consequence, the DPJ faced a historic, devastating defeat in the lower house election held on 16 December 2012. If a group of lawmakers skilled at systemic policy analysis had been in charge of drafting the manifesto, or a certain number of professional policy analysts from outside organisations had been added to the manifesto development team, the result would have been less disastrous.

A second phase of systemic policy analysis is to examine the consequences of implementing a policy as systematically as possible. When implementing a certain policy in a certain field to achieve a certain objective, its positive and negative impacts will reach a number of different fields, as well as within the field. Serious impacts can take complex paths and unexpectedly reveal themselves where least expected. The quality of policy proposals is heavily dependent upon how thoroughly policymakers have predicted the various types of consequences that the policy in question may bring about.

Energy policies may give us a good example. No one, including those in the nuclear industry, would oppose a plan to discontinue the operation of dangerous reactors that have no prospect of passing the safety standards stipulated by the Nuclear Regulatory Authority, an independent regulatory commission established in September 2012, and to raise the ratio of renewable energy to total energy supply. However, it is quite doubtful that the DPJ government's announcement in September 2012 of aiming to be a zero-nuclear state by the end of the 2030s (completely abandoning the option of nuclear power generation) was based on a careful deliberation of all possible consequences.[10] As of July 2013, of the 50 commercial reactors in Japan, only two of them – Unit 3 and Unit 4 at the Ooi Nuclear Power Plant in Fukui Prefecture – are in operation, and the rest are all offline.[11] In order to avoid the worst-case scenario of blackouts at all costs, power companies and the government have been urging business entities and households to conserve energy while fully utilising decrepit thermal power plants and other facilities. Furthermore, the government launched the new Feed-in Tariff (FIT) system in July 2012, requiring electricity utilities, which have a regional monopoly over power generation and transmission, to purchase electric power from renewable energy suppliers at a high, fixed price in an effort to achieve the rapid and large-scale prevalence of renewable energy.[12] The implementation of this series of policies will surely cause energy rates to rocket, forcing more small- and medium-sized businesses unable to afford to equip themselves with an in-house power generation system to go bankrupt, and see the acceleration of plant relocation to developing countries and the subsequent 'hollowing out' of industries. Will it not increase the so-called 'working poor', and, consequently, spur the nation's falling birth rate? Will it not aggravate already-perilous pension and health-care finances, threatening the very existence of systems? Were they 100% sure that their decision would not negatively impact our national security and alliances with other countries? The point of the argument here is not that giving up the nuclear power option was a mistake, but that such a drastic policy change must always be preceded by careful and systemic prediction of the consequences and thorough discussions of appropriate countermeasures that can cushion negative effects.

However, conducting systemic analysis and enhancing the quality of policies are not easy matters, especially in Japan, which lacks an institutional framework that demands and encourages quality systemic analysis. Japan is yet to see the establishment of independent policy analysis institutions and think tanks with excellent policy analysis capabilities. Policy analysis conducted in bureaucrat-led policy networks has been far from systemic and their scope of deliberation has been limited to a single policy field.

Analysis of long-term policy goals

We have to admit that the deliberation on long-term policy goals has been generally insufficient and inadequate, lacking critical elements of policy analysis, including developing a feasible timetable, which specifies to what extent, by when and with what kind of method objectives should be accomplished, and modifying these specifics according to circumstances.[13] A good example is the concept of sustainable development. This concept is widely accepted in most developed countries, including Japan, as one of the most important long-term policy guidelines that ought to drive policy decisions. Even politicians who come up with policies that would please the voters but are hardly compatible with sustainable development (eg one that would make future generations pay a large portion of the cost) pay lip service to this concept.

The problem is that the political and economic systems of most countries, including Japan's, are only designed to tackle short-term or, at best, medium-term policy issues, lacking a system or the organisations necessary for the development, formulation and execution of long-term goals, such as sustainable development. Even in the few countries that do have special organisations designed to address long-term goals, they rarely serve their functions. Ultimately, long-term goals for society can be achieved only through a continuous effort to flexibly and appropriately tackle individual problems at a given time. This being the case, policy analysis for short-term and medium-term problems needs to be in line with the nation's long-term goals. In other words, the validity of policies that have been formulated, adopted and implemented to solve short-term and medium-term problems needs to be constantly verified in the context of long-term goals, and modifications need to be made whenever necessary. This is the only way in which long-term goals can be achieved.

However, conducting policy analysis with a long-term perspective is no easy task for the Kantei (composing of the prime minister and cabinet secretariat members) and the bureaucrats, who are constantly swamped with various issues that require immediate actions. Furthermore, the majority of lawmakers without a stable support base, whose actions are naturally motivated by how to increase the chances of their re-election, are not motivated to take long-term perspectives on policy issues. This makes the role of policy analysts even more important, and seeking and formulating long-term goals for society are yet another important set of duties for policy analysts.[14] A succession of 'improvements' for impending issues, ones that please myopic politicians and voters, may turn out to be detrimental to society in the long run. Therefore, policy analysts are required to constantly monitor measures taken to handle each issue at a given time and ensure that each of these measures helps bring society one step closer to a better future.

Priority-setting among policies

Setting priorities among policies vying with each other over available resources is an unavoidable part of government responsibilities. However, policy analysts have hardly ever reached out to the government to offer their informed, rational advice. As pointed out in Chapter Four, policies formulated across policy networks led by bureaucrats with little background in policy analysis may have provided some interested groups and stakeholders with access to decision-makers and policy influence. Yet, piecing together partially optimal policies does not necessarily deliver full optimisation for society as a whole.

Setting priorities among policies is no easy task for any government whose power base is not stable enough. This is why Japanese governments have so often attempted to delay unpopular decisions for as long as possible. However, reaching the point where they could not delay unpopular decisions any longer has not prompted them to take the initiative to do what needs to be done. Instead, they have tended to leave potentially unpopular tasks to be dealt with through the budget formulation process, led by the ruling party's Policy Research Council and the Ministry of Finance. The former Prime Ministers Nakasone and Koizumi, who strived to achieve political and administrative reforms through their leadership skills, backed by influential brain-trust advisors, are exceptions.

The ruling party's Policy Research Council is essentially nothing but a collegial, idea-coordinating organisation, having rarely asserted leadership; even the chairperson of the council is not given much authority. Consequently, the coordination of ideas and priority setting within the Policy Research Council has tended to be poorly developed and ingratiatory by nature. Similarly, the budget formulation conducted by the Ministry of Finance was not necessarily based on in-depth analysis of policy priorities in view of the long-term interests of society as a whole. Power balances within the policy network and influential politicians' meddling has never been something bureaucrats could easily ignore.

Ultimately, the Kantei should take on the difficult task of setting priorities among policies, using their value judgements and convincing the Diet and the public of the validity of their judgements, with advice from policy analysts. Historically, it has usually been the case that the Japanese Kantei has neither the courage nor intention to do this; instead, they respond to as many policy requests from policy networks as possible, but do not take a lead in setting the policy agenda. At the same time, there has been a tendency to shy away from raising taxes, relying instead on government bonds or resorting to cheap tricks such as making across-the-board budget cuts. In fact, they have often failed to even adopt the very policies that they accorded top priority and ardently hoped to put into practice due to strong resistance among Diet members and the public.

Conclusion

This chapter has overviewed six major problems, or flaws, of policy analysis in Japan. These problems are not exclusive to Japan. Most countries that have attempted to introduce policy analysis into their systems have similar problems. Even in the US, the very birthplace of policy analysis, not all the analysis conducted is thorough and appropriate. That being said, problems tend to be more serious and escalated in Japan, where policy analysis has long been left primarily in the hands of bureaucrats, who are in a position both to formulate and to implement policies. This is why the final chapter of this book has focused on acknowledging the problems within the policy analysis culture in Japan.

It has been a long time since the social significance of policy research in general and policy analysis in particular was first recognised in Japan. It is almost 20 years since academia started to realise the necessity and urgency of fostering highly knowledgeable and skilled policy professionals, and major universities and graduate schools soon started to introduce new public policy programmes, which feature policy analysis as part of their core courses. After all these years, however, policy analysis has yet to establish itself as an independent profession. Most public policy programmes are still struggling to attract intellectual and public-minded candidates, while surprisingly few graduates trained in policy analysis manage to find a job in a relevant field. Moreover, the cursory and inappropriate application of policy analysis has tended to be linked with the birth of problematic policies due to analytical mistakes. Policy analysis scholars and practitioners can no longer sit back and watch this situation unfold.

First, in order to break through the status quo, we should think about how to restructure the curriculum in public policy programmes in a way that will provide students with even more advanced and practical policy analysis skills. Second, we should urge the government, market and citizen sectors to work together and push for a significant increase in the employment of those who have acquired advanced skills in policy analysis. Additional measures we must advocate include: (1) the establishment of an independent research unit specialised in budgetary analysis, akin to the Congressional Budget Office in the US, as a Diet-affiliated organisation, which should be required to hire a substantial number of policy analysts as its full-time staff; (2) the recruitment by governmental ministries and agencies engaged in policy analysis activities of policy analysis experts who have passed a special screening process other than the regular national civil service examination;[15] (3) reform of the nominal policy-secretary system so that it can engage in its original function;[16] and (4) helping to establish highly independent and prestigious think thanks and policy-oriented NPOs and NGOs that can afford and are willing to hire high-quality policy analysts.

Ultimately, policies are, and should be, made and implemented through politics (the political process), in which extra-rational factors such as ideology, bargaining and compromise often play a vital role. In fact, few policies are the pure products of intellectual (rational) analyses. How can we increase the possibility of better (ie more efficient, effective and ethical) policies being adopted and implemented? It may sound somewhat paradoxical but the first thing that must be done is to explore fully the possibility of making democracy more substantive and engaging. Specifically, attempts need to be made to remove, to the greatest extent possible, factors that may inhibit the proper functioning of substantive political transactions among key policy actors, and the number of opportunities for citizen participation in the policy process needs to be expanded.

What I have argued thus far in this chapter – the urgent need for an improvement in the level of policy analysis – never implies that policy analysis is to be a substitute for democracy. Rather, the primary mission of policy analysis is to complement democracy. We can reasonably expect that public-minded high-quality policy analysts intelligent enough to provide key policy actors – including the citizenry in general – with evidence-informed policy options will make a substantial contribution to facilitating political transactions that are more informed, thereby improving the likelihood that better policies will be adopted and implemented in democracies.

Notes

[1] For more detail on the 'democratic myopia', see Adachi (2014).

[2] Dror (2001: esp chs 13, 14) provides important insights into this matter.

[3] Another example of poor cost projection is the one regarding the construction of the city subway Tozai line in Kyoto City. The total construction cost of this Tozai line, which opened in 1997 and runs between Daigo and Nijo, amounted to ¥451.5 billion, ¥200 billion more than the original projection.

[4] For the head of the local government, who is directly elected by the voters, it is not impossible to exert his/her leadership with the support of the voters if they wish to by suppressing the resistance of agencies that have planned and promoted policies.

[5] Let me mention two exceptions. The first case is when the former Prime Minister Yasuhiro Nakasone separated and privatised Japanese National Railways through his strong leadership (April 1987). He achieved this by marshalling excellent and sincere policy-oriented bureaucrats mainly from ministries not committed to policies of any particular field (eg Ministry of Internal Affairs and Communications). He did not give in to formidable resistance from the opposition party and labour unions. The other exception is the case of Prime Minister Junichiro Koizumi. Although the privatisation of the postal service was not the top issue for many voters at that time (ie according to the Census conducted in January 2005, voters' top issue was pension/welfare system reforms; postal privatisation was only eighth in the ranking), and the postal privatisation bills were rejected by the House of Councillors in August 2005, Koizumi dissolved the House of Representatives and called a general election, focusing entirely on the postal privatisation. He won a landslide victory by a far greater margin than expected.

[6] After the 1993 Southwest Hokkaido Earthquake and Tsunami, the Agency for Natural Resources and Energy in the Ministry of International Trade and Industry (currently the Ministry of Economy, Trade and Industry) ordered the Federation of Electric Power Companies of Japan (FEPC) to conduct a tsunami safety evaluation. The FEPC used the latest methods to estimate the size of a possible tsunami and examined its potential influence on nuclear power plants. Taking the margin of error into consideration, they checked whether water levels of 1.2 times, 1.5 times or twice the estimate would impact the emergency equipment. This test revealed that at the Fukushima Daiichi Nuclear Power Plant, the seawater pump would shut down when the water level reached 1.2 times the estimate, impairing cooling functions (it was only the Shimane Nuclear Power Plant in addition to the Fukushima Power Plant that was affected by this water level). In July 2002, the government organisation Headquarters for Earthquake Research Promotion published 'On the Long-Term Evaluation of Seismic Activities Off Eastern Japan between the Sanriku Coast and the Boso Peninsula', in which they stated that there was a 20% chance of a magnitude-8-class tsunami/earthquake occurring along the Japan Trench within 30 years. The Tokyo Electric Power Company (TEPCO) was also

aware from the estimate they made around May 2008 that the earthquake predicted by the aforementioned evaluation would bring tsunami waves of OP (Onahama Pile) + 15.7 metres to the property of the Fukushima Daiichi Nuclear Power Plant, and that the Unit 4 reactor building area would be inundated by 2.6 metres of sea-level rise. What is more, TEPCO presented a report on 11 May to the Spill Overtopping Study Group, established by the Nuclear and Industrial Safety Agency and the Japan Nuclear Energy Safety Organisation in January 2006, that tsunami waves of OP + 10 metrers at Unit 5 would cause its emergency seawater pump to shut down, which might lead to reactor core damage, and that OP + 14 metre tsunami waves would flood the building and impair the power supply system, including the emergency diesel generator, external alternating-current source and direct-current source, resulting in a total outage of electricity. In other words, they were aware of the necessity to take immediate action (The National Diet of Japan Fukushima Nuclear Accident Independent Investigation Commission, 2012: 1.2.1).

[7] Adachi (2002) recounted the criticality accident on 30 September 1999 at the Tokai uranium enrichment facility owned and operated by JCO Co. Ltd, and emphasised the vital need for the government to take every possible measure to prevent catastrophic accidents.

[8] Systemic thinking requires understanding a partial system in relation to the whole system and incessantly going back and forth between the parts and the whole. In this sense, it can also be called 'holistic thinking'. For more details on systemic policy thinking, see Adachi (2011).

[9] It goes without saying that cost–benefit analysis and cost-effectiveness analysis are useful analytical tools to help this process.

[10] The LDP-led coalition government, which won a landslide victory in the 2012 lower house election, overturned this decision and allowed the resumption of the existing reactors whose security had been confirmed, as well as the construction of new reactors.

[11] Both of these two reactors at the Ooi Nuclear Power Plant were shut down for regular inspection in September 2013. Since then, no commercial nuclear reactor has been allowed to re-operate (as of 1 May 2014).

[12] The buyback price for solar power over 10 kW was set at ¥42/kWh over a period of 20 years, wind power over 10 kW was set at ¥23.1/kWh for 20 years, and geothermal power over 15 MW was set at ¥27.3/kWh for 15 years. The prices will be modified depending on the level of the prevalence of renewable energy.

[13] Long-term policy goals requiring re-examination include, to mention just a few: what energy mix should be attained in the long run; on what timetable and with what method should the government debt be reduced; what measures should be taken against the falling birth rate; on what timetable and with what method should sustainable pension/health-care systems be achieved; what short-, medium- and long-term measures should be taken against the 'hollowing-out' of industries and subsequent job loss; how should land devastation be prevented, including rapidly increasing deserted croplands and forests going unkempt; and with what funds and on what timetable should aging infrastructures be renewed.

[14] The author does not mean to imply that all policy analysts should do these things, nor that they are competent enough to do so, but, rather, that the examination of long-term goals for society should be considered an important part of policy analysis.

[15] The latest literature that provides a close examination on this matter includes Ueno and Penner (2004) and Ueno (2012).

[16] A policy secretary employed with public funds is institutionally expected to serve his/her employer, a Diet member, as a policy analyst/adviser. However, in reality, policy secretaries have been forced to devote most of their time to routine secretariat work.

References

Adachi, Y. (2002) 'Can the Japanese Nuclear Sector Survive?', *Seisaku-kagaku*, vol 9, no 2, pp 1–12.

Adachi, Y. (2011) 'What Are the Core Knowledge and Skills for Policy Professionals? Public Policy Studies in Japan', *Seisaku-souzou-kenkyu*, vol 4, pp 37–46.

Adachi, Y. (2014) 'Democracy in Transition Management for Sustainable Development', in K. Ueta and Y. Adachi (eds), *Transition Management for Sustainable Development*, Tokyo: United Nations University Press, pp 137–53.

Curtis, G. (ed) (2002) *Policymaking in Japan: Defining the Role of Politicians*, Tokyo: Japan Center for International Exchange.

Dror, Y. (2001) *The Capacity to Govern: A Report to the Club of Rome*, London: Frank Cass.

Headquarters for Earthquake Research Promotion (2002) 'On the Long-Term Evaluation of Seismic Activity off Eastern Japan between the Sanriku Coast and the Boso Peninsula' (in Japanese), http://www.jishin.go.jp/main/chousa/kaikou_pdf/sanriku_boso.pdf

Stigler, G. (1971) 'The Theory of Economic Regulation', *Bell Journal of Economics and Management Science*, vol 2, no 1, pp 3–21.

The National Diet of Japan Fukushima Nuclear Accident Independent Investigation Commission (2012) 'Reports'. Available at: http://warp.da.ndl.go.jp/info:ndljp/pid/3856371/naiic.go.jp/en/report/

Ueno, M. (2012) 'What Is Missing in Japan's Budget Policy Debates: Institution, Policy Analysis, and Policy Analysts' (in Japanese), *Journal of Policy Studies*, vol 41, pp 115–40.

Ueno, M. and Penner, R. (2004) 'An Institution Model for Reforming Japan: Capacity to Budget', *NIRA Research Output*, vol 17, no 1, pp 16–36.

Index

Policy analysis in Japan

Ministry of Education, Culture, Sports,
  Science and Technology (MEXT) 252–4,
  264, 265, 271–5
  key features 106
Ministry of Finance 34, 66, 97, 106
  features 106
  role of PRI 108–9, 110–15
Ministry of Internal Affairs and
  Communications 106
Ministry of Justice 106
Miwa, Y et al 79
Miyakawa, K 104, 114
Miyakawa, T 19, 142
Miyamoto, T 59
Miyoshi, Y 79
Morgan, MS 33
Mori, D 79
Mori, K 42
Morita, A 265–6
Morita, A and Kanai, T 151
Morton, RB 35
Murakami, J 78
Murakami, K 61
Muramatsu, M 150, 157
Muramatsu, M and Inatsugu, H 152
mutual adjustment approaches *see*
  'incrementalism'
Myung-bak, Lee 177

N

Nagasu, Kazuji 47
Nakajima, M 75
Nakamura, M 111
Nakamura, M and Maeda, H 75
Nakamura, T 79
Nakasone, Prime Minister 139–40
Nakauchi, Y 281–2
Nakaumi reclamation project 293
Nakishima, M 136
National Commission on Educational
  Reform (NCER) 253
National Graduate Institute of Policy Studies
  (GRIPS) 24
National Institute for Research Advancement
  (NIRA) 23, 215–16
National Personnel Authority (NPA) 253,
  266–7, 277, 279
National Public Service Recruitment
  Examination 276, 277
NDL (National Diet Library) 177
neoclassical monetarism 33–4
networking research 21
New Public Commons 204–5, 206–7, 273
'New Public Management' (NPM) 20–1,
  257–8

newspaper and television reporting 235–6
  see also media and policy analysis
NHK *see* Japan Broadcasting Corporation
  (NHK)
NIAD-UE (National Institution for Academic
  Degrees and University Evaluation) 265
Nihon Keizai Shimbun 238–46
Nihon Toshi Center 46–7
Nikkeiren 188–90
Nippon Keidanren 188–90
Nishide, Y 214
Nishikawa, S 133
Nishio, M and Matsushita, K 41, 49
Nishio, T 104–5
Noda, A et al 265
Noda, Prime Minister 205, 209
Noguchi, Y 29, 185
non-profit organisations (NPOs) 21, 199–213,
  219–21
  and Civil Code revisions 199–201
  current state of sector 203–4
  key organisations 202
  main activity fields 203
  and the media 247
  and NPO Law revisions 201–2
  recruitment of PPAM graduates 276–9
  role in New Public Commons 204–9
    public awareness of sector 209–13
  and think tanks 225
  training and education 211–13
  trends and future issues 213
Nonprofit Academic Centers Council
  (NACC) 212–13
normative theory research 68
NPO Law (1998) 199, 201–2
nuclear industries
  disaster management efforts 97, 204–9,
    225–9, 242–3, 293, 294
  protest movements 209
  regulation 97, 294, 296
nursing care insurance systems 20, 58

O

objectives of policy analysis 7–9
Office of Committee on Administrative
  Reform 186–7
Ohashi, Y 59
Ohmy News 247
Ohtake, F et al 80
oil crisis (1970s) 19
Okabe, S 139
Okada, Katsuya 225–6
Okada, Y and Hayashi, S 79
Oliver, MJ and Pemberton, H 188
Omori, M and Kamata, K 75
Omori, W 151, 153

representing business interests 188–90,
190–4, 279–80
roles in Japanese Society 219–26
NPO vs for-profit bodies 219–21
policy markets 221–2
social levels 223
Think Tanks to Japan project 223
time frames 8–9
time series analysis 33
Tinbergen, J 32–3
Tohoku Disaster 228–9, 230–1
Tokyo Electric Power Company (TEPCO)
293–4
Tokyo Foundation 23
'Toyama Plan' 273–4
trade unions *see* labour unions
training *see* education and training
trinity reform 77
Tsubota, T 247
Tsuchiyama, K 41, 44
Tsujinaka, Y and Ito, S 151
Tsuneki, A 79
Tsuru, T 59
TT2005 178–9

U

Uchida, T 79
Uchiyama, Y 111
Ueno, M 215, 217, 223–4, 280, 302
Ueno, M and Penner, R 302
Ueyama, S 159
uncertainties, risk evaluation 226–9
United Kingdom
legislative support agencies 125–7
policymaking processes 176–7
types of think tanks 180
United Nations, employment of PPAM
graduates 281–2
United States
legislative support agencies 125–7
policymaking processes 176
social welfare systems 70
think tanks 180, 219–23
training centres for NPO subjects 212–13
universities and policy analysis
history of 15–16, 24
see also professional graduate public policy
schools (PPAM)
University of Tokyo 15, 24
Urabe, H et al 78
Usami, M 79, 81–2
Uzuhashi, T 59

V

value analysis 62–4
deficiencies in 64–9
see also policy analysis
Vinken, H et al 214
Virtual Think-Tank 243
voluntary forms of local policy analysis 153–4
see also non-profit organisations (NPOs)

W

Wandel Report 61
Waseda University 257–63, 267
Watanabe, S 44, 273, 275, 279–80
Weimer, D and Vining, A 1, 10, 29, 117
welfare policies 59, 65–6, 292
background history 57–9
characteristics and inconstancies 59–60
causes 61–4, 64–8
international comparisons 58–9, 292
Williamson, O 30
World Think Tank Forum 223

Y

Yakushiji, K 174
Yakushiji, T 29
Yamada, A 75
Yamada, K and Tsukahara, S 280
Yamaguchi, J 174, 176–7
Yamaguchi, M 77
Yamakoshi, A 188, 194
Yamauchi, H 190
Yamauchi, N 214
Yamauchi, N et al 201, 209, 211
Yamaya, K 35
Yamazaki, O 195
Yanagawa, N 79
Yano, M 79
Yashiro, N 80
Yomiuri Research Institute 237
Yomiuri Shimbun 241, 275

Z

Zaikai 188–90
Zenjhoren 192–3
Zenjikohren 192–3